Great Cathedrals

Great Cathedrals

Bernhard Schütz

with photographs by

Albert Hirmer, Florian Monheim,

Joseph Martin

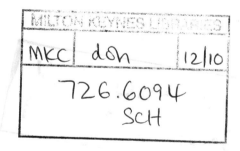
Harry N. Abrams, Inc., Publishers

Project manager, English-language edition: Kate Norment
Editor, English-language edition: Alexandra Bonfante-Warren
Jacket design, English-language edition: Judy Hudson
Design Coordinators, English-language edition: Judy Hudson, Arlene Lee
Translated from the German by Translate-A-Book, Oxford, England
Typeset by Organ Graphic, Abingdon, England

Library of Congress Cataloging-in-Publication Data

Schütz, Bernhard.
  Great cathedrals / Bernhard Schütz.
    p. cm.
Includes bibliographical references and index.
  ISBN 0-8109-3297-0
  1. Cathedrals–Europe. 2. Architecture, Medieval.
  3. Architecture, Gothic. I. Title.
  NA5453 .S39 2002
  726.6'09'02–dc21

                              2002006823

Printed and bound in Italy
10 9 8 7 6 5 4 3 2 1

Harry N. Abrams, Inc.
100 Fifth Avenue
New York, N.Y. 10011
www.abramsbooks.com

Abrams is a subsidiary of  LA MARTINIÈRE
                                               GROUPE

Contents

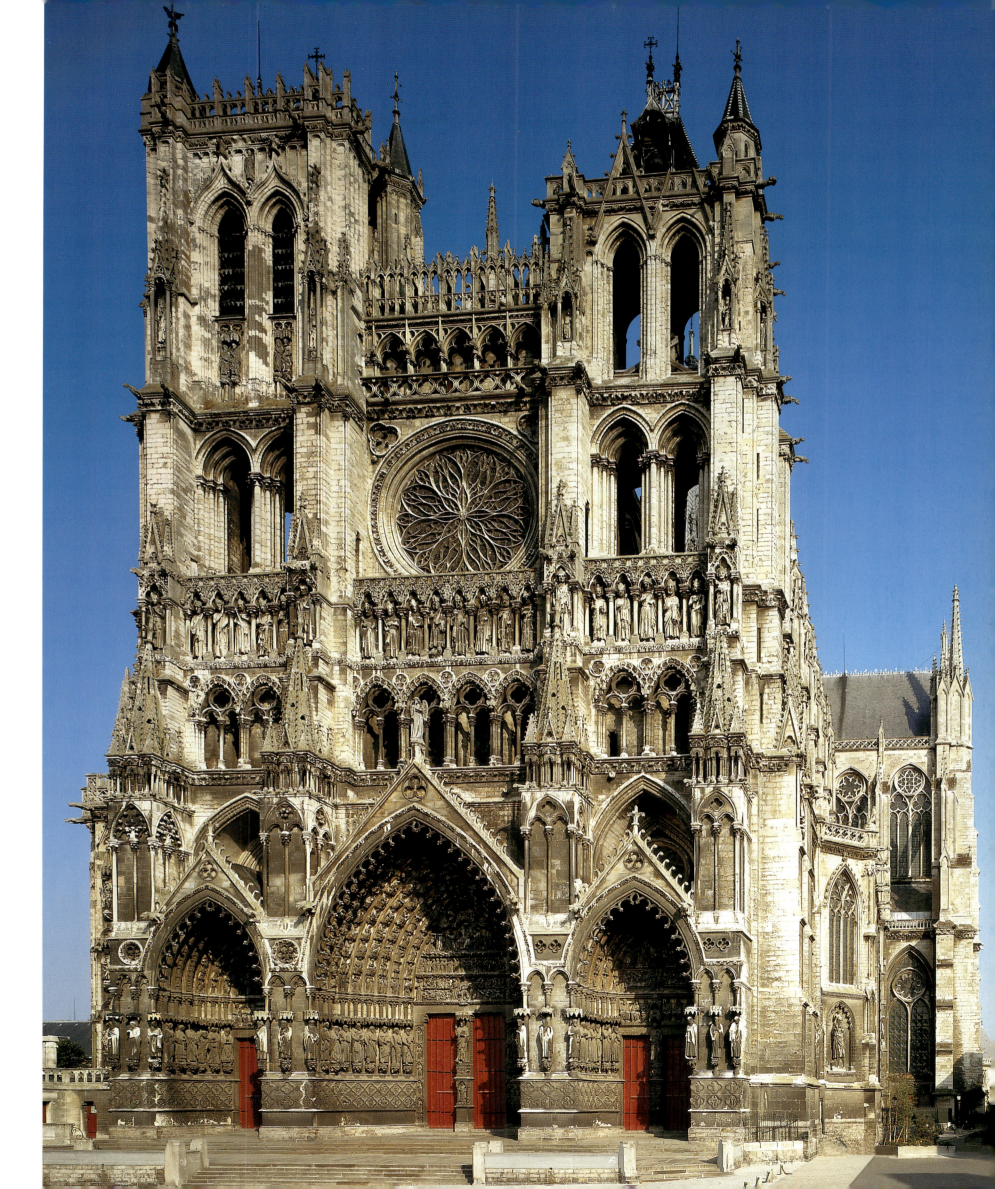

Introduction

This book provides an overview and an appreciation of the great medieval cathedrals of Europe: those of France and England, Spain and Italy, as well as Germany and adjoining countries, the former Holy Roman Empire. The cathedral is the greatest achievement of medieval European architecture, a work in which architecture and fine arts are united in a comprehensive whole, a purpose-built ecclesiastical building.

What is a cathedral?

Undoubtedly, most people think first of the French Gothic cathedrals: Notre-Dame in Paris, Chartres, or Reims. For many, "cathedral" is synonymous with "Gothic," and logically "Gothic" is first and foremost "cathedral Gothic." This view is bound up with mental images of extremely rich and finely decorative architecture, with interiors comprising pillars, arches, stained-glass windows, and rib vaults, and exteriors characterized by exposed buttressing and pointed pinnacles and gables. The motifs that recur everywhere are the pointed arch, the rounded shaft, and tracery.

In their construction, the Gothic cathedrals are mere frameworks, in comparison to the massive stone-wall heaviness typical of the preceding Romanesque style. They represent, from a technical viewpoint, bold, at times risky architectural engineering, in which the wall fabric is reduced to what is strictly necessary; this gives an impression almost of weightlessness, as if the laws of gravity, bearing, and load, in some inexplicable and miraculous way, do not apply here. This not only makes the building as light as it can be, but sometimes even gives the impression of a titanic upward surge.

Perhaps the most profound impression we receive from cathedrals in their original condition, like Chartres, is the surreal power of the illumination, from the colored beams emanating through glass windows that twinkle like precious stones; these are surely intended to give the observer an idea of the splendor of the light of heaven, the divine light.

The architectural structure and the windows together create an aura that has something mysterious and numinous about it, and is also an expression of the transcendental. Thus, even today's cultivated visitors detect with the same powerful immediacy as the Romantics before them, when they rediscovered the Gothic cathedrals and praised them in hymns, that this is the house of God. It is a holy place, to which reverence is due. Never before or after has the vision of sacredness so magically affected the mind.

Step by step the cathedral becomes a towering house of glass with fragile, thinly partitioned lattices; at this point the High Gothic cathedral looks like an enormously oversized shrine. The epitome of this is the high choir of the cathedral in Cologne, ideally represented in the cross-sectional drawings of the early 19th century from the engravings of Sulpiz Boisserée (see ill. page 14). This is, perhaps, the most accurate reproduction of a cathedral ever, because it captures not only the building and its typical Gothic cathedral construction, but also the spiritual soul, indeed the very idea of the cathedral. Here, we can see what every Gothic cathedral really is: a phenomenal achievement, always overwhelming, and never quite attainable.

The Gothic cathedrals of France soon inspired emulators in neighboring countries, first in England, then in Spain, and finally in all of Central Europe, and north as far as Scandinavia. A certain resistance emerged only on the part of Italy, still dominated by Classical antiquity, yet there, too, the Gothic-style cathedral found followers, for example in Milan and Florence, though admittedly in an Italian adaptation.

Nevertheless, by no means all cathedrals were Gothic. The word "cathedral" actually has nothing to do with Gothic, but simply describes the main church of a bishopric. That is why there are also cathedrals in the Romanesque, Renaissance, Baroque, and every other style, including contemporary, up to the present. In the Holy Roman Empire, the Romanesque cathedrals were highly valued; they were built by the greatest men in the empire, and were proudly erected with many towers, often with a defiant appearance, for architecture was effectively used to convey an image of power. In England, the naked, sometimes threatening, attitude of power adopted by the Norman ruling class was more pronounced; in contrast, the highly cultured inheritance of the Classical period lived on in the Romanesque cathedrals in Italy. Here, the aesthetic was concerned less with the demonstration of might than of pomp.

A cathedral, regardless of country or age, is the seat of a bishop or archbishop, and of the clergy attached to this church, the chapter, which is made up of canons. The origin of the word "cathedral" is the Latin *cathedra*, the thronelike seat of the pontificate, which is a symbol of both the bishop's teaching role and pastorate. The bishop's church is called a "cathedral" in France, England, and Spain; in Germany and in Italy it is known as a *Dom* and *Duomo* respectively. These terms are derived from *domus episcopalis* and *domus canonicorum* (house of the bishop or house of the canons), comprising the living areas of the bishop and the chapter, as well as the church. During the Middle Ages, the word *domus* was carried over in its old German form, *thuom*, to the church buildings formerly called the *ecclesia maior* (main church), *mater ecclesia* (mother church), or *ecclesia episcopalis* (bishop's church).

A term for a bishop's church that is only used in the southern part of the area where German is spoken, for example, in Basel, Constance, and Strasbourg, is *Münster*. Etymologically, this derives from the Latin *monasterium* (monastery), and it expresses the fact that the cathedral concerns the whole chapter, not just the bishop. Nonetheless, several large cathedral-like churches count as a *Münster*. Although these were only parish churches when they were established, they had a clergy with an especially strong membership, equivalent to a cathedral chapter. The most famous examples of this are the *Münster* of Freiburg (a bishop's church since 1827) and that of Ulm. In other regions, a city church with numerous clergy would be called *Dom*, even if it was not, and is not, the seat of a bishop, for example, in Erfurt or Brunswick. It has become the norm in everyday speech to glorify as *Dom* or *Münster* a church that is simply an important structure of a certain size, even if it is a monastery church. Altenberger Dom near Cologne, formerly a Cistercian church, or Weingarten Münster, a Baroque Benedictine church, belong in this category. In this expanded sense, the two words imply nothing more than structural

rank, the artistic quality of the church without regard to its function. The misnomer is a way to upgrade a church, usually for reasons of local partisan pride. A parallel to *Münster* in England is the word "minster." Among English cathedrals, it is used only in York, the lesser of the two archbishoprics in medieval England. As in Germany, several collegiate churches, for example, Beverley and Southwell, are also referred to as minsters. In the case of Westminster Abbey, the word is incorporated into the name.

The chapter of a cathedral not infrequently had the considerable strength of 40 to 80 canons as well as a great number of assistant clergy: the deacons and subdeacons. The canons, also called prebenders, lived together according to set rules and privileges ("canon"), which included prayer in the choir and the use of the refectory and the dormitory. This communal life, the *vita communis*, differed from a monk's life in that it was not subject to the stricter rules of a monastic order.

Inside the cathedral, usually at the east end, the choir was separated from the rest of the church for choral prayer and other activities of the chapter during divine service. Barriers were erected on the long sides, and a rood screen or other barrier was placed facing the aisle. During choral prayer the canons sat in their places in the choir stalls, which stood in front of the screens on the long sides, as a rule in two rows, just as in the monastery churches. Laypeople were excluded from acts of worship in the choir. The nave was the place for the people, and that is why the pulpit was placed there.

In cathedrals with two choirs, a style that spread in the Holy Roman Empire, mostly before the high Middle Ages, there logically could be two rood screens and two choir stalls. Such a double arrangement survives only in Naumburg. Today, only the English and Spanish cathedrals still boast nearly unadulterated views of medieval canons' choirs and their liturgical fixtures, which mainly originated in the Late Gothic. Elsewhere, especially in France, the rood screens at least were later removed because they were disruptive. This opened the canonical choir to the people, but it also detracted discernibly from the original concept of the cathedrals.

The living area of the chapter corresponded to that of a monastery with cloisters, utility rooms, and communal halls, which were grouped around the cloisters, including, especially in England, the very lavish Chapter House. The cathedral precinct, bounded by a wall, was often in the outlying areas of medieval cities. Both these factors protected the cathedral clergy from the recurring rebellions of the urban population. In addition, the surrounding wall was an expression of "immunity," that is, the special status that the law granted a cathedral precinct, which was under its own jurisdiction.

The overall layout of such a cathedral precinct can best be studied today in England and Spain, and here and there in Germany. In France and Italy, the buildings adjacent to the cathedral have for the most part not been preserved, although in Italy one of these was especially prized for religious purposes: the baptistery. The most important examples are in Florence, Pisa, and Parma. These baptisteries are buildings that stand next to or in front of the church, and which may display even greater architectural merit than the cathedral itself. In these, a Late Classical–Early Christian tradition lived on, which had died out in other countries.

Over the course of time, the chapter's *vita communis* was observed less strictly. The canons, who were often from the nobility, moved out of the communal rooms, and had their own palaces erected around the cathedral, like wordly nobles around a ruler's palace.

Many bishops had their own palaces, just like temporal princes. The palace, which could have its own chapel of considerable size, as in Reims, was by preference laid out on the other side of the cathedral from the chapter buildings. It was distinguished by a magnificent hall, like the *salle synodale*, for example, that is preserved in Sens. The bishops were, not infrequently, determined people of great power, as well as the spiritual shepherds of their bishoprics. At the same time, as vassals of the crown, or as peers, sometimes even dukes, they had the positions of temporal reigning princes. They often supported royal power in territorial conflicts with other rulers. Whether in the Holy Roman Empire or in Norman England, in the crown lands of France or in the divided domains of Spain, without the bishops, royal power could be asserted, and maintained, only with great difficulty, if at all.

This close connection to royalty is manifest in the cathedrals' fixtures and in the royal galleries of the facades; whole series of royal statues are particularly common in France. Here, it is hard to decide if the focus is intended to be regal Old Testament prefigurations of Christ's Passion and the Redemption, or French kings, or perhaps both at the same time. They look French, which may have prompted their popular identification as French kings, such as Philip Augustus in the northern transept in Reims. The west facade of the cathedral in Wells, England, also has a sequence of kings. In the clerestory windows of the Cologne Cathedral choir, there is a sequence of 48 kings with crowns, scepters, and orbs, but here, too, it is not clear who they are supposed to be. The kings in the glass window sequence in Strasbourg, despite the haloes to which only saints are entitled, are rulers

Royal figure (traditionally identified as Philip Augustus) on the facade of the north transept, Reims Cathedral

of the Holy Roman Empire, according to the inscriptions (see Plate 56). The most famous king of cathedral sculpture, the knight in Bamberg Cathedral (see ill. page 11), could be one of them.

The bishops were the sole authority in the cities where they had their residence, and, from the late Middle Ages, the people of the cities frequently tried to free themselves from their rule through bloody uprisings and wars. Sometimes these succeeded, for example, in Cologne, but not in other cities like Mainz or Würzburg. In Italy, the position of the bishops within their cities of residence was much weaker.

Here, from as early as the 12th and 13th centuries, citizens' councils increasingly established democratic or guild styles of government in the cities, which might be taken over by the violence of individual families, a sequence of events that became typical of the Italian city-states. The bishops, who even in the early days in Italy usually had the city government in their own hands, were now disempowered and politically unimportant. In contrast, the bishops of the Holy Roman Empire were increasingly temporal lords of their

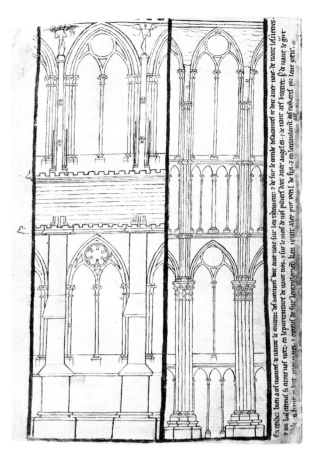

From the site log of Villard de Honnecourt, around 1220–40: *Ecclesia triumphans* (the Church Triumphant); west tower of Laon Cathedral, perspectival view; unexecuted plans for the nave elevation at Reims Cathedral. (Paris, Bibliothèque Nationale ms.fr 19093)

own territory, independent of the empire, in effect, bishop-princes; three of them, the bishops of Mainz, Cologne, and Trier, even became Electors.

The importance of the bishoprics depended, on the one hand, on their location and, on the other, on their size. A favorable location was at the heart of a kingdom, for example, in the crown lands of France, or in an economically prosperous region, such as northern Italy or on the Rhine. Less favorable locations were in the outlying areas, perhaps on the eastern frontier of the Holy Roman Empire. The size of the bishoprics, which was just as important to their incomes, differed considerably in the various European countries, because the bishoprics were unevenly distributed through them. Italy, with 170, had by far the most. In France, which was much larger, there were only 75, and in Spain close to 50. The German-speaking areas had about 40, and England, excluding Scotland and Wales, just 20. The number changed constantly, for bishoprics were abandoned or combined with others, and new bishoprics were created. Nevertheless, the number stayed consistent enough to show that the Italian bishoprics on average were the smallest, and the English were the largest; yet within countries, whether according to area or to the number of inhabitants, the size of the bishoprics varied considerably.

The financial might of a bishopric was an important precondition for the building of a new cathedral. The sponsors, at least in the Gothic period, were not only the bishop, but the whole chapter, who put their fortunes and incomes behind him. The city, on the other hand, was responsible not for the cathedral, but for the parish churches. Bishop and chapter had to rely on other sources of money, for example,

donations. When a cathedral such as Santiago, Chartres, Cologne, or a number of cathedrals in England was a well-visited site of pilgrimage, the donations from the pilgrims could be used for building work. Otherwise, the usual practice was to take the reliquaries owned by the cathedral in procession through the country to display them, offering their healing properties for money; sometimes processions from several cathedrals got in each others' way. Last but not least, the city guilds were also donors; they preferred to endow the expensive glass windows, keeping the memory of the donors alive by depicting in the window their symbol, for example, a tailor's scissors. The general population contributed with unpaid tasks, such as being wheelbarrow men. At Chartres, for example, the inspiration of piety was such that even the nobility joined in.

A few cathedrals in England were financed by Norman bishops, who were both tax collectors and the king's governors. Monarchs all over Europe energetically supported the construction of cathedrals, in some instances by monetary contributions and privileges, as in Spain and France, and in others by taking over the entire financial burden, like the emperor of the Holy Roman Empire with the *Kaiserdomen* (imperial cathedrals) in Magdeburg, Bamberg, and Speyer. Other examples were the Norman king William II in Monreale and the Late Gothic emperor Charles IV and his house in Prague. Dukes also sponsored cathedrals, notably Henry the Lion in Saxony, who financed the construction of three cathedrals, and, later, the duke of Milan with Milan Cathedral.

In Italy the situation was generally different from the rest of Europe. Here, as a rule, it was neither the bishop nor the chapter, but the city that pressed on with building the cathedrals, after the government had come into the hands of the citizens. In Pisa, the city used the immense plunder from the naval victory against the Saracens. In Florence, on the other hand, the responsibility for cathedral building lay not with the entire city, but with a single guild, which had become rich enough through the wool trade to finance such an enormous work.

The works were urged on and carried out by the masons' lodge. The architect, the *magister operis* or *magister fabricae* (master of something skillfully produced), is seldom named in sources from the Romanesque period. Sometimes this overseer was a cleric, as in Speyer, although it remains unclear if this person was responsible for the finances of the building site or for the actual building work. The names of the architects are more frequently known in Italy, and definitely through laudatory inscriptions, for example, in Pisa and Modena. During the Gothic period, the picture of the master becomes increasingly clear. In Chartres, Reims, and Amiens, the names are preserved in a labyrinth set into the floor. Other architects' names appear in archival sources. The Late Gothic record is nearly complete. The two most important sources for both the building activities and the architects' appointments for the period around 1200 are the report by Gervase of Canterbury about the construction of the cathedral choir there, and the site logbook, dating from 1220–40, by the French architect Villard de Honnecourt. He was very well traveled, and knew Reims especially well. His book is an instructive annotated collection of sample drawings, from which we learn that the architect was responsible for all the tasks that arose on the site. These included the building work, the construction machinery, and the fixtures and fittings, from the sculptures to the choir stalls. There are also several pictorial reproductions of medieval building activities, primarily in book illustrations and stained-glass windows. Apparently the architect was, in many cases,

also the head of the sculpture workshop, as with the west choir in Naumburg and demonstrably in the case of Peter Parler in Prague (see ill. page 200).

The basis for the architects' plans was geometry, not just for the floor plan and building shapes, but also for the graphic arts. Even the God of Creation depicted at the world's beginning is presented as an architect with a compass. Statics did not yet exist; trusting to experience, the architects became ever bolder. Drawn plans are not known until 1211, when window tracery was invented in Reims. This made precision in the individual parts so necessary that it was no longer possible to work without a plan drawing or even a template at a scale of 1:1. With the development of tracery, the plans, often drawn like documents on parchment, were also refined more and more, and became correspondingly larger, until with the design of the cathedral facade in Cologne, they reached a height of 13 ft. (4 m). Not infrequently, the plans were also scratched into the walls or stone floors. Several architects might oversee different building sites at the same time. In the 13th century, isolated complaints surfaced that the architects were not pitching in, but only standing around deep in thought and giving instructions. Nevertheless, some renowned architects had international reputations and were called abroad, for example, to Milan or, in many cases, to Spain.

Viewed as a whole, the medieval European cathedrals of the Romanesque period offer an extremely variable picture of strongly imprinted characters varying from region to region and from realm to realm. The scene unifies with the Gothic cathedrals of France. The new architecture extended into the other European countries, making the Gothic, despite regional specialties, an "international style."

The overwhelmingly powerful effect of the cathedrals was so great that, for the first time and of its own free will, Europe was united from Norway to Andalusia—at least in its architecture.

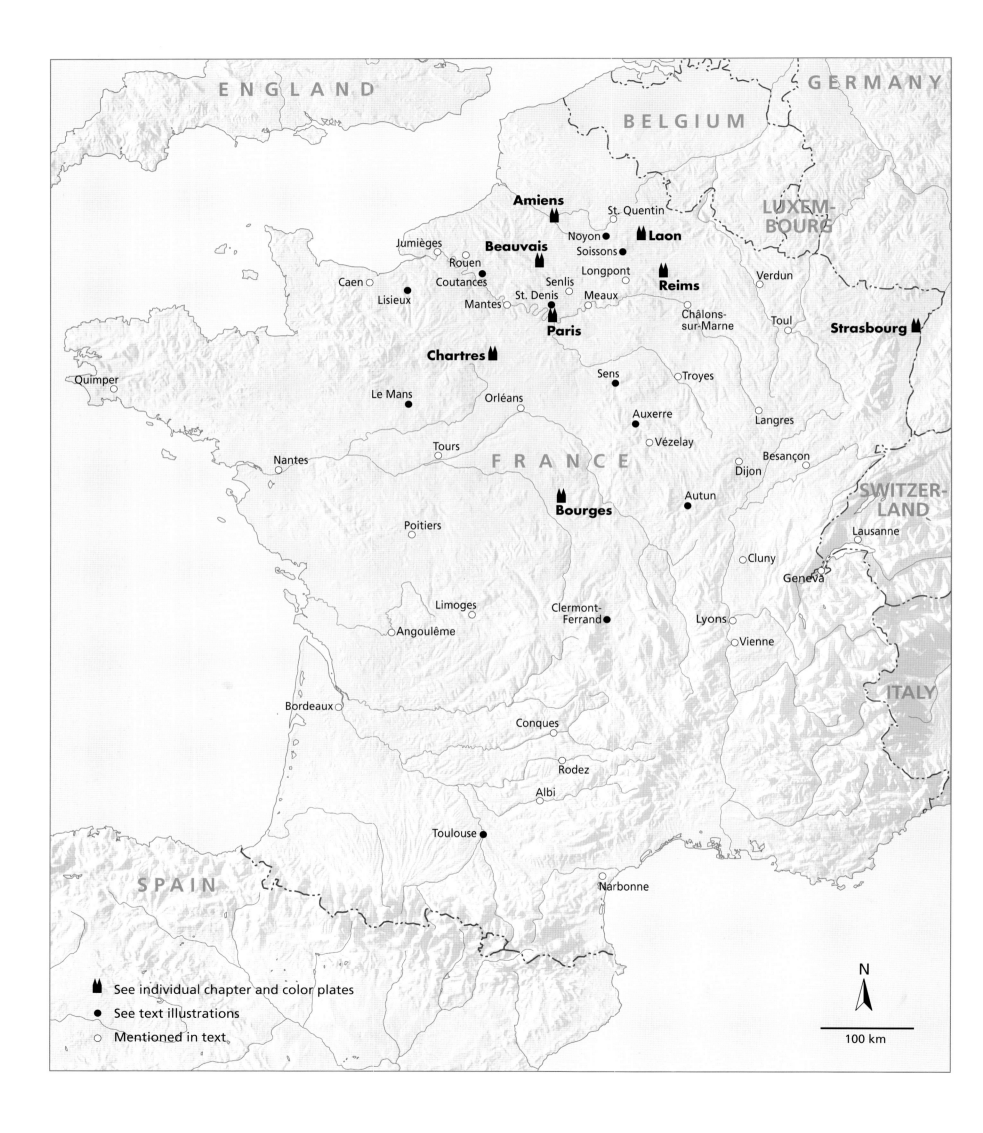

ENGLAND

GERMANY

BELGIUM

LUXEM-
BOURG

Amiens

St. Quentin

Jumièges

Noyon ● **Laon**

Beauvais Soissons ●

Rouen Longpont

Verdun

Caen ○ Coutances ● Senlis **Reims**

Lisieux ● Mantes ○ St. Denis ○ Meaux ○

Châlons-
sur-Marne

Toul

Strasbourg

Paris

Chartres

Sens ● Troyes ○

Quimper ○

Le Mans ● Orléans ○

Auxerre ●

Langres ○

Vézelay ○

Besançon ○

Nantes ○ Tours ○

FRANCE

Dijon ○

SWITZER-
LAND

Bourges

Autun ●

Poitiers ○

Cluny ○

Lausanne ○

Geneva ○

Limoges ○

Clermont-
Ferrand ●

Lyons ○

ITALY

Angoulême ○

Vienne ○

Bordeaux ○

SPAIN

Conques ○

Rodez ○

Albi ○

Toulouse ●

Narbonne ○

N

See individual chapter and color plates

● See text illustrations

○ Mentioned in text

100 km

France

Architectural History

The history of the kingdom of France begins with the Merovingian ruler Clovis. Following the collapse of Roman Gaul in 486, he founded the Frankish royal dynasty and, after he was converted to the Christian faith in 499, united church and crown in the kingdom of the Franks. Under the Carolingian ruler Charlemagne, whose coronation as emperor in Rome in 800 restored the ancient imperial title, the Frankish kingdom became the heart of a great empire encompassing half of Europe. However, this centrality of power was lost by Charlemagne's heirs. Under the Treaty of Verdun, the empire was divided into three separate kingdoms. The middle one, Lotharingia, was a long, narrow territory stretching from the North Sea to Italy. In 870 and 880, under the Treaty of Mersen, Lotharingia was dissolved. From that time on, Charlemagne's former empire consisted of two adjacent territories: the kingdom of the Western Franks, which more or less corresponded to today's France, and Louis the German's kingdom of the Eastern Franks, later the Holy Roman Empire of the German nation. In 875, shortly after this division of power, the West Frankish king, Charles the Bald, gained the title of emperor, even though the kingdom of the Western Franks was already in the process of breaking up under the last of the Carolingian rulers. The region between the Loire and the Pyrenees, which was still inhabited by the old Gallo-Roman peoples, and Celtic Brittany declared themselves independent. Provence and the Jura region, or Lower and Upper Burgundy, joined together with the kingdom of Burgundy to form the kingdom of Arles, named for its capital city. This kingdom fell in 1034 by testamentary contract, that is, was bequeathed, to the Holy Roman Empire, then ruled by Conrad II. In 884, next to the kingdom of Burgundy, the duchy of Burgundy came into being and remained closely associated with the French crown for centuries, its dukes belonging to a collateral line of the royal house (the Capetians). Finally, in 911, Normandy was handed over to the Normans as a duchy, nominally as a royal fief, but in reality it became an independent power.

In 987, when Hugh Capet took over the hereditary monarchy, and in so doing founded the royal dynasty of the Capetians, the crown lands amounted to only a fraction of the old kingdom of the Western Franks: the Ile de France around Paris and areas around Orléans, Sens, and Bourges. In 1152, Louis VII divorced his wife, Eleanor of Aquitaine, an event that was to have serious consequences for French history, since Poitou and Gascony both belonged to her territorial possessions in western France. The situation became threatening for the French royal house, when

Eleanor then married Henry Plantagenet, count of Anjou, Touraine, and Maine, who in 1154 became king of England, thus duke of Normandy. After he had also acquired Brittany in 1169, the whole of western France was in the hands of the House of Plantagenet, which made it an English, rather than a French, zone of influence, even though Henry's continental possessions were French fiefs.

The power base of the French monarchy was extremely narrow at that time, with the constant feuds and robberies by the barons bringing the country to the edge of chaos. However, the crown did have one influential supporter in the form of the "royal" dioceses in the crown lands. They were subordinate to the king, who had the right to invest whom he chose as bishop. And it was in these dioceses that the Gothic cathedrals were constructed. As vassals of the king, the bishops or archbishops of six of these dioceses held the rank of a peer of France (equivalent to that of a count): Reims, Laon, Langres, Châlons, Beauvais, and Noyon. These bishops filled half of the places in the college of the crown council, which consisted of 12 peers.

During the next generation, the traditional lineup of the rival powers altered in favor of the French throne. When Philip Augustus came to power in 1180, he took advantage of the struggle for power in the House of Plantagenet between the brothers Richard I, "the Lionheart," and John, and, on occasion resorting to military means, gradually won back almost all the regions under English control. The decisive blow was struck at the great Battle of Bouvines in 1214 against the allied forces of the English king and the Holy Roman Emperor Otto IV. In the period following the bloody Albigensian Wars in southern France, the powerful lands of the counts of Toulouse also fell to the king, along with Provence and Poitou. By around 1285 almost all the lands of the old kingdom of the Western Franks had been won back or had formed family alliances with the House of the Capetians, which in 1328 was succeeded by the House of Valois. In the Hundred Years' War, which began in 1339, the regions of western France to which England had laid claim were finally retained despite catastrophic defeats.

The political fragmentation of France can be visibly traced in the various Romanesque building styles that were employed. In every region—in Normandy, Poitou, Provence, Burgundy, the Auvergne, and Aquitaine—marked singularities are revealed. There was a great deal of building everywhere at that time, and much of it has been preserved, but there are only a few Romanesque cathedrals. The foremost examples are those of Autun and Langres, both of which belong to the highly developed Romanesque style

of Burgundy. In Beauvais, only the nave of the early Romanesque cathedral has survived; compared with the Gothic choir, it crouches much lower, and seems relatively tiny in scale. The cathedral in Angoulême has a very different appearance: a single-naved building with a succession of domes on pendentives, typical of southwestern France. At Le Mans, a Romanesque nave was converted in the very early Gothic period, and raised to the then fashionable height by means of vaulting added to the central nave.

Almost all the older cathedrals were replaced in the Gothic period by new buildings, as happened at Reims and Chartres, which in the pre-Gothic period, that is, before the late 12th century, had claimed the most important and largest cathedrals. Such a drastic clean-slate policy can only be explained by the probability that most pre-Gothic cathedrals were seen as too small and too unambitious, and also may have been structurally inadequate.

The great Romanesque monastery churches were more important in terms of historical and art-historical significance, particularly the religious centers built to honor the tombs of saints and famous relics, such as St. Martin in Tours, St. Martial in Limoges, St. Bénigne in Dijon, St. Benoît-sur-Loire, Ste. Madeleine in Vézelay, and St. Rémi in Reims. They were also places of pilgrimage, and were especially popular if they lay on one of the pilgrim routes to Santiago de Compostela. In these centers, churches of massive proportions were built, and also in Toulouse, where the five-aisled monastery and pilgrim Church of St. Sernin surpassed by far, both in size and quality, the Gothic cathedral that was begun later, but never completed.

Beginning around the year 1000, a special style of building evolved for the pilgrim churches along the route of the pilgrimage dedicated to St. James the Great: a fine galleried nave with a transept, choir, and ambulatory with radiating chapels, and the distinctive feature of side aisles and galleries grouped in a U-shape around the arms of the transept. To start with, these churches had flat roofs, like St. Rémi in Reims; then later, in buildings such as Ste. Foy in Conques, St. Sernin in Toulouse, and Santiago de Compostela (see Plates 232, 233), they were given barrel vaults placed directly over the galleries, thereby dispensing with a clerestory.

Very important flat-roofed buildings were constructed in the abbeys of Normandy, most notably the church begun around 1040 in Jumièges, and the later one in Caen, then the capital city of Normandy. The Abbey Church of St. Etienne in Caen, commissioned by the count of Normandy, with its great galleried nave and west front with two towers, was shortly to become the model for the development of the colossal Norman churches of England (see pages 213–295).

The most important abbey—politically as well as structurally—was that of Cluny in Burgundy, a monastic establishment that had the special status of its own Cluniac order within the Benedictine order, and in its heyday comprised up to 1,450 monasteries. In the dispute between the monarchy and the papacy over lay investiture, Cluny was the central church body responsible to the pope with a mission to liberate the church from secular dependence. Pope Gregory VII (1073–85) tried to impose papal supremacy over all secular sovereigns, including the emperor, and was the first to excommunicate a ruler of the Holy Roman Empire—Henry IV, who had himself been a monk at Cluny. The great wealth of the abbey can be seen from its church, begun in 1089, and consecrated in about 1132: a barrel-vaulted, five-aisled basilica of immense length and narrow, steep proportions. The five aisles were graduated in height. The showpiece was the eastern section, with its many towers, two transepts, ambulatory, and radiating chapels. The three-story walls consisted of tall, extremely steep dividing arcades, a blind triforium, and clerestory; the entire church was richly decorated. This gigantic building, with its total length of 613 ft. (187 m), including the antechurch, completed later (as a comparison, the Cathedral of Speyer is 440 ft. [134 m] long), exceeded all contemporary church buildings in Europe both in size and splendor. After the French Revolution, the church was demolished up to the south transept, which was left standing as a final remnant.

The ascetic, strictly reformist order of the Cistercians, founded in 1098, marked a reaction against Cluny, which had become too worldly and extravagant. The Cistercians were named for their earliest establishment, Cîteaux, founded in a remote forest near Dijon. Thanks to the charismatic personality of Bernard de Clairvaux, the order grew quickly, and developed its own simple, severe style of church architecture. Somewhat earlier, in 1084, the Carthusian order came into being, when its founder, Bruno of Cologne, withdrew to the site of today's Grande Chartreuse, the chief house of the Carthusian order, in the mountainous area of Grenoble; there, forsaking the world, he led a communal contemplative hermit's existence, which eventually led to the establishment of a school. Another order to achieve European significance was that of the Premonstratensians, which developed from a monastery foundation that Norbert of Xanten set up in 1120 in Prémontré, near Laon. In the Romanesque period, France was above all a country of monasteries, whose renunciation of the world found widespread appeal.

Another monastery was to prove decisive in the development of architecture, especially that of cathedrals: the ancient Benedictine Abbey of St. Denis on the outskirts of Paris. Its church was completed in 775 under Abbot Fulrad. According to legend, it was already standing in the sixth century under the Frankish king, and was believed to have been consecrated by Christ himself, which gave it an aura of special holiness. Under the Carolingians, St. Denis was the foremost abbey in the West Frankish part of the empire. Here Pépin the Short, father of Charlemagne, was crowned king of the Franks in 754; he is also buried here, along with the later emperor Charles the Bald. Here too is where Charlemagne originally wished to be buried, next to his father. The church was, in addition, the burial place of Denys, or Dionysius, the patron saint of France, the legendary first bishop of Paris, who was identified with the biblical figure Dionysios Areopagites of Athens, a disciple of St. Paul. A third Dionysios also comes into the picture: a Syrian theological philosopher of the late fifth century, who in his writings had passed himself off as Areopagites, and today is known as "Pseudo-Dionysius the Areopagite." People were taken in by this deception, so three different people with the name "Areopagites" came to be merged in a single figure. This theory was established in writing by Abbot Hildouin of St. Denis, who wrote a biography of Dionysios in the reign of Louis the Pious, the son of Charlemagne, with a supplementary Latin translation of the original writings in Greek. Charles the Bald in turn commissioned the most learned man of his day, John Scotus Erigena, to carry out a new translation with a commentary, and in 1137 Hugh of St. Victor wrote a new commentary in Paris. These writings formed an important basis for the intellectual life of theologians, particularly at St. Denis where the relics of the saint were venerated. The idea that the first bishop of Paris could be identified with the biblical Areopagites and the philosopher remained irrefutable throughout the Middle Ages; only the critical theologian and philosopher Abelard (1079–1142) dared to cast doubt on it.

Suger was abbot of Cluny from 1122, and a close confidant of two kings, Louis VI and Louis VII. When the latter set off on the Second Crusade in 1147, Suger took over the regency of the kingdom in his absence. He had already become a powerful force in the movement to reposition the French kingdom against the Holy Roman Empire and its legal succession to the dominant Carolingian empire. Suger knew both Normandy and Rome from personal experience;

Right:
West facade

Below left:
Ground plan of the choir
(by D. v. Winterfeld)

Below right:
South side of the double
ambulatory seen from
the west

reworked at St. Denis, and would have great significance for the buildings of the future. In Romanesque ambulatories the radiating chapels, never more than five in number, projected out from the semicircle of the ambulatory, with a section of the ambulatory wall between them. At St. Denis, these separate chapels became a cohesive crown of seven shallow-vaulted apses, each furnished with two large-scale stained-glass windows. The windows formed an almost continuous screen around the whole space, interspersed with narrow shafts. The ambulatory had two aisles. The inner aisle, next to the choir, served as the ambulatory proper, while the bays of the outer one did not form a true ambulatory, but demarcated a series of chapels together with their adjoining apses. The chapels were separated from each other by low barriers, rather than by walls. The available space was thus given maximum transparency, and the monolithic columns between the ambulatory and the row of chapels were as thin as possible. The columns of the inner choir were also just as thin to begin with, in the old Romanesque tradition, but they could not bear a sufficient load, and in the 13th century were

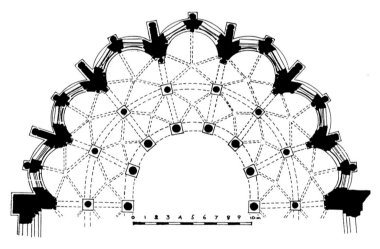

before 1140 he built the abbey's new twin-towered west front with its three large portals decorated with sculptures, and between 1140 and 1144 added a new choir. These two architectural achievements served as models for every new development in what became the French Gothic style in the age of cathedral building. Suger himself made written reports of the buildings' measurements, but with no mention of the master builder.

The pride of French churches in the Romanesque period had been the ambulatory and radiating chapels, or chevets, with their exceptionally tall, slender columns (occasionally too slender, as at Cluny) in the semicircular space around the inner apse of the choir. This old approach was thoroughly replaced by thicker round pillars. The abaci of the capitals could thus be retained—which was a great technical achievement. The inner columns portrayed the Apostles, according to Suger's own report. To this end, Suger had imported marble columns from Rome, just as Charlemagne had done at Aachen and Centula.

The vaulting of the ambulatory created the pattern for future buildings. The vaulted areas of the bays in the ambulatory were given a trapeziform shape, surrounded by strong box-shaped transverse and dividing arches. The diagonal ribs were bent in such a way that the boss, where the ribs crossed over, lay in the middle of the bay. This made it possible for the four segments of the vault to be approximately the same size. For the arches of the vault, the old problem of the vertices being at different heights was convincingly resolved: the diagonal ribs, the radius of which is considerably greater than that of the other arches, were given a round-arched form, while the others were pointed. The pointed arches have a lesser radius, but their pointed shape allowed the vertex of each one to be of a height comparable to those of the diagonal arches. In the western section of St. Denis, the same problem was solved partly with imposts and partly with pointed arches, and in other buildings with stilted arches. The choir of St. Denis now made these experiments out of date, however. The solution of the pointed arches proved to be so perfect and variable that it remained generally valid for all Gothic cathedrals of the future, applicable to every situation.

Apart from such technical improvements, a further important innovation was that windows could now be made larger to form colored, self-illuminating walls of light. Light became a constructional element of architecture: the builders composed with light. Suger himself said of the ambulatory chapels that the full, wonderful, continuous light of the bright, glittering windows (*clarissimarum vitrearum*) revealed the beauty of the inner space and the splendor of the choir. In another version, the windows are even *sacratissimae*, "extremely holy" or "hallowed."

The way the light made the architecture glow and sparkle was a completely new discovery in the context of Romanesque architecture. This view and use of light seems close to the Neoplatonic metaphysics of light of the Pseudo-Areopagite, and lead by analogy to the Light of the World, that is, rising up in recognition of Christ as the true, though invisible, light. This concept is touched on in the inscription on the portal, where it says that this noble, shining work may illuminate our spirits so that they move through its lights to the true light, to which Christ holds the key. Suger did not actually quote the writings of the Pseudo-Areopagite, but it seems clear that at St. Denis the abbot, and very likely all the other monks, with their knowledge of Latin, were at least aware of the content of these writings. Thus, it seems that St. Dionysius, alias the Pseudo-Areopagite, had an influence on the design of the building. Suger could certainly have been influenced by other sources, for example by the inscriptions on Roman apse mosaics, in which a comparable metaphor of the shining, illuminating light can be found.

Suger's writings played an important role not only at St. Denis, but for all future Gothic cathedral architecture, because they were the only source from that time in which a kind of theology of church architecture was expressed, which ultimately was a theology of light. As the buildings testify, it was to remain valid for several centuries.

Only the ambulatory, with the crown of apses, remains of Suger's choir, which rose up over a crypt. The upper choir was replaced by a new one in 1231, as were the nave and transept. That the upper choir is no longer in existence is an irreplaceable loss, in this founding building of the Gothic period, even if the present choir is of the highest quality, and itself served as a founding building for a later phase of Gothic architecture (see page 31). Whether Suger's choir had three or four stories, that is, whether it had galleries or not, is disputed. The buildings that succeeded it leave no clue.

After St. Denis, where the consecration of the choir in 1144 was attended by numerous neighboring bishops, new cathedral buildings appeared one after the other in their dioceses, as though Suger's choir had unleashed a new enthusiasm for building. These dioceses were subordinate to the crown, even though some did not stand on crown land. It seems, therefore, that there was a historic connection between the emergence of the early Gothic cathedrals and the French kingdom, before the cathedrals expanded further in the 13th century.

In 1140, at the same time as the choir of St. Denis was built, the Cathedral of Sens was begun; it was the seat of an archbishop, who had the rank of a primate of Gaul. In its original version, the bath-shaped ground plan had no transept or crown of chapels leading from the ambulatory; it had a closed, uniform atmosphere. The central nave is designed with double bays with sexpartite rib vaults and supporting elements, the main supports being compound piers, awkwardly interspersed by pairs of circular pillars. The walls rise to three stories by means of dividing arcades, a low false gallery, and a clerestory that was later increased in size. The weightiness of the stone walls is still reminiscent of the Romanesque, although something new can be seen in

Right:
Sens Cathedral, choir and
sanctuary from the west

Below:
Noyon Cathedral, central
nave looking east

the rigor and conciseness of the system of supporting ribs and in the sexpartite vaulting. This was very early Gothic. Following St. Denis, Sens was the second building in the new style.

The next cathedrals—except for Senlis—had four stories: as well as the arcades and the clerestory, they had a gallery and a triforium. The first of these was Noyon, possibly begun about 1145, a building with thin, fragile columns surrounding the choir and tightly clustered, round columns braced with shaft rings, or annulets. Unlike the choir, the nave, as at Sens and Senlis, has double bays and supporting columns, which disturb the unity of the structure as a whole.

Not until Laon (see pages 50–59), begun around 1155–60, were efforts made to unify the choir and nave properly by giving the whole cathedral circular columns on which the rest of the design was based. Laon was a model for Early Gothic architects and stonemasons, with its powerful, though not thickly clustered, circular columns, which stand like tubes *en délit*, that is, free from the wall, and thus needed considerable bracing to bind them to it. The side aisles and galleries are also designed throughout with rounded forms, which give this type of architecture a singularly three-dimensional character, as though it were the work of a sculptor rather than an engineer.

Early Gothic cathedral architecture was quickly refined, as the columns, pillars, and profiles became increasingly slender, but without losing their circular, sculptural quality. An ingenious example, verging on the precious, can be seen in the double-niched apse of the transept at Noyon, which is a reworked Early Gothic version of the Romanesque transept of the cathedral at Tournai, now in Belgium. This structural affinity came about because Noyon and Tournai once formed a double bishopric.

Noyon was surpassed by the south transept of Soissons Cathedral, which is also apsidal. Here there is not only a triforium and clerestory, but also a side aisle and gallery running around the apse. The ensemble forms a concluding spatial zone that is a perfect example of the "diaphanous," that is, transparent, use of space that is characteristic of Gothic cathedrals. The southern transept at Soissons displays a singular architectural delicacy. The fully mature Early Gothic style can also be seen in the systematic use of columns, pillars, and arches.

The same can be said for the cathedral-like choir of the Abbey Church of St. Rémi in Reims, with its particularly original triple-column arcading separating the crown of chapels from the ambulatory. This choir was soon regarded as a complete masterpiece, and was imitated almost entirely

Far left:
Noyon Cathedral, south
transept and junction
with the nave

Left:
Soissons Cathedral,
south transept

Below:
Reims, Abbey Church
of St. Rémi, choir

in the pilgrim church of Notre-Dame-en-Vaux in Châlons-sur-Marne.

Notre-Dame in Paris, begun in 1163, was designed on a very different scale from all previous Early Gothic cathedrals (see pages 70–79); it is a five-aisled structure, like Cluny, with a double-aisled ambulatory, like St. Denis, but originally without a crown of radiating chapels, as at Sens. Its increased size is the visible expression of royal and metropolitan ambition. Like most other Early Gothic cathedrals, the structure has four stories, though the usual triforium above the gallery was replaced by circular windows. These were later removed when the clerestory windows were enlarged and rebuilt, at least in the area of the transept and crossing, when Viollet-le-Duc restored the cathedral in the 19th century. In building the central nave and choir, the architects aimed for a greater degree of unity than usual, and employed the same sturdy circular columns, the same tripartite system of arches, and the same sexpartite vaulting. Variations occurred only in the side aisles and galleries. A typical feature of Notre-Dame is that individual parts of the building lack the sculptural force of rounded forms while, conversely, the very thin walls occupy more space. The design is chiefly concerned with displaying a united ensemble rather than individual pieces. This was the essence of the next Gothic era.

After the Early Gothic style had made its mark in numerous abbey and collegiate churches, even parish churches, as far as Normandy and Burgundy, a new phase was launched

Chartres Cathedral,
buttressing on the nave

of the central nave. Only the broader, lower outer side aisle is a real "nave." When the naves are seen together, the structure is five-storied. All these things and, not least, the dizzying height of the columns of the central nave make Bourges a spatial miracle of endless fascination.

At Chartres (see pages 80–95), begun in 1194, the whole layout is much more lavish: a three-aisled basilica with a five-aisled choir, a double ambulatory, and a crown of radiating chapels that alternately interlink with the outer ambulatory bays or project outward as independent apses. This alternating design was dictated by the presence of a Romanesque crypt. The transept has three aisles, like the Romanesque pilgrim churches, but unlike them has three portals at both the north and south ends, as is usually found in west facades. The allocation of bays is made according to a strictly ordered pattern. The double bays with their sexpartite vaulting are everywhere replaced by oblong bays with quadripartite vaulting. These harmonize better, in terms of mass, with the bays of the side aisles, and unify the ground plan, which seems to conform to a carefully plotted overall grid. This ground-plan system became from then on the norm for cathedrals.

In the structure of its walls, Chartres Cathedral is more tightly organized than the Early Gothic style. All the parts of the vaulting—the transverse, diagonal, and wall ribs—were "served" by circular pilasters, or engaged columns, which literally "engaged" with them. At the end of each bay was a cluster of five shafts. These branched out above the piers. On each of their four sides the piers had a row of shafts, making them into a clustered pier. These were alternately paired, each circular pier with octagonal shafts being followed by an octagonal pier with circular shafts—a specialty of the architecture at Chartres. The clustered pier was a further development of the Early Gothic circular pillar. The engaged columns did not run all the way to the cathedral pavement, as the older compound piers had done, but now were supported on the pillar, sometimes by a corbel. Compound piers would have been more appropriate for the upper shafts, but suffered from the disadvantage that they could not be installed in the most important part of the cathedral: in the corners of the polygon formed by the choir, where the columns stand very close together. Clustered piers were a compromise between compound piers and circular pillars, aimed at uniting the polygon of the choir and the rest of the cathedral, and thereby promoting the engaged-column system over the Early Gothic circular pillar.

The construction of the stories at Chartres also reveals crucial innovations compared with the Early Gothic, with

like a thunderbolt around 1200 with two cathedrals of opposing styles: Bourges and Chartres.

Bourges (see pages 96–105) is a five-aisled basilica with no transept and a double ambulatory, so that the radiating chapels are reduced to bays of relatively tiny size. The structure constitutes an outstanding, highly inventive achievement, with no trace of Early Gothic. The aisles are graduated in height, which means the dividing arcades are extremely high, but there is no gallery on the upper wall; only the triforium and clerestory survive. In this respect, Bourges is a Gothic Cluny. The way the inner, higher side aisle next to the central nave is placed in relation to it is extraordinary and original. It has its own clerestory and triforium, and is so narrow that it looks less like an independent nave than a background space enclosing the whole cathedral, set behind the dividing arcades

everything being simplified, and then systematized. The gallery is left out. They did not need it. The walls are thus three-storied—as at Sens, for example—but with the difference that the clerestory windows are much larger. They are now as big as the dividing arcades, which, compared with Early Gothic, were a gigantic size, and dominate the entire wall area. Moreover, the windows were subdivided into an upper rosette and two lancet windows that form a "composite window." This innovation ensured the maximum enlargement of the self-illuminating light-wall. The colored light is more of a constructional feature than at St. Denis. The blind triforium, in the form of an arcade with a passage behind it, was now moved to the middle of the wall to bring the upper and lower parts into harmonious balance.

The increase in size of the glazed area was only possible because the clerestory windows extended down a good way below the position of the impost. This left the base of the vault with hardly any support walling. For this reason, the lateral support of the vaulting and the outward thrust needed to be buttressed externally. There had already been flying buttresses reaching up to the clerestory in the Early Gothic period, to some extent at St. Rémi in Reims and at Notre-Dame in Paris, but not until Chartres did open buttressing become indispensable, determining from then on the way cathedral exteriors were built.

It was planned that Chartres should have no fewer than nine towers, which would have been a record for all cathedrals. In addition to the two west towers, which were a legacy of the previous building, two more towers were planned for each of the transept facades, another over the crossing, and two more over the choir. Earlier, seven towers had been planned for Laon, of which five were built. This ambitious program was taken still further at Chartres, but in the end the builders settled for the two existing west towers, and brought the transept and choir towers only as far as roof level.

The way Chartres was built marked a radical new departure. Apart from the attached shafts, the same innovations are to be seen in a more or less contemporary new building, the cathedral at Soissons. This is generally regarded as a lesser architectural achievement, though technically it is more mature, since it was here that the buttressing was given a second, upper arch from the beginning, to protect the upper areas against wind forces. In Chartres, the upper arch was not introduced until later, after the buttressing had proved inadequate. Chartres was certainly begun earlier, though there is much to be said for Soissons having been first to resolve the problem. This question is still disputed.

Chartres was essentially the model for the next era of cathedral building. It marked the beginning of "Classical" Gothic. Later cathedrals such as Reims and Amiens are variations with alterations and improvements, but contain no fundamental innovations. At Reims (see pages 60–69), begun in 1211, tracery was introduced instead of the three-light window, a discovery that was widely taken up throughout Europe. At Amiens (see pages 34–43), begun in 1220, the triforium was finally pierced when the choir was built, and

Le Mans, former cathedral

Above:
Exterior view of the choir

Above right:
Interior view of the choir

the clerestory windows were decorated on the outside with triangular gables. Both were widely emulated. With the choir at Beauvais (see pages 44–49), efforts were made to produce a *tour de force*, that is, to make something new by taking elements from both Bourges and Chartres, giving the upper choir the elevation of Chartres and the ambulatory the graduated structure of Bourges. In the choir at Le Mans, too, begun in 1217 after the Battle of Bouvines, the graduated structure of Bourges is employed, though the upper choir is still only two-storied because the triforium was left out in favor of a steep extra elevation of the piers and dividing arcades.

A conspicuous feature of the development of these cathedrals is that the height of the central nave and choir increased from building to building in an almost even curve: Noyon, 75 ft. (23 m); Laon, 79 ft. (24 m); Paris, 107 ft. (32.5 m); Chartres, 120 ft. (36.5 m); Bourges, 121 ft. (37 m); Reims, 125 ft. (38 m); Le Mans, 112 ft. (34 m); Amiens, 138 ft. (42 m); Cologne, 144 ft. (44 m); Beauvais, 157 ft. (48 m). Beauvais is thus more than twice the height of Noyon, whereas the width of the naves has only increased from 30 ft.

(9 m) to 51 ft. (15.5 m). This explains why Beauvais, with its width-to-height ratio of 1:3, seems so extraordinarily narrow and steep. The quest for height did not make for spatial harmony. The tolerable maximum was reached at Amiens and, just about, at Cologne. Beauvais was Gothic's "Flight of Icarus," and managed it twice over, for in 1284 the choir collapsed, and in 1573 so did the approximately 492-ft. (150 m)-high spire over the crossing, built on four piers and arches, then the highest tower or spire in the world, 26 ft. (8 m) higher than the one at Strasbourg Cathedral.

Around 1230, the "Classical" Gothic influenced by the Carthusians took a new direction in Paris, known as the "Rayonnant" or High Gothic style. This was the age of Gothic tracery, when the ornamental tracery patterns, whether on windows or in the blind version, now determined the appearance of cathedrals. The first truly High Gothic building was the new building of St. Denis, begun in 1231, with its tracery windows of massive dimensions and its pierced triforium, and above all the most beautiful and noble achievement of this period: the great glowing rose window in

the transept. The same architect also designed Troyes Cathedral, which, after its collapse in 1228, was rebuilt in a manner almost identical to St. Denis

The high point of Parisian High Gothic, to which the royal Sainte Chapelle also belongs, are the facades of the transept at Notre-Dame with their pointed gables and rose windows contained in square fields, where the radiating power of the spokes and the ornamental rose patterns on the periphery are most beautifully balanced (see Plates 30, 31). These inspired the even more dramatic rose window on the west facade of Strasbourg Cathedral and the over-refined tracery grille, the famous "harp strings" (see Plates 49, 51), which provided High Gothic with a quite unsurpassable ideal image of its tracery, which in its unfathomable beauty seems like a dream of eternal heavenly riches and heavenly order.

The Late Gothic, the Flamboyant style with its wavy tracery forms, produced no new cathedral buildings, but was occasionally used to enrich buildings with new show-piece windows, such as the west facade at Amiens (see ill. page 9).

On the periphery of the lands controlled by the kings of France, and in regions bordering them, cathedrals of high quality came into being, including Tours, begun about 1235, which offers a cross section through the development of Classical Gothic to Late Gothic, and Auxerre, begun in 1215, which has a pronounced, unmistakable character of its own with its Burgundian double wall, high triforium, and carefully measured spatial layout (see ill. page 20). In addition, it offers a rectangular eastern chapel, uniquely sumptuous with a thin, fragile, and highly refined structure, and entrance columns. In the east of France, the cathedrals at Châlons-sur-Marne and Metz also display important examples of Gothic tracery, the latter with its strikingly steep vaulting plan.

The Gothic cathedrals of Normandy are also as noteworthy as those built elsewhere, particularly Coutances, where the structure of Bourges has been adapted in an original way, and which has an octagonal lantern tower of remarkable height over the crossing. Also worth mentioning are Rouen Cathedral, with its highly original false galleries

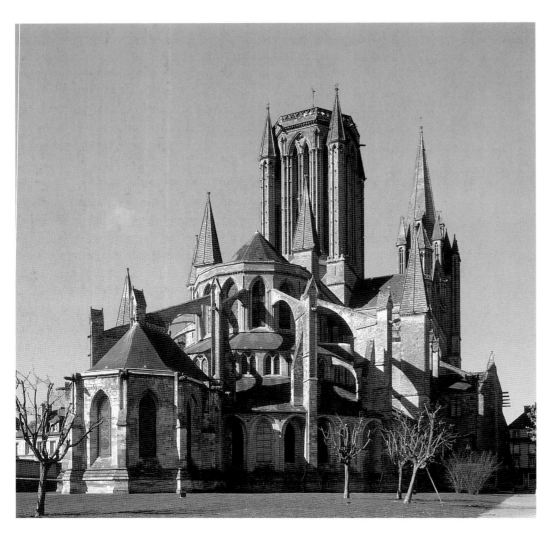

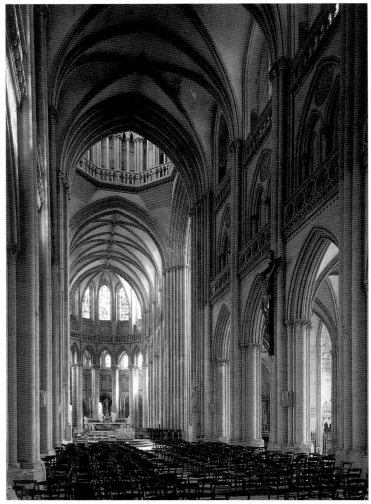

Coutances Cathedral

Above:
View from the east

Above right:
Central nave and choir

in the nave and the rampant Flamboyant magnificence of the western section, and the cathedrals of Sées and Evreux for their tracery work.

The cathedrals of Bayeux and Lisieux are also different, with their Romanesque foundations, while Lisieux has an Early Gothic nave and a High Gothic choir, almost metallically sharp in its use of forms. These buildings suffered destruction and damage in the Hundred Years' War and during the Wars of Religion, and constantly had to be repaired and altered up to the 19th century. Seen as a whole, they are unusually varied and rich. The most northerly cathedrals in France, those of Arras and Cambrai, were once very important buildings, but were destroyed in the French Revolution.

While the buildings of northern France present a variety of styles, the picture in the south is much more unified. There, in the second half of the 13th century, building was begun on large cathedrals in Clermont-Ferrand, Limoges, Narbonne, Toulouse, and Rodez, all designed with the same layout, including an ambulatory and radiating chapels and a

similar ground plan. Even the structural elements, such as compound piers and a modest triforium abutting the clerestory, are so similar that the buildings seem interchangeable. By contrast, the cathedrals of Poitiers and Albi are striking exceptions. In Poitiers in the second half of the 12th century, a large-scale hall church was built that is wholly in keeping with the Romanesque hall churches of the Poitou region, and in Albi a single-naved brick building was begun in 1282 that from the outside looks like a powerful fortress with round bastions.

There are a few other cathedrals that in France and Switzerland are assigned to the second rank, but in other countries would be rated first-class: Meaux, Lyons, Vienne, Bordeaux, Quimper, Nantes, Toul, Verdun, Lausanne, Geneva, and Besançon. Some monasteries and collegiate churches are also really cathedral buildings, such as those in Mantes, St. Quentin, St. Bénigne in Dijon, and the Cistercian cathedrals of Longpont, Royaumont, Valmagne, and Ourscamp.

The final stage of cathedral building in France is marked by Orléans. Here the still uncompleted Gothic cathedral,

which itself had replaced an uncompleted Romanesque cathedral, was destroyed in 1568 by the Huguenots with little left standing. Its reconstruction lasted with interruptions from 1601 until the 19th century, with Louis XIV personally selecting a Gothic-style design for the facade. In this way, a Post-Gothic style emerged during the Baroque period, which after the Revolution was succeeded by the Gothic style of the Restoration years. Orléans must be the only cathedral whose construction extended from the Romanesque style of the 12th century to the Neo-Gothic of the 19th.

Amiens

Amiens, located in the far north of France in Picardy, and since about 340 the seat of a bishop, did not fall to the crown of France until 1190. The cathedral had been newly built after a fire in 1137, and consecrated in 1152. In this relatively recent building, which had certainly once been vaulted, another fire broke out in 1218. Bishop Evrard decided to turn this fire to his advantage, and, instead of repairing the damage, he obtained the approval of the clergy and the people to build a new and much larger cathedral, which, with its total length of 476 ft. (145 m) and 138-ft. (42 m)-high nave, surpassed all other cathedrals. It remains the largest cathedral in France to this day. Only the Abbey Church of Cluny was larger.

Building began in 1220, nine years after Reims and 26 years after Chartres. An inscription in the "labyrinth," or symbolic pattern inlaid in the pavement of the building, names Robert de Luzarches as the first master builder, Thomas de Cormont as the second, and his son Regnault as the third. It was Regnault who had the labyrinth installed in the middle of the nave in 1288. They began, unusually, not with the choir but with the nave and west facade, for which a foundation frame of up to 39 ft. (12 m) was laid, which at that time caused amazement The nave was completed in about 1236, and the bell cages of the towers on the facade followed in 1243. The eastern section seems to have been built by about 1270. In later Gothic periods, the top sections of the towers and the nave chapels were completed, and finally, after a fire in 1528, the tall, lead-covered wood flèche, which soars far above the towers like a pointed needle.

Together with Chartres and Reims, Amiens belongs to the triad of "Classical" French cathedrals. Many admirers of Gothic, one being the architect and restorer Viollet-le-Duc, preferred Amiens because of its structural precision. Today, the compelling atmosphere of Chartres has caused it to be more appreciated, whereas Amiens is accused of being too smooth and cool, its perfection having lost the attractiveness of the original building, and in the process much of its fascination.

The whole complex relates strongly to the other two Classical cathedrals: a three-aisled nave with a twin-towered west facade, a three-aisled transept, a five-aisled choir with a polygonal east end, an ambulatory, and radiating chapels. The towers on the ends of the transepts were begun like those at Chartres and Reims, but are missing today, and with them the idea of equipping the transept with two facades was also abandoned. The choir is a 7/12 polygon with the usual trapezoid bays in the ambulatory and apsidal chapels forming five sides of an octagon. The central Lady Chapel does not conform to the symmetrical semicircle of the other radiating chapels because it projects a good deal further outward; it is a kind of Sainte Chapelle, not freestanding, but integrated into the choir as a whole.

The characteristic elevations of the walls in the central nave, the work of Robert de Luzarches, present a new, enriched version of the three-storied structures of Chartres and Reims with dividing arcades, triforium, and clerestory. The most important difference lies in the proportions. At Amiens, the bottom story, measured from the pavement to the bottom ledge of the triforium, is about as high as the triforium and clerestory together. This means that not only had the dividing arcades become taller and steeper, but so had the entire nave.

To support the nave, the architect used the clustered circular pillars of Reims, though while the pillars there seem a little stocky and sturdy, at Amiens they are slender and tall. They raise the upper part of the building to a height that seems to be beyond the physical grasp of people standing underneath. The clerestory appears to be completely removed from this world.

Compared with Chartres and Reims, the upper part of the wall is clearly different; here, the forms employed by Robert de Luzarches are completely comprehensible. In the triforium, the columns of the arcade are divided into pairs of arches with three openings each, surmounted by a trefoil and a pointed arch. Through these openings, which look like windows, the triforium is enhanced and made richer. In the clerestory windows, the twin-arched tracery with an upper circle adopted at Reims was developed further into a four-arched setting, and in the transept and nave given six arches, even eight in some places. Hardly had tracery been invented at Reims than its motifs were being increased at Amiens in both variety and magnificence. Here, it was immediately recognized that more could be done with tracery than had been realized at Reims.

Apart from these innovations with motifs, which made a much more distinctly architectural use of tracery, the architect also introduced innovations in his system of attached shafts and ribs. The attached shaft above the pillars was no longer in five parts, but had only three. The central shaft extended upward in the same thickness as the projecting shaft in the main pillar. This ran, as compound piers had done previously, from the pavement up to the base of the vaulting, and first appeared at Chartres and Reims. The accompanying shafts, intended for the diagonal ribs, engage with the pillar higher up the wall.

What was missing were the shafts for the wall ribs, but these could be left out because there were no wall ribs. They were replaced by the window arch, which was a constituent part of the tracery. The architect had realized that wall ribs were superfluous in tracery windows of this sort, and would only have overcomplicated the profile. The window arch could take over the function of the wall rib, and at the same time serve as a vaulted arch. This solution was something fundamentally new.

The window arch was equipped to the left and right with an extremely thin, perpendicular pilaster, the same size as the mullion in the center of the window. These three uprights and the connecting pointed arches provide a basic support for the tracery. Above them sits the great upper circle. These forms are set on the leading or foremost layer of the tracery, and are the main elements of the first "order," while subsidiary or filler forms of the second and third order are set back behind them. This layering of tracery first appeared at Reims, but what was new at Amiens was the systematic consistency with which it was carried out. As a result, tracery acquired its own set of rules based on these different orders. In addition, the bars of the first order reached down to the bottom ledge of the triforium. In this way, both triforium

and window were brought into a perpendicular relationship, an idea that was first realized in the apse of the upper choir at Reims, and now was transferred to the whole cathedral. Despite agreeing basically with what had been done at Chartres and Reims, the master builder succeeded in creating something architecturally new at Amiens: a cathedral with its own pronounced character.

The choir was made by the successors of Robert de Luzarches. The structure was changed here, in that the triforium was pierced, and given tracery openings crowned by gables. The tracery became even more magnificent in the clerestory windows, which from now on had six lights. This made it inevitable that for the windows of the polygon, at the focal point of the entire cathedral, and despite the narrow space available, they would put in four-light windows of equal magnificence.

The upper choir has the same clustered circular pillars as the nave. Unlike Chartres and Reims, they also continue around the polygon. As a result, these pillars are not aligned on the main east-west axis, but on the angles of the polygon, and thus are spaced at unequal intervals from each other around the inner choir. In Chartres and Reims this had been avoided by installing circular pillars with only one attached shaft.

The pillars in the double side aisles of the choir were designed differently. Here they used a new type of pillar, derived from the clustered circular pillar, which provides a shaft for each of the eight vaulted arches rising above. This is the extended clustered circular pillar, with four strong shafts for the transverse and dividing arches and four thinner ones for the diagonal ribs. The wish to have pillars serving all the vaulted arches was clearly present at Amiens, but in the upper choir compound piers would have been preferable to the clustered pillars that were installed. After Amiens, this course was not taken until Cologne.

For the external structure, Robert de Luzarches followed the style of buttressing for the nave that had been proven at Soissons and Reims, with two flying buttresses one above the other. However, he did not follow the hallmark of Reims, the angels' tabernacles. The choir offers a more ambitious external appearance. The clerestory windows are distinguished by triangular gables, and the tops of the flying buttresses have cross shapes, or at the end of the choir a Y-shape and additional blind tracery. On the flying buttresses, angled openwork tracery windows were inserted between the weight-bearing bridge and the upper buttress, making the buttresses more airy and transparent. On the upper choir there is a shrine in filigree tracery. This treatment was taken

Above left:
The *Golden Virgin* on the pier of the south transept portal

Above:
The *Beau-Dieu* on the pier of the middle portal in the west facade

up soon after in Cologne, where the structure of the choir was in parts literally copied, and elesewhere enriched even further.

The only part of the structure that did not quite reach the highest standards was the west facade, especially when compared with the facade at Reims, begun more than 30 years later. The towers, of which the right-hand one was not completed, are scarcely higher than the roof of the central nave, and seem to cower in front of the cathedral. The rose window, elsewhere set proudly in the middle of the facade, is placed much too high in relation to the extreme height of the central nave, and is too small compared with the structures beneath it to be appropriately effective. However, the three gabled portals making up the portico put all previous portals to shame. No other cathedral, not even Reims, has an entrance of such compelling power. The cycle of figures, more extensive than any before it, has been completely preserved, but one has a feeling that the execution is rather mechanical. The 52 wall figures represent a worthy collection of saints, but artistically are sublimely tedious, all different and yet all the same. By contrast, in terms of subject matter, the divinely serene Christ figure on the pier of the middle portal, the *Beau-Dieu*, a second version of the destroyed *Beau-Dieu* from Notre-Dame in Paris, is an immediately convincing work. The only first-rate sculpture at Amiens is the Madonna on the portal of the south transept, the famous *Golden Virgin*, whose elegance, posture, and robe with its long pleats provided the model for numerous later Madonna statues, as far away as Marburg and Wimpfen in Germany.

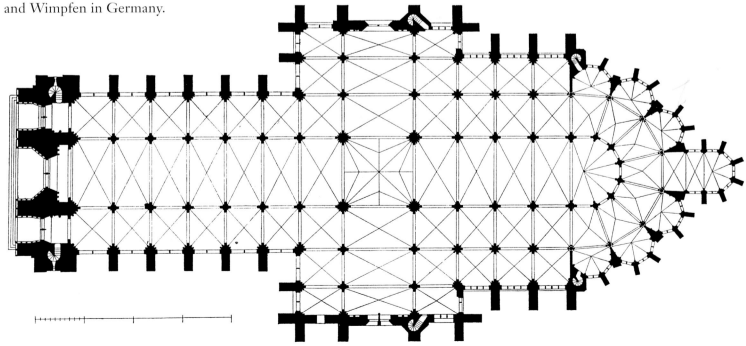

6

Beauvais

Beauvais is famous for being the tallest cathedral in France, with a nave height of 157 ft. (48 m), but the slur of hypertrophic excess also clings to it, for which it has been severely punished, not once but twice.

The old 10th-century cathedral was a low, modest building, the nave of which still exists rather miserably in the shadow of the new building. It was damaged by fire in 1180, and again in 1225. The second of these fires provided the opportunity for a new building, the foundation stone of which was laid in the same year, five years after Amiens and 31 years after Chartres. As a result of serious social unrest in the city, which even required the intervention of Louis IX (St. Louis), the works proceeded slowly, and at first building was confined to the choir. Not until about 1255, three centuries after building had first begun, could construction be started above the side aisles and the ambulatory, under the leadership of a new architect. In 1272 the choir was completed.

Then, 12 years later, in 1284, the first disaster occurred, when the vault of the upper choir and part of the clerestory collapsed. Only the apse was spared. Even today, the causes of the collapse have not been clearly established. The restorer, architect Viollet-le-Duc, suspected bad mortar but, most of all, negligent work on the upper parts of the building. Construction errors were also considered, and there had certainly been something foolhardy in the way the inner pillars of the buttressing, which rise up between the upper choir and the outer buttresses, do not stand on their own independent base; instead, they rest on the outer wall of the choir, supported by the transverse arches of the inner side aisle and the ambulatory.

When it was reconstructed, a process that dragged on until the end of the 14th century, the building was strengthened, and the arcades of the four bays of the choir were subdivided into double arcades with the help of intermediate pillars; this can be seen clearly in today's building. This subdivision was continued into the clerestory, where the original window layout was halved. Two windows were made out of each of the original ones. Finally, the vaulting was given an additional transverse rib in order to halve the crowns of the cross vaulting, which were far too large. The formerly quadripartite vaulting now became sexpartite. The new structure has proved its durability to this day, even though no further buttressing was added, which in fact left the new transverse ribs without support.

Building was not extended westward until the end of the Hundred Years' War. The south and north transepts and crossing date from 1500. Then, however, instead of going on to build a nave, it was decided in about 1560 to erect a colossal crossing tower, which was completed in 1569. It had four stone stories and a wooden spire reaching a height of about 492 ft. (150 m), even taller than the cathedral tower at Strasbourg, which is 466 ft. (142 m) high. It soon became clear, however, that the weight-bearing pillars on the west side of the crossing, where there was still no nave, really needed further support. In 1573, when work was about to start on this, the western pillars gave way, and the tower collapsed. After this second disaster, the damage was repaired, and work started to extend the building. The nave, which was planned with five aisles and was therefore bound to be something special, was later set aside. The cathedral has thus remained a naveless torso, comparable to the cathedrals of Narbonne and Toulouse in southern France.

When building began in 1225, the plan provided for a five-aisled choir with a seven-sided polygon, an ambulatory, and a symmetrical semicircle of radiating chapels. The ground plan of the choir corresponded closely to that of Amiens. The latter was certainly begun after Beauvais, although it is possible that the whole layout of the cathedral was established as early as 1220, when building began there. At Beauvais, the three bays of the choir were noticeably deeper than those at Amiens, and the wall sections correspondingly wider. It seems the builders were aiming to achieve a greater sense of space, to make an intentional contrast with the apse and its more tightly spaced pillars and stilted arches. At Reims they had avoided this contrast by every possible means. What one masons' lodge felt to be unsatisfactory was especially emphasized in another. After the collapse of the tower at Beauvais, however, ideas about spaciousness were reversed, as the newly installed intermediate pillars actually halved the depth of the bays, and produced very narrow wall sections, closer to those on the sides of the apse of the choir. Breadth became narrowness. In addition, the clustered circular pillars correspond to those at Amiens in their tall, narrow section and triple clusters of shafts.

Beauvais Cathedral differs from Amiens, and the two other Classical cathedrals of Chartres and Reims, in that the side aisles are not of the same height but graduated. The inner side aisle and the ambulatory have their own clerestory and triforium. This solution ultimately goes back to Bourges, the outsider among the earlier cathedrals, but the idea could also have come from Le Mans Cathedral, begun in 1217, or the slightly earlier, cathedral-like collegiate church at St. Quentin, for both of these adopted the graduated system of Bourges ahead of Beauvais.

How the first architect, who started the building, conceived the upper parts is not known. The model may have been Le Mans, where there is no triforium and the clerestory sits directly above the arcades. That would have led to a nave with less steep proportions. The second architect opted for the three-storied structure of the Classical cathedrals, and placed a triforium above the arcades, piercing it like the choir at Amiens, and building a tall clerestory above it. The triforium is positioned about halfway up. The imposts for the vaulting were placed high up in the window area, higher than at Chartres, Reims, and Amiens. The whole structure can be seen as a synthesis between the structural system of the Classical cathedrals, which characterizes the upper choir, and that of Bourges, which is limited to the side aisles and the ambulatory. As a synthesis, it sought to unite what could not be unified. The Classical tradition was the decisive factor, however. Earlier, at St. Quentin, the design had proceeded on similar lines, putting the same synthesis into operation.

Left:
Top of the choir from the south

Below:
Cross-section through the choir

This concept had consequences for the proportions of the building. Since the staggering of the side aisles made very tall dividing arcades necessary, the choir had to be similarly lofty to ensure that the clerestory was about the same size as the arcades. This not only produced a record height of 157 ft. (48 m), but also made the building extremely steep and narrow. It is not so much the steepness as the narrowness that most visitors find excessive in the interior, to the point that some are so impressed by the building's boundless height that they cannot breathe properly.

This extreme effect is almost more striking on the outside of the cathedral. While both the graduated lower levels retain a sense of human proportion, this is completely lost in the upper choir, which soars even more steeply upward. There is a break between the lower levels and the upper choir. With the buttressing, too, new and undreamt-of dimensions were opened up, which previously had been impossible in the engineering of buildings. The outer buttresses seem so solid in the way their lower parts are raked back but then soar upward like thin wall screens, while the inner columns look like slender, excessively extended columns. The flying buttresses sweep at dizzying heights from the outer to the inner pillars and from there onto the clerestory. They are so thin, they seem more like mere struts. Along the sides of the choir, near the angle with the crossing, the buttress columns are strengthened by their cruciform shape, and are themselves buttressed by the arms of the crosses.

All in all, the buttressing is such that it sends the viewer into a state of bemused wonder that anything like it can actually stand up. Today, for safety reasons, iron ties have been employed throughout the structure. As we know, the architect's flight of fancy has already caused the choir to collapse once. Since then, the buttressing has done its work, however skeptically many observers may have looked skyward.

Plates 8–10

8 Choir and transept from the south
9 Looking into the choir
10 Vault of the choir

Right:
Ground plan of the choir before its collapse in 1284

Far right:
Ground plan of the building today with intermediate pillars in the choir

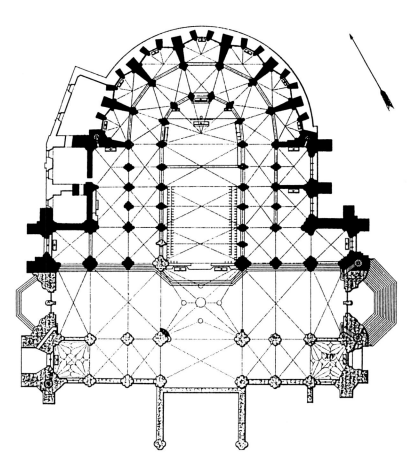

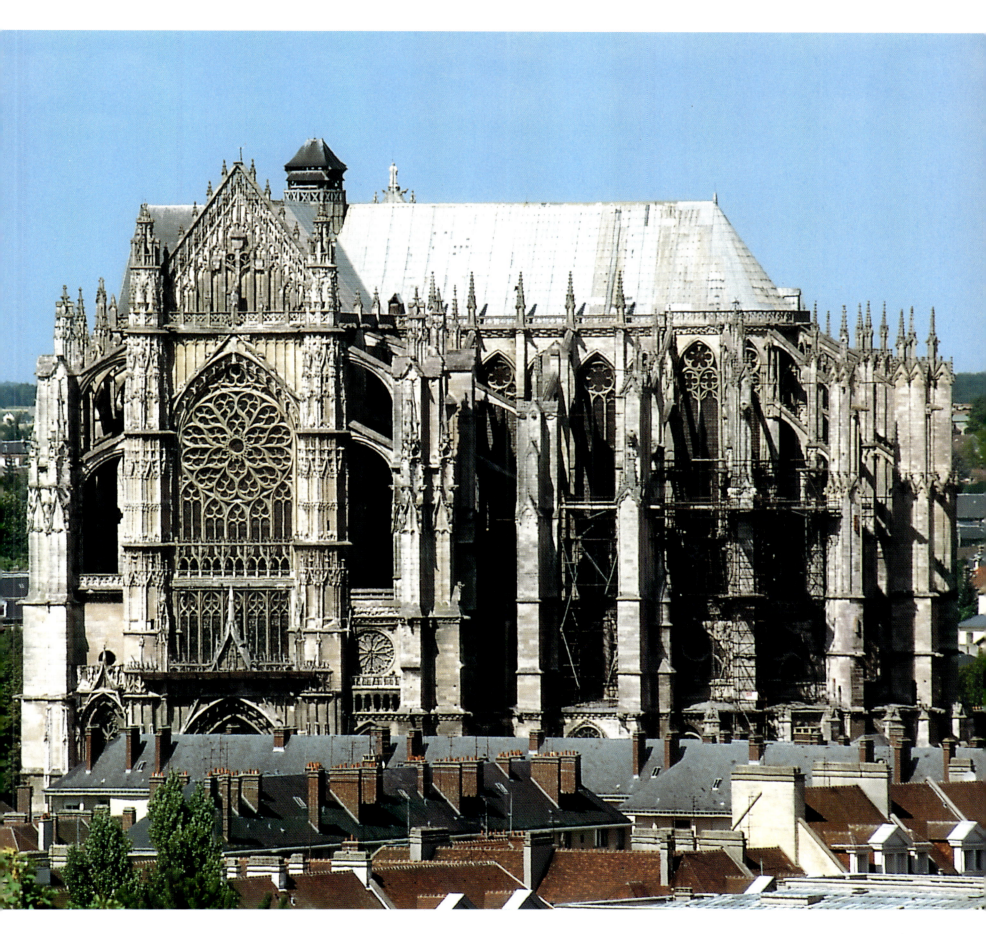

Laon

Located on a rocky outcrop, the city of Laon is visible for miles around. In the late Carolingian period, it was the capital of the kingdom of the Western Franks. Later the bishop claimed the title of duke, and ranked as a peer of France. At the royal coronation, he came directly after the archbishop of Reims in the hierarchy. The old cathedral, which was also a place of pilgrimage dedicated to the Virgin Mary, was damaged by fire in 1111. Bishop Gauthier de Mortagne began the new building soon after 1155. The cathedral would have been completed around 1200, when the works on the west facade were concluded, but, immediately after that date, the choir and ambulatory, which, unusually, had no chapels, were replaced by a choir almost as long as the nave and with a similar structure. At the east end it has neither apse nor ambulatory, but is square-ended and distinguished by a large rose window. Related rose windows were built in both arms of the transept and in the west facade, thus giving the cathedral rose windows on all four sides. The south rose window was later replaced by a tracery window.

The square-ended choir is a unique curiosity among French cathedrals. In 1106, Gaudri, former chancellor to the English king Henry I, became bishop (he was murdered in 1111), and perhaps for that reason the building program in Laon took its lead from England, where the square-ended choir was gradually winning acceptance. The open, square crossing tower follows a similar pattern. In France such towers were rare, although they were common in England.

Laon is the best example of a French Early Gothic cathedral, with its four-storied structure consisting of side aisle, gallery, triforium, and clerestory. The dividing arcades have sturdy circular columns. The gallery opening in the story above is a double arcade with enclosing arches, the so-called biforium motif, which was often used in Carolingian times. The low triforium is, by contrast, a blind arcade with small pillars. The back wall of the triforium is built so far back from these pillars that the passage behind the blind arcading became a rather wider, box-shaped walkway—hence the term "box triforium." Finally, the clerestory has fairly small windows set within the vaulted area. The bottom ledge of the clerestory is level with the springing line of the nave vaulting. The vaulting is also typical of the Early Gothic: quadripartite cross-rib vaulting in the side aisles and galleries, and sexpartite vaulting in the central nave and upper choir. The sexpartite arrangement was needed because one section of the vault had to connect with two wall sections in an almost square bay, not unlike the double bays of the intersecting system commonly used in German Romanesque architecture. The ends of the double bays were marked by the transverse arches. In the middle of the bay an additional transverse rib crosses the nave exactly like the transverse arch. The transverse rib crosses over the diagonal rib at the boss. With the help of the transverse rib—which is what it is there for—the two lateral panels of the vault adjacent to the clerestory windows are divided into two halves. The advantage is that the panels are only half as big as they would be in a quadripartite vault, and are easier to construct.

The engaged pillars for the vaults only begin above the capitals of the circular columns, and thus the whole wall system seems to be thrust upward by these pillars. At Laon, a unified structure was favored, and for that reason the architects avoided putting in alternating supports that used composite main columns and circular intermediate pillars, as, for example, had been employed at Noyon Cathedral, which was begun at a slightly earlier date. The choice of circular columns probably stemmed from the original plan for the choir, which terminated in an apse and was derived from the apses used at Noyon and St. Denis with their semicircle of columns.

There is a hint of additional supports being employed on the circular columns at Laon, where the pedestals and the abaci of the capitals alternate between being square on the main supports and octagonal on the intermediate supports. In both the eastern bays of the nave the architects tried to emphasize the main supports by giving them thin, tubelike pillars fashioned as individual pieces, and standing slightly clear in front of the column, in the manner of a downpipe. To tie them into the column, they used the pedestals, the abaci of the capitals, and, most conspicuous of all, shaft rings, or annulets. The projecting, unattached pillars are fixed *en délit*, that is, not in the same places as the stone columns behind them. This *en délit* technique is a characteristic of French Gothic and in particular of Laon. It is used to maximize the amount of circular mass contained in the projecting pillars. The form of pillar tried out in the eastern bays of the nave was not continued when the building was extended westward, and remained an experiment. It was, however, important for future developments in that these pillars acted as a predecessor to the pillars of Classical Gothic: the clustered pillars that were widely used after Chartres.

The *en délit* solution was also generally used in the engaged columns of the upper wall, which were braced from top to bottom by no fewer than five shaft rings, which at first had been no more than a technical device for masonry work, but now became a structural element and thus part of the architectural design. Above the main columns are loosely grouped clusters of five engaged shafts, which correspond exactly to the arches of the vaulting to which they are linked: the transverse arch, the two diagonal ribs, and the wall ribs. In between these, a group of three shafts that extends upward over the intermediate columns needs to serve only the transverse rib and the two wall ribs. The alternation of columns in the arcade below corresponds to the alternating pattern of shafts used above them. A circular shape was used everywhere for the shafts, the columns of the gallery, and the triforium, and this was continued in the design of the columns in the side aisles and galleries and also in the shape of the arches and ribs. It is this circular form that lends the architecture a particularly vigorous, richly structured relief. It was also a distinguishing feature of Early Gothic elsewhere, but it was in Laon that it reached its zenith.

A conspicuous feature of the cathedral is the unity of the structure, which is rigorously preserved from the nave through the three-aisled transept to the choir, making it comparable to the Romanesque pilgrims' churches of France, such as St. Sernin in Toulouse. In the arms of the transept, the side aisles and galleries are also grouped around the transept, as they were in the pilgrims' churches, although here the gallery is not an independent space, but just an open platform set against the wall beneath the great rose window. The platform forms a kind of raised forecourt for a chapel added to the transept on the east side and extending outward with a polygonal apse, and has an underchapel at ground level. This double chapel, perhaps originally built with pilgrims in mind, is again something unique.

Above all, the exterior is unparalleled. The facades of both transepts were originally planned as facades with twin towers on the front of each. These, together with the crossing tower, would have made for a group of five towers. The model for this idea was Tournai Cathedral, now in Belgium, an extraordinarily rich Late Romanesque building, which with its transept and choir, unlike Laon, formed a triple apse. At Laon, only the eastern one of each tower remains, its substructure concealing a double chapel that was never built, although the pillars would have been strong enough to support towers on top.

The towers are unmistakable, with their multistoried tabernacles placed at right angles to each other on the four canted edges of the towers. These open structures, transparent even from a long way away, alternate on the north tower between rectangular and octagonal. On the south tower they are all octagonal. This tower later supplied

South transept and wall elevation in the nave

the model for the west towers of the cathedrals in Bamberg and Naumburg (see Plates 86, 95).

Laon's greatest fame is derived from the twin-towered west facade. Shortly after the towers were built, they were praised by the architect Villard d'Honnecourt as something unique. The most important motifs since the facade of St. Denis—the three portals, the rose windows, and the tops of the towers—were here brought into a new relationship. In this they were helped by an additional characteristic motif: the rhythmic, three-part architecture of the pillars projecting boldly from the wall of the facade like an aqueduct on two levels.

Taking its lead from the circular rose window, the round arch is here predominant. At ground level are the three arches of the portal, with their tunnel vaults and gables; above the rose window is a row of deep niches, the middle one wider and taller than the others, wider even than the middle portal beneath. The porch and the niches break up the shape of the facade, cutting into the structure with a certain impetuous wildness, and giving the whole west front a spatial depth that no facade had possesed up to that time. This depth is continued by the gallery, with its staggered variation of height, and in the open corner tabernacles of the towers. Originally there were also pointed turrets on the towers and all their tabernacles. One of these survived until 1793, but then was pulled down because it offended the eyes of the honest burghers, who saw it as a symbol of feudal arrogance.

The architect of the west facade was, according to Georg Dehio, "a genius still encumbered by a trace of barbarism, but a genuine genius, full of originality and joyful boldness." Since the west facade was completed, along with five of the seven towers planned for it, the cathedral has stood on its rock like the vision of a heavenly mountain. The effect is emphasized by the way the heavens are visible through the openwork towers, lighting the building with a special aura.

Plates 11–17

11 General view of the town from the southwest
12 View from the northeast
13 West facade
14 Choir looking northeast
15 Central nave looking east
16 View into the crossing tower
17 North transept and upper wall in the nave of the choir

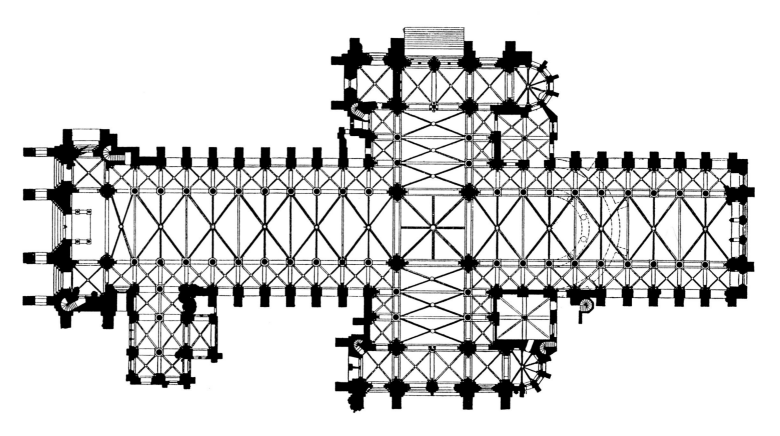

Reims

The archbishopric of Reims was founded as early as the third century. Its spiritual heads included saints such as Nicasius and Remigius, the patron saints of the two large abbeys in Reims. The archbishopric had the right to a special status in the kingdom: the archbishops were not only primates of *Gallia Belgica* and peers of France, but they also had the privilege of crowning the king. Coronation ceremonies took place in Reims Cathedral from 936 until 1825.

Around the middle of the 12th century, and very much in the spirit of the age, Archbishop Samson began building a new cathedral in the Early Gothic style to replace the old building, which probably had a Carolingian western arm. This had not been completed when in 1210 a fire broke out, allegedly an act of arson by Archbishop Albéric de Humbert. Faced with all the latest developments being admired in Chartres, Soissons, and Bourges, the archbishop was no longer satisfied with the cathedral then under construction. He had to have something more modern and splendid, and in due course his wishes were fully granted.

After a year spent planning and setting up the organizational side, the present building was begun in 1211, 17 years after Chartres. The works had to be financed by numerous collections levied throughout the country, and were interrupted in 1233 by a popular rebellion that drove out the archbishop and canons, who were not allowed back until 1236. In 1241, 30 years after the building was started, the choir was made over to the canons. This meant that the east bays of the nave were finished; the choir itself was not placed at the east end, as was usual, but in the central nave, right next to the crossing. The west facade was completed later, in about 1255, but construction of the towers dragged on until the 15th century. The names of the master builders were commemorated in a labyrinth inlaid in the pavement, taking up two full bays in the western part of the nave. In 1779 it was removed because the canons were disturbed by the noise of children playing on it. Similar labyrinths were installed at Chartres and Amiens. The one in Chartres has been preserved, though the names are missing, and the one in Amiens has been reconstructed. The form of the labyrinth at Reims and the names of the master builders are known from written records. The "head of the church," the polygon of the choir, was begun by Jean d'Orbais. Jean le Loup carried on the works for 16 years, then Gaucher de Reims, and finally, for 35 years, Bernard de Soissons was the architect. The last two were responsible for the western arm and facade.

The model that provoked the new building in Reims was Chartres Cathedral. The whole program followed that of its predecessor: a three-aisled nave with a twin-towered facade, a three-aisled transept, also with two towers, which did not rise above roof level, and a five-aisled presbytery with an ambulatory and radiating chapels. The eastern arm at Reims is, however, much shorter than the one in Chartres, while the nave at Reims is longer. The reason for this is that the canons' choir was in the nave, so that less space was needed in the eastern arm and more in the nave.

Jean d'Orbais, the first architect, developed his architectural plan based loosely on Chartres. The presbytery terminates with five bays rather than seven, as a result of which the radiating chapels are bigger and the arcades of the main apse are less narrow. In his allocation of space in the ground plan, the architect concentrated on joining the sides of the polygon as smoothly as possible to the east–west walls of the presbytery. The depth of the three bays is gradually reduced going toward the apse, and the wall sections are correspondingly narrower until the last one, which almost matches the width of the next bay in the polygon. This makes for a smooth progression into the apse. Clearly, the architect's chief objective was to unify his structural elements.

This objective applied equally to the structure as a whole. The three-storied structure of Chartres is repeated here in similar proportions, with dividing arcades, a triforium, and large-scale clerestory windows, but the clustered pillars, also taken from Chartres, were treated differently, the alternating supports being abandoned in favor of the sustained unity of circular pillars. In the polygon, the pillars are circular, and carry only one shaft.

For the engaged ribs in the upper wall, the cluster of five shafts was the same as at Chartres. Although the windows were also similar, both in the side aisles and the clerestory, at Reims an innovation of great consequence was made, which from then on became a distinctive mark of the Gothic style: tracery. The windows were subdivided, like the window groups at Chartres, with two main lights and a top circle with a sexfoil ornament, although these were no longer made with thick posts and stone slabs, but are slender and for the most part circular. At Chartres the spandrels were still massive, but now they, too, could be pierced and glazed. The windows have the same tracery in every part of the cathedral, even in the chapels and the main apse. Tracery was a further means of establishing unity.

This unity was also sustained in the handling of individual details. Circular shapes predominate everywhere, strong but not thick, and retaining a sculptural element. The architects steered a middle course in every respect in their design decisions, looking always to achieve a happy balance.

In their handling of space, too, and the relationship between height and width, they attained a polished harmony hardly to be found in any other cathedral.

One of the typical features at Reims is the design of the walls in the chapels and side aisles. Here, the windows are set so far back in the surrounding wall that deep wall niches emerge, framed by pillars. The pillars provide space for a passage, the *passage rémois*, a motif adopted from the Early Gothic Abbey Church of St. Rémi in Reims.

Compared with Chartres, its model, the architects of Reims sought their own design solution in the external buttressing. Technically, they went back to the scheme used at Soissons with two superposed arms, the upper one running up to the eaves. At the five-aisled eastern end, the buttressing had to be further subdivided with an intermediate support. Unusually, the inner and outer arms are not in line with each other, and do not run parallel at the same angle, but rise at different angles. There is no convincing explanation for this irregularity, though it may be that the architect decided intentionally to stagger the points of intersection between the inner and outer arms.

The great distinguishing feature of the exterior is supplied by the tabernacles on the columns of the flying buttresses, each one topped by a pointed pinnacle, and containing the figure of an angel. These tabernacles, as well as the fronts of the transepts and the west facade, also contribute to the unity of the building, for they surround it completely. The upper part of the cathedral is surrounded by an army of angels, which keep watch in the tabernacles like sentries in their boxes. On the transept, kings take the place of the angels (see ill. page 15). Mainly it is the tabernacles that give the whole cathedral its unique, uplifting majesty, particularly at the eastern end, where the concentration of sculptural power is nothing short of grand.

The high point of the exterior is the rightly acclaimed west facade with its three deep, enormous portals crowned with triangular gables, its radiant rose window, the tops of the towers, and octagonal openwork structures with canted corners, like the towers at Laon. It seems as though this facade represents a synthesis, a bringing together in one facade of the two earlier masterpieces at Laon and Notre-Dame in Paris, although they are different from each other. Here, the impetuousness of Laon is refined by the clearer harmony of Notre-Dame, and enriched still further by the bell-shaped portals at Amiens. The overall effect is also helped by the fact that the pointed turrets planned for the towers, and on which work had already begun, were never completed.

The *Beau-Dieu* on the portal of the north transept (archive photo taken before the head was destroyed)

Like Chartres, Reims is a place famous for sculpture. Increasingly it became a center that could have been called Europe's academy for sculptors. In Reims, an old Roman city, people turned first to Roman sculpture, and on the portals of the north transept created an antique style of handling drapery, full of hollows and loops, especially in the figures of Peter and Paul, which represents the first high point in the sculpture of Reims, raising it above the mediocre quality of previous years.

Long before the portals were built, work was under way on a magnificent series of wall figures, including the famous *Visitation of Mary* group, in which the antique style was mastered. The sculptor obviously had no completely preserved Roman figures to use as models, only torsos. He copied their postures, then placed Gothic busts of his own invention on the bodies, in which there is still a trace of the antique *contrapposto*, or counterpoise, adding his own Gothic liveliness to the compositional balance.

When the portals were finally built, the figures were transferred to them and supplemented with new ones. This meant that their value as pieces of art counted for more than their place in the continuity of the series. Thematic parallels were seen as less important than overall symmetry. The sculptor responsible for the end product was the so-called Master of Joseph. His figures, and particularly the angels, have a completely new elegance in their bearing and movement and, in addition, are given enchanting smiles (see ill. page 10). This is an expression of French wit, a worldly quality that would have been unthinkable in Chartres Cathedral.

The masterpiece of another sculptor is the *Beau-Dieu* that later replaced an older figure on the portal of the north transept. The figure embodies the serious and at the same time gentle beauty of Christ. Unfortunately the head, one of the most impressive divine images of all time, was destroyed in World War I.

The cathedral is alive with sculpted figures, even around the rose windows of the transept and on the inner side of the west wall, illustrating themes from the Old and New Testaments and other sources. The most surprising works are to be found high up, for example, in atlantes and consoles bearing figures of prophets and apostles, in which the workshops constantly surpassed themselves, and gave European sculpture a new drive that lasted until Bamberg and Naumburg (see ills. pages 176–87, 188–99).

Plates 18–24

18 West facade

19 *Visitation of Mary* group from the middle portal of the west facade (see also Plate 20)

20 Middle portal of the west facade

21 Choir and south transept

22 Central nave looking west

23 Interior of the west wall (see also Plate 22)

24 Choir from the southeast

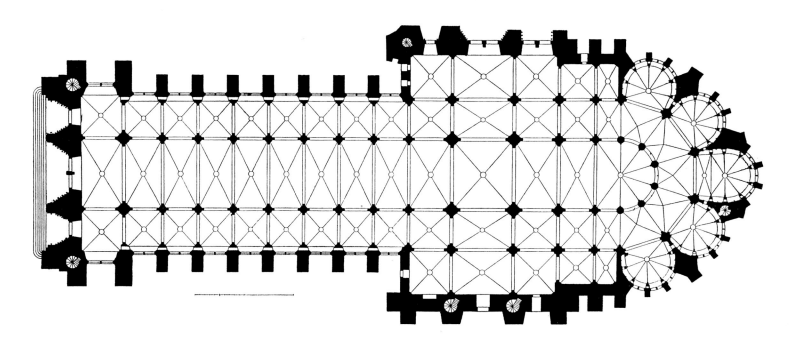

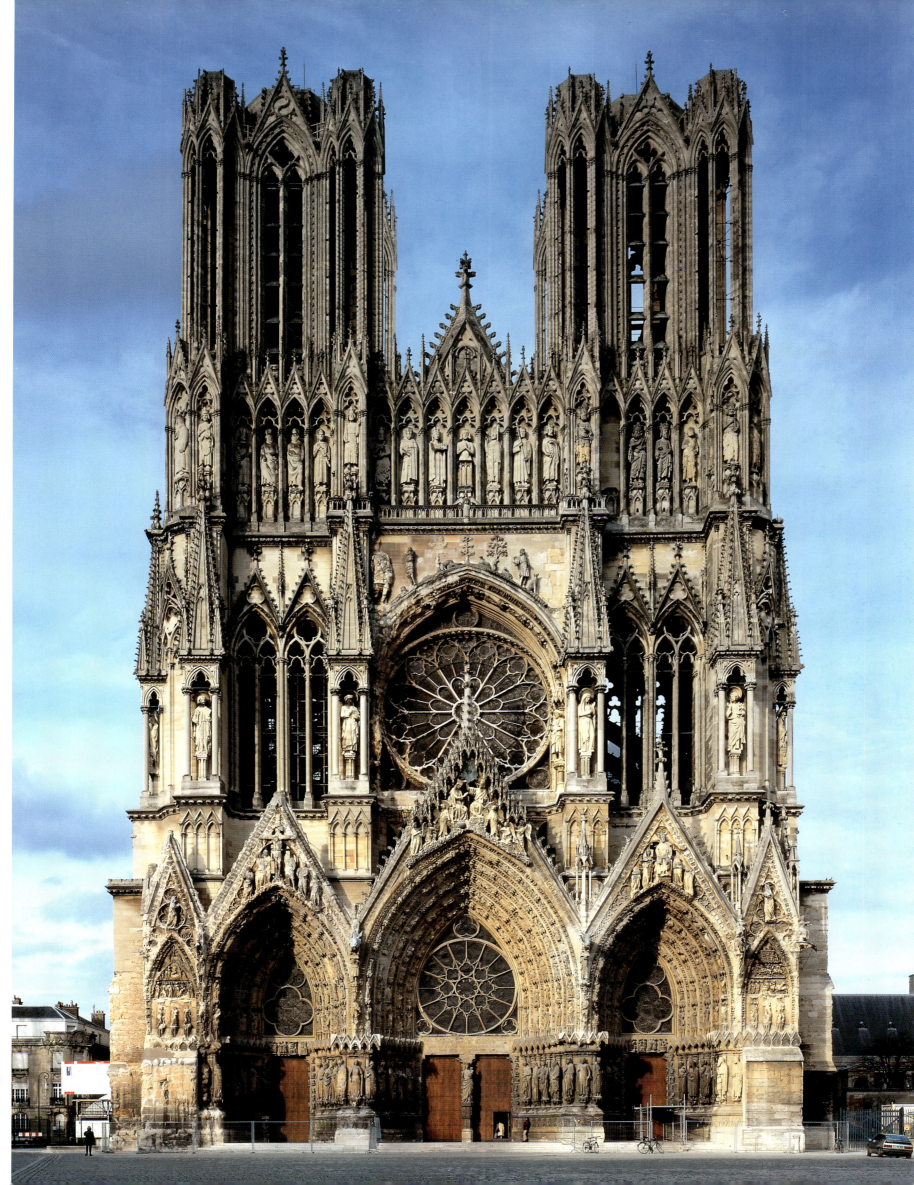

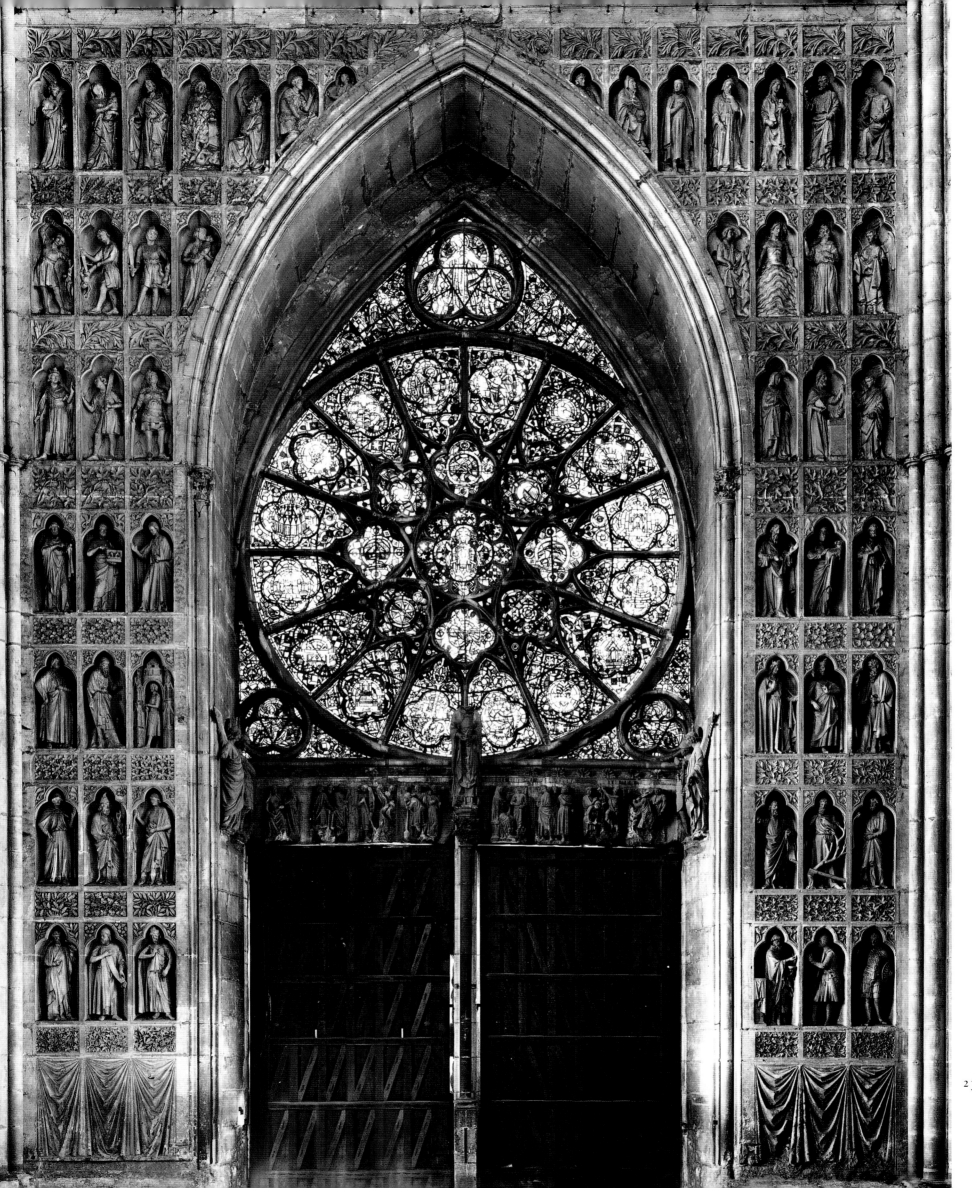

Paris

Paris once again became the capital of France under the ruling dynasty of the Capetians, taking over from Laon. The bishop of Paris was subordinate to the archbishop of Sens, but, because of his association with the kings of France, his standing was higher, particularly since the university was also under his supervision. The diocese of Paris was, in addition, one of the richest in the country. This special position found its outward expression in the Cathedral of Notre-Dame. Bishop Maurice de Sully began building it in 1163 to replace the very old previous foundation. With its grand dimensions—426 ft. (130 m) long, with a nave 115 ft. (35 m) high and a five-aisled layout—its builders determined from the outset to outdo by a clear margin all previous Early Gothic cathedrals. To this could be added its undeclared ambition to be a worthy royal metropolitan cathedral. In 1182, the choir was consecrated, and the whole of the interior was completed by about 1218.

Notre-Dame is a five-aisled, galleried basilica with double side aisles of equal height, a single-aisled transept that does not project beyond the outer perimeter, and a west facade with two towers. The then obligatory ambulatory formed a semicircle, like the main apse, and was only later transformed into a polygon when that style became the norm. The double side aisles are continued evenly around the main apse, as at St. Denis, but are incomparably larger, and have a different ground plan: the bays in the semicircle are divided into five sections, like the Early Gothic cathedrals at Sens, Senlis, Noyon, and Laon. The advantage of this five-part division was that the wall sections and arcades of the main apse and the choir retained the same width. This was done to assure the greatest possible unity between the choir and the apse.

The bays in the ambulatory take the form of curved trapeziums. The trapeziums of the outer aisle were so large that they had to be subdivided. The number of supports between the inner and outer aisles were double those in the main apse. This meant that for every arcade in the apse there were two in the semicircle in the middle of the ambulatory, and consequently there were usually three wall sections in the outer encirclement to each trapezium-shaped bay. In the middle section, each bay formerly housed a small chapel added on like a projecting minichoir, the whole group forming a set of miniature radiating chapels.

Within the individual segments of the ambulatory, the layout of the supports and wall sections gave rise to a simple but unusual vaulting pattern. Instead of the trapezium vault with sharply curving cross ribs, as used at St. Denis and which was increasingly becoming the accepted solution, here there were triangular vaults: over each trapezium in the inner aisle of the ambulatory there were three, and five over the outer aisle, each one facing away from its neighbor.

The wall elevation in the upper choir and nave is now three-storied: at ground level are the dividing arcades with their sturdy circular pillars; above them the high gallery with double openings surmounted by a blind arch; this runs through the choir as a double arcade, and in the nave has three openings. Above the gallery are the slender clerestory windows with very simple tracery consisting of two lights and a top circle. The windows reach down to a point well below the impost of the vaulting. In their present form they date back to about 1230. Originally they were much smaller, with their bottom ledge located slightly above the impost. In the wall space between the gallery and the windows, today occupied by the lower part of the windows, was a circular rosette that opened onto the roof truss of the gallery. These rosettes were an unusual variation on the more customary triforium story, and were soon replaced because the tiny clerestory windows let in too little light, and so had to be enlarged. The rosettes were reconstructed in the 19th century by Viollet-le-Duc, at least in the area of the crossing.

The vaulting in the choir, nave, and transept is all sexpartite. This design made for an elegant transition to the quadripartite vaults of the radiating chapels, because the vaulting in the nave part of the choir is semisexpartite. The engaged columns are tripartite throughout, however, though strictly speaking they should have had five shafts at the ends of the bays, because they have to serve five arches in the vault. Thus, they could not avoid having two ribs, the diagonal rib and the upper wall rib, branching out of one shaft. In the middle of the bay the three shafts are sufficient, because here there are only the transverse rib and the two wall ribs on either side of it. This inconsistency in the shaft-rib system was accepted. It is a clear instance of how careful they were to preserve unity in Paris, which also explains why the shafts as well as the gallery openings and the tracery windows maintain the same form around the semicircle of the apse.

Unlike Laon Cathedral, which was begun at a slightly earlier date, the shafts in the choir at Notre-Dame are very thin, while in the central nave they are almost wafer-thin. Even the wall, much of which has survived, is thin. Their thinness and flatness are typical of this architectural style, and provide a further means of unifying the structure.

In the nave an alternating system of supports was used, not in the dividing arcades but between the double side aisles. Every other pillar is surrounded by 12 individual tubelike shafts, giving the pillar the appearance of an architectonic sculpture. They bring a lively rhythm to the double-aisled naves of the side aisles, which is very different from the side aisles in the choir, with their monotonous sequence of similar pillars.

On the exterior, the fragility of the walls and the great height of the building made extensive buttressing essential, with deeply projecting buttress pillars on the side aisles and open flying buttresses over the lateral roofs. Originally there seem to have been intermediate supports for the arches above the pillars dividing the side aisles, which did not continue uninterrupted up to the clerestory, but were divided in two. These double flying buttresses were replaced around 1300 by single ones, which seem extremely thin as they boldly span the space between the buttress pillar and the clerestory. The intermediate supports then became unnecessary, and were removed.

The most famous part of Notre-Dame, and at the same time a Parisian landmark, is the twin-towered west facade, built some time between 1200 and 1245. This is the opposite of the facade at Laon. Each of the towers covers the area of four bays in the side aisles, and is as wide as a double side aisle. The five-aisled layout of the cathedral is not reflected in the facade; it is uncompromisingly divided into three parts with three exemplary portals at ground level. Above them is a radiant rose window. The fame of the facade rests on the way that its various parts are so harmoniously balanced: the side parts and the middle, the towers and the various stories, the vertical and the horizontal, the upright stance and the lateral cohesiveness. This was achieved with the help of an immediately clear grid of various rectangles, divided by two galleries: the Gallery of Kings above the portals and the considerably deeper openwork tracery gallery in front of the gable of the central nave roof and the lower section of the tower. The contrasts provide a synthesis in which none of the elements is overbearing or too robust. The result is completely harmonious, the proportions classically elegant; nothing could be added or removed without spoiling the balance. It is fortunate, given the form in which we see the cathedral today, that the turrets originally planned for it were not carried out.

Finally, tracery in the Flamboyant Gothic style gave the exterior a new look, when, after about 1225, chapels with rich tracery windows were added between the buttresses of the side aisles and the ambulatory, and triangular gables appeared above the windows and blind tracery on the fronts of the buttress pillars. These chapels, 37 in all, completely surround the cathedral.

The arms of the transept were then extended outward to align with the chapels, and were given magnificent new facades. In 1258, according to the inscription by Jean de Chelles, the north facade was begun. The somewhat later south facade was the work of his successor Pierre de Montreuil (d. 1267), who built the nave at St. Denis and possibly its transept. The immediate model for Notre-Dame was provided by the transept fronts of St. Denis, with their splendid rose windows placed above a pierced triforium; the spandrels of the windows were also pierced. The north rose window in Paris, which has a diameter of 46 ft. (14 m), is an even more refined reworking of the north rose window at St. Denis, turned through half a segment; its 12 inner spokes were increased to 16 and in the outer section doubled to 32. On the periphery, the radiating petals of the rose terminate in a band of pointed arches and trefoils. The ensemble is a complete treasure with all the refinement of a piece of jewelry.

The south rose window is a variant of the north one. It was changed by Viollet-le-Duc, who turned it, so that the

North transept and choir from the southwest: in the area of the crossing, the original four-story elevation with rosettes has been reconstructed.

spokes, unlike those of the north window, are arranged along a vertical and horizontal axis, making it correspond to the north rose window at St. Denis. Each of the transept facades of Notre-Dame has a portal with a pointed gable flanked by smaller, narrower gables. The gables and the circle of the rose window determine the appearance of the whole facade. Both have a luminosity that outshines the rest of the building, making the cathedral seem from a distance like one of the crowning glories of Gothic tracery, although it is really one of the pinnacles of Early Gothic.

The sculptures on the portals were extensively destroyed in the French Revolution, but on the west facade parts of the archivolts and the tympanums have survived, and on the portal of the south transept facade all the sculptures are still in place, as is the Madonna on the north transept. On the west front, the damaged figures were replaced during the cathedral's restoration in the 19th century.

Ground plan of Notre-Dame, the upper half shown with chapels in the buttresses

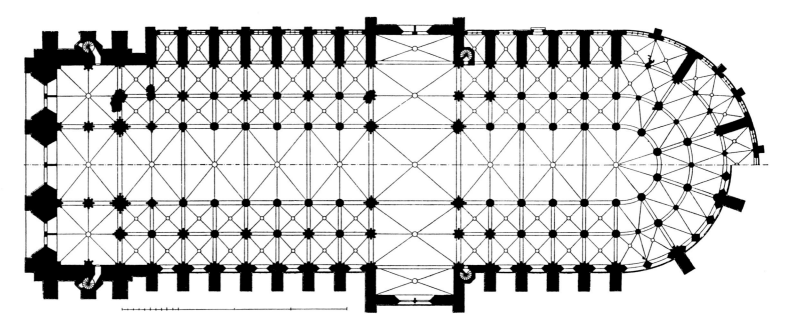

74 *France*

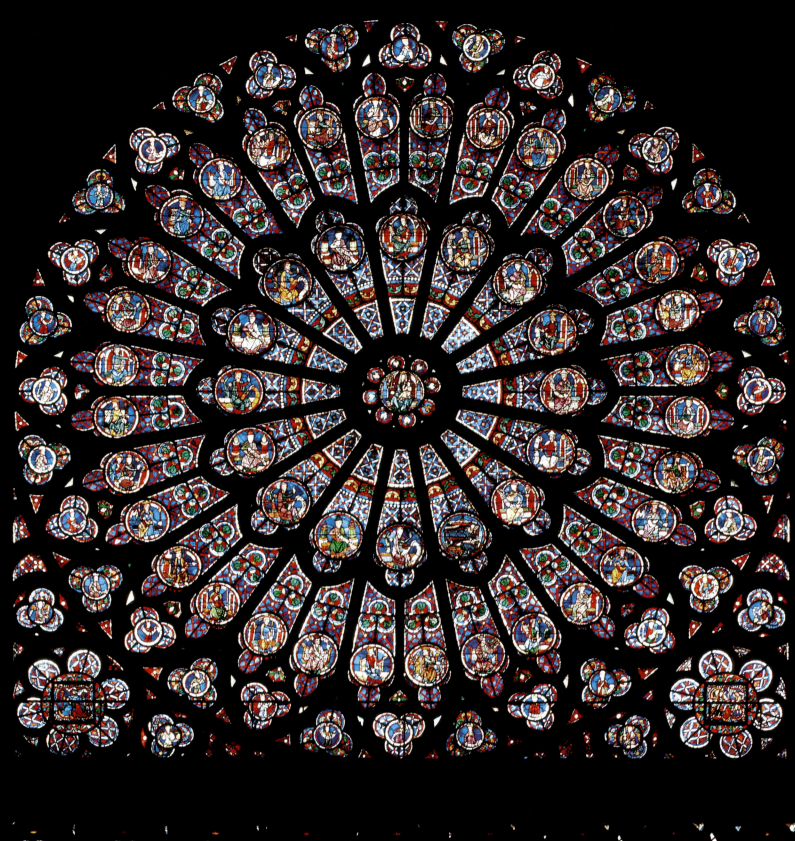

Chartres

Much more than any other cathedral, Chartres has its own very special aura. This comes on the one hand from its architecture, which is one of the greatest achievements in the history of architecture, and on the other from the fact that its original design and furnishings have been almost completely preserved, whereas in other French cathedrals they have been completely or partly lost. These treasures include the comprehensive sculpture cycle of the portals and, even more important for the overall effect, the stained-glass windows. These bring a mystical hyperreality to the interior that the architecture alone could never convey.

The windows are no mere openings, but self-illuminating walls. The light breaks through a mysterious deep-blue or violet darkness, and lets the brighter colors, such as the reds and yellows, shine even more clearly. This light gives the windows the effect of being sparkling walls of precious stones, which in many places really glow. The interior itself lies in a dim half-light. Surrounded by radiant walls, it has a sacred feeling of something blessed in a secular world that captivates even the most rational people today. This impression reaches us in a twofold manner, as something both fascinating and overpowering. People feel imperatively and irresistibly drawn to it, as though by some hidden power, and at the same time experience a holy awe as they contemplate it.

All the colors are today richer and deeper than elsewhere as a result of being cleaned. Older stained glass, such as that in the west window group at Chartres, was brighter, and after Chartres became even more bright, as can be seen very clearly at Strasbourg and Cologne. A cathedral such as Amiens, which later had all its stained glass destroyed, has lost the best and the most important quality of all: its atmosphere of holiness. For that reason, the restorations carried out in other cathedrals in the 19th century were careful to copy the old style when they replaced any missing glass, and were often deceptively successful at this. Because of its stained glass, Chartres is the only cathedral that can convey an almost perfect image of how it was when it was built. The losses and alterations are not easy to discern. Like most other French cathedrals, it no longer has the almost indispensable choir screen between the canons' choir and the main nave, and the arcaded pillars in the inner choir have been redesigned in a Baroque style.

Chartres was not only the seat of a bishop and the home of the most famous cathedral school of the High Middle Ages, of which Bishop Ivo of Chartres, among others, was a member from 1090, but it was also the greatest pilgrimage center in France. Here, the Robe of Mary, which Charles the Bald had inherited from Charlemagne and donated to Chartres, was kept as a healing relic. In 1020 the Carolingian cathedral was damaged by fire, and Bishop Fulbert had a new cathedral built on the site of the old one. The Carolingian nave was leveled, but the side aisles were used as a crypt. In the east part Fulbert added an ambulatory, also with a crypt, and three boldly projecting radiating chapels. All Fulbert's crypts were absorbed into the present-day church, which to a certain extent dictated the ground plan.

After a fire in 1134, which affected the western part, a new west facade was built in stages. First the north tower was started, then around 1145 the slightly different south tower, which has been completely preserved right up to the spire. While the lower parts of the towers were being built, the three portals were erected in the middle and the three-window group above them. Together these form an ideally balanced and unified whole. The portal seems to have been planned originally for a site set further back within a portico or vestibule, but then was brought forward to its present position.

In 1194 the Fulbert building went up in flames during a damaging citywide fire, but the western arm and portal were saved. When the cathedral's most important relic, the Robe of Mary, surprisingly turned up again after it had been thought lost, there was unlimited joy. The new building was begun immediately, supported by the bishop, the cathedral chapter, the king, and, not least, by the people of the region who, regardless of their social position, freely undertook manual labor duties; one trade or profession after another funded part of the expensive stained glass for the windows. By 1220 the vaulting of the choir was completed, and a year later the choir moved into it. Consecration followed, though not until 1260, in the presence of Louis IX (St. Louis). Soon, however, faults began to appear in the building. In 1316 a building commission pleaded for the best architects in France to build an upper row of flying buttresses, which were then installed. The original buttressing had been constructed in such as way as to absorb the lateral thrust of the vaults, but not the wind pressure transmitted from the roof onto the unbuttressed clerestory walls. The last important building work, following a lightning strike in 1506, was the new upper part of the north tower on the west front, designed in the Late Flamboyant style by Jean Texier, also known as Jean de Beauce.

More recent research has indicated that all parts of the cathedral were begun at the same time, but not completed together. The architects, whose names and origins are unknown, managed to devise a total design for the cathedral that would prove influential right into the Late Gothic period: a three-aisled nave, a three-aisled transept, and a five-aisled choir, with rectangular bays in the central nave and square bays in the side aisles. As in previous buildings, the central nave is twice the width of the side aisles. Unlike the Early Gothic double bays, which with their sexpartite vaulting belong to the past, this division of the bay areas forms a symmetrical, almost standardized grid, which was so convincing in its simplicity and regularity that it was later imitated countless times.

The ambulatory posed special difficulties because it had to be built over an existing crypt formed by the ambulatory and three radiating chapels of the Fulbert building. The ground plan was largely based on the old one. Despite this, the architects succeeded in making the single-aisled ambulatory into a two-aisled structure, as in St. Denis and Paris, and in increasing the number of chapels from three to seven. New foundations were needed only for the chapels. The three chapels inherited from the Fulbert building were given new exteriors, and allowed to project beyond the outer ambulatory as independent, single-vaulted apses. The four newly added chapels are only shallow bulges, however, their vaulting combined with that of the adjacent bay in the ambulatory, as was done at St. Denis. Thus in the vaults, too, there is a rhythmic alternation between the shallow and the deep chapels.

For the ground plan for the apse of the choir and the ambulatory, the architects took an important step away from previous Early Gothic architecture. Where the polygon had always been subdivided into polygonal parts, they treated the semicircle itself as a polygon. This consisted of seven sides of a 14-sided figure (the sides were not completely regular, because of the underlying crypt). In contrast to this, the apse in the upper choir is designed as if it was made from seven sides of a 12-sided figure. The latter structure proved successful. From then on the 7/12 apse became generally accepted for larger buildings.

No less important than the rationalization of the ground plan were the new elements that appeared in the elevation. The gallery was done away with. The structure was three-storied, consisting of dividing arcades, triforium, and clerestory. There had been three-storied structures before, such as Sens Cathedral, but the groundbreaking innovation at Chartres was the treatment of the clerestory windows. Previously, these had been very small, but now they became

as large as the dividing arcades. The increase, at the expense of the gallery, was the decisive quantum leap in cathedral architecture. It showed that what matters most in cathedrals is the light. From now on, in the nave and upper choir, glass was just as important as stone, if not more so.

The triforium was placed exactly in the middle of the structure and divided the main stories like a running horizontal border. As before, it provided a passage with an arcade of small pillars and a closed back wall. Because of the lean-to construction of the roofs over the side aisles, it was impossible to install windows. A generation later, from around 1230, an alternative way of roofing the side aisles made it possible to light the triforium.

The hitherto undreamt-of size of the clerestory windows, which had only slightly been foreshadowed by the ambulatory at St. Denis, was immediately taken up as an architectural idea of great appeal. Taking their cue from the large rose windows at Laon, the architects also gave Chartres magnificent rose windows on the fronts of both transepts and on the west front, where it was placed above the older group of three windows. In a smaller format—another new idea—the rose window was transferred to all the clerestory windows in the shape of a circular rosette placed at the top above two lights and a central mullion. This was a new type of window, its three parts sharing a closer relationship than, for example, the three graduated west windows, which were merely grouped together. The rosettes, a forerunner of tracery, have ornamental patterns in the form of an octofoil. Unlike the circular forms employed in tracery since it was invented in Reims in 1211, these patterns were carved from flat plates of stone. The overall effect of these windows is to surround the whole of the upper part of the cathedral with rose windows and rosettes, except in the choir where the narrowness of the openings prevented their inclusion. The circular form of the rosette also caused the clerestory windows to be reshaped with round arches rather than pointed ones.

In every cathedral, the questions of which shaft-rib system to use and which type of column were two of the most important design problems. At Chartres, clusters of five shafts were used, with one for each part of the vaulting: for the transverse arch and, on either side of it, the diagonal ribs and the wall ribs. The shafts begin above the columns, as was done at Laon and Paris. They could have started at ground level, as on the window walls of the side aisles, and also on the pillars at the crossing, which at Chartres are clustered piers with a stepped core, and have no less than seven shafts, each one designed to serve a vaulted arch or the profile of an arch. Clustered piers of this type would have been best for the nave, harmoniously uniting the clusters of shafts and the columns, and so creating a system in which the components all matched from the pavement up to the vaults. However, this was not done, and there must have been an important reason. It is to be found at the place that was the most difficult design area in almost all French cathedrals, their Achilles heel, so to speak: at the apse of the choir and the ambulatory. The polygon formed by the choir at Chartres is so narrow, and has so many angles, that clustered piers would have been the worst type of column imaginable, because it would have been impossible, or nearly so, to get them to go around the polygon. For that reason the architects resorted to the tried circular column, which for these angles was the ideal form and also provided support for the upper choir.

This type of column could also have been used in the nave, for reasons of unity, as was done during the same period at Soissons Cathedral, which is structurally closest to Chartres, almost a twin. But in Chartres the circular type of column, even with its attached shaft, was seen as too bare and unstructured. In the nave, therefore, the architects increased the number of shafts to four, all with the same alignment. This had two advantages: on the one hand, the core of the column could be retained, and aligned on the same axis, and on the other the arches that connected with the other three sides of the column, namely the dividing arches with their profiles and the vaulting of the side aisles, at least had a support. The result was the clustered pier. It was a compromise, born out of two dissimilar constraints: the problems with building the polygon and the need to have as much harmony as possible between the columns, shafts, and arches.

The clustered piers were an innovation, despite certain earlier developments in, for example, Laon, Blois, and Canterbury. The inventive urge revealed itself still further in the way the piers alternate between a circular core with octagonal shafts and an octagonal core with circular shafts, so that the form of the supports is continued consistently in the main shaft of the cluster placed above it, although the latter is much thinner. This alternation of forms is a classic example of a chiasmus, the inversion of elements in a structure. The idea was not taken up elsewhere. Later architects took exception to this kind of variation, which was at odds with their desire for unity, or they did not want to be seen as mere copyists. In any event, the

core of the piers and the four shafts of later buildings were always circular, which is why, for cathedrals such as Reims and Amiens, the term "clustered circular pillar" is used.

The enlargement of the clerestory windows, which was the most important of all the innovations at Chartres, influenced the external structure. The upper walls of the nave and choir had very little walling between the windows, and had to be buttressed with arches reaching high over the roofs of the side aisles. While there had already been openwork buttresses, for example at Notre-Dame in Paris, Chartres was the first place it was used as a structural element that determined the overall external appearance of the building. The multistage projecting buttress piers are astonishingly massive, suggesting that no risks were to be taken with a construction such as this, for which there were no precedents.

The arches also reveal the architects' inventiveness, for this is not a matter of simple buttressing, but a structure consisting of two superposed arches with, between them, an arcade of small columns. The arcades follow the curve of the arch, and increasingly tip over in an outward-leaning direction, as if they had no firm base. Instead of standing up, they seem to sway like a bridge lifted up into the air. This idea too, for all its originality, found no successors.

In addition, it was very important for the general appearance of the exterior that the fronts of both transepts should have twin-towered facades, each with a large rose window, placed above a row of five windows, and three portals crowned with gabled porches. Previously, facade building had been confined to west facades, as at Laon, for example, but now the whole program was transferred to the transepts. The transepts at Laon, with their large rose windows and planned towers, provided a direct model from which only the three-portal layout was missing. The transept towers at Chartres were built no higher than roof level. The same thing happened to two other towers, due to be placed over the side aisles before the beginning of the ambulatory. Similarly, the tower planned for the crossing was never begun. In Chartres, the Laon seven-tower plan was to have been increased to nine. But when they were at the point of being built, the enthusiasm for towers vanished, perhaps for financial reasons and perhaps also because so many towers would have been seen as too arrogant.

The cathedral has a total of nine portals, including the three portals that had been erected in 1145. It was planned to decorate these with extensive cycles of figures and reliefs. The west portal in particular is a milestone in the history of sculpture, with its Porte Royale, or *porta regia*, as it was called in the 12th century. This is the earliest extant example of a portal design that was later taken up everywhere. The recessed portal was given a revolutionary funnel shape and decorated with statues, and the tympanum, lintels, and curved niches of the archivolts were covered with reliefs. The original model for them was the triple west portal at St. Denis, built under Abbot Suger, whose sculptures were for the most part destroyed in the Revolution.

The sculptures of the Porte Royale are the main works characterizing the archaic phase of Gothic cathedral sculpture. The extremely elongated figures in the recesses, representing kings, queens, and figures from the Old Testament, are mounted on columns, on which they seem to sway rather than stand. The robes, under which the shapes of the bodies are clearly delineated, have narrow folds and hollows. All the figures are completely motionless. Side by side they form a closely fused phalanx running into the recesses, each one offering an eternal witness. Although the figures are as unmoving as the columns themselves, their faces and expressions reveal an unusual watchfulness, as though they are filled with their own inner life, and gaze down at the observer from another, timeless world.

The spiritual center of the portal is the Christ figure in the middle tympanum: surrounded by the symbols of the four Evangelists, he sits enthroned in the mandorla, an almond-shaped panel. The right hand is raised in majesty, and the left hand holds the Holy Book. The subject is the Apocalypse of Christ in Glory, the *Maiestas Domini*. It shows a figure of unending gravity with an expression that promises neither vengeful punishment nor forgiving gentleness, but justice from which none can escape. In this figure the sculptor succeeded, in a way seldom found in the history of art, in conveying at least a sense of foreboding, thereby reconciling the twin nature of Christ, the divine and the human, in one image. The figure elevates both natures in equal measure, and is unique in Gothic cathedral sculpture.

Along with this sculptor, others were working on the Porte Royale, one of whom was a sympathetic figure, but with a completely different mission: to decorate the archivolts of the two side portals with representations of the signs of the zodiac, the monthly occupations, the liberal arts, and their famous ancient representatives. The program begins by embracing the cosmos and the holy teachings as a whole. This sculptor gave these images an endearingly fresh originality, the magic of a silent, spiritual poetry, in which people are happy as the children of God are in a golden age, free from cares and stress. The observer looks on as though

seeing a paradise lost, but one that continues to have an effect, like memories of childhood.

On the portals of the transepts, the Last Judgment is portrayed on the south transept, with the figures of the apostles in the recesses of the central portal. On the north transept is the *Coronation of the Virgin*, with the Prophets and other figures. Here the sculpture becomes strangely doctrinaire, like a theological reaction. In place of the physical liveliness found, for example, in the archivolts at Laon and Sens, there is a somewhat joyless severity and a unifying similarity of forms. The figures here are all spiritual brothers and sisters, lacking their own characters or individual traits, or even their own faces. Although no figure is the same as any other, and there is always some variation, they all look very similar. This produces a kind of solemn monotony, particularly in the center of the South Portal, where the apostles are gathered around the figure of Christ on the pier, a representation of Christ made human and conveying a mild and gentle impression that became famous as the *Beau-Dieu*, the "fine" or "handsome" God.

On the side portals, the sculpture is more free, particularly on the right-hand portal on the north side, where the sculptor of the fat Solomon was one of the "pioneers of studies from nature" (Wilhelm Vöge), and on the left-hand portal on the south side, where the later figures of St. George and the so-called St. Theodore show two contrasting knightly figures: George, the grim, older fighter, and

Theodore, the handsome young hero, the ideal of moral purity and noble courage. With these two figures, and with that of the *Holy Modesta* in the north porch, a female figure with a certain erotic appeal, the portal sculpture at Chartres concluded on an almost masterly note, as it had begun just a century before on the west portal.

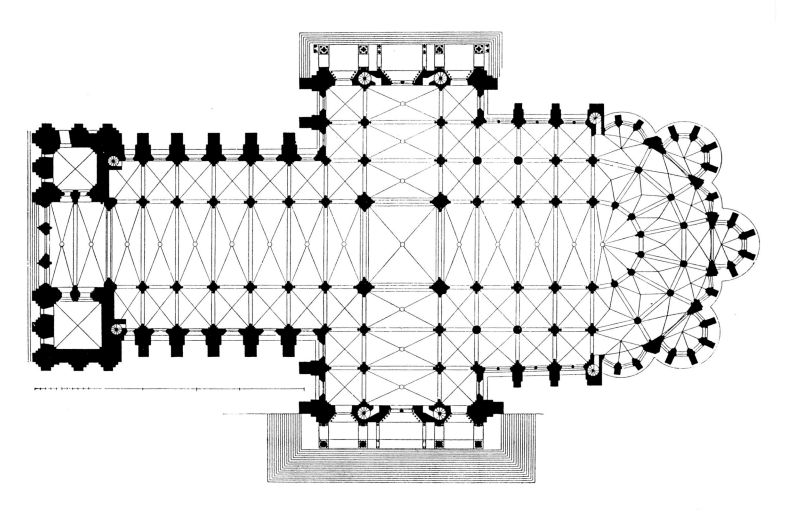

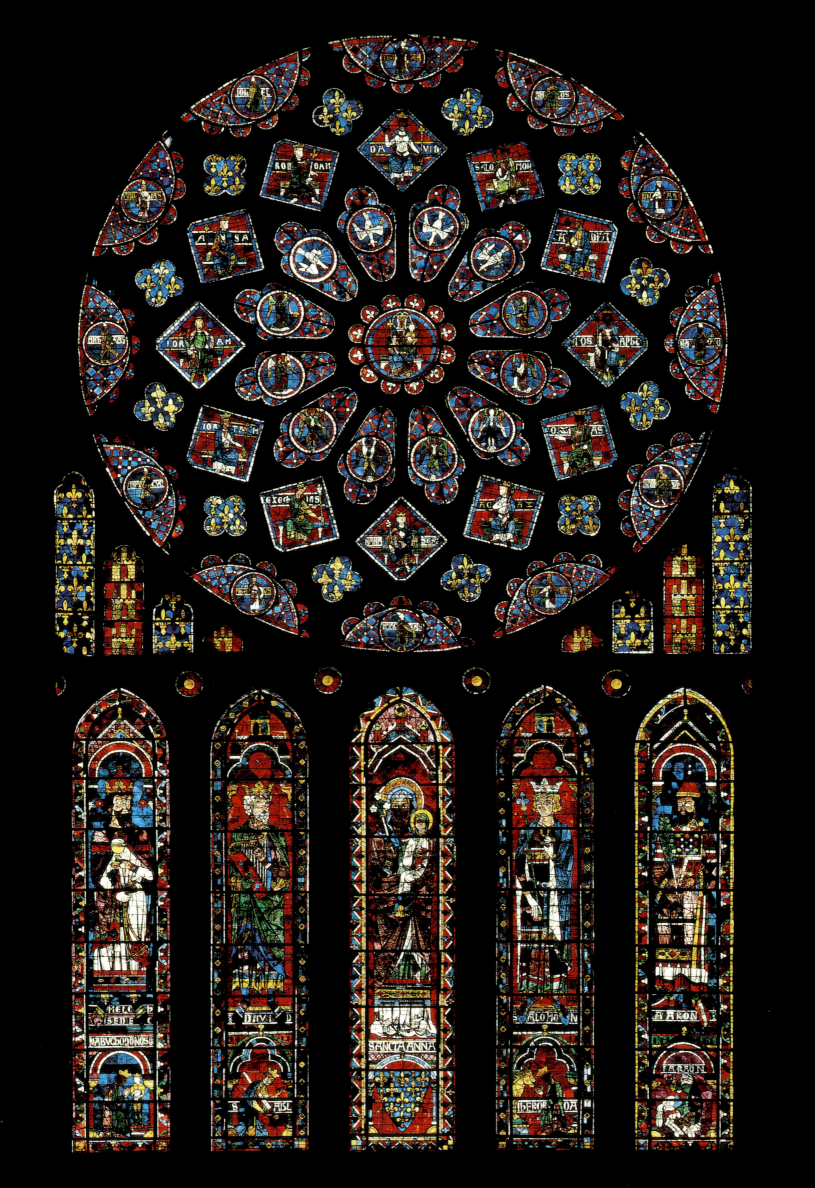

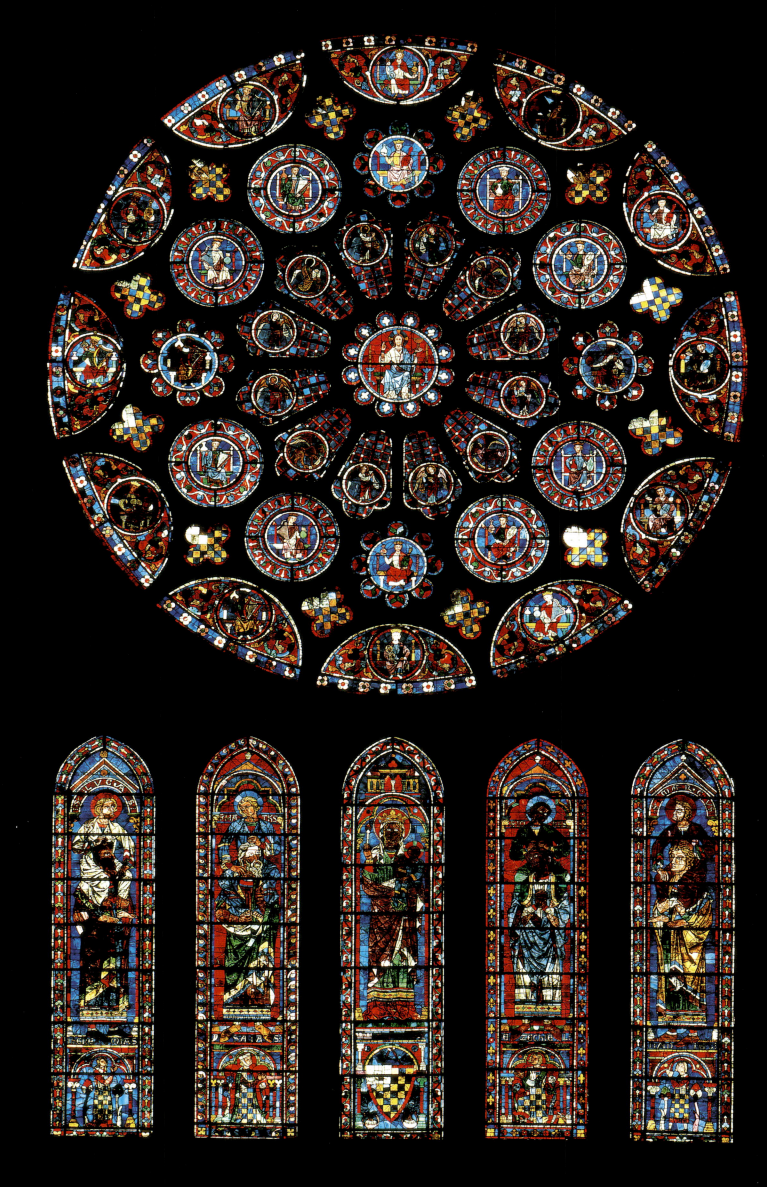

Bourges

The development of French cathedrals changed course shortly before 1200: on the one hand there was Chartres, and on the other Bourges, which lay farther south. Both cathedrals were begun at about the same time, but were very different from each other. They each displayed so many innovations that both could have been taken as models for future buildings. However, the main route, the royal route, as it were, was signaled by Chartres. Bourges remained an outsider, and found only a few imitators on the fringe, to some extent at Coutances in Normandy and at Le Mans, though chiefly in Spain.

Bourges had been a crown possession since around 1100, and the archbishop residing there held the rank of a primate of Aquitaine. In about 1195, the cathedral was begun by Archbishop Henri de Sully, a brother of the bishop of Paris and a nephew of an earlier abbot of Cluny. By 1214 the choir was completed, as was the whole cathedral by about 1250. Many problems involving statics were encountered with the west towers, right up to the collapse of the north tower in 1506. The west facade now has a heterogeneous appearance, the result of various repairs and alterations, as, for example, when the duc de Berry, the famous patron of the arts, had a magnificent tracery window inserted toward the end of the 14th century, which does not go with the rest of the facade at all.

Only the two portals with figures remained from the earlier cathedral, modeled on the west portal at Chartres; those on the north and south side of the nave were replaced by new ones. The present building was laid out on such a huge scale that the choir reached beyond the old Gallo-Roman city wall onto a lower-lying area, which necessitated building a crypt on the other side of the wall to provide a substructure.

Looking at the whole design, the lack of a transept is particularly noticeable. Because of this, the ground plan is bath-shaped, and corresponds to the original layout of the archbishop's cathedral at Sens. Bourges, however, unlike Sens and most other cathedrals, is not three-aisled but has five aisles, together with a double ambulatory and tiny radiating chapels. This layout goes back to Notre-Dame in Paris. The chapels are most unusual constructions. They are covered with steep stone turrets, and are no bigger than tiny recesses, jutting out like bays between the buttress columns. At Bourges, the radiating chapel received a new and highly original treatment.

The essential feature of Bourges is the way it embraces the unusual and the innovative. The process began in the crypt which, although only a substructure, is as architec-

turally ambitious as the church above. The plan for the apse of the choir forms a semicircle with no polygonal breaks, but the semicircle in the double ambulatory is subdivided into five segments like a 5/10 polygon. In the upper part of the building the semicircular theme is maintained in the apse of the choir as far as the eaves. Each segment of the outer ambulatory consists of three interlocking triangles, which together form the usual curved trapezium. This pattern is the same as for the inner ambulatory of Notre-Dame in Paris. In contrast, the trapeziform bays of the inner ambulatory have cross ribs with a boss in the middle of the bay. These cross ribs are of an unusual design. The position of the central boss was usually arrived at by bending the course of the ribs. In Bourges, however, the ribs follow a curved ground plan. This curve makes it possible for the ribs to meet in the middle of the bay without being bent. There was nothing new about arches with a curved plan. They had been present in French ambulatories since the Romanesque period in the arcades around semicircular apses, and in the main apse at Bourges, and also in the arcades separating the two ambulatories in the crypt and the main church. The new feature of this vault ribbing was that the curve of the dividing arches was transferred to the ribs. This new solution to an old problem was clearly better than the usual solution of bent ribs in terms of sweep and elegance. Nevertheless, it was not taken up elsewhere, because it was much more difficult to make ribs with a curved plan than a straight or bent plan.

The ambulatory in the main church differs from that in the crypt, in that the wide spans of the arched trapeziums in the outer ambulatory are not divided into three interlocking triangles but into two side triangles and a central trapezium, which mirrors in reverse the shape of the adjacent trapezium in the inner ambulatory. This outer trapezium leads to the tiny exterior chapels which, seen from the inside, have the shape of a rounded apsidiole. All these details make for an unusual and ingenious set of inventions.

However, the most important invention concerns the five-aisled elevation of the cathedral as a whole. Unlike Notre-Dame in Paris, where the double side-aisles are the same height, in Bourges they are graduated. The outer side-aisle is wider than the inner one and very low, while the inner one is narrower but more than twice as high. The graduation of the five aisles indicates what the whole concept was aiming for: Bourges was to be as large in terms of ground area as the largest cathedral to date, Notre-Dame in Paris; and at the same time as large in terms of structure as the largest abbey church—the five-aisled graduated church at

Cluny. Finally, the whole building was to be as unified as possible, hence the absence of a transept, so that the inner space was not interrupted by transept and crossing.

This graduated scheme made it necessary for the dividing arcades, especially their columns, to be very tall. Above them in the nave and choir is a triforium, whose arcading was contained within a larger relieving arch, and a clerestory. This is sited, just as in Early Gothic cathedrals, in the inner wall, and does not extend down over the vaulted area. It is also remarkably low. The windows, unlike those in the Early Gothic period, consist of groups of three lights—only two in the apse—with a top circle in the form of a sexfoil. This kind of window group is a parallel development to the clerestory windows of Chartres. The three-storied structure, with dividing arcades, triforium, and clerestory, is repeated in the walls surrounding the inner side aisles, although the dividing arcades leading to the outer aisle are very low. The three stories share the same height as the dividing arcades of the central nave. When you look at the central nave and the side aisles together, the structure seems to be five-storied.

This impression works because the inner side aisles are so narrow and tall that they take up less space than a normal nave, and form a background space for the central nave and choir, surrounding them behind the dividing arcades. Meanwhile, the central arcades are just the right width and height to fit precisely with the three-storied structure of the inner aisles.

The presence of a surrounding space behind the nave and the overly tall columns was both unusual and, up to then, new in this kind of architecture. If you look straight down the nave into the choir, the space seems rather top-heavy with the triforium and clerestory placed so high up. However, if you see it together with the background space of the inner side aisle, especially from the apse of the choir, this impression of top-heaviness gives way to a feeling of enclosing harmony, a spaciousness that, in the nave, is given extra elevation by the clerestory. It then seems like a spatial miracle, our sense of wonder increased as we walk around and look at it from different points of view.

While Bourges is about space, Chartres is about its window-walls. That is the fundamental difference. However, the achitect of Bourges was also inventive in his design of the walls and the shaft-rib system he employed. For his vaults in the central nave and choir, he used the then common sexpartite rib system. As had already been done in Paris, these combined seamlessly with the more varied vaulting in the apse. The dividing arcades consist appropriately of main columns and intermediate columns, which are barely

distinguishable in terms of thickness. Their shape, however, a circular core with eight slender engaged columns, is the same everywhere, even in the apse. This shape was something new, and led to a surprising further effect which came about by letting the columns on the upper wall of the central nave and choir, and also on the walls of the side aisles, run up with projecting shafts as far as the imposts of the vaulting. The way this was done makes the columns look somehow split, while the intervening wall areas seem like no more than space-fillers. The circular shaft, which looks like part of the column, was ideal for the purpose of supporting all the engaged columns needed to connect with the vaulting: five over the main columns and three over the intermediate ones. The column and wall system enhanced the unity of the building, and made it possible for the structure of the choir to be continued almost unchanged around the apse. The cardinal problem of cathedral architecture was resolved here for the first time.

The exterior is equally unified, its three-layered structure no less marked by the unusually steep openwork buttressing with its two superposed arches, so slender they seem almost fragile. The buttresses, their outer columns crowned with ornate pinnacles added in the 19th century, are basically a sober piece of architectural engineering, but their consistency and sinewy tautness lend them a considerable aesthetic value of their own. There is a good, open view of the walls, and here it is not ultimately the clerestory windows but the buttresses that unify the cathedral into a single structural body. The ideal of unity was pursued in many cathedrals, but at Bourges, both internally and externally, it was realized more decisively than anywhere else.

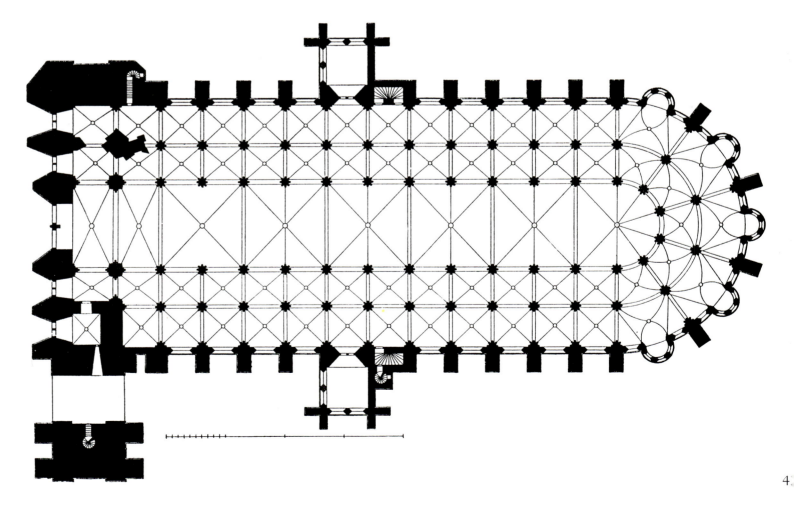

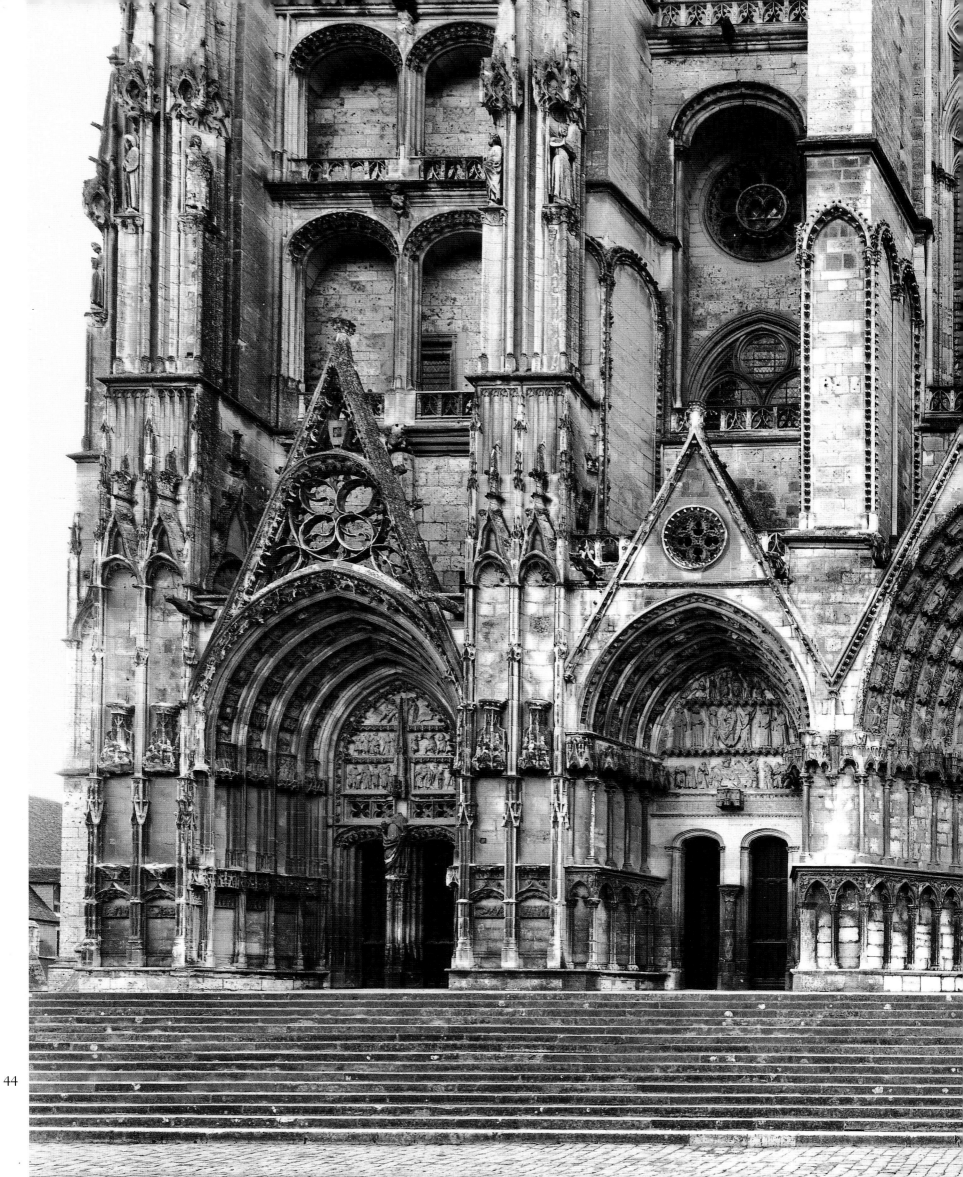

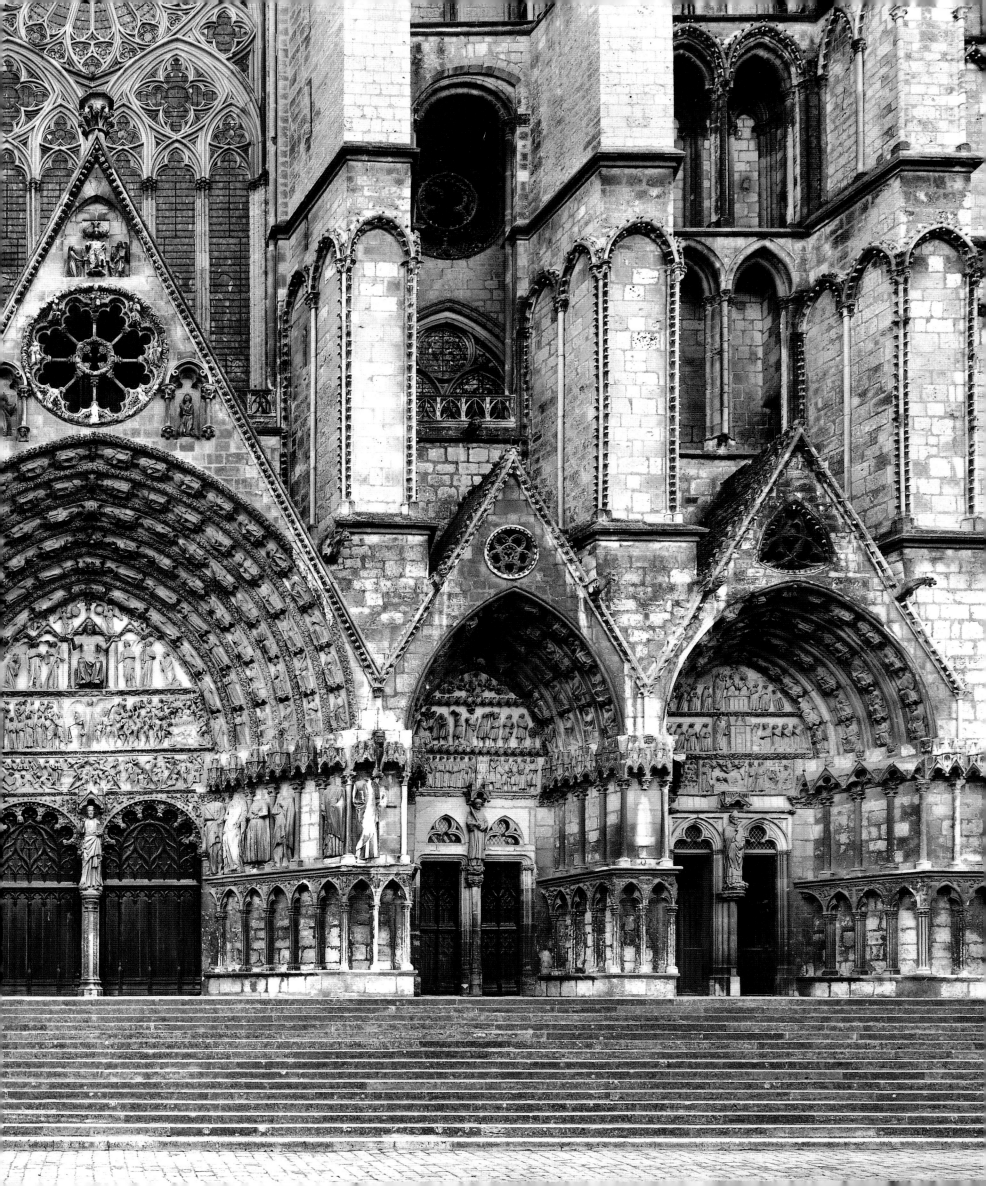

Strasbourg

Strasbourg, the Roman city of Argentoratum, had been the seat of a bishop since about 500. Until the late 17th century it belonged to the Holy Roman Empire. Around 1015, Bishop Wernher, one of the founders of the later house of Habsburg, launched the building of a new cathedral inside the area of the old Roman fortress. Built in the style of the late Ottonian period, it was a columned basilica with a pronounced transept, and culminated at the east end in an apse with a rectilinear external design. The west front had two towers, one of the first such treatments in Romanesque architecture. Today's cathedral has the same dimensions as Wernher's building.

Shortly before 1200, a Late Romanesque building was started at the east end. The crossing was vaulted with an octagonal dome, and the arms of the transept were each subdivided into four vaulted areas. To do this it was necessary to build a double arcade at the crossing, and install a support in the middle of each transept arm. This was a most unusual approach. The arms of the transept, which were inherited from the Late Ottonian building, were so large that the architects did not dare cover it with a single vault. To achieve their ends, they introduced a strangely crude, inconsistent structure characterized by enormous circular columns. This Late Romanesque eastern part of the cathedral was preserved as a remnant of the first phase of building, and, together with the Early Romanesque decorations in the apse, forms a sharp contrast with the Gothic building we see today, with the nave and facade to which the cathedral owes its fame.

In about 1225, a French workforce took over the building, and completed the south transept in the then prevailing French Gothic style. The central column was converted into a kind of extended clustered column with eight circular detached shafts, and decorated with a triple-layered cycle of figures: the four evangelists, four cherubs with trumpets, and three angels bearing the instruments of the Passion that flank the seated figure of Christ. The column is a monument to the Last Judgment. As such, it refers to the ecclesiastical court that took place in the south transept, its raised rostrum preserved with a graduated triple arcade in the east wall. The sculptor of these figures was definitely the architect—as with the founder's choir at Naumburg (see pages 188–99)—and certainly one of the great artistic personalities of that time.

The same architect also began the new building in the nave, and erected the surrounding walls of the side aisles in the two eastern bays. Here, the structural system is difficult to analyze because of chapel annexes added later. The foundations of the Wernher building were used again throughout the nave, and for this reason the three aisles have unusually spacious proportions.

In about 1240, another French master builder took over the nave. He perfected an architectural system that was highly modern, and completely thought through. The three-storied elevation of the walls, with its large tracery windows in the clerestory and pierced triforium with barred tracery, is closely related to the founding structures of the French Flamboyant style, for example the naves at St. Denis and Troyes Cathedral. The shaft-rib system, however, goes beyond these. The main supports were provided by compound clustered columns, which are fully symmetrical, with each side of the column carrying five engaged columns of varying thickness. The builders were able to ignore the usual problems posed by columns in the apse of the choir, because in Strasbourg there is no such apse. Thus, the architect did not give his columns the circular shape, which is the easiest to use in the apse, but a canted and raked-back form of the type used in Romanesque and Early Gothic times, though on a much larger scale. The raked-back steps and the fronts of the columns were ideal for housing the engaged columns.

At the end of each bay, a cluster of five engaged columns runs up to the base of the vaulting. The thick main shaft and the two thinner accompanying shafts were connected to the transverse arch, which did not have the usual simple profile but a triple one. The architect at Strasbourg was alone among French cathedral architects in designing the transverse arches of the nave with three shafts, thereby relating them more closely to the dividing arcades beneath, which had the same triple cluster of shafts. The remaining shaft in the middle of the side of each column connects with the diagonal rib, whereas the wall rib does not begin until the ledge beneath the triforium. The shape of the columns and their shafts and arches were united in complete, functional accord. This was a system that could not have been improved on.

However, in the side aisles the system is not right. The columns and their shafts were designed for the same vaulting layout as was used in the central nave, but the arches do not conform to the system. The wall ribs have one profile and one shaft too many, but the transverse ribs connect with only one shaft despite their triple profile. As a result, the diagonal rib is not connected to the middle shaft, as it should have been, but to the thin shaft next to it. Shafts and ribs do not match each other. It is all too obvious that this was an emergency solution. The reason for it was that the previous designer of the Angels column had already begun the surrounding walls of the side aisles in the two eastern bays,

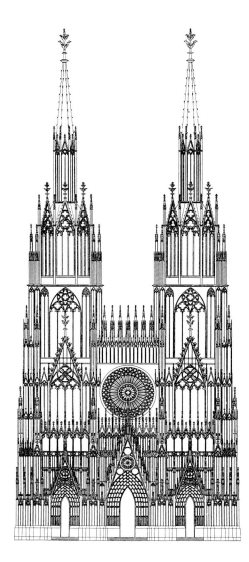

and had done so using an earlier conventional system, which provided only one shaft for the transverse arch. For reasons of unity this solution had to be retained in the side aisles. Only in the nave was a new design possible, and only there could the architect realize his concept of total perfection in the shaft-rib system.

In 1275, the nave was completed, and in 1277, the west front was begun. At first the work was still the responsibility of the cathedral chapter, but from 1286 the city took charge. At the heart of the plans was the facade with its rose window and three figured portals. Several large parchment drawings have been preserved, including the famous "Drawing B," which, because of its fine balance, is generally considered to be the most beautiful design produced for a twin-towered facade using Gothic tracery.

The design was changed during building, the rose window being set slightly lower down. This was the work of Master Erwin, who took control in about 1284, and bore the legendary, unofficial name of "Stonebrook" (von Steinbach). The outstanding features of Erwin's facade are the tracery stretched like the strings of a harp in front of the side towers, and, in particular, the extraordinarily radiant 16 petals of the rose window, set in a square frame above the steeply sloping gable of the portal with its array of pinnacles. This wonderful creation, one of the most fascinating in the history of architecture, inspired Goethe in 1772 to write his

hymn of praise to Erwin von Steinbach, and thus launched the enthusiastic rediscovery of the Gothic in Germany and its proclamation as the national style. Since the Italian Renaissance, the Gothic style had always been seen as somewhat German, and at the same time somewhat barbaric. Goethe was firmly convinced of its German origins, and his hymn was critical only of the accusations of barbarism. That the Gothic style's true origins lay in France was only recognized and acknowledged a little later.

From 1382, the two towers were connected by a middle block to form a solid rectangle, the work of Master Michael of Freiburg, a nephew of the master builder of Prague Cathedral, Peter Parler; then from 1399 Ulrich von Ensingen, the cathedral builder from Ulm, built up the north tower in the form of an octagon with four accompanying corner newels. It was not planned to have a counterpart on the south tower. From 1419 Johannes Hültz of Cologne finally added the highly original steeple with its seven stepped newels on each of the eight tiers. In 1459 the tower was completed, its dizzyingly tall structure held together in the upper parts by a great number of iron ties. Once the somewhat taller crossing tower at Beauvais collapsed soon after its erection, the Strasbourg tower—at 466 ft (142 m)—became the tallest church tower in the world and remained so until the 19th century.

From 1459, the masons' lodge at Strasbourg presided over all the other masons' lodges in Germany. In 1697, Strasbourg passed to France as part of Louis XIV's expansionist policies; some one hundred years later during the French Revolution, some wished to demolish the tower because it offended against equality, but fortunately they settled for declaring the cathedral a "Temple of Reason," and then a "Temple of the Supreme Being."

Many of the decorations and furnishings at Strasbourg were lost during the Reformation and again during the Revolution. The stained-glass windows survived, however, including the series of 20 emperors and kings of the Holy Roman Empire, made in about 1250–70, all of whom wear haloes as though they were saints. The sculptures on the three west portals, dating from 1280–1300, were also largely preserved—the wall figures of the Virtues and Vices, the Prophets, and the Wise and Foolish Virgins, among them a particularly naive virgin who gazes adoringly at her seducer as the Prince of the World.

During the Revolution, the figures of the apostles in the recesses of the two portals of the south transept were destroyed; these dated from about 1220. Also lost from the same place was the seated figure of King Solomon, which

Above: Angels or Judgment column in the south transept
Above left: "Drawing B" of the west facade (later copy with additions)

was designed for the secular tribunal that took place in front of the portal. The two figures of Ecclesia and Synagogue, which belonged to this group, have been preserved, along with the tympanums with the *Death* and *Coronation of the Virgin*, and the whole series of columns from the court in the interior. These are works by one of the best French cathedral sculptors, notable for the admirable quality of the delicate, veil-like delicacy of the robes, and the calm, sensitive heads filled with deep inner feelings and gentle pain.

The sculptor surpassed not only himself but all other comparable previous works with the female figures of Ecclesia and Synagogue. The figures admit so many viewpoints that they seem to turn as the viewer walks around them. A lively interaction arises between them that extends over the width of the whole double portal. The Synagogue figure cannot return Ecclesia's proud look as she turns her head toward her, and so she must look away full of shame, her head lowered. The victorious figure does not enjoy her triumph, however, and the defeated one is in no way made contemptible, as though the ideals of chivalry applied also to women. The marked physicality of the figures, accentuated by belts reflecting current French fashion, is not without erotic appeal. A little earlier, Gottfried von Strasbourg had described Isolde in a similar way in his *Tristan* epic. The sculptor's portrayal of the noblewoman, visibly characterized by the *Minnesang* (song of courtly love), was the same as the poet's.

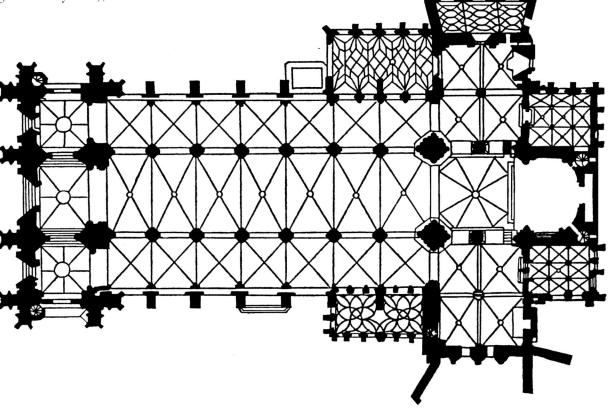

49

52

54

55

See individual chapter and color plates

See text illustrations

Mentioned in text

N

100 km

POLAND

Stralsund

Rostock

Lübeck
Ratzeburg
Wismar

Schwerin

Bremen

Verden

Berlin

NETHERLANDS

Utrecht

Osnabrück
Minden

Königslutter
Braunschweig
Magdeburg
Halberstadt

Münster

Paderborn

s'Hertogenbosch

GERMANY

Ghent
Antwerp

BELGIUM

Mechelen

Cologne
Altenberg

Aachen

Naumburg

Tournai

Fulda

Limburg

Mainz

Prague
Kuttenberg

Trier

Bamberg

CZECH REPUBLIC

Worms

Speyer

Nürnberg

FRANCE

Schwäbisch
Hall

Regensburg

Eichstätt

Strasbourg

Schwäbisch
Gmünd

Passau

Vienna

Thann

Freiburg

Salem

Salzburg

Basel

AUSTRIA

SWITZERLAND

Chur

ITALY

SLOVENIA

Germany

and Neighboring Countries
(The Former Holy Roman Empire)

Architectural History

The region of the Federal Republic of Germany belonged in the Middle Ages to a much larger state organization, the Holy Roman Empire, which continued in name until 1806. Charlemagne, its founder, succeeded in uniting the area covered today by France, large parts of Germany, its eastern border regions, and northern Italy into one single kingdom. Charlemagne's declared aim was the *renovatio imperii Romanorum*, in other words, the restoration of the ancient Roman Empire, and with it the rights of inheritance of the ancient emperors. For Charlemagne, who at first was only a king of the Franks, the title of Roman emperor brought with it the inalienable assertion of his political power in the West. However, unlike the ancient emperors, Charlemagne and his successors acceded to the title of emperor on the instructions of a second and different authority, that of the pope, the spiritual leader of the Church of Rome. In this way, the papacy was able to establish itself as an independent spiritual power beside the secular leadership, and this quickly led to the popes claiming equal authority alongside the emperors and then absolute pre-eminence over them. This conflict of interests determined the politics of the Holy Roman Empire for centuries, and finally weakened royal-imperial authority to such an extent that the independent powers of landowning princes and the bourgeoisie gained the upper hand, and the historical development of Germany was marked, unlike that of France, by particularism, as is borne out to an important extent by the cultural variety of the individual regions. When a German king was awarded the title of emperor by the pope, he assumed the role of *Patricius Romanorum* (patrician of the Romans), and was bound to the obligation to protect the Church of Rome. This gave emperors seniority over all other secular princes in the region of the Church of Rome and placed them on the same level as the Eastern Byzantine emperors of earlier times in their relations with the Orthodox Eastern Church. The ruling structure in the Holy Roman Empire was based on two essential features: in their capacity as king, the rulers were regents of the Roman empire; and, in their capacity as emperor, they were protectors of the Church and thus the supreme secular rulers of the Western world.

Charlemagne's various divisions of the empire (at the Treaties of Verdun, 843; Mersen, 870; and Ribemont, 880) produced two lasting states: the kingdom of the Western Franks and the kingdom of the Eastern Franks. In 921, the rulers of both kingdoms agreed on a contract in which the possessions of each were mutually recognized. This document confirmed the political separation of Germany from France. In 962, after the end of the Carolingian dynasty, Otto I the Great (936–73), in his role as ruler of the Eastern kingdom, was able once more to revive the title of Roman emperor, which from that time remained with the Eastern kingdom. In so doing, the Saxon ruler established the idea of a permanent Holy Roman Empire—which from the end of the 15th century carried the additional wording "of the German nation." But not all the rulers of the Eastern kingdom—who from the early 12th century reinforced their claim to the emperor's title with the title "king of Rome"—were crowned as emperor in Rome. (Unlike the French kings, the German rulers had to be elected.) After the death of Emperor Frederick II in 1250 and the ensuing decline of the ruling house of Hohenstaufen, there was a long period when the Holy Roman Empire and the whole of the Western world had no emperor at all; this ended with the coronation of Ludwig of Bavaria as emperor in 1328. In the 16th century, during the Habsburg dynasty, the title of emperor was made hereditary, and was no longer bestowed by the pope.

In the Middle Ages, the heartlands of the Holy Roman Empire were the German duchies of Saxony, Franconia, Swabia, Bavaria, and Lorraine, previously part of the shortlived Carolingian middle kingdom created in 843. In addition, the empire possessed the kingdom of Bohemia, as well as modern Austria, Switzerland, the Netherlands and Belgium, Alsace, parts of eastern France, and for a time Burgundy and the Arelat (Lower Burgundy, whose capital was Arles in Provence), its territories stretching to the Mediterranean. Finally, it also owned the always hotly disputed region of northern Italy as far as the Papal States, and for a time southern Italy and Sicily.

The extent of the territory and the variety of peoples and languages show that the Holy Roman Empire was anything but a unified nation state limited to German tribal regions. Its largest revenues came from northern Italy, the Netherlands, and what today is French Alsace, which then was described as *vis maxima regni*, "the greatest strength of the empire." In the later Middle Ages, the capital of the empire, that is, the residence of the emperor, was Prague, today in the Czech Republic, and finally Vienna, today in Austria. The area covered by the Holy Roman Empire, despite the addition "of the German nation," was thus not at all like the area covered by the "German Empire" in its 19th- and 20th-century forms.

The kings were elected, often long before they acquired the title of emperor, by the five leading dukes, and from the 14th century by the college of the seven princes: the archbishops of Mainz, Cologne, and Trier, the king of Bohemia, the duke of Saxony, the count palatine of the Rhine, and the margrave of Brandenburg. Because the secular territorial rulers always pursued their own special interests, royal policies had to be made by other powers, on the one hand by secular leaders with land rights, but far more so by those vassals of the empire whose office was not hereditary, and was newly awarded each time: the bishops. First Charlemagne, then, in particular, Otto the Great developed an imperial church system by which the bishops were appointed by the king or at least confirmed in their office. This was important because the kingdom needed loyal followers to help it cope with the secular rulers. Royal power would have had hardly any firm basis without the support of the episcopate. That was the reason why conflicts over investiture, when the popes disputed the right to appoint bishops with the king, posed a threat to the existence of the kingdom during the Holy Roman Empire. At the same time it became clear during these disputes how important it was to be appointed a bishop, an office that made its holder a combination of both spiritual and temporal leader. As such they were specifically appointed to further imperial political aims. As soon as Charlemagne had organized the regions of his empire to the east of the Rhine, he started founding bishoprics and monasteries. Otto the Great continued this tradition when he sought to secure the eastern borderlands of his empire with a string of bishoprics, and a new arch-bishopric at Magdeburg. In so doing, he hoped to start converting the heathen Slavs to Christianity, and colonize the regions to the east of the Elbe. This policy of founding bishoprics encountered many severe setbacks, but was finally successful.

The high status of the bishops was later evident from the fact that three of the seven princes were archbishops, including the most senior of them all, the archbishop of Mainz, who was entitled to the office of imperial chancellor, and had the privilege of crowning newly elected kings. The archbishopric of Mainz was by far the largest in the Holy Roman Empire. The metropolitan establishment of Mainz was supported by no less than 14 suffragan bishoprics, from Chur in the Rhaetian Alps of modern Switzerland as far as Verden near Bremen in north Germany. The other arch-bishoprics—Cologne, Trier, Bremen-Hamburg, Magdeburg, and Salzburg—were much smaller.

From the beginning, their cathedrals were the visible and enduring expression of the high rank of the archbishops and bishops. In the first three centuries after Charlemagne, cathedrals in the Holy Roman Empire were generally larger and more massive than those in other European regions. Even in the Carolingian period new buildings such as Salzburg were marveled at for their impressive size. The largest of all was the so-called Old Cathedral of Cologne, almost 328 ft. (100 m) long, which was then outstripped by the Carolingian abbey church in Fulda, which had a massive 230 ft. (70 m) transept. In Fulda they set their standards by nothing less than St. Peter's in Rome, creating for St. Boniface, the apostle to Germany who is buried there, a church modeled on the burial church of St. Peter.

The great period of cathedral building did not begin until the era of the Saxon-Ottonian imperial house, between 950 and 1025. None of the cathedrals built at that time is still standing, but some of today's buildings give us a certain picture of them in that they were built on the foundations of their Ottonian predecessors.

Sometimes it was the emperor himself who ordered the building. In 955, Otto the Great made a highly ambitious and extravagant start on the cathedral in Magdeburg, which he had elevated to an archbishopric. He had splendid ancient columns brought from Italy, just as Charlemagne had done earlier for the palatine chapel in Aachen and the abbey church in Centula. The Ottonian Cathedral of Magdeburg, the first "imperial cathedral" in the Holy Roman Empire, in which its founder was buried in 973, was a columned basilica with an east transept and in style went back to two late basilicas of ancient Rome, St. Peter's and St. Paul-outside-the-Walls, which were both five-aisled, columned basilicas with a west transept. Magdeburg was to be a new Rome. This reversion to Rome occurred frequently during the Holy Roman Empire, starting in the Carolingian period with Fulda and Aachen, continuing in the Ottonian period with Cologne Cathedral, and finally with the second "imperial cathedral" after Magdeburg, endowed at Bamberg in 1003–4, and consecrated in 1012. This was founded by Henry II (1014–24), the last of the Saxon emperors, who created the bishopric of Bamberg and had himself buried in the cathedral. Henry's cathedral at Bamberg was a "Roman" basilica with a west transept and probably had columns. The massive cathedral of Archbishop Willigis in Mainz also reflected the Roman style, with its broad, protruding western transept. This building burned down on the day of its consecration in 1009, and was rebuilt shortly afterward by Archbishop Bardo. Finally, another building bearing a strong Roman influence was the Romanesque cathedral begun in Strasbourg by Bishop Wernher in 1015, a massive structure with columns and a protruding transept, though this was now placed at the east end.

All these buildings have disappeared in their original form, but they show that in the time of the Holy Roman Empire there was a distinct architectural preference for the Roman style, modeled on the Early Christian columned basilica. None of these basilicas erected from the Carolingian period onward reached the dimensions of the late Roman period. Around 800, liturgical reforms were responsible for introducing structures with double choirs, of which Cologne Cathedral was a good example. While Early Christian churches had developed a purposeful *via triumphalis* from the entrance to the apse, churches were now surrounded at both east and west ends, their two polarities, by a sanctuary with an apse. Each of the sanctuaries had its own system of privileges. The old, widely held view that double choirs were an illustration of *regnum* and *sacerdotium*, the two poles of the Holy Roman Empire, has been proved false, the product of romantic historical fantasy.

Until the beginning of the Gothic period, an important part of cathedrals and monastery churches was the crypt, an underground room usually located beneath the sanctuary, which served primarily for the worship of relics, but was also used for burials. With two choirs, churches could have two crypts, mostly in the form of a many-aisled hall with columns.

The Cathedral of Trier was an exception. It dates back to a square building from the 4th century that had four monolithic columns more than 39 ft. (12 m) high. After it had been repaired many times, this late ancient structure was converted into a pillared building under Archbishop Egbert toward the end of the 10th century. From 1030, Archbishop Poppo had an identical square building added to the house of the Babenbergs to the west, and built today's four-towered west facade with its protruding middle apse, a mighty example of defiant power building that clearly demonstrates that the city of Trier was the seat of one of the great archbishops of the Holy Roman Empire. At the time of the Hohenstaufens, the interior of the cathedral was converted to its present form and embellished with a newly added west choir, which is a magnificent example of the mature Rhenish Late Romanesque style.

The cathedrals of Carolingian and Ottonian times were without exception flat-roofed. Not until the Salian (Franconian) dynasty, which followed the Ottonian, did architects begin to span the naves with arches. The pioneering construction, the imperial cathedral of Speyer (see page 140–49), was the Salians' showpiece, which at the same time served as their burial site. It had a total length of 440 ft. (134 m), and was the largest new building in the Western world, until it was surpassed by the Abbey Church of Cluny.

Speyer Cathedral, begun around either 1025, 1029, or 1031 under Conrad II, completed in 1061 under Henry III, and converted in about 1080 under Henry IV, was the first completely vaulted large-scale building of the Middle Ages. During the first phase of building, only the side aisles in the nave were vaulted, but during the conversion the central nave was also given vaults, in which two wall sections were joined together by a cross-vault covering a double bay. Each side aisle to the left and right of the double bay had two single bays. This was the so-called intersecting system, a layout that was invented in Speyer, and led the way for future vault systems in the Holy Roman Empire. To counteract the vaulting and its thrusts, massive piers were required instead of columns, and a system of attached columns to connect with the vaulting. Speyer launched a completely new development, which brought with it further innovations. Instead of using cross-vaults in the arms of the transept, cross-rib vaulting was employed with simple box-ribs in a very large format, the first of its kind. This immediately

Trier Cathedral, west facade

Right:
Königslutter, former
Benedictine abbey church,
from the northeast

Below:
Ratzeburg Cathedral, from
the south

On the Rhine, two other six-towered bishop's churches with intersecting vaults followed Speyer Cathedral, their appearance qualifying them as imperial churches: the cathedrals of Mainz and Worms (see pages 156–61 and 150–55). Both have modern cross-rib vaults in the nave, and both are especially remarkable for their octagonal tower at the crossing. This group of three Rhenish imperial cathedrals was unsurpassed during the Holy Roman Empire by later cathedral buildings of the Romanesque period.

The active building program of the Salians was immediately taken up by the next emperor, Lothair von Supplinburg from Saxony, when he had the collegiate church of Königslutter built near Brunswick as his burial site, a vaulted structure that challenged the great cathedrals in its ambitiousness. After the emperor's death the building, then consisting only of a choir and transept, was completed after a fashion with a meager nave and a flat roof.

The emperors of the next ruling house, the Hohenstaufens, did very little in the way of cathedral building in the North Alpine region of the empire. Meanwhile the Hohenstaufens' great rival, the Guelph duke Henry the Lion, worked flat out to construct, or at least to sponsor, three new cathedral buildings in his North German territory (Lübeck, Ratzeburg, and Schwerin), and, at the same time, had his burial site built in the form of the cathedral-like collegiate church at Brunswick. During the Hohenstaufen period, the bishops also pursued a vigorous building policy. Around half the cathedrals then in existence were now replaced by new, vaulted buildings, which had the advantage of being less vulnerable to fires than the older, flat-roofed structures.

The largest of the Hohenstaufen cathedrals, also in the Romanesque style, was built in the archbishopric of Salzburg: a five-aisled, galleried basilica, which in the 17th century was replaced by the slightly smaller Baroque building that still stands today. However, the other Hohenstaufen cathedrals have mostly survived: Münster, Osnabrück, Naumburg, Bamberg, and Basel. Also from this period are the east ends of the cathedrals in Minden, Trier, and Strasbourg, and the immense west front of Mainz Cathedral. These cathedrals were so well built and were so impressive that they have satisfied all later requirements up to the present day.

In many cases, building extended well into the 13th century, and it is notable that almost all the masons' lodges remained faithful to the old inherited building methods of the Romanesque period and its intersecting vault system. In Osnabrück, they continued building in the Romanesque

found many imitators, as did the octagonal domical vault at the crossing, which on the outside of the building looks like a tower. The exterior with its six towers offered an unavoidable demonstration of imperial power, and set a standard to which subsequent buildings would have to aspire.

manner into the second half of the century. This almost defiant allegiance to a past tradition gave the buildings a squarish, thick-walled heaviness, and, on occasion, when the workforces were trained in the Rhine area, was responsible for the opulent decorativeness of the small columns, arches, and blind windows seen in Rhenish, especially Lower Rhenish, Late Romanesque buildings. By around 1250, the Romanesque period was generally finished, this date coinciding with the decline of the Hohenstaufens and a temporary end to the imperial period.

The persistence of Romanesque architecture is even more remarkable given the fact that in France the Gothic style had been adopted since 1150, and after 1200 had become the fully developed Classical Gothic of Chartres Cathedral and other buildings that imitated it. Almost all the cathedral builders in the Holy Roman Empire remained resistant to French Gothic for more than a hundred years. In some cases this may have happened through lack of awareness, but in others it was entirely intentional, as, for

example, in Bamberg, Trier, and Mainz, where the new French method of building cannot have been completely unknown. For the clients and their architects, the style we now call Romanesque was their well-tempered tradition, which they clearly wanted to hold on to, seeing it as part of the tradition of the Holy Roman Empire. The roots of the Romanesque reached back through Charlemagne to ancient

Above:
Brunswick Cathedral, from the north
Below left:
Osnabrück Cathedral, nave looking east
Below right:
Münster Cathedral, from the south

Rome, making it a visible testament to the empire's history, which seems to have taken on something of an untouchable, if not sacred, nature. In this light, the obstinate fidelity to the Romanesque style can best be understood as a wish to preserve a kind of Roman imperial style. However, the result was that even though the buildings were of high quality, they must have seemed hopelessly outmoded when compared with the modern developments being achieved in France.

The first clear signs of eclipse came with the French Gothic collegiate church in Limburg an der Lahn, which today is the cathedral, and Magdeburg Cathedral on the Elbe. In Limburg, an impressive seven-towered basilica was begun around 1190, or slightly later. It has a transept and ambulatory, but no radiating chapels. The elevation is four-storied like some French Early Gothic cathedrals, and consists of dividing arcades, gallery, triforium, and clerestory. The sexpartite rib vaulting has a transverse rib in addition to the cross ribs, and also corresponds to French Early Gothic. Limburg is closest to the cathedrals of Noyon

Regensburg Cathedral

Far left:
View from the east

Left:
Interior looking east

and Laon, the latter also having many towers. However, at Limburg it was only the type of building that was borrowed from France: its formal vocabulary is not French Gothic, but a model example of the rich, decorative Late Romanesque style of the Rhine area. A building thus came into being that was a cross-border synthesis of a French type dressed in the robes of its native Rhineland.

For the cathedral in Magdeburg, the archbishop, who had studied in Paris, had a choir built in 1209 in the style of French Early Gothic cathedrals, together with an ambulatory, radiating chapels, and a gallery (see ill. page 122). At ground level the design is still squarish and massive, a Gothic style in Romanesque garb; the gallery, however—the so-called bishop's way—is a fine piece of French Early Gothic, commonly found in Cistercian foundations, with its tubelike shafts, annulets, and rib vaults, their imposts set at different heights. While it is true that the old imperial church of Otto the Great was uniformly designed at ground level, several antique columns were introduced to line the walls of the inner choir, put on display like relics of their own history, and made additionally remarkable by figures of saints. At Magdeburg, the advent of Gothic manifested itself as a laborious transition from the Romanesque period.

Some three decades later, between 1230 and 1240, the ground for Gothic was so well prepared that the local Alsatian masons who were building Strasbourg Cathedral, and had produced a choir, crossing, and transept arms in a heavy Romanesque style, could be replaced during the building process by a French workforce with a completely contemporary approach. The nave is a purely French Classical Gothic structure, which rates as one of the best and most modern works of French architecture and one of the finest achievements in world architecture (see pages 106–19).

The same goes for the somewhat later Cologne Cathedral, begun in 1248 (see page 162–75), one of the greatest cathedrals of all, which, with its transept, five-aisled nave, and two-towered front, was not completed until the 19th century. Only the east end of the choir was finished in the Middle Ages. New heights were reached at Cologne, built at a time when French Gothic had matured after a hundred years of trial and error. The result, in terms of ground plan and structure, is an example of advanced French system building carried out with tremendous rigor. The complex problems that had always arisen in the building of Gothic cathedrals were resolved in Cologne to an optimal extent, whether in the ground plan of the choir polygon, with its ambulatory and radiating chapels, or in the shapes of pillars, engaged columns, and ribs, which had to be fused harmoniously throughout. Many regard Cologne Cathedral as the finest piece of systematic architecture to be found in any cathedral to that date, and as the zenith of a development process that had always striven for increasing perfection.

The cathedral in Regensburg is also based on the French Gothic style. After a completely unsuccessful start, which by about 1250 had produced an east end with three graduated

Right:
Doberan, Cistercian monastery church, from the southeast

Below:
Freiburg im Breisgau Cathedral, from the southeast

were not confined to Ulm, where the 528-ft. (161 m) tower, completed in the 19th century, is the tallest church tower in the world, nor to St. Stephen's in Vienna, but were also manifested in Thann in Alsace, in Landshut in Bavaria, and, again, in Freiburg, whose cathedral tower is thought by many to be the most beautiful in the world. Sometimes the Cistercians also built churches in the manner of cathedrals, though always without towers. These can be found in the brick region of the Baltic, as at Bad Doberan; or near Cologne at Altenberg, where the monastery church is clearly an offspring of Cologne Cathedral; in southern Germany at, for example, Salem on Lake Constance or Donauwörth in Kaisheim; and, last but not least, in the kingdom of Bohemia at Sedlec near Kutná Hora, where the church was laid out with five aisles.

Among the Gothic cathedrals of the Holy Roman Empire, the one in Halberstadt also follows the layout of French cathedrals, albeit on a reduced scale: an ambulatory with no radiating chapels and openwork buttressing on the exterior. In the elevation of the steeply proportioned central

apses but no ambulatory, a first-class architect who had studied in France took charge of the building. Instead of a cathedral choir with an ambulatory and radiating chapels, he designed a several-storied apse with large windows, a glass-house of perforated tracery that retains its original stained glass and counts as one of the magical wonders of Gothic cathedral architecture. The nave also attains the high standard of French cathedrals. In southern Germany, however, Regensburg Cathedral was, and remained, a foreign intruder; this kind of Gothic was not generally accepted in the region.

The French Gothic style found its closest imitators in the region of the Holy Roman Empire that was the farthest removed from France: in the Hanseatic cities of the Baltic, particularly in the brick buildings of Lübeck, Wismar, Rostock, and Stralsund. Here, several astonishingly large brick churches—as many as three in one city—had the same layout and scale as cathedrals, but always remained parish churches. The most magnificent was the Marienkirche in Lübeck. The inhabitants of other cities were clearly competing with one another, as were the bishop and cathedral chapter of Schwerin, who replaced the old cathedral of Henry the Lion with a new building on the model of Lübeck.

In southern German cities, the citizens also built parish churches with all the appearance of cathedrals, particularly in Freiburg and Ulm. The lofty ambitions of such citizens

nave and choir, the windows—the pride of every cathedral in France—are so small that a large area of masonry is left visible. This can be found elsewhere in Gothic buildings in German-speaking regions. In Halberstadt, the French-inspired Gothic cathedral has been similarly Germanized.

Other new Gothic cathedrals reveal no French influence at all. Here, bishops and cathedral chapters took the same course as city rulers did elsewhere with their city churches: they built hall-churches rather than basilicas, that is, churches with aisles of equal height. Such cathedrals were little different from parish and other churches, except that some were rather larger. An early example, built around 1225–75, is the massive cathedral at Paderborn, Westphalia, equipped with stout columns, followed soon after by the spacious, light-filled hall of the cathedral at Minden on the Weser (1250–90), and around 1260 by the cathedral in Meissen on the Elbe.

The Late Gothic cathedral in Eichstätt, Bavaria, has five aisles and a double choir, which is rare among cathedrals. At Verden, near Bremen, building started around 1297 on a

cathedral using the same ground plan as Reims Cathedral, with an ambulatory, but no radiating chapels. The building was then completed as a hall-church rather than a basilica, characterized by its new type of choir: the hall ambulatory. This style was soon followed in the new choir built in the cathedral of the Hanseatic city of Lübeck. In the Late

Right:
Passau Cathedral,
view of the choir

Below:
Tournai Cathedral,
from the north

200–09). Long after the Salians, this was another imperial cathedral, as well as the coronation and burial church of the kings of Bohemia. Charles IV was from the house of Luxembourg, and had been brought up in France. In 1344, he brought the Frenchman Matthieu of Arras to Prague as his architect—Matthieu would design a totally French cathedral with an ambulatory and radiating chapels. However, his successor, Peter Parler, from Schwäbisch Gmünd, appointed in 1353–56 at the age of 23, gave the cathedral a quite individual character. Even though its basic design was already fixed, Parler conceived a completely new vaulting configuration that united all the internal spaces, and tracery windows of a kind that had never been seen before. In this way he replaced the rigid schematization of Matthieu with imagination and variety. Peter Parler brought new life to the doctrinaire, desiccated Gothic of the French, and pointed the way to a new era: the Late Gothic.

During the Late Gothic period, new cathedrals were not built on a lavish scale, except for one latecomer: the east end of the cathedral at Passau on the Danube. The single-aisled choir with its polygonal apse, a Late Gothic answer to the cathedral choir in nearby Regensburg (see page 129), is an extravagant glasshouse with a profusion of tracery. In addition, the architect went back to a concept that had been developed at Regensburg but not carried out: over the crossing was built an octagonal, domelike structure similar to those that, centuries earlier, crowned the Rhenish imperial cathedrals. This happened at a time when, in Italy, the cathedral dome in Florence had already been completed, and the dome of St. Peter's in Rome was being planned. Now, at the end of the Gothic period, an idea was coming to fruition that would become fundamental to the future development of new churches. It is possible, therefore, that the last medieval cathedral buildings of the Holy Roman Empire received a certain impetus from new Italian architecture, at least in their domes.

In the Early and High Middle Ages, the regions of modern Holland and Belgium also belonged to the Holy Roman Empire. Here, too, they built very ambitious cathedrals of considerable size, as well as several monastery and city churches that rival the cathedrals architecturally, and in fact are indistinguishable from them. Tournai Cathedral has great richness. Dating from around 1160, it is a Late Romanesque building with a four-storied nave and galleries. The east end, which was extended in the Gothic period with a French-style cathedral choir, was originally a central structure with three transepts and three apses connected to ambulatories. It has a very striking

Gothic period, the hall ambulatory was to become the hallmark of several churches in southern Germany, for example in Nuremberg, Schwäbisch Gmünd, and Schwäbisch Hall.

Emperor Charles IV brought the medieval cathedral to a brilliant conclusion with the choir of St. Vitus's Cathedral in Prague, situated above the city on Hradcany Hill (see pages

exterior with a group of five towers, like those planned for Laon Cathedral in France, but only partly carried out (see Plate 11).

In the Gothic period, the five-aisled cathedral at Utrecht, begun in 1254 by Bishop Hendrik van Vianden, was closely modeled on Cologne Cathedral. It has a three-aisled French choir and ambulatory and a 368-ft. (112 m)-high west tower, which ranks as one of the most beautiful Gothic towers, a Lower Rhenish counterpart to the Upper Rhenish cathedral tower at Freiburg. The cathedral was completed in 1517. As early as 1674, however, the nave was destroyed by a tornado, and not reconstructed. A view of it was made by the painter Pieter Saenredam.

Most of the large church buildings in Holland and Belgium date from the Late Gothic period. Some of them were elevated to cathedral status in the ecclesiastical reforms of 1559, as happened in Mechelen, Ghent, Antwerp, and s'Hertogenbosch. Unlike the large church buildings in German-speaking regions, those in Holland and Belgium, influenced by French architecture, generally have an ambulatory and often radiating chapels as well. The most lavish have five aisles, following the lead of Utrecht Cathedral. They are the cathedrals of Antwerp and s'Hertogenbosch, the latter a magnificent building overflowing with filigree refinement.

The Gothic church towers in these regions have a special character. Their chief model was Utrecht Cathedral. The towers sometimes reach astonishing heights, and in their upper parts tend to be decorated with increasingly fine perforated masonry, as can be seen in the north tower of Antwerp Cathedral. In Melchelen, they set out to build the tallest tower in the world, but it was not completed; nevertheless the stump of the tower alone is just as imposing in size as the Gothic churches of the region. They are a testament to the mature opulence that had been achieved by the time they were built.

Basel (Switzerland)

Basel, situated on the Upper Rhine, is today the capital of a Swiss subcanton. It grew on the site of the Roman fortress of Basilea into one of the most important cities of the Holy Roman Empire. At the end of the fifth century, it joined the Frankish kingdom, and became the seat of a bishop in the eighth century. The bishopric was subordinate to the archbishopric of Besançon. Bishop Hatto (Heito), concurrently the abbot of the monastery on the Lake Constance island of Reichenau, was a friend and adviser to Charlemagne, and, in 811, undertook an ambassadorial journey on behalf of the emperor to the Byzantine emperor in Constantinople. In Basel, he had a cathedral built that drew paeans of praise, and on Reichenau he built the new monastery church of Mittelzell. The famous monastery plan for St. Gall has also been traced back to Hatto.

After the collapse of the Carolingian empire, Basel fell in 912 to the kingdom of Burgundy. Its last ruler, Rudolf III, was childless, and, in 1006, transferred his empire by testamentary contract, that is, bequeathed it, to his nephew, the German king, Henry II, who in 1014 received the title of emperor, and was later canonized, as was his wife, Kunigunde. In the 13th and 14th centuries, Basel freed itself gradually from the bishops in favor of guild rule, and sought the status of a free city. In 1356, an earthquake destroyed large parts of the city, bringing a major setback to its political development.

From 1431 to 1449, the Ecumenical Council sat in Basel —though not with the pope—with the aim of reforming the Church from top to bottom. A short time later, in 1459, Pope Pius II founded the University of Basel. From that time, Basel became one of the most important centers of humanism and book printing. In 1501, the city joined the Swiss Confederation, and left the Holy Roman Empire. In 1529, with the onset of the Reformation there was an outbreak of iconoclasm in the churches. The bishop and cathedral chapter left the city for ever. From then on the cathedral, known as the *Münster* (minster), in Basel, became the chief parish church, while the city parliament was made responsible for its maintenance.

Today's minster was preceded by two earlier buildings, which were mostly buried beneath it. The first building, which had two circular towers in the west, dated to either the time of Hatto or to the early 10th century, after the Hungarian invasion of 916. The second one is known as "Henry's Cathedral," because Henry II sponsored it, partly by donating the famous *Golden Antependium of Basel* (today in the Musée de Cluny, Paris), considered one of the greatest and most significant pieces of artistic metalwork of the

Ottonian period. The Henry Cathedral was consecrated in 1019 in the presence of the emperor and empress. It stood on the foundations of the first cathedral; it no longer had west towers, but did have towers flanking the choir to the east, which together with the apse looked down from on high over the Rhine. Beneath the choir there was an extensive crypt, five-aisled in the west part and three-aisled in the east. After a fire in 1085, a west facade with two towers was added to the Henry Cathedral. The two lower sections of the north tower were preserved, each a square ashlar block with a flat surface. The direct model for the two-towered facade may have been the west elevation of the slightly earlier Wernher Cathedral in Strasbourg.

The present cathedral was begun around 1170, under the Hohenstaufens, and completed in about 1200 or soon after. Again, this third cathedral stood on the foundations of its predecessor, but now a new transept was added. The choir, rebuilt from the old crypt, was laid out as a polygonal choir with an ambulatory but no radiating chapels, and flanked at the side by towers in the corners between the choir and the transept. Together with the crossing tower, this produced an east group of three towers like the imperial cathedrals in the Rhineland. The older west towers seem to have been integrated into the new cathedral.

In the earthquake of 1356, parts of the cathedral collapsed, bringing down the vaulting of the central nave, choir, and transept, the upper stories of the west and east towers, and the apse, as well as the crossing tower, which shattered the crypt. However, the vertical stone walls, made throughout from solid ashlar blocks, survived without much damage, as did the rib vaulting of the side aisles and the ambulatory. The master builder Johann von Gmünd was appointed to organize the reconstruction of the destroyed parts of the building. He was a member of the famous Parler family of master builders, and had led the building of the minster choir at Freiburg im Breisgau, begun in 1354.

The nave at Basel is a galleried basilica with double bays using the intersecting system. The dividing arcades have pointed arches, and they, along with the narrow side aisles hemmed in by huge pillars, are closely related in their heavy, powerful forms to the Late Romanesque style of Alsace. One can imagine that the original nave vaulting, as it stood before the earthquake of 1356, would have had heavy, squarish transverse arches, like those in the side aisles. This would have given it a much more weighty appearance than the present Late Gothic rib vaulting. Galleries were unusual in the Upper Rhineland. With their round-arched triple arcades, double pillars, and broad relieving arches, they recall the Romanesque architecture of northern Italy. In type the nave is also comparable with the archbishop's cathedral in Sens, a founding building of the French Early Gothic style, which had just been completed at that time. A notable feature of the central nave is its great width, in marked contrast to the narrow side aisles. The nave has an internal width of some 39 ft. (12 m) and a height of some 67 ft. (20 m). The spatial relationship is similar to that of the previous building, the architect having adopted the old ground plan for the nave.

The east end is a major work of Late Romanesque architecture. The crossing, with its compound piers—which have no fewer than five massive circular front columns on each side—seems not to have been spanned originally by a cross-rib vault, as it is today, but probably by an octagonal drum cupola raised on pendentives, similar to that in the east end of the minster at nearby Freiburg im Breisgau, which followed directly after Basel. The east apse with its ambulatory was formerly a masterpiece of Late Romanesque inventiveness, and in part remains so today. In its original state, the ambulatory was not at ground level, like the choir, but was set lower down, at the level of the crypt; later it was raised up to the height of the galleries, and connected to the choir with five arcades. The present intermediate vault, which makes the ambulatory two-storied, perceptibly altered the original concept. The five arcades of the ambulatory, whose width and height gradually increase toward the middle, are a most unusual design. Instead of employing columns, like those generally used in France for ambulatories, or massive pillars, the architect combined small individual columns and smaller sections of pillars in a less tight grouping that one can see through. The arcades have no flat intrados, but are like a stepped portal, each with three stepped arches and freestanding wall columns. In France, the home of the ambulatory, such rich and originally conceived ambulatory arcades are nowhere to be found. This richness could have been extended to the galleries. Thus, the apse in its original state can be imagined as a showpiece that clearly surpassed the conventional styles used up to then in the Upper Rhineland.

The galleries of the apse were so badly damaged in the earthquake of 1356 that Johann von Gmünd replaced them with new ones. These are distinguished on the outside by round windows, and, on the inside, next to the choir, by simple pointed arches ranged in a gridlike row with extremely thin shafts. These shafts extend the tracery posts of the clerestory windows downward. The galleries and the clerestory are decorated with extremely delicate tracery. The

arcades of the lower part form an optically solid base for the windows, a real glasshouse, and the posts of the gallery. Despite the stylistic contrast, the upper part is so harmoniously joined to the lower that Late Romanesque and Late Gothic appear to form a new and comprehensive unity. Master Johann's reconstruction of the apse is a successful design solution that is both innovative and respectful of the past.

The most important decorative piece in the Late Romanesque building is the Gallus Portal in the north transept, which was put up in the 12th century, and much added to later. This is a Romanesque stepped portal with a rectangular frame, a tympanum with relief figures, pillars in the recesses, and a richly carved surround. The portal is enclosed on each side in a most unusual way by five-storied tabernacles with figures representing the Four Evangelists.

Above:
Romanesque panel with Apostles

Below:
St. Vincent panel: four reliefs with scenes from the legend of St. Vincent

In terms of historical development, the portal is important because this is the first time in the German-speaking region that large-scale figures were used in the recesses. The inspiration for the portal came not so much from the highly developed figured portals of the Early Gothic period in France as from the Romanesque portal designs of northern Italy. The program, which centers around the Last Judgment, was supplemented by figures in the lateral tabernacles.

Also preserved from the Henry Cathedral are two highly significant relief panels: one shows pairs of apostles in dispute, the other relates the legend of St. Vincent in four reliefs. Both panels reveal the influence of relief sculptures on ancient Roman sarcophagi, which enabled the sculptor of the apostles to capture the postures of toga-wearing Romans, and—the story of St. Vincent—to portray the architecture and landscape in a lively and realistic fashion that is unique in Romanesque sculpture. The reliefs date from some time between 1000 and the Late Romanesque period, and seem to have served previously as choir screen panels, with the apostles panel, together with a second panel, possibly enclosing the *Golden Antependium* of Henry II.

Plates 60–62

60 Cathedral from the east looking across the Rhine
61 The Gallus Portal in the north transept
62 View through the nave to the choir

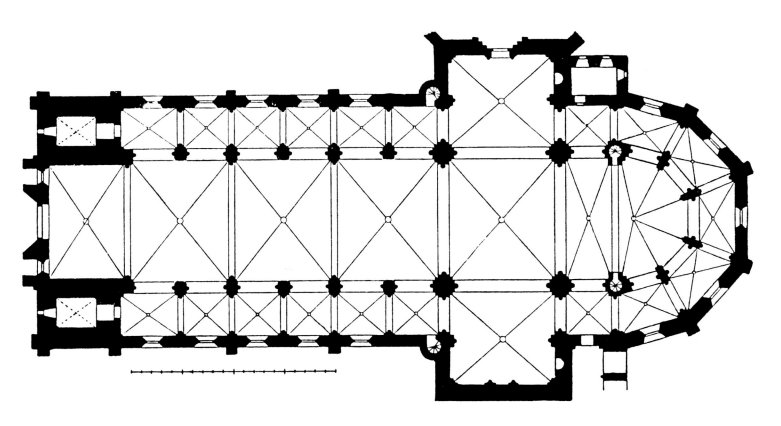

138 *Switzerland*

Speyer

The cathedral of Speyer on the Rhine, the largest of the so-called imperial cathedrals, was both the showpiece of the Salian emperors and their burial site. Conrad II (1024–39) began the cathedral around 1025–31, and Henry III (1039–56) continued the work. In 1061 came the consecration of "Speyer I." Only two decades later, Henry IV (1056–1107) had hardly settled down again after his pilgrimage to Canossa in 1077 before he had the cathedral redesigned to give it a more splendid appearance. This building ("Speyer II") is very like the present version in the east end. Workers were recruited from all over the empire and from other regions. The emperor himself appointed as his building manager Bishop Benno von Osnabrück (d. 1088), famous as the *architectus praecipuus* (architect extraordinary), and after him Otto von Bamberg, who in 1102 became bishop of Bamberg, and later was canonized.

The western parts were blown up by invading French troops in 1689, during the War of the Grand Alliance. In the late 18th century, Ignaz Michael Neumann, son of the great Baroque architect Baltasar Neumann, rebuilt the west bays of the nave to the original design. In the 19th century, on the initiative of the regional ruler, King Ludwig I of Bavaria, the west block was also restored, with its three towers. The plans submitted by the director of building, Heinrich Hübsch from Karlsruhe, were close to those of the original, but then he strayed so far from them that the whole western elevation has a very individual, Neo-Romanesque appearance.

The cathedral is a columned basilica with a transept, choir, and crossing. In accordance with the emperor's wishes, it exceeded all other buildings of that time in size. It now has an overall length of 440 ft. (134 m), with a central nave some 108 ft. (33 m) high and 46 ft. (14 m) wide. The crypt has remained unaltered since Speyer I, and is the largest in the world. It extends over the whole area of the choir, crossing, and both transept arms. Each of these sections, which are separated from each other by colossal arcades of columns, is an individual compartment with pillars—a crypt by itself, as it were. To the west, the vault of the Salian kings was added to the crypt in 1906. This is the resting place of Conrad II, Henry III, Henry IV, and Henry V, as well as Rudolf of Habsburg (1273–91), the founder of the Habsburg royal and imperial dynasty, and his successors Adolf of Nassau (1292–98) and Albert of Austria (1298–1308). Originally the tombs were laid in the ground in front of the Altar of the Cross.

The most admired part of Speyer I is the nave. The side aisles have been preserved unchanged, and in the central nave the original layout can easily be recognized despite later rebuilding. At the time it was built, when it was still customary in the Holy Roman Empire to build columned basilicas in the antique tradition or simple piered basilicas, its design concept was completely new. It was not only that the side aisles were completely vaulted, and each bay systematically given a four-arched framework with engaged columns on the walls and piers; far more crucial was the way in which the walls of the central nave were organized with rows of 12 gigantic openings, their arches symmetrically aligned beneath the clerestory windows. In this way the horizontal story divisions of previous columned basilicas became a tightly organized combination of stories with a vertical emphasis. The openings, reminiscent of ancient Roman aqueducts, turn the elevation into a single, very high arcaded wall. The nave itself was flat-roofed, however. Its atmosphere was that of a *via triumphalis* lined with gigantic arcades, and in its size and magnificence had a character that was unmistakably related to the imperial style of the ancient Romans.

In the next phase of building (Speyer II), the nave was also vaulted with slightly domed cross-vaults, each of which joined two wall openings to a double bay. The vaulting was a pioneering technical feat of the highest order. The walls and the openings were altered, with every other pier being strengthened with a sturdy engaged column that supported the transverse arch and the barrel vault. With the help of the double bays, which take up the same space as two smaller bays in the side aisles, a perfect ground plan and elevation scheme were achieved right away, the so-called intersecting system, which was to be very influential in the Holy Roman Empire.

very primitive, and was then improved at this building's successor, the cathedral at Worms.

The crossing at Speyer would also go beyond conventional designs. Here, the architects erected an octagonal dome over an inner drum with openings, mounted on pendentives. The exterior was given a dwarf gallery. This proved a model for later Rhenish crossing domes.

Taken as a whole, the exterior of the east end at Speyer has an apse, protruding transepts, a domed crossing tower, and two tall square towers that together convey the image of an optimistic, proud sensibility, confident in its power. Here, the Salian ruling house demonstrated, a few years after the pilgrimage to Canossa, not only its devotion to the Church, but, even more, a visible sign of the continuity of imperial sovereignty. Whoever built in such a manner would surely prevail.

Until the former three-towered western facade was destroyed, the counterpart to the east end was a rather cold block, set crossways to the nave and surmounted in the middle by an octagonal dome similar to that over the crossing. Behind the main block stood two square towers,

Also during this phase the east and west ends were redesigned. The choir was given an apse with interior and exterior blind arcading and the new motif of a dwarf gallery under the eaves. This form of apse was widely adopted, for example, immediately afterward at Mainz Cathedral. Both transept arms were newly built as monumental cubic blocks with especially thick walls and deeply recessed intrados in the windows. The broad lesenes, or pilaster strips, used on the walls look like firm pier columns, and increase the impression of monumentality to something even more colossal. At the same time, the stonemasons from Lombardy working on the exterior were responsible for the very rich decorative effects and the air of imperial splendor. The ambitiousness of this architecture was as great as the age could conceive. The same is true of the vaulting in the interior. Here, the concept was changed during the building process, so that the first plan for cross-vaults was not carried out. Instead, the hip was underlaid with simple box-shaped ribs to increase the vault's stability in view of its size. The art of rib-vaulting in the Rhineland started with these ribs, which were still technically

placed on each flank, and set back like sentinels. This gave the cathedral a group of three towers in the west as well, which balanced with the other group. The west front must have conveyed a message of pride similar to that of its counterpart in the east. The interior of the transverse block was given an entrance hall with a gallery above, which had a large round-arched arcade opening on to the nave. Whether the gallery served as a chapel or as the emperor's loge (box), or both, is not clear.

Since its rebuilding in the 19th century in the Neo-Romanesque style, the west front conveys only a faint impression of its original state, as this was recorded in old views, particularly in a drawing by Wenzel Hollar of about 1635. The defiant massiveness of its appearance could not be recaptured. But the cathedral as a whole has reacquired its two three-tower groups, giving it six in all, and fulfills the high ambitions of the Salians, as it stands, visible from afar, looking over the Rhineland plain.

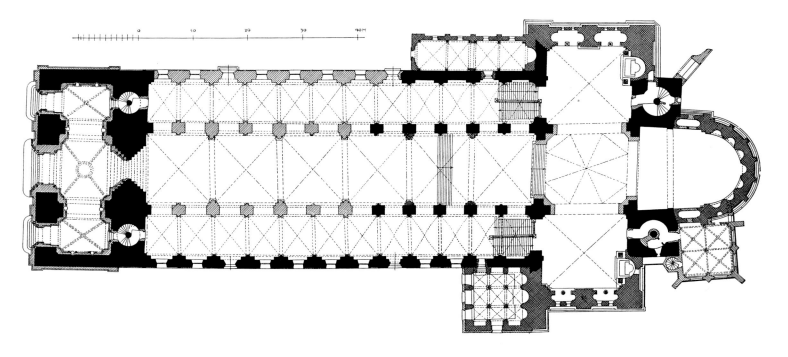

Worms

The bishopric of Worms, situated between Speyer and Mainz on the Rhine, was one of the oldest, but also one of the smallest, bishoprics in the Holy Roman Empire. In contrast, the largest bishopric in the empire, Constance, was ten times larger. In an earlier period, Worms was, for a short time, capital of the kingdom of Burgundy and thus the scene of the Nibelungen saga. The city achieved greater historical significance in the early Middle Ages as the seat of the duchy that produced Conrad the Red, a son-in-law of Otto the Great. Conrad fell at Lechfeld in 955 in the victorious battle against Hungary, and was buried in Worms Cathedral. He was the progenitor of the later imperial house of the Salians. They derived their claim to the title of emperor from Conrad's connection to the Ottonians.

In Worms, the conflict over investiture was ended in 1122 by the Concordat of Worms, which struck a compromise between the claims of the pope and the emperor. The city's constant support of the emperor was rewarded in 1181, when the Hohenstaufen emperor Frederick Barbarossa exempted Worms from all taxes, a privilege that was announced in the cathedral on a bronze tablet. This made Worms one of the seven free imperial cities in the Hohenstaufen period. Worms also received great historical glory through the more than 40 imperial and court assemblies that were held there, the most famous of these being the Diet of Worms of 1521, which in practice sealed the splitting of the Church into two camps: Catholic and Evangelical.

Worms was already the seat of a bishop in late antiquity, but there is no evidence of cathedral buildings until the Merovingian and Carolingian periods. After 1000 a large building appeared that was typical of the Ottonian era. This was consecrated in 1018 under Bishop Burchard, one of the most important religious politicians of the late Ottonian epoch, who in the end collaborated significantly with the Salians when they took over the monarchy. The present cathedral has exactly the same dimensions as the Burchard cathedral, except for the west apse, which was added later. Like other Ottonian cathedrals, the Burchard cathedral was a basilica with a double choir, and had a transept in the east. Four round towers, positioned on either side of the east and west apses, gave it its particular character. The west towers have been preserved up to a certain height, and incorporated in the present building.

The four round towers were then kept as the symbol of Worms when the Burchard cathedral was replaced by the present one. This happened in the Late Romanesque period, and for that reason the question of dating is especially important. The year 1181 offers a clue, for a service of con-

secration took place then. But when was the new cathedral started? In contrast to Speyer Cathedral, which was certainly almost completed by the time of the death of Emperor Henry IV in 1106, the formal vocabulary and the stonework at Worms are so much more advanced that research has now moved forward the date when building began to around 1170. The western apse at Worms would then have been built around 1220–30, at the same time as the western apse of Mainz Cathedral.

In fact, however, Worms Cathedral is half a century older. This was not established until 1979 through the dendrochronological dating of old scaffolding poles. Building began in the eastern part around 1120–25, only a few years after Speyer Cathedral was completed. By the time it was consecrated in 1181, the east end and nave were completed and the western apse was well advanced, if not already finished. These discoveries caused a sensation, and threw much-needed light on the developmental history of Romanesque architecture from the Upper Rhine to the Middle Rhine.

Speyer Cathedral acted as a measuring stick for Worms, even though Worms is not as large. With its total length of some 354 ft. (108 m) it is about 85 ft. (26 m) shorter than Speyer, and the height of the central nave is about 20 ft. (6 m) shorter at about 90 ft. (27 m). It is clear from a long distance away, however, that Worms as well as Mainz, with their groups of three towers, were measuring themselves against Speyer. This relationship to Speyer is the reason why Worms Cathedral bears the title "imperial cathedral," even though no emperor made his presence felt there. But at least the progenitor of an imperial house, Conrad the Red, was buried there. The decisive factor that won Worms its proud designation as an imperial cathedral was that its overall appearance was no less imperial than that of Speyer.

Unlike Speyer, where small pieces of hammered undressed stone were used in places, the exterior and interior of the new Worms Cathedral were both built with cleanly cut blocks of housing stone and precisely shaped structures such as pilaster strips, friezes for round arcades, and blind arches. Romanesque architecture had now adopted a purer form of stonemasonry, and as a result the corners of structures are lavishly adorned with torus moldings, grooves, and ogival forms. This improves their sculptural force, which is further strengthened by their deep brownish-red sandstone colors. This rounded sculptural effect is carried over from the structural elements to the larger constructional shape and from there to the whole cathedral. The physical and sculptural quality of the architecture at Worms has a strong individual character, which has progressed beyond the cubic blockiness of earlier buildings, particularly on the exterior.

The east end faces the city with a panel-like, massively framed gable front with a three-storied window group and dwarf gallery, flanked by round towers. Massiveness, severity, and pride characterize this front, reflecting a high-minded, sovereign sense of security that has an imperial ring about it. Strangely, though, the two towers are asymmetrical in the treatment of the stories, which is typical of the cathedral as a whole.

The western apse presents an alternative program. Here, instead of the apse of the Burchard cathedral, a choir block with an octagonal domed tower was set between the round towers, modeled on the eastern apse at Mainz, and beyond it a polygonal apse consisting of five sides of another octagon. This creates the impression of two graduated octagons with towers boldly ranged behind one another, both with stone roofs and sturdy dwarf galleries. (The apse was taken down in 1906–7, the stones were numbered, and the apse was rebuilt.) Everything in this western section is packed with great richness, especially in the apse with its blind arcading and singular group of three rosettes and a rose window. The whole section seems full of stored-up energy, a pressing, forceful mass that has always been an object of fascination. The west choir at Worms ranks as highly in terms of innovative achievement as the most modern design of that time

in European architecture: the French cathedral choir with ambulatory and radiating chapels.

The interior of the cathedral is a three-aisled basilica using the intersecting vault system discovered in Speyer with cross-vaults in the side aisles and cross-rib vaults in the eastern apse, transept, and in the double bays of the central nave. The strong influence of Speyer can also be seen in the dome over the crossing, which is a second version of the one at Speyer, and in the wall system of the central nave, where the distinctive motif of Speyer—the large openings—determine the elevation. The Speyer wall system is almost exactly repeated on the north side, though slightly simplified as well,

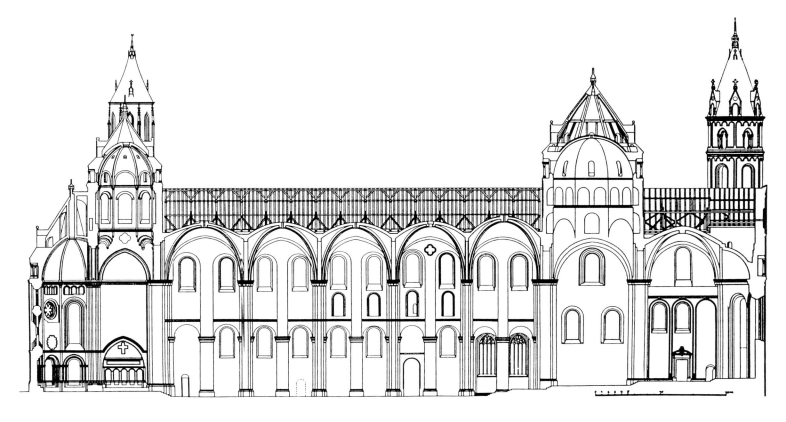

but not on the south side. Here, the elevation is two-storied, the openings beginning above the dividing arcades. This solution corresponds to the original concept at Speyer, which was later rejected there. In Worms it was taken up again. In addition, the wall was embellished beneath the clerestory window with recessed blind arcading. Thus, the north side of the central nave is substantially different from the south side. Furthermore, the wall sections are not completely uniform, especially on the south side, where each bay is different. That may seem displeasing in a building of such ambitiousness, and the building's planners have been accused of uncertainty, because clearly they changed the plan many times. In fact, however, this lack of uniformity in the walls, also evident in the eastern towers, must have been intentional. Faced with the monotonous uniformity of Speyer, in Worms they set out to achieve the exact opposite: constant variation and with it a lively variety. Compared with others in the Romanesque period, the masons' lodge at Worms was more or less the only one to implement this concept.

Plates 69–71

69 View from the northeast

70 West choir

71 View through the nave to the west choir

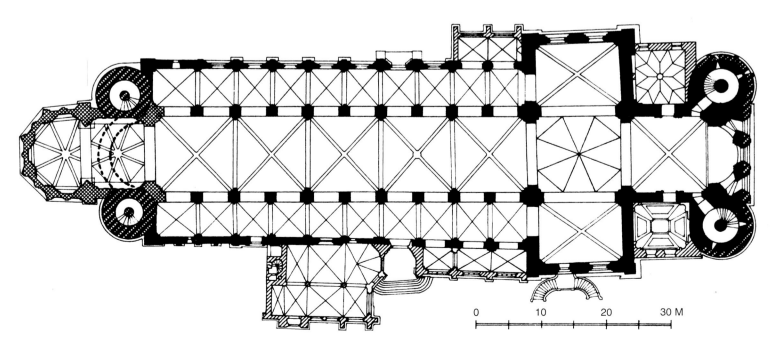

0   10   20   30 M

69

Mainz

The cathedral at Mainz is the second largest of the so-called imperial cathedrals on the Rhine. In terms of ecclesiastical history, it ranks supreme among the cathedrals of the Holy Roman Empire. The bishopric of Mainz had 13 suffragan bishops, for a short time 16, which was far more than any other in the empire. In addition, the archbishop of Mainz had the right to crown the king, and also from 965 held the rank of imperial chancellor; then, from the 14th century, he was the highest-ranking of the electoral princes.

Archbishop Willigis (975–1011), one of the mainstays of Ottonian politics, had a large cathedral begun shortly after 975, but this burned down on the day of its consecration in 1009. It was rebuilt soon afterward under Archbishop Bardo and consecrated in 1036. The Willigis-Bardo cathedral was a basilica with two choirs, a large projecting west transept on the Roman model, and a transverse block in the east, to each side of which towers with staircases were added. These towers still stand today.

After a fire in 1081, Emperor Henry IV commissioned the rebuilding of the affected parts; he also carried out the rebuilding of Speyer Cathedral at the same time. Before Henry's death in 1106 only the eastern section was completed. On the exterior, this consisted of a transverse block with a magnificent apse, with an older tower on either side. Like Speyer, the apse has blind arcading and a dwarf gallery, surmounted by an octagonal tower. Unlike Speyer, the tower was not over the crossing, but over the square eastern choir, which connects to the apse and has galleries on each side.

The nave was laid out, like Speyer, as a columned basilica using the intersecting system. The wall openings of Speyer were again adopted here; however, they did not continue up and around the clerestory windows, but ended a good deal lower down by their ledges, beside the position of the imposts for the vaulting. The openings are not the great, governing motif here, but just a smaller wall structure with a shallow profile. As the openings did not encompass the clerestory windows, the architects were able to group the windows in pairs in the wall, and place the feet of the vaulting lower down than had been done at Speyer. Compared with Speyer, this is a simplified and flattened type of wall, just as the nave is some 16 ft. (5 m) lower. The soaring verticality of Speyer, and its powerful, almost excessive character is here replaced by spaciousness, a balanced unity, and a calm, measured scale.

When the central nave was built, the vaulting originally planned, with cross-rib vaults, was no longer used. Instead, the nave was given rib vaults in about 1200. In the first half of the 13th century, a new west section was added, with a transept, a tall octagonal crossing tower, and a square choir flanked by smaller towers, which was extended by three apses. These parts of the building were consecrated in 1239, and with their varied blind arcading, friezes, and galleries represent a decorative peak in Rhenish Late Romanesque architecture. Despite their late date—by this time purely Gothic buildings were being started, for example, in Trier and Marburg—the rounded Romanesque arch defiantly still held sway. The opulent richness of its forms clearly indicates the builders' desire to outshine all previous buildings.

The Gothic style did not appear at Mainz Cathedral until the consecration of 1239 when a choir screen was added to the front of the western choir. This was the work of the best sculptor of the time, who later went to Naumburg and became known as the "Master of Naumburg." Very little remains of the choir screen, which was destroyed in 1682, except for a wonderful piece of Gothic cathedral sculpture, the famous head wearing a headband, and some other pieces.

After the nave was extended from 1279 with very modern Gothic chapels with rich tracery windows, the east stair towers were erected in 1361, and the Romanesque eastern dome, which was too low compared with the west tower, was given a tall windowed octagon, the spire of which then far exceeded the height of the west tower. To even them out, in 1482 the west tower and the western satellite towers were also increased in height. The present Baroque-Gothic terminations of the three west towers were built by Ignaz Michael Neumann in 1769 after the church had been struck by lightning. These new additions give the whole of the west part an unmistakable character of its own.

The eastern section suffered severe damage in 1793, when the French-occupied city was bombarded by imperial troops and the spires burned down. In 1828, the octagonal choir tower was given a new roof, designed to plans by Georg Moller. This was not a Gothic pointed tower but a dome made of iron, then a pioneering achievement. The eastern group of towers was pulled down from 1870, and replaced by the present octagonal tower in the middle and the terminations of the two circular towers. These were designed by Petrus Cuypers, a Dutch architect who sought to give the eastern section a Romanesque purity of form, but the result was a very mundane, railroad-station brand of Romanesque, which, worse still, spoiled the previously well-calculated balance between the eastern and western tower groups. Since then the cathedral has had only one ruler: the overpowering middle tower in the west, which completely dwarfs the two satellite towers.

The Gotthard Chapel, built under Archbishop Adalbert, at the north end of the western transept (consecrated in 1137) is joined to Mainz Cathedral, although it is really a

separate building. This was the old church of the archbishop's palace, built as a two-storied double chapel in the form of two superposed rooms with an opening connecting them in the middle bay. The design is similar to the older double chapel built in 1080 on the south side of Speyer Cathedral. Double chapels such as these go back to the storied western sections of Carolingian churches, divided into upper and lower churches, and were built from around 1000 in episcopal, royal, and ducal palaces. The double chapel at Mainz, which has piers in the lower church and columns in the upper church, is one of the best-preserved examples.

The archbishops particularly liked being buried in their cathedrals. Many of them were given sculptural tomb memorials, which from the 13th century took the form of a tomb with a relief, then after about 1400 just the relief, which was put up on a pier. Mainz Cathedral has 29 examples, many of high-ranking officials, which show the development of sculpture from about 1250 up to the 18th

and 19th centuries. Only Würzburg Cathedral has more. On the relief, the archbishop is usually portrayed in his full pontifical robes. The two earliest examples show the archbishop carrying out what was then his most important office: crowning the kings of the Holy Roman Empire. Siegfried von Eppstein (d. 1249) crowned Henry Raspe and William of Holland, and Peter von Aspelt (d. 1320) crowned Ludwig the Bavarian, Henry VII of Luxembourg, and his son John of Bohemia.

Another most unusual piece is the bronze door in the market portal of the north aisle. It was part of the Willigis-Bardo cathedral, and according to an inscription on the edge of the frame was donated by Archbishop Willigis, and cast by a certain Berenger. The inscription also proudly notes that this is the first cast bronze door since the time of Charlemagne and the doors of the palace chapel at Aachen. A later addition from 1119–22 is the inscription running above the double door: a bronze-engraved document describing a privilege granted to the townspeople by the archbishop.

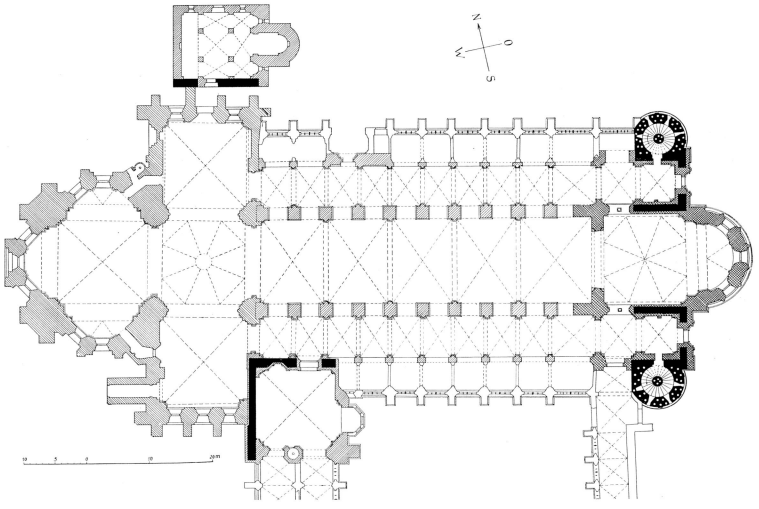

72

Cologne

Cologne, the old Roman city of Colnia Agrippinensis and the seat of a bishop by the fourth century, was the largest city in Germany in the Middle Ages. By around 1500, it had some 50,000 inhabitants. Under Charlemagne, Cologne was raised to the status of metropolitan see of a newly created church province that stretched from present-day Belgium up to northern Germany. The archbishops of Cologne had the right to anoint the king at coronations; from 1031, they held the title of chancellor to Italy, and from the 14th century were electoral princes. In rank, they came directly after the archbishop of Mainz. Soon after Cologne was raised to an archbishopric, a new cathedral was begun before 818 and consecrated in 870. Known today as the "Old Cathedral," it is a columned basilica with two choirs and two low transepts; its total length of 312 ft. (95 m) and frontal atrium some 328 ft. (100 m) long, made it the largest new cathedral of the Carolingian empire. Archbishop Brun, a brother of King Otto the Great, had the cathedral expanded to five aisles around 960, in an attempt to make it a second St. Peter's. Its cultic importance was increased when Archbishop Rainald von Dassel, the chancellor of Frederick Barbarossa, stole the relics of the Three Magi from Milan in 1164, and had them brought to Cologne Cathedral, where they were later kept in a magnificent gold reliquary. The reliquary, a masterpiece by the Meuse goldsmith Nicolaus von Verdun, is the most magnificent of the gold reliquaries of the High Middle Ages, particularly noted for the classical poses of the seated figures of the prophets and apostles along its length. According to old records, it was more or less completed in 1191, when the relics were placed in it. In 1204, the Guelph king Otto IV, later emperor, donated further precious materials. The front dates from this time, including the Adoration of the Kings, in which Otto had himself portrayed as the fourth king.

After all the great foundations in Cologne had been granted a costly Romanesque or Late Romanesque church, resulting in a number and architectural quality unequaled in Europe, the Old Cathedral lost its preeminence. Around 1220, therefore, Archbishop Engelbert resolved to build a new cathedral, and sought to finance it through large annual donations; however, the start of building was prevented by the archbishop's murder in 1225. This cathedral project was probably envisaged as a Late Romanesque showpiece, something that the other churches in Cologne had already surpassed.

Not until 1248, under Archbishop Conrad von Hochstaden, did the cathedral chapter finally decide to undertake the new building. The archbishop, one of the most powerful imperial princes of the time, was at first a follower of Emperor Frederick II of Hohenstaufen, but in 1239 joined the papal camp, and, together with the archbishops of Mainz and Trier, secured the election of the anti-Hohenstaufen rulers Henry Raspe (1246) and William of Holland (1247). Given such militant anti-imperialism, it was perhaps to be expected that the new cathedral would not be built on the time-honored model of Roman architecture—in the Romanesque style, in other words—but that its sponsors would make a point of adopting the completely different building methods of France.

The master builders in charge were Gerhard, who worked out the basic concept, then from 1271 Arnold, and finally his son Johannes (from 1296). The choir was structurally completed around 1300, but was not consecrated until 1322, after most of its decoration and furnishing had been carried out, in particular the stained glass and the choir stalls (both preserved today).

When the choir was approaching completion, planning turned to the two-towered facade in the west, which was to be more gigantic than any previously seen. The towers were to be almost 500 ft. (150 m) tall. For the facade and its infinite quantity of details, a 13-ft. (4-m) parchment plan (Plan F) was drawn up around 1300, perhaps even earlier, on the model of the one made by the masons' lodge at Strasbourg, which with a few changes was largely kept to in the final version. The builders began with the south tower. Only two of its stories were completed in the Middle Ages, while the north tower did not get beyond the preliminary stage. The task faced by the builders was very daunting, not least because of the massive 49-ft. (15 m)-deep foundations. The four side aisles in the nave were built in the Middle Ages, partly with vaults and partly without, as were the dividing arcades of the central nave and the eastern clerestory in the transept, until work was discontinued in 1560.

Not until national sentiments were aroused in the Napoleonic period was there any enthusiasm for completing the cathedral. It was seen at that time as a shrine of the German nation, a national memorial, particularly suitable now that Gothic was generally regarded as the German national style. This doctrine, in existence since the Italian Renaissance, had never been seriously examined. After the cathedral had been publicized as a finished building with plans and cross sections (see ill. page 14), building was continued in 1842. The State of Prussia under King Frederick William IV took over responsibility for the building (the Rhineland had been a Prussian province since 1815), supported by Cologne's Central Building Union and by lotteries in aid of the cathedral building fund. In 1880 the work was completed when the finial was placed on the south spire, which had now reached a height of 512 ft. (156 m).

The design of the western facade remained faithful to Plan F. The facades of the transept, for which there were no medieval plans, were designed by cathedral architect Ernst Friedrich Zwirner, who followed the cathedral's original formal vocabulary.

In terms of architectural history, Cologne Cathedral is a culmination of French cathedral Gothic. It is a five-aisled basilica with side aisles of equal height, a three-aisled transept, and a choir and ambulatory with radiating chapels. The crossing was earlier chosen as the site for the shrine of the Three Magi. The cathedral's ground plan was at first close to the original plan for Beauvais Cathedral. During construction, however, the choir at Amiens was increasingly favored as a model, as can be seen in the double flying buttresses on the exterior and in the tracery decorating the gabled windows of the clerestory, which form a symmetrical line at the level of the eaves.

The interior elevation is three-storied like the Classical cathedrals of France, with a pierced triforium like the one in the choir at Amiens. In Cologne, the wall system completely solved a problem—the form of the piers—that until then the French had only got around by compromising. In the side aisles of the choir, extended compound piers were used, like those employed in the choir at Amiens, that is, a circular pier with four main shafts for the transverse arches and four adjacent shafts for the ribs. In the upper choir, however, where in Amiens they had employed a compound pier with only four shafts (even though many more shafts were needed), in Cologne they developed a composite compound pier with a circular core, around which were arranged as many shafts of varying sizes as were required to support the arches, namely four on each side of the pier and five on the thicker piers at the crossing.

The value of such compound piers was completely proven in the corners of the choir polygon, the Achilles' heel of all cathedral-building systems. In order to lead the piers around the polygon, the architect changed the core, replacing the circular form with the flatter shape of an egg, the broader end of which points outward to the ambulatory. This kind of core, which looks circular, made it possible to install as many shafts as were needed to support the arches, and in the process to keep the shafts equidistant from each other, which had always seemed to be an insoluble problem. The discovery of the egg-form was a stroke of genius. A similar pier shape can be seen in the Cistercian abbey church of Valmagne, in southern France, which was begun in 1252.

There was further inventiveness in the design of the two approaches to the polygon, something that had always been a critical element in cathedral architecture. On the outer side of the ambulatory the plan was for a regular seven-sided structure, but the inner side of the apse of the choir is not regular: the sides of the first bay are not only longer than the others, but also turn slightly inward. The purpose of this irregularity was to ease the connection between the main choir, with its longer wall sections, and the much narrower sections in the apse. This avoided the sudden break between the main choir and the apse that was so often the case. Another, but different type of transition was chosen for the upper wall. In the triforium the tracery shapes of the apse are continued into the first bay of the main choir; in the clerestory windows, it is the other way around, with the tracery of the main choir being continued into the first bays of the apse. In this way the main choir and apse were linked smoothly together.

In every part of the choir it is clear that the design is a summation of earlier experiences. The result is complete perfection, with everything working in close accord. Here, the move toward an architecture of glass, and structures reduced to extreme vertical soaring slenderness, reached its zenith. The proportions are correspondingly steep, on the one hand with a nave height of some 144 ft. (44 m) against a width of 46 ft. (14 m), and on the other with the steep incline of the vaulting, which is even more precipitous than that in Amiens. The impressive verticality of this dematerialized glasshouse is somewhat overwhelming. And yet—and this is something that people find very hard to imagine—the five aisles of Cologne Cathedral, for all their height and width, would still fit inside the ancient Roman Pantheon (though not lengthwise). There, absolute size was the overwhelming factor, whereas in Cologne it was the vertical thrust upward.

To make sure that the building stood up, it was given a particularly strong buttressing system, in which the flying buttresses abutting the clerestory wall were located, for the first time, at the ideal point in terms of statics. On the north side, the buttressing is simpler, but on the south side, facing the city, it is symmetrically covered by a web of tracery, as though the stone had begun to give off shoots. Such richly decorated buttressing had never been seen before, buttressing having previously been thought of as an exercise in engineering. But Cologne Cathedral was to be the cathedral to beat all cathedrals.

The west front is the extreme expression of this ambition. Unlike the facades of French cathedrals, where the emphasis was on the portals and the rose window, and the towers were seen merely as attachments, in Cologne a closely positioned pair of colossal towers was planned, which, in both their height and magnificent tracery, would make every previous facade look modest. Even the spires were to be covered in tracery, an idea that was then followed up in Freiburg in the Upper Rhineland and in Burgos, Spain. The portals, however, the pride of all French facades, are submerged in the towers. Originally, there were to have been five portals, requiring room for 77 wall statues (in Reims there are only 33). The tower concept became so far removed from anything else that, as happened in Babel, it became excessive, even in the fact of its being executed in duplicate. This love of gigantism was bound to fail, however, because a building like this could not come to terms with human dimensions. That it actually happened can be attributed to the Romantic enthusiasm of a new era and especially to Frederick William IV, king of Prussia. But who, in the beginning, could have foreseen that the Prussians would get involved with it?

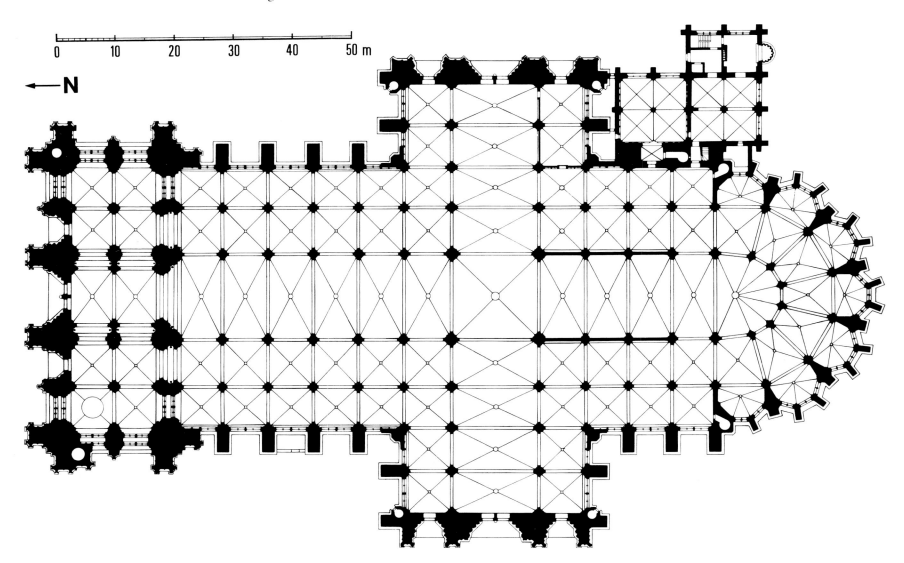

84

Bamberg

The bishopric of Bamberg was founded by Emperor Henry II (1002–24), the last of the Ottonian emperors. In Frankfurt in 1007, when he was still king, permission for the foundation was granted by the bishops' assembly, although, in fact, Henry had already begun building the cathedral some years earlier, and parts of it were already completed. The consecration took place in 1012, five years after the bishopric was founded. This cathedral, which Henry had chosen as his burial place, stood in the northern district of Bavaria in a fortified town of the margraves of Babenberg, to whom the place had belonged.

Henry's cathedral was a three-aisled basilica with a double choir, a west transept, and, facing the city, east towers on either side of the choir. The Church of St. James in Bamberg is clearly a smaller version of the cathedral: this is a columned basilica with a remarkably similar ground plan, built after 1072. Henry's cathedral stood on the same site as the present building, but was somewhat smaller, and had a different axis. Its cultic significance grew after Henry and his wife, Kunigunde, were canonized, in 1146 and 1200, respectively. Another local saint was Bishop Otto von Bamberg (d. 1139), the missionary to Pomerania, who had earlier directed the building of Speyer Cathedral.

The present cathedral is a completely new building erected in the early 13th century. It was commissioned by Bishop Ekbert (1203–37) of the then very important, but soon to be extinct, princely line of Andechs-Meranier. One sister of the bishop married the king of France, another the king of Hungary, a third the duke of Silesia; one of his brothers was patriarch of Aquileia, and thus the highest-ranking religious leader after the pope, while another brother married the granddaughter of Emperor Frederick Barbarossa, heiress to the palatinate of Burgundy. Bishop Ekbert remained loyal to the emperor in the increasingly violent conflicts between Emperor Frederick II of Hohenstaufen and the popes.

The cathedral was built in an astonishingly brief time. It was probably begun some time before 1220, perhaps even a little earlier, and was consecrated in 1237, shortly before Bishop Ekbert's death. In France at that time the east end of Reims Cathedral was being built. Set beside the Gothic of Reims, Bamberg Cathedral is remarkably conservative: one only has to compare the Late Romanesque eastern apse, flanked by four square towers, with the choir of Reims Cathedral. There is a more serious reason for Bamberg's conservative appearance: the planners wanted to preserve the memory of Henry's cathedral in the new building. Therefore they retained the old layout, with a double choir and towers flanking the east apse and west transept. Their ambivalent intentions also explain why the cathedral was strangely beset with constant changes of plan, despite the very short time it took to build.

The way the building progressed shows that there must have been two factions in the cathedral chapter, who opposed each other with varying degrees of success. On one side were the traditionalists, who wanted a new version of the sacrosanct Henry cathedral, and on the other were the progressives, who preferred a modern style of architecture. The main source of conflict was whether to have flat roofs, as in the Henry cathedral, which would by then have been a hopeless anachronism, or up-to-date rib vaulting, which was more fireproof. At first the traditionalists held sway. Apart from the bay between the eastern towers, the eastern choir and nave were to be flat-roofed. Then the progressives pushed through a sexpartite rib vault, at least for the eastern choir, though not for the nave. When this was begun, the vaulting had been erected because the shaft system was designed to take vaulting. Then the planners changed their minds, and decided to have a traditional clerestory with a flat roof. In the end, however, a fire came to the aid of the progressives, and the vaulting plan, which had already been prepared, was then carried out, which meant walling up every other clerestory window.

Later, a workforce from the nearby Cistercian monastery of Ebrach took over the task of building the transept and the west choir, and here too the plans were changed at least twice. For the counterparts to the east towers, the planners finally departed from the model of the Henry cathedral, and built two west towers with storied, openwork, columned tabernacles at the four corners of each tower, for which Laon Cathedral provided an already well-known model. The same design was taken up a little later at Naumburg Cathedral. Finally, the builders raised the low east towers by two stories to balance the difference in height between them and the west towers. In the 18th century the Baroque architect Johann Michael Kuechel built up the east towers once more to make them exactly the same height as the west ones.

Despite the many changes of plan, the cathedral is a unified building designed on the intersecting system. It is massive, with a large surface area like the old cathedrals of the Hohenstaufen period, and a model of the last days of the Late Romanesque style. The western choir represents a timid attempt to switch to French Gothic, but the new did not go well with the old, especially on the exterior. The eastern apse between the towers, which is an absolute architectural masterpiece, is unequaled. It is opulent and magnificent, its lofty crown of large windows looking out over the city, both satisfying to look at and evocative of the lordly might of earlier large imperial buildings. The eastern apse is one of the last and richest peaks of a great tradition, a Hohenstaufen counterpart to the French cathedral choir.

The sculpture at Bamberg is also of high quality, some of it exceptionally so. It is the work of two sculpture studios, where the training was completely different. The first came from the German Romanesque school, the second from French cathedral Gothic. First, the tympanum over the door in the northeast tower was given an enthroned Madonna and Child in the middle; the cathedral patrons, St. Peter and St. George, are on her left, and the patrons of the bishopric, Henry and Kunigunde, are on her right. These saints are portrayed in strictly hieratic postures, but also evoke an ideal image of equidistance to the papacy (St. Peter) and the empire (Henry), a subject that had a certain explosive force at the beginning of the reign of Frederick II.

The first studio developed quickly, as can be seen in the reliefs on the side screens in the eastern choir, where pairs of Apostles in dispute are on the south side, while on the north side are the prophets. The dispute gathers momentum from the dignified restraint of the Apostles to the wild, passionately aroused quarrel of the Prophets, from peaceful postures to twisted, curiously confused movements. More important still, the expressive vitality and strength of the figures increase from relief to relief, finally reaching a climax of urgency.

On the Prince's Portal on the north side of the nave, the older studio created most of the figures in the recesses, where the Apostles stand on the shoulders of the Prophets, as the New Testament on the Old. In the right-hand recesses, the new sculptors make their appearance, having come directly from the masons' lodge at Reims Cathedral—they must have arrived in 1225–26. They also created the tympanum on the Prince's Portal, with its very human portrayal of the Last Judgment, in which there is joyous laughter as well as heartrending wailing and moaning. The new studio brought laughter to Bamberg. In no other cathedral in Europe is so much laughing and smiling to be seen, a feature also of the Blessed Children, safe and secure in Abraham's bosom on the Prince's Portal. The figures of Ecclesia and Synagogue were also part of this portal at one time (the originals are today inside the cathedral), two female figures whose lively physicality reflects the sublimated eroticism of the Minnesinger period.

In the interior, the *Visitation of Mary* is a first-rate piece of sculpture. Mary's robes have a sweeping Hellenistic

fullness, and Elizabeth is portrayed as a gaunt old woman, who seems to be contemplating eternity with her deeply introverted gaze, like a blind seer, as though she is not Elizabeth, but a prophetess or a sibyl.

The gaze of the Bamberg Knight is quite the opposite. His head is turned as he looks searchingly for something in the distance. His youthful figure represents the eternally young king, a portrait of great magnanimity, gentle righteousness, and fearless deeds, his noble appearance standing for the absolute ideal of kingship. Whether the Knight is meant to represent Henry II, Stephen of Hungary, Conrad III, Frederick II of Hohenstaufen, Philip of Swabia, or Constantine the Great is still unclear. As an ideal figure, he will always remain impossible to identify. At the time, though, regardless of whom the figure actually represents, Bishop Ekbert may have been referring indirectly to Emperor Frederick II, the outstanding personality of his age, who was praised and worshiped by his followers as the great wonder of the world.

Finally, the second studio also produced the six figures on the Adam doorway in the southeast tower (today in the museum): the naked figures of Adam and Eve, St. Peter, Henry and Kunigunde, and Stephen. Henry stands opposite

Above left:
The founding couple, Emperor Henry II and Empress Kunigunde, in the left-hand recess of the Adam doorway, about 1230–35

Above right:
Emperor Henry II and Empress Kunigunde on the lid of the marble tomb by Tilman Riemenschneider, in front of the east choir (see Plate 89), installed in 1513

St. Peter, who looks anxiously at him, but he turns brusquely away. If contemporary history is also concealed in this portrayal, it may be that Henry's posture reflects the destruction of the sworn unity of papacy and empire, as it is depicted on the sanctuary doorway. If this is so, then the sculpture at Bamberg can be seen as a seismograph of political events.

The saintly imperial couple, Henry and Kunigunde, are also portrayed on the tomb made by Tilman Riemenschneider in 1499–1513. The couple are shown recumbent on the lid in magnificent robes; to either side, events from their lives are depicted in a series of reliefs. Thus, the cathedral's founders received a commemorative monument worthy of their rank, though not before the second studio had created a similar memorial for a pope, Clement II (d. 1047), previously Bishop Suidger of Bamberg, who in 1046 was raised to the papacy by Henry III at the Synod of Sutri.

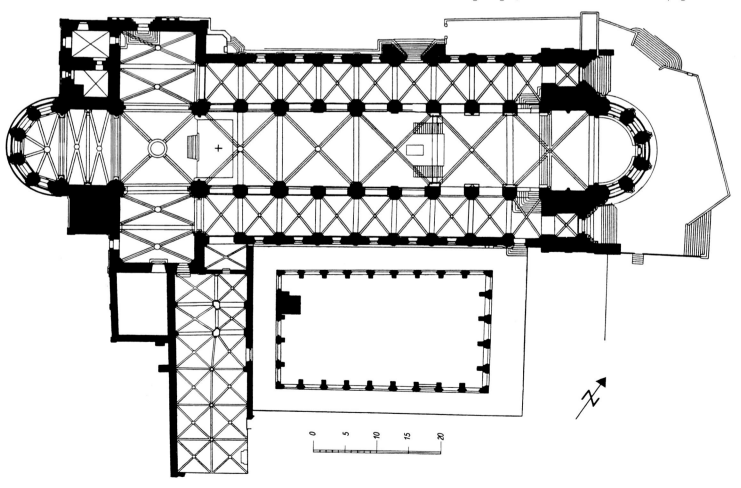

186 *Germany*

Naumburg

Naumburg on the Saale takes its name from a walled town known as "New Burg" on the border of the Slavic territories, which Margrave Ekkehard I of Meissen had built in about 1000. As one of the most powerful princes in the empire, Ekkehard was the most likely candidate to be elected emperor after the death of Otto III, but he was murdered, which left the way open for Henry, Duke of Bavaria. Ekkehard also founded a seminary in Naumburg. Its church stood on the site of the present cathedral's west choir. The town was raised with papal approval to a bishopric in 1028, when at the request of Emperor Conrad II the missionary bishopric of Zeitz, founded by Otto the Great, moved to the safety of Naumburg after its exposed position had made it all too easy for the Slavs to plunder. The bishopric was now in the protective care of the margraves Hermann and Ekkehard II, the sons of the murdered Ekkehard I.

Immediately after the move, the first cathedral was built (consecrated before 1044). This was a barely 160-ft. (50 m)-long basilica with two apses, an east transept, and west towers, which stood to the east of the older seminary church on the same axis. Only the crypt has been preserved from the first cathedral: this was a later addition dating from about 1160–70, located under the eastern apse, a magnificent example of its type with lavishly decorated capitals and richly ornamented columns. The first cathedral was replaced between 1210 and the middle of the 13th century with a considerably larger new building almost 295 ft. (90 m) long, built from the outside around its predecessor so that services could continue to be held for as long as possible.

In its external appearance the cathedral is a square, purely Romanesque building. With its arch friezes, round-headed windows, and pilaster strips, it seems so old-fashioned that it could well have been built 50 years earlier. Only the octagonal stories of the east towers flanking the apse are more lavishly structured. Later—certainly after the fire of 1532—these were made higher and in the 18th century given rather awkward Baroque domes with lanterns.

Inside, the cathedral is a vaulted basilica built by the intersecting system. Even though all the dividing arches and transverse arches are pointed, the basic form remains Romanesque, as are the massive crossing piers with their circular shafts, and the vaults, which are still old-fashioned cross-vaults. The entire edifice, designed by a master builder trained in Cologne in the Late Romanesque period, is as austere as a Cistercian church.

Only the western bay of the central nave has a rib-vault. This was built in conjunction with the west choir, which was

added in about 1250 on the site of the old seminary church. The choir is a single-naved Gothic structure, consisting of a square bay with sexpartite rib-vaults and a five-sided apse. On the north side of the choir, a tower was added later, erected on an older base with openwork, polygonal-columned tabernacles at each corner, as had been done shortly before in Bamberg and even earlier in Laon. The three stories with the tabernacles were built one after the other in the 13th, 14th, and 15th centuries, as though a new story had to be added every hundred years. The matching tower on the south side did not get beyond the first stages of building, which indicates that the cathedral's finances were uncertain after the completion of the west choir. The present south tower was not built until the end of the 19th century.

All the same, its builders managed to construct a new Gothic apse for the eastern choir in about 1320–30. This is an unusual four-sided structure, closed off at the center, which acts as a counterweight to the western choir. These two apses became even more pronounced when a screen was added in front of each of them. It is extremely surprising that both of these have survived.

Naumburg Cathedral is famous not for its architecture, which is relatively unspectacular, but for its sculpture, which is the best to have been produced by European sculptors in the mid-13th century. The sculptor who had previously created the west screen in Mainz Cathedral in about 1239 was summoned from France. The west choir and screen were his work, establishing beyond question that this "Master of Naumburg" was not only the chief sculptor but also the chief architect.

The leaf capitals in the screen's blind arcading are true miracles of natural observation in the way they faithfully render the local flora. The screen itself contains a cycle of reliefs with scenes from the Passion. Christ is portrayed here as a humble human being, and maintains in every scene a wise and quietly patient remoteness and an untouchable dignity, while, in contrast, the whole spectrum of human behavior and emotion is played out around him, from simpleminded guzzling during the evening meal to Peter's fearful feelings of guilt at his betrayal of Christ, and the murky, guilt-laden atmosphere when, amid much muttering, Judas is paid in pieces of silver. The sculptor evidently understood nature as a biologist does, and also the psychology of human beings, whose behavior and characters he saw into and managed to portray so successfully.

The high point of the Passion is the life-sized Crucifixion group in the portal: Mary and St. John the Baptist are moving embodiments of inconsolable grief, their pain clear to see in both body and soul, but Christ embodies the idea of the Promised Land, since anyone entering the choir must pass beneath his outspread arms, as though he is blessing them. The cross bearing the crucified figure, which had earlier hung in triumph above the nave, has now come down to earth. Humanity is brought face to face with it and cannot escape it, and thus is summoned to be constantly compassionate.

The west choir itself, the famous Foundation Choir, has an undeserved reputation for outrageousness because of its cycle of statues: the figures here are not statues of saints, but secular princes and nobles, the men even bearing arms. They represent actual people from the region who lived 200 years earlier and made donations to the cathedral building fund, none more so than the margraves Hermann and Ekkehard III, seen here with their wives, the ancestors of the 13th-century ruling margraves of Meissen, from the house of Wettin.

The sculptor created extremely lively people out of these historical figures, each with his or her own characteristics. Hermann and his wife, Reglindis, the daughter of a Polish king, and Ekkehard with his wife, Uta, are almost inconceivably unlike each other. Hermann, a gentle, sensitive weakling, is clearly outshined by his strapping, hearty, smiling wife. In contrast, his brother Ekkehard is a well-fed bear of a man who plants himself firmly beside his wife like

Dietmar and Sizzo, figures of founders in the west choir

a warrior, while she is a highly cultivated but completely emotionless beauty who draws up the collar of her cloak on the side next to her husband, as though he made her shiver. It is not surprising, therefore, that Ekkehard murdered the father of Timo, who stands next to him and for that reason glares at Ekkehard in a furtive way, full of hatred. Obviously, the sculptor was using the figures to make a historical interpretation.

Little is known about the founders, except that some of them were murderers and others were rabble-rousers. The worst of them all was Dietmar, who stands on the far left in the apsidal polygon: he assassinated the king, and was made to suffer the punishment of God in single combat. Dietmar stands next to the figure of a knight called Sizzo; no fewer than five of the other figures, including Ekkehard and Uta, are shown looking at him, and the whole focus of the group seems to be concentrated on him. It is possible, therefore, that the idea of guilt and atonement could have been part of the whole concept, the atonement to be achieved by founding the church.

Why, though, did the bishop and the cathedral chapter build a costly and unusual choir for the founders, some of whom lie buried there? Other cathedrals had similar founders, but did not give them such a memorial. Who was so interested in this cycle of figures, and what was the point of having them made? Concern for the spiritual well-being of the founders, which is mentioned in an episcopal manuscript, cannot have been the decisive factor. It seems rather to have stemmed from a political decision, taken on the personal initiative of the then margrave of Meissen, Henry. In 1244, Henry had pushed an illegitimate half-brother, Dietrich, into office as bishop of Naumburg against the will of the cathedral chapter. The half-brothers had a further connection. In 1247 the pope had to exhort Henry to leave the church at Naumburg alone, his father having already seized some of its properties. In 1254, the margrave sent troops into the Naumburg area and caused such devastation that in 1259 Bishop Dietrich abandoned his independent imperial-religious status and surrendered the bishopric to the care of the margrave. That status was restored in the time of margraves Hermann and Ekkehard to the way it had been at the very beginning, after the bishopric of Zeitz had moved to Naumburg.

Given this background, it is easy to make sense of the founders' choir, which had been built shortly before these events. The founders, particularly the two margraves, were used to legitimize the planned takeover in advance. As the founder figures indicate, the takeover restored the original status of the bishopric, as embodied by the founders, and thereby made it legal.

Plates 95–103

95 General view from the southeast, looking over the city

96 Looking along the nave to the west screen of the west choir

97 The west choir with figures of the founders

98 Scenes from the west screen. Top: *Last Supper*. Bottom: *Christ before Pilate* (see Plate 99)

99 West screen, portal to the choir with the Crucifixion group

100 Hermann and Reglindis, founder figures, in the west choir

101 Ekkehard and Uta, founder figures, in the west choir

102 Reglindis (detail; see Plate 100)

103 Uta (detail; see Plate 101)

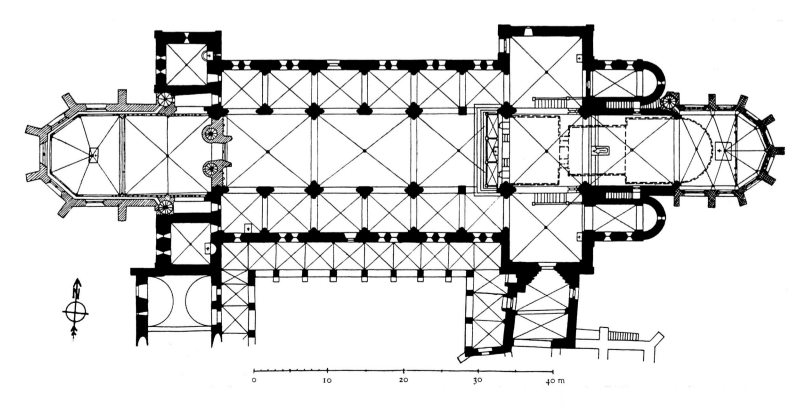

Prague (Czech Republic)

The cathedral at Prague, now the capital of the Czech Republic and formerly that of Bohemia, was always very closely associated with the rulers of Bohemia. Duke Wenceslas of the Premyslid dynasty was presented with the relic of the arm of St. Vitus by Henry the Fowler I (919–36), the founder of the Ottonian dynasty, to whom Wenceslas owed an oath of allegiance. This is why in 926 he had a rotunda with four apses, the St. Vitus Rotunda, built on Hradcany Hill in Prague (consecrated in 930). In 929, Wenceslas was murdered by his brother. After he had been canonized as a martyr, he was quickly promoted to rank alongside St. Vitus as patron saint of Bohemia. In 932, his mortal remains were transferred to the St. Vitus Rotunda, which then became the most important cultic site in Bohemia. In the 11th century, another patron saint of Bohemia was laid to rest there: St. Adalbert, bishop of Prague, who died a martyr's death in 997 as a missionary to pagan Prussia, and whose remains were transferred to the Rotunda from Gniezno in Poland.

The bishopric of Prague was founded in 973, separating it from the diocese of Regensburg, to which it had belonged. The Rotunda served as cathedral, until the Premyslid duke Spytinhew II had a new cathedral begun in 1061 in the form of a columned basilica with two choirs, a west transept, and two crypts. Its east choir was dedicated to St. Vitus. On the south side of the choir one of the four apses of the old rotunda was preserved—this being the burial site of St. Wenceslas—and incorporated into the new building as a chapel.

Prague rose even further in power as a royal capital, when, in 1085, Henry IV (1056–1106) made Duke Vratislav II king and Bohemia a kingdom. St. Vitus's Cathedral was and remained the favored burial place of the Premsylid dynasty.

The kingdom of Bohemia fell in 1310 to the house of Luxembourg, when the last Premyslid daughter, Eizabeth, married Count John of Luxembourg, the son of the king of Rome, and later Emperor Henry VII. The principal patron of St. Vitus's Cathedral was their son Wenceslas, later Emperor Charles IV. Wenceslas was educated in Paris at the court of the French king Charles IV, his uncle, and thereafter called himself Charles. In 1333, at the age of 17, he went back to Prague as governor of the kingdom of Bohemia. Thanks to his and his father's efforts, Prague was raised to an archbishopric in 1344. Up until then, the bishopric of Prague had been subject to the archbishopric of Mainz. In 1346, the pope, who had been one of Charles's teachers in France, awarded the archbishopric of Prague the important right to crown the kings of Bohemia, which put it on an equal footing with Mainz. Charles himself was elected king of Rome in 1346. One year later, after the death of his father, he succeeded him as king of Bohemia, and, finally, in 1355, he was crowned emperor as Charles IV. Prague, where the emperor resided, was now the capital of the Holy Roman Empire.

The rebuilding of St. Vitus's Cathedral in the Gothic style was the work of the two Luxembourg kings. Earlier, in 1341, John had ordered one-tenth of the proceeds from the silver mine at Kuttenberg to be put toward maintaining the tombs of St. Wenceslas and St. Adalbert, and also toward building a new cathedral. Hardly had Prague become an archbishopric in 1344 than the foundation stone was laid for the new cathedral, in the presence of the ruling house, to the northeast of the old cathedral. Charles had commissioned the French architect Matthieu of Arras in Avignon in 1342, and in 1344 he came to Prague. Matthieu supervised the building until his death in 1352. After him, Charles appointed Peter Parler, then only 23 years old, as architect. He was the son of Heinrich Parler, based in Gmünd, who had previously worked at Cologne Cathedral. It seems that Peter Parler had been employed on the Frenkirche in Nuremberg, which was also one of Charles's foundations, before he was summoned to Prague. The choir was completed in 1385, seven years after the death of Charles IV.

Peter Parler remained in charge of the works until his death in 1399. When Charles's son and successor, Wenceslas, showed less and less interest in continuing the building, progress faltered. The three lower stories of the south tower were built, and in the transept the south wall with its vestibule and the east wall, but neither had its tracery windows. In 1419, after the Hussite Wars had broken out, the masons' lodge was disbanded, and the workforce went to Vienna, taking the building materials with them. After further building had been seriously considered in the 17th and 18th centuries, the cathedral was restarted only in 1872 with a Neo-Gothic building plan, and completed in 1929. In the nave, the architects concentrated on building the choir bays. New plans were needed only for the west towers, which are small and fairly insignificant.

The appointment of a Frenchman as architect leads one to think that Charles favored a French-style cathedral for the new archbishopric. Matthieu of Arras began a choir, which was wholly modeled on the most modern cathedrals of southern France. Narbonne, Toulouse, and Rodez had been begun around 1270–80 and had similar ambulatories and radiating chapels. The whole ground plan of the choir, with its 5/10 polygonal apse, was taken from them, and, more unusually, not only the chapels in the ambulatory but those in the main part of the choir were also apsidal, with a 5/8 structure. In the parts built by Matthieu, the formal vocabulary is decidedly southern French, marked by great slenderness. The windows of the ambulatory chapels have a somewhat schematic tracery typical of that found everywhere in the 14th century. If St. Vitus's Cathedral had been completed according to Matthieu's plans, it would have been another example of the almost unalterably doctrinaire style of cathedral Gothic from southern France, which had begun after 1248 with the cathedral of Clermont-Ferrand and its architect, Jean Deschamps.

It is to Peter Parler's credit that St. Vitus's Cathedral was then given a completely different look, which made it one of the first buildings in the German Late Gothic style. Where it was still possible, he changed the concept for the chapels, and made them rectangular. On the north side, in two bays set aside for the sacristy, he tried out difficult figurations, with ribs hanging down freely from the vaulting, the so-called pendant-vaults. On the south side, projecting irregularly into the transept, is his rectangular chapel over the place of the ancient cult of Wenceslas, which is a shrine in its own right. In his work on the chapels, particularly in his new rib vaults, Parler showed himself to be an innovative virtuoso.

For the vaulting of the choir he devised a solution that was later so often imitated that it can be regarded as the

Nineteenth-century view of St. Vitus's Cathedral from the southeast before its completion. Engraving by Vinzenz Morstadt, 1826

direction of the future. The shell of the vault is no longer made up of single crowns but is a barrel with lateral crowns let into it. The ribs are laid on the vaulting surface. The transverse arches separating the bays are dispensed with. Instead, the ribs, with two diagonal ribs running parallel to each other, form a pattern that is repeated at the ends of the bays and produces a rhomboid shape at the vertex of the vault. The basic figure, from which all else follows, is a gable, or Y-shape. The long arms of each Y-shape span two wall sections, which takes care of the ends of the bays. The Y-shapes overlap each other from either side, and thus form a dense network of ribs containing smaller and larger rhomboids. In the apse, however, the overlapping arms of the Y-shapes form half a ten-pointed star. This vaulting system in Prague launched the Late Gothic tradition of net vaults in the southern countries of the Holy Roman Empire.

In the clerestory and triforium, too, Parler sought new solutions for this old problem, which had been rather neglected. Here, he placed angled tracery lanterns at the end of each bay that form triangular spurs and bring a certain movement to the walls as they project outward from them. In the tracery windows of the clerestory, the inner four mullions are enclosed by an outer section, which incorporates a window within the window. As for the tracery on the window, and also on the buttresses and the outer wall surfaces, Parler devised new, often fluid, and lightly floating forms, such as no masons' lodge had ever tried before. Although the geometry of the tracery was still constructed using compasses and spirit levels, it was handled much more freely by Parler than ever before, expressing an almost boundless fantasy restrained only by the rules of the compass, and building to a climax in the tracery curtain over the great window of the south transept.

Special emphasis was placed on the triforium, with its sturdy columns and rectangular framework. The narrow passage of older triforiums is here turned into a deeper gallery with much better access through openings in the piers at the ends of the bays. What also makes the gallery outstanding is the row of portrait busts above the doorways. Here, Charles IV and members of his family are commemorated, as well as the archbishops who helped with the building, the building managers, and finally the two architects, Matthieu of Arras and Peter Parler. Busts of Christ and the most important Bohemian saints are placed on the walls of the passageway in front of the clerestory. The cycle of portrait busts is unique, both in itself and in the realistic way the busts are rendered. Like other heads of masons' lodges and other members of the Parler family, Peter Parler was also a sculptor. In 1373, his son Heinrich created the very elegant knightly figure of St. Wenceslas for the Wenceslas Chapel.

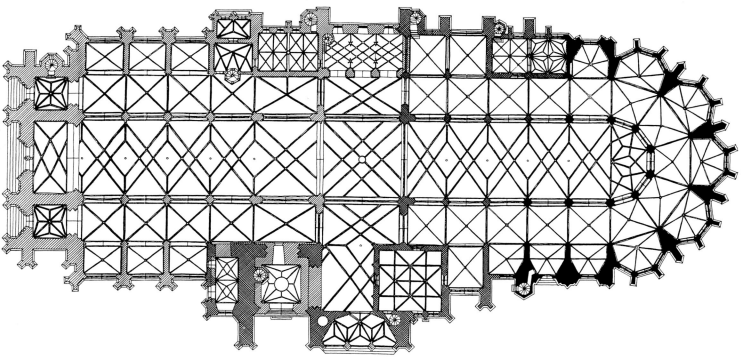

0   5   10m

SCOTLAND

▲ See individual chapter and color plates
● See text illustrations
○ Mentioned in text

N

50 km

Durham

● York

Lincoln

○ Lichfield

Norwich ●

Peterborough

Ely

WALES

Cambridge ○

○ Bury
St. Edmunds

○ Hereford

E N G L A N D

● Gloucester

○ Oxford

St. Albans ○

London ○

Rochester ○

● Bristol
○ Bath

Canterbury

Wells

Salisbury

● Winchester

○ Chichester

● Exeter

FRANCE

England

Architectural History

Anglo-Saxon England played almost no part in medieval European politics before 1000. The reason for this was that the monasteries of Britain and Ireland controlled theological education and spiritual life from the post-Roman period until the early Middle Ages, and it was from there that missions set out for Gaul and Germany. There were numerous missionaries, wandering monks like Columba, Boniface, Willibald, and Kilian, who hastened the spread of Christianity. The monks also brought an early flowering of art and culture to the Continent, particularly with their illuminated manuscripts.

After the end of the Roman period, the British Isles were defenseless, their Celtic populations open to invasion. In the middle of the fifth century, England was conquered and christianized by Germanic Angles, Saxons, and Jutes. Under their Anglo-Saxon rulers, who divided the land into several kingdoms, England remained so weak politically that, in the early Middle Ages, it fell to the raids of the Scandinavian Vikings, and finally to the Danish king Canute. He conquered the island soon after 1000, and incorporated the country into his Greater Scandinavian Empire. This foreign invasion did not last long, however.

A more lasting invasion was that of the Normans. William, known as "the Bastard" because of his illegitimate birth, was given the dukedom of Normandy by the king of France. In 1066, he crossed over to England, defeated Harold, last of the Anglo-Saxon kings, at the Battle of Hastings, and in a short time overran the entire kingdom. These events are recorded like a military campaign report on the famous 230-ft. (70 m)-long Bayeux Tapestry.

King William I, now called William the Conqueror, secured his rule over England, building a total of 50 stone castles, and dividing the country up among his followers, including the seats of bishops. Within 20 years, almost all of the bishops and abbots were Norman. To William, it seemed obvious that he should install spiritual dignitaries himself, although on the Continent the dispute between emperor and pope over investiture was then reaching its stormiest phase (see page 124). Norman England was practically unaffected by the dispute: at the end of William's 21-year reign, England was like a colonial empire in the hands of a very small group of Norman lords, no more than 300 in number. At court and among the Norman nobility, French was still spoken until the 14th century. The Norman rulers were, and remained, a body of foreigners, making no attempt at assimilation. After the Norman line had died out, a new French dynasty established itself in 1154 with Henry Plantagenet, count of Anjou, who at the same time controlled large parts of France. This led to a lasting conflict with the French throne and finally to the Hundred Years' War, in which England finally gave up its claims on the Continent.

Before William, English churches had been small and insignificant. Soon, though, the Normans began to build churches in the grand style near their castles. Without exception, these churches were pure demonstrations of power, and for people in England at that time their massive, completely unaccustomed size must have seemed imposing, if not intimidating. It is more apparent in the construction of churches than anywhere else that the architecture employed was a means of legitimizing Norman rule and securing power. Political ends can also be achieved with architecture, for it is more intrusive and lasting than short-lived treaties. Perhaps for this reason, the Norman churches in England are the most eloquent examples in the entire Middle Ages. Even today, these buildings clearly convey the idea that those in charge of the builders were a tremendous centralized ruling power.

A direct predecessor of these great Norman buildings was the monastery church at Westminster in London, built by King Edward the Confessor, who was buried there in 1066. At the Christmas celebrations of the same year, William the Conqueror had himself crowned there as king. Nothing remains of this church, which seems to have been a second version of the great abbey church at Jumièges in Normandy: a galleried basilica with a two-towered front, transept, and graduated choir. This Norman building type remained the main one in England after 1066.

At the beginning of the Norman building program, the archbishop of the new cathedral at Canterbury was Lanfranc, whom William installed in 1070, as soon as he had been able, following some trouble, to dismiss the sitting archbishop, Stigand. Lanfranc had previously been abbot of one of William's foundations, the Abbey of St. Etienne in Caen, capital of Normandy. As archbishop of Canterbury, and thus primate of the English Church, Lanfranc was the supporting pillar in William's ecclesiastical policies.

In the next phase, the Norman building program went ahead at a great pace. In an astonishingly short time, one gigantic building after another was begun, and, for the most part, completed just as quickly. St. Augustine's in Canterbury, Bury St. Edmunds, Lincoln, Old Sarum (the predecessor of Salisbury), Rochester, St. Albans, Winchester, Worcester, Gloucester, Old St. Paul's in London, Norwich, Ely, Durham, Chichester, York, and Hereford, and then—as late arrivals in the 12th century—came Lichfield and Exeter, and finally Peterborough in 1118.

Right:
Winchester Cathedral,
Norman north transept

Far right:
Norwich Cathedral,
nave looking east

Some of these churches at first had only the status of monastery churches, and were not made cathedrals until later. The boundaries between a cathedral and a monastery church were not as clearly defined in England at that time as they were on the Continent. Only about half the bishops' churches were occupied by secular canons, with a provost at their head, as was usually the case on the Continent. The other half were mainly Benedictine monastic establishments with a prior at their head. The role of abbot was filled by the bishop.

Some of the Norman buildings were later extended with a new nave and other additions, for example, Durham, Ely, and Old St. Paul's in London, which then reached a length of some 591 ft. (180 m). Others were pulled down and replaced by new buildings, like York, Exeter, Lichfield, Worcester, and London's St. Paul's. Still others have vanished, apart from a few remains: St. Augustine's in Canterbury, Bury St. Edmunds, and Old Sarum. Finally, some Norman churches were later given vaults, for example, Gloucester and Norwich.

Common features of these Norman buildings in England are the extremely long naves, the long transepts, and the square tower at the crossing, which, as at St. Albans, rises like a real Norman fort above the church. Crossing towers like this were almost obligatory, even though they led to building problems and sometimes collapsed, because the crossing piers were too weak. Later still, up to the end of the

Middle Ages, the crossing tower was an essential part of English church architecture, sometimes surmounted by a soaring spire.

In the more lavish Norman buildings, the west front was given a facade with two towers, as at Canterbury and Durham (see Plate 157) or an entrance front with highly monumental niches, as at Lincoln, or later in the Early Gothic period at Peterborough (see Plates 152, 145). The high point of Norman west fronts came with the extravagantly decorated yet powerful west front at Ely, which formerly had five towers, a large central one and four flanking satellites (see Plate 140). Externally, these buildings all convey an impression of defiant, fortresslike impregnability and an almost abrupt forcefulness. When people looked at them, they were clearly meant to understand that the lords who had them built were not to be trifled with.

In the interior spaces the picture of Norman architecture is at its most impressive, and least distorted, in Durham and Peterborough, in the transept at Winchester, and in the nave at Ely, while farther off in Norwich one can see the beginnings of Gothic vaulting (see Plates 161, 147, 148, 141).

Inspiration for the Norman churches in England came from Duke William's prestigious building in Normandy: St. Etienne in Caen, formerly a flat-roofed, three-storied, galleried basilica with a recessed clerestory with a containing arch, and especially large-scale openings in the galleries, their dimensions in line with those of the main arcade. This elevation was adopted in England, but enriched by raising the profile of the dividing arcades. The clerestory keeps its earlier form, and is usually distinguished by a graduated, rhythmic triple arcade, with the window wall set back to allow a passage in between. The arcades of the gallery form the main story. These have a large, round-arched opening, after the model of Caen, and, for the most part, a double arcade with a central column, which produces the so-called biforium motif, a design commonly found on the Continent, and noted for its excellent proportions; the proportions, seen from the central nave, make the gallery an elegant, very grand story, comparable to the *bel étage*. However, the gallery space itself, which lies behind, is structurally as inconspicuous as a cheap shed or storage space. The nobility hardly ever used the gallery; it was purely a status symbol, fulfilling the need to create an imposing effect in the nave with its showpiece biforium. Taken as a whole, the elevation strongly resembles a three-storied aqueduct with three different styles of arcade placed on top of each other: the dividing arcades at ground level, the biforium in the gallery, and the graduated triple arcade in the clerestory. The walls consist almost entirely of arcades, with no large, flat spaces.

This type of architecture cannot be compared with anything else in Europe in terms of its imposing appearance and the massive power of its masonry. It even surpasses the churches of Normandy. The ethos behind these buildings was always to think large, sometimes excessively so. At the same time, though on a smaller scale, the builders were very keen on rich decorative forms, as can be seen in the blind arcading, intersecting arches, zigzag strips, carved moldings, and other ornamental forms. Thus, an impression of richness was added to that of power, and in time became even more opulent.

To avoid a feeling of monotony in the apparently endless arcades, architects eagerly seized on the tried and true method of alternating main and intermediate piers. On the sides forming the arches, the main piers are equipped with a cluster of circular engaged columns, whereas the intermediate piers have a sturdy cylindrical shape or a more decorative variation of this. The alternating piers correspond to the intersecting system in the vaulting of the Holy Roman Empire. As the three stories of the more lavish buildings were connected by long perpendicular shafts, which could have connected with arched vaults, the wall system of Norman buildings would have been ideal for vaulting. However, only the side aisles were vaulted at that time.

The great exception is Durham Cathedral, begun in 1093 (see pages 286–95). Here, the architects took the logical step,

Gloucester Cathedral, pier arcade in the nave

and decided to risk vaulting the choir, nave, and later the transept. From the beginning they used highly developed rib vaults, so that Durham became the earliest large building in Europe to be completed with rib vaults, a sensational, pioneering achievement, the ribs seeming suddenly to arise out of nowhere.

A parallel development in Norman architecture, though confined to southwestern England, favored another type of wall: arcades with narrow arches and soaring circular piers that are real colossi. The main example is Gloucester. If these piered arcades are compared with the Romanesque kind on the Continent, the Normans' passion for power can be seen as almost brutal. As the stories above the arcades are tiny, the enormous piers are totally dominant.

Norman architecture is the English Romanesque. The designation "Norman" was coined in 1817 by Thomas Rickman, who was trying to record the development of English architecture from the Norman Conquest, in 1066, to the Reformation by labeling each stylistic phase. The categories introduced by Rickman continue to be commonly used today. Norman was followed by Early English, in other words, English Early Gothic, then came Decorated, which is the same as Classical Gothic, and finally Perpendicular, for Late Gothic. These distinctions, of course, are not hard and fast.

The Early English period lasted until around the middle of the 13th century, while its beginnings can be precisely

dated to the year 1175. This was when the rebuilding of the choir at Canterbury Cathedral began, following a devastating fire (see pages 222–33). William of Sens, a Frenchman, had been summoned as architect from the home of Early Gothic, then in its early stages, and it was he who brought the new style to England, admittedly in a completely independent version. In 1178, William of Sens was badly injured when scaffolding collapsed, and he returned to France. The cathedral was completed in 1185 by William the Englishman. Thus, the Gothic style was established very quickly in England, or at least in Canterbury.

A little later, from about 1180, a Gothic counterpart to Canterbury appeared at Wells Cathedral (see pages 246–57), and, with this building, the typical English Gothic style was launched in earnest. It is preserved intact in the nave and transept—the only French element here is the cross-rib vaulting in oblong transverse sections. The wall, however, is in the old English tradition, a three-storied, aqueduct-like arcaded structure, boldly divided into bays. The clear divisions between the stories, to emphasize the horizontal aspect, was, and remained, a hallmark of English Gothic. In addition, the piers are surrounded by very dense clusters of slender shafts, and the arches are richly outlined. Wells is far removed from the logical shaft-rib system employed in France. These Gothic engaged columns and circular shafts are not distributed in a functional or systematic way, but are purely decorative. This tendency is characteristic of English Gothic.

The main example of Early English is Salisbury Cathedral, a completely new building that did not have to take into account any earlier parts, and was built quickly in 48 years, between 1220 and its consecration in 1268. It was constructed on a green meadow in the middle of its own isolated close, which also happened quite often elsewhere in England, but is unique among English cathedrals for its air of complete harmony. The building program can be regarded as the ideal type for English Gothic cathedrals. Compared with the more or less contemporary Classical French cathedrals such as Reims and Amiens, it seems to take a deliberately opposite course, for here almost everything is different. The building is not only extremely long, much longer than was usual in France, but has two transepts, instead of one three-aisled transept: a larger one that projects out a long way from the middle of the building, and a smaller one by the choir; both are single-aisled and have a row of chapels on the east side. The east end is even more distinctly different from French churches: instead of ending with an apse, the choir is square-ended with a straight arcaded wall; instead of an ambulatory with radiating chapels, the choir has a low retro-choir, linked to a similarly square-ended east–west chapel. Instead of a polygonal ground plan for the east end, right angles prevail everywhere. The building descends in three stages from the choir transept to the east chapel. What is more, instead of having a facade with two towers and large portals, the nave ends in a towerless screen facade with tiny portals. This makes the crossing tower with its soaring stone spire seem even taller.

Salisbury Cathedral has a highly individual character, especially the exterior, which in its architectural effect is almost the equal of the French cathedrals. The distinctive motif, characteristic of the whole cathedral and all other Early English buildings, is the plain lancet window. Sometimes it is used singly, sometimes in pairs or in rows, now and then in tiers, and finally as a rhythmic group, perhaps graduated at the top. It is surprising how many effects can be achieved with this simple motif, right up to the most famous example: the Five Sisters in the transept at York, a row of five tall, symmetrical lancet windows.

Not only Salisbury, but other English cathedrals, too, have strongly marked individual characters—even though in Europe the similarities common to a particular nation tend to predominate, and produce a relatively homogeneous overall picture. While the cathedrals of France became increasingly alike, and finally were almost indistinguishable, every English cathedral maintained its own personality, always preserving its distinctiveness, as though each was a living individual with both positive and negative features that suited only that one building. There are two reasons for this individuality: on the one hand, most cathedrals do not adhere to a uniform design because the various parts of the building come from different periods, and therefore can reveal the most violent contrasts, for example Norman set against Perpendicular. We can sense how, in the course of its history, the cathedrals grew and were altered, each in its own way. That is never concealed. In England, there was little inclination to unify the whole of a building, as there was in France, except in those buildings that were most closely allied to France: Westminster in London, and York, which for that reason seem the least English of England's Gothic buildings. On the other hand, English architects developed astonishingly imaginative designs, far more and much earlier than their colleagues on the Continent, often with completely unorthodox, almost exotic fantasies. The great period for this was that of the Decorated style. As the name suggests, the delight in ornamentation increased, sometimes in floral decorative sculptures and also in the use of black Purbeck marble for shafts and small columns, something that had been favored during the Early English period at Canterbury. The most important innovations of the Decorated style were in two other areas, however: in tracery windows and rib designs for vaults.

The Decorated style was primarily concerned with Gothic tracery, stemming from Westminster in London, which was begun in 1246, and where, for the first time, the windows were covered with tracery after the French model. The early tracery shapes consist of simple compass constructions such as circles and trefoils, which is why this first phase of Decorated is described as Geometrical. One of the best examples is the Angel Choir in Lincoln Cathedral (see Plate 156). Then, however, from about 1300, tracery designers were increasingly allowed to indulge their fantasies. They introduced curved, fluid shapes with sweeps and flourishes, flamelike and increasingly fine creations, which sometimes competed with natural forms, and were barely reminiscent of the earlier strict geometric designs. This second phase of the Decorated is the Curvilinear. Famous examples are the west window at York and the Bishop's Eye at Lincoln (see Plate 153).

Buildings in the Decorated style are characterized by a feature even more distinctive than tracery: their vaulting. Here, the English architects soon proved themselves to be virtuosos. Conventional cross-rib vaults were enriched with additional ribs, some of them ridge ribs, running lengthwise

Exeter Cathedral, interior looking east

and across the vault, which came in at the end of the Early English period, and some the so-called tiercerons. These ribs depart from the same point as the transverse arches and cross-ribs, but, instead of meeting at the boss, connect with the ridge ribs. Using tiercerons, architects could devise particularly good four-pointed star shapes, as at Lichfield and in the nave at Lincoln. The masterpiece of this type can be seen at Exeter Cathedral, where there are so many tiercerons that the ribs, all with the same profile, shoot from the wall in a tight sequence like jets from a fountain, and then spread out like a fan. This motif is continued over the whole length of the cathedral.

The abbey church, later the cathedral, at Bristol (1298–1330), contains a unique example of English Gothic vaulting. The building is, most unusually for England, a hall church, and has especially complicated and imaginative

vaults, particularly in the side aisles. Lightweight transverse arches span the aisle like bridges, supporting horizontal struts and, above them, a small rib vault over each bay. Each bay is divided into four compartments by cross-ribs. The visual delights of this vault are increased by the fact that the pointed arches above the struts are subdivided into two smaller arches. This produces a bewildering array of overlaps and views through the vaults, as well as rib formations that seem to hang down from the top over the struts. The transverse pointed arches make the vaulting high up in the bays look strangely remote. This arrangement is in contrast to the east–west aisle beneath. Such original, almost addictive boldness, which also stands in contrast with the broad layout of the nave and choir, could be found only in England at that time. It is one of the absolute peaks in the art of vault design.

Besides the tiercerons, the English had a second kind of additional rib, the so-called liernes. These are short connecting pieces between the main ribs, which gave an inexhaustible range of possibilities. Using liernes, dense webs

of ribs could be spun, along with rhomboids, honeycombs, and continous patterns along the ridge rib. The high point of lierne vaulting is the choir at Wells, with its great net vault spanning the whole area, and the tightly woven star shapes in the retro-choir and the Lady Chapel (see Plates 135, 137).

Lady Chapels, located at the east ends of cathedrals, or sometimes, as at Ely, separate buildings, were an almost indispensable part of the overall plan, and were often, as at Wells, an architectural treasure on which no expense was spared. This was also true at Ely and Gloucester, where the chapels are true jewels of the mature Decorated or early Perpendicular styles. In other cathedrals, the Lady Chapel is more in line with the rest of the building, but is still treated as a precious ornament.

However, the noblest and most beautiful achievements of English medieval architecture are the Chapter Houses built next to the cathedrals, the assembly rooms of the cathedral chapters, or the monastery. All of these would be worthy of a gathering of kings. They are mostly designed as polygons

Gloucester Cathedral

Far left:
Lady Chapel looking west

Left:
Stained glass in the east
wall of the choir

with a central pier, beginning at Worcester with a circular structure belonging to the Norman period.

The Chapter House at Lincoln is a 10-sided building in the most opulent Early English style, with lavish use of black Purbeck marble on the shafts of the central pier. Later examples are octagonal. Without exception they are high points of Decorated architecture, and include Southwell, famous for its naturalistically decorated capitals, and the particularly large and magnificent structure at York (see ill. page 12), both of which manage to do away with the central pier. The Chapter Houses at Westminster and Salisbury (see Plate 128) both have central piers, and are closely related. Here, one can experience that complete purity that is only to be found when form and proportions fuse together in supreme artistic harmony. Here, and only here, the genius of England seems to have reached a peak, and become France's equal. In Wells, too, the multirib vaulting above the central pier never ceases to fascinate, unmatched in its radiant power (see Plate 136). All these buildings came into being at a happy time for architecture. It is as though English Gothic,

and particularly the Decorated style, sought and found perfection in this period of cathedral building. The results are wonders of world architecture.

The Decorated style depended to a great extent on the art of the stonemasons. The small columns and arch profiles of the wall structures, as well as the tracery shapes and ribs, were constantly refined, and made even more slender. This approach was taken still further in the choir of the abbey church, later the cathedral, at Gloucester, the burial place of Edward II, who was murdered in 1327, and where some 10 years later his son Edward III had the old Norman choir converted into a filigree tracery screen. The east wall, wholly taken up by a gigantic single window, and the side walls are made from wafer-thin horizontal and vertical bars that form great schematic grids. This Rectilinear style was the opposite of the Curvilinear from the Decorated period. The grid leads to a rigidly maintained uniformity. The principal guidelines are the vertical ones, which fall dead straight like plumblines—this strict emphasis on the perpendicular is where the style's name comes from. The vaulting at

Right:
York Cathedral, nave
looking east

Below:
Winchester Cathedral,
nave looking east

Gloucester features a net design that is more tightly woven than any before it, and also forms a grid (see ill. page 212). The stone of the bars and moldings has become so slender that the observer today may be reminded of modern iron constructions. This refinement of the stonemason's work, taken to a point of almost dangerous fragility, can be seen as an expression of courtly elegance, a tribute to the royal sponsors. Indeed, St. Stephen's Chapel at Westminster Palace, part of the royal court, was where the style evolved.

The Perpendicular was a special variety of English Gothic that has no parallel on the Continent. After it took further remarkable shape in Gloucester, it was widely pursued in the second half of the 14th century in countless parish churches.

In terms of cathedrals, the move toward verticality had been prefigured in the nave of the archbishop's cathedral at York, begun in 1291, an unusually large and spacious building, where, in the nave, the horizontal division of English stories had given way to a more French-looking elevation with continuous shafts and a clerestory, which is placed together with the triforium to form one story. This elevation was repeated in the choir, which was built from 1361.

Among the cathedrals, the stylistic purity of Perpendicular architecture is evident only in the naves of Winchester and Canterbury. From about 1360, the Norman nave at Winchester, the walls of which were mainly preserved, was so extensively redesigned with taut vertical structures and then surmounted by a complex vault that the overall impression is of a new building. In Canterbury the entire nave was newly built, beginning in 1377 (see Plate 114). It replaced the Norman nave of Archbishop Lanfranc, and is again distinguished by the taut vertical lines of the shafts, further emphasized by the unusual height of the arcades.

In the last phase of Perpendicular, English architects developed a new specialty, the fan vault, which, in virtuosity alone, easily outshines the richest rib vaults of the Continent. It was first conceived around 1370 in the cloister at Gloucester, and was produced on a larger scale after 1500 in King's College Chapel, Cambridge, the choir at Bath Cathedral, and in the retro-choir at Peterborough (see Plate 149). In a fan vault, the vault crowns to left and right of the ends of the bays are inverted half-cones, and support all the ribs and tracery shapes. These radiate outward and form semicircular fans. The fans run elegantly across the ends of the bays, and touch each other. Between them, the remaining space is filled with tracery in the form of squares or rhomboids with concave sides.

The fan vault is a rigorous, systematized development of the fan-shaped radiating tiercerons of the Decorated style. Their rows of adjacent triangular crowns are replaced by a single shape, the half-cone with its circular shape, which makes all edges superfluous, and unifies the vaulting still further. These virtuoso creations arouse tremendous fascination, particularly because the ribs and tracery shapes are as slender as the veins of leaves. The architect goes beyond nature—a very ambitious aim—and in the end negates even the laws of gravity. In Henry VII's Chapel in Westminster Abbey, begun in 1503, the fans hang down weightlessly, or so it seems, from the ceiling like lamps, not unlike the earlier bosses in the Divinity School at Oxford, dating from about 1480, and the choir of Oxford Cathedral, built in about 1500. Here, the decoration becomes a work of art, virtuosity becomes acrobatics, and the architect a sorcerer, whose art arouses astonished disbelief.

After that, English Gothic made no further advances. Instead, architecture after the Middle Ages became more Classical than anywhere else in Europe, as though in some kind of antimedieval protest. In secret, however, the Gothic lived on, inspiring the Romantic imagination and a continuing admiration for its structural achievements, until the Gothic revival of the 19th century when it again emerged triumphant.

Above:
Westminster Abbey,
Henry VII's Chapel,
fan vault

Left:
Gloucester Cathedral,
cloisters with fan vault

Canterbury

The archbishopric of Canterbury has always been the ecclesiastical center of England. As early as about 600, Augustine (not to be confused with the Doctor of the Church) converted the Anglo-Saxons, and made Canterbury his seat. Canterbury has maintained its primacy in the Church of England, and its consequent right to crown the monarch, despite rivalry with England's second archbishopric, York. William the Conqueror installed his favorite, Lanfranc, abbot of St. Etienne in Caen, Normandy, as archbishop in 1070. In Caen, the new abbey church had been built under Lanfranc; it was a galleried basilica with an east transept and west front with two towers. In Canterbury, Lanfranc immediately started rebuilding the cathedral. Only seven years later, in 1077, it was consecrated. There is almost nothing left to be seen of this cathedral, which had a five-part graduated choir east of the transept. The area of the Lanfranc building is occupied by the transept, the nave, and the west front of the present building. The north tower of the west facade remained standing until the 19th century, supported by powerful projecting flying buttresses. As far as one can judge, the facade of the Lanfranc building was one of the most modern structures in European architecture of the day, essentially a more developed version of the west front at St. Etienne in Caen, a Gothic prototype. The tower was replaced in 1834 by the present one, which matches the Gothic south tower.

In 1093, after a four-year vacancy, Anselm of Canterbury was appointed as Lanfranc's successor. He was one of the greatest scholars of the time, known as the father of scholarship, and was later canonized. Anselm had a new, much larger choir built for the 150-strong monastic community; by 1107, two years before his death, the choir already had its wooden ceiling in place. It was not consecrated until 1130, however. The new choir was laid out with galleries, like Lanfranc's nave, and was designed with an ambulatory and chapels; the outer walls are still largely in place. Both side chapels have been preserved. These are not radial, as commonly found in France, but lie parallel to the ambulatory with their apses pointing to the east end of the choir. Strangely enough, the chapels were originally surmounted by towers, which is a fairly singular concept. Trinity Chapel was added at the east end of the ambulatory, and later the east end was extended still further in its present form.

Shortly before the beginning of the ambulatory, the two arms of the transept were built projecting outward with two apses on the east side of each and a tower in the angle of the west side. The arms of this unusual structure form a choir transept, and are in addition to the transept of the Lanfranc building. It has the same height as the inner choir, but with no crossing, the transept being emphatically separated from the inner choir by arcades. On the Continent, the choir transept is to some extent paralleled by the third church at Cluny. In England, it was later much imitated.

The choir acquired early fame because of its magificently painted wooden ceiling and wall paintings. The exterior is similarly splendid; the angle towers' ornamentation, for example, seems like embroidery in stone. Here, English architecture begins to be decorative, and would remain so until the end of the Middle Ages. Only the spacious, three-aisled hall-crypt with its lavishly decorated columns has been preserved complete from Anselm's choir, enclosed by the broad walkway of the ambulatory, which opens onto the hall of columns via arcaded piers.

In the second half of the 12th century, Canterbury acquired another saint, who soon became extremely popular: Thomas Becket. In 1162 he had been declared archbishop by Henry II, whose controversial rise to the throne had been supported by Becket. Four years later, however, Becket went into exile after his relations with the king became tense. Among other places, he went to Sens, the seat of one of the French archbishops. In 1170, Becket returned in triumph, but, in the same year, he was murdered by knights loyal to the king in the north transept of the cathedral. His body was buried in the crypt. Becket was canonized shortly afterward, after which his grave became the destination of countless streams of pilgrims.

In 1174 the choir of Archbishop Anselm burnt down, but the crypt with Becket's grave was unscathed. The horrified monks appointed an international commission of English and French architects for the purpose of rebuilding the choir. After controversial discussions, the French architect, William of Sens, was successful with his compromise proposal to keep the surrounding walls, which were still usable, but to build a completely new inner choir. William's proposal was accepted, and he supervised the works until 1178. His successor, William the Englishman, completed the choir in 1184, after only 10 years. A monk, Gervase of Canterbury, produced a vivid report in the form of a year-by-year journal of the building operations and related matters, which among other things contains descriptions of the building that for their time are unusually accurate.

The works began at the crossing, and moved eastward step by step. The whole of the east end is thus not the work of William of Sens, but of his successor. Looking at the entire plan, the architects had to take into account that the building had several liturgical functions to fulfill, and this can, in fact, be clearly seen in the nature of the structure. The five sections attached to the transept and crossing of the Lanfranc building were ready to move into as early as 1180, and were specifically for the monks' choir. To the east of these, the transverse arms of Anselm's choir were converted into a real transept with a crossing. Behind this came the sanctuary, where the high altar stood. Then the next area funnels eastward, leading to the raised Trinity Chapel. Gervase called this part the Thomas Becket Chapel, for here was the sumptuous shrine with the remains of the saint, the destination of the pilgrims. Thus, the ambulatory could serve as a pilgrims' way. It also revealed a second shrine, the tall rotunda added directly to the ambulatory, which, as early as 1199, was known as the Corona, or crown, and today is generally called Becket's Crown. Preserved here as a relic is the crown, or top, of the saint's head, cut off when he was murdered, hence the appropriate circular shape of the chapel. When work on the Anselm crypt continued, it was necessary to build an underchurch for the Trinity Chapel, the ambulatory, and the Corona. This corresponds exactly to the ground plan and placement of the piers of the upper church, and clearly increases the height of their floor levels in relation to the western part of the choir.

William of Sens brought the Gothic style to England when he built the new choir, but the new designs had to harmonize with the external walls, which were Norman. Once again, the choir was given galleries. As Gervase stresses, it is higher than the old Anselm choir. The architect chose this course while he was raising the arcades and side aisles a considerable height; now they are as high as the old side aisles and galleries combined. The gallery openings contain two biforiums to each wall section, and are in themselves relatively low, as is the clerestory, which stands in the vaulted zone, and, in the old English-Norman tradition, has an inner passage. The imposts for the vaulting are set unusually low down the wall, at the height of the capitals of the gallery openings, which in effect limits the height of the clerestory windows. William of Sens opted for sexpartite vaulting throughout, as was then usual in France, and joined the transverse ribs to only one shaft, although the other arches have a cluster of three shafts. The shafts' splendid appearance is enhanced by the use of luxurious black Purbeck marble, which was widely adopted in the English Gothic period. These begin above the piers.

The architect employed such an astonishing variety of piers that they look like something from a pattern book; in the process he showed such inventiveness that some pier types that only later became important in France were anticipated here. In the monks' choir, octagonal and circular piers were used in alternation. For the choir crossing the architect switched to an octagonal core surrounded by eight extremely slender engaged columns, a combination that is repeated in the upper story to give the piers a two-storied structure. These forms are closely related to those used in Bourges Cathedral, which was begun a decade later. At the point where the choir slopes upward, there is even a clustered pier with an octagonal core and four circular attached columns, which was to become the predominant shape in Chartres. Finally, the Trinity Chapel was given angled transverse pairs of circular piers, as were used earlier at Sens. These paired piers are enriched in some places by circular columns placed between the two halves of the pier, a form that reappeared later in the choir at Le Mans. At Canterbury, all the paired piers were originally to have been built with these circular columns.

The proportions in the monks' choir are not at all French. Compared with the gallery and clerestory, the piers seem much too tall, although they do not stand out so much today because of the choir stalls. Seen on its own, the monk's choir is top-heavy and out of proportion. This was, however, the architect's precise intention, for the height of the stories in the monks' choir was calculated in relation to the east end, where the Trinity Chapel stands on a higher level. The stories are the same height in the chapel as in the monks' choir, although the piers are much shorter, to allow for the raised floor level, which makes the arcades precisely the right height. Viewed as a whole, the Trinity Chapel achieves a high degree of equilibrium and harmony. Since the chapel terminates our view, this impression is transferred to the whole choir. Even though the Trinity Chapel was built under William the Englishman, who moved the steps farther west, credit for the planning of the essential elements should be given to William of Sens. His task was to create a space in which the most important part was the eastern end, and he even built the narrow funnel shape into his plans. Our view travels without interruption from the wide sanctuary into the narrower chapel at the end. Thus, from the handicap of the old Anselm choir an excellent idea was born that is to be found nowhere in France, although the whole of the Trinity Chapel is a clear reference to the cathedral at Sens, the city from which William of Sens originated.

The Corona, the rotunda at the head of the building, is in the best French Early Gothic style, with its arc of lower windows, triforium, and upper row of windows, which with the radiating sections of the vault form a crown of light over the shrine of Becket's Crown. From the outside, the Corona is the same height as the sanctuary, and with its ring of pinnacles looks like a castle tower or armed fortress.

According to Gervase, the inner structure of the east transept was designed by William the Englishman. Its several-storied columned galleries are purely decorative, with their pattern of columns and variety of arches flanking the wall. Here, for the first time, the imported version of Gothic took on an English character: Early French turning into Early English.

Almost two centuries later, in 1377, it was decided to pull down the nave, and build a costly new one. This was to be one of the masterpieces of the Perpendicular style: a basilica whose dividing arcades are as tall as combined arcades and galleries were in the past. This was exactly as William of Sens had done earlier. The distinctive feature of the nave's architecture is the continuous vertical "pull" of the piers and engaged columns, whose densely clustered profiles soar upward in a slender procession, then at the foot of the vaults transfer into fanlike radiating ribs, and finally terminate in star patterns along the ridge. The marked formal precision of the nave gives it a special character. It was completed in 1405. Soon after, the south facade tower was built, and the transept—except for the north tower, the only part of the structure still standing from Lanfranc's original building—was replaced by a new version. Finally, from 1433, the magnificent crossing tower was built in two stages: at first, it had only one story, then acquired a second one after the piers at the crossing were strengthened. In 1504, John Wastell introduced one of the wonders of Late Gothic English vaulting in the inner part of the tower, the crowning glory in the long history of fan vaulting.

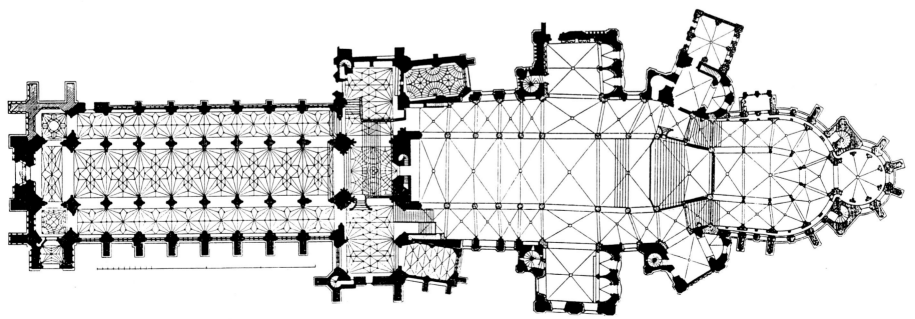

111

Salisbury

Salisbury Cathedral is the most unified of all England's cathedrals. This is due on the one hand to the short time it took to build, and on the other to the fact that there were no older buildings on the site to reckon with. Originally the bishop's seat had been in the nearby hill town of Old Sarum, where there was a cathedral as early as the 12th century. Osmund, one of the bishops of Old Sarum, had previously been William the Conqueror's chancellor and was later canonized. The rules that he laid down for the monastery, the "Uses of Salisbury," were followed up to the Reformation and served as a model elsewhere.

In 1218, the bishop's seat was moved into the valley at Salisbury. The new cathedral was built in a single phase on a green meadow from 1220 until 1268, when it was consecrated. In the same year, Amiens Cathedral was consecrated on the Continent. The architect at Salisbury had the rare opportunity to design the whole building as he chose, and in this sense the cathedral is representative of the architecture of its time, the mature Early English style. When building began, the Early English style had been established for almost half a century, since the rebuilding of the choir at Canterbury.

In typical English fashion, the cathedral has two transepts with two crossings: one projecting far out from the middle of the complex, with the crossing tower at the center, and a second one by the choir, which is narrower and shorter by one bay. A row of chapels is added to the east side of each transept, and structurally forms a continuous side aisle because there are no walls dividing the chapels. This, too, is an English peculiarity, occurring also in the Norman cathedrals at Durham and Peterborough.

The choir is divided into separate functional areas in a masterly way. The western part between the two transepts served as the canons' choir, while the three bays east of the choir crossing are the sanctuary and at the same time the bishop's area. The head of the choir is square-ended. Behind it lies the retro-choir, which runs around the head of the choir in a U-shape and is also an ambulatory. At the east end it is two bays deep.

Occupying the easternmost part of the choir is a chapel as wide as the head of the choir but with a square end and extending two bays beyond the retro-choir. The chapel is not, as was customary elsewhere in England, the Lady Chapel but the Trinity Chapel. A Lady Chapel was not needed because the whole cathedral is dedicated to the Virgin Mary. The interiors of the retro-choir and the Trinity Chapel occupy the same spatial area, the chapel extending outward from behind the east end of the choir. The nave is the plainest part of the building. It has three aisles and takes up about the same area as the choir.

The whole building has a strongly rectilinear quality. The characteristic English cathedral plan, as formulated earlier, is here resolved in an ideal manner. It differs radically from the French cathedral plan, with its polygonal choir, ambulatory, and radiating chapels. The English solution is much more subdivided than the French, but at the same time simpler, because the heavy French polygonal construction has been replaced by the simplest shape that geometry has to offer: the right angle.

Salisbury's role as a model building is also very purely expressed on the exterior. The choir and choir transept seem to act as a unified, cruciform central structure. Seen from the east, each arm of the cross occupies three bays and has a gabled front with small towers. In addition, the windows of the clerestory are all the same, namely graduated triple lancet windows. This unity of form is the supreme rule. Despite being the central part of the building, the east front is emphasized as the showpiece. It offers a rich, multilayered perspective, governed by steep pointed gables and groups of lancet windows. In France, the east end of the cathedral is apsidal, but at Salisbury it is very firmly a front.

The middle part is stressed, but not overly so. The Trinity Chapel, placed between the set-back gables of the retro-choir, has three graduated gables of its own that can be seen as representing the Trinity. The three gables are embedded in the overall view of gable fronts and form an unobtrusive but significant point of emphasis within it. The whole view is a masterly exercise in the distribution of weights. The graduated gabled fronts stand in front of the transverse block of the choir transept, which in turn is backed by the transverse block of the main transept, the whole plan dominated and pulled together by the gigantic crossing tower with its stone spire pointing to the heavens. Seen from here, the nave seems far away.

At the west end the cathedral has just its facade, rather than a whole prospect: a gabled front extended sideways by walls and corner towers. These two slender, four-cornered towers provide firm support, but to the eye seem little better than square, pierlike blocks. The principal motif is the group of three graduated windows in the middle. The rest of the space is studded with numerous galleries of figures. These are used to clad the facade like regalia in a lavish, extensive relief. The portals, however, are less effective. As a whole, the facade stands like a screen in front of the nave set behind it, and is, in fact, a good example of the screen facade, a type seldom found in England.

The interior, where the arcades and upper stories of the triforium and clerestory are strictly separated and the columns are slender, is a strangely austere version of Early English. The architect seems to have viewed the flowering richness that then characterized English architecture as an ascetic would, all taste for the exuberant leaving him cold. A certain richness is nevertheless evident here, partly in the piers with their four engaged shafts and in the double biforium in the upper story. At the same time, however, the architect gave them a strict feeling of spareness, a clarity that has something puritanical about it. The interior looks as though the architect had wanted to unite the decorative instincts of Early English with the more exacting spirit of French cathedrals.

In the choir and nave, the interior has a uniform appearance. The conspicuous buttressing of both crossings was done later, the western piers joined lengthwise to the eastern ones, forming a barrier in front of the transepts. The additions to the main crossing were not carried out until the 15th century. The tower, which at 403 ft. (123 m) is one of the tallest built in the Middle Ages, had begun to lean toward the southwest under its own weight (some 7,050 tons), and these measures were intended to prevent the crossing pillars from slipping further. Today it still has a lean of about 2.5 ft. (75 cm). In the 14th century, buttressing was installed at the choir crossing to counteract the lateral thrust of the arcades and triforium arches, an inverted pointed arch being placed over the pointed arch underneath. These measures provided a model for the famous strainer arches introduced later at the crossing in Wells Cathedral.

One part of the building does not conform to the overall unity: the Trinity Chapel. This is a lavish, shrinelike structure, enclosed by tall windows and dressed in columns of a fragile slenderness, precious lengths of black Purbeck marble. The chapel is a three-aisled hall, but the columns stand so close to the walls that the side aisles are less aisles than a special kind of outer shell, peculiar to England, the columns seeming to step inward from the side walls.

At the point where the Trinity Chapel meets the retrochoir, the space broadens into a structure occupying several bays, with a regular alternation of broad and narrow bays. The columns, which in the chapel are simple and circular, here become more varied: columns with four shafts and other varieties of circular posts, thin as pipes, are grouped in fours and detached from the middle post so that one can see daylight through them. Such refinements of the stonemason's art embody the design principle that underlies the whole of the Trinity Chapel: the desire for transparency,

Salisbury Cathedral from the Bishop's Garden, John Constable, 1825. Oil on canvas, 35 x 44 in. (89 x 112 cm). (The Frick Collection, New York)

for looking through to the other side, and for constantly changing perspectives. The chapel is definitely one of the most beautiful treasures of the Early English period. Whereas on the Continent an impression of sumptuousness would have been created with tracery, here it is conveyed solely by the columns.

Salisbury's second jewel is the Chapter House by the cloisters. This was built about 1270–80 as an almost precise copy of the Chapter House at Westminster in London, which was completed by 1257 at the latest. Both are regular octagons enclosed by large tracery windows and have a central support from which the ribs fan outward. The octagon with central support had already produced an Early English *pièce de résistance* in the Chapter House at Lincoln. This time, though, the architects pursued the idea of having a glasshouse, and completely covering the wall area with tracery windows in the French manner—as, for example, in the Sainte Chapelle in Paris. Here the central support is less important than the cladding of the perimeter with windows, for which a continuous band of glowing stained glass was proposed. The English opulence of Lincoln was replaced by French brilliance. The Gothic style of both countries is united here, and the result is an amazing, utterly beautiful room. That was certainly the view of contemporary observers, who praised the Chapter House at

Westminster as an "incomparable work." Such was its builders' pride in their achievement that an inscription on the floor at Westminster praises it in these poetic words: "As the rose is the flower of flowers, this is the house of houses." This image is equally appropriate to the Chapter House at Salisbury.

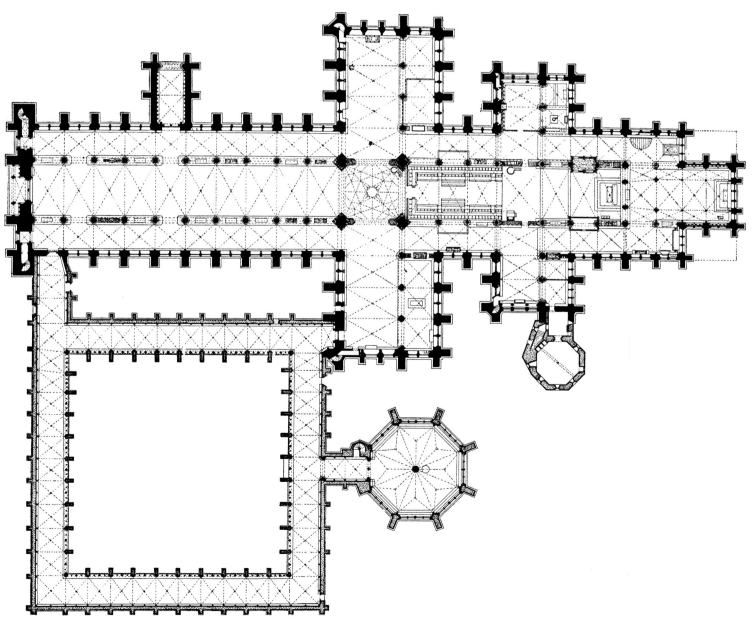

120

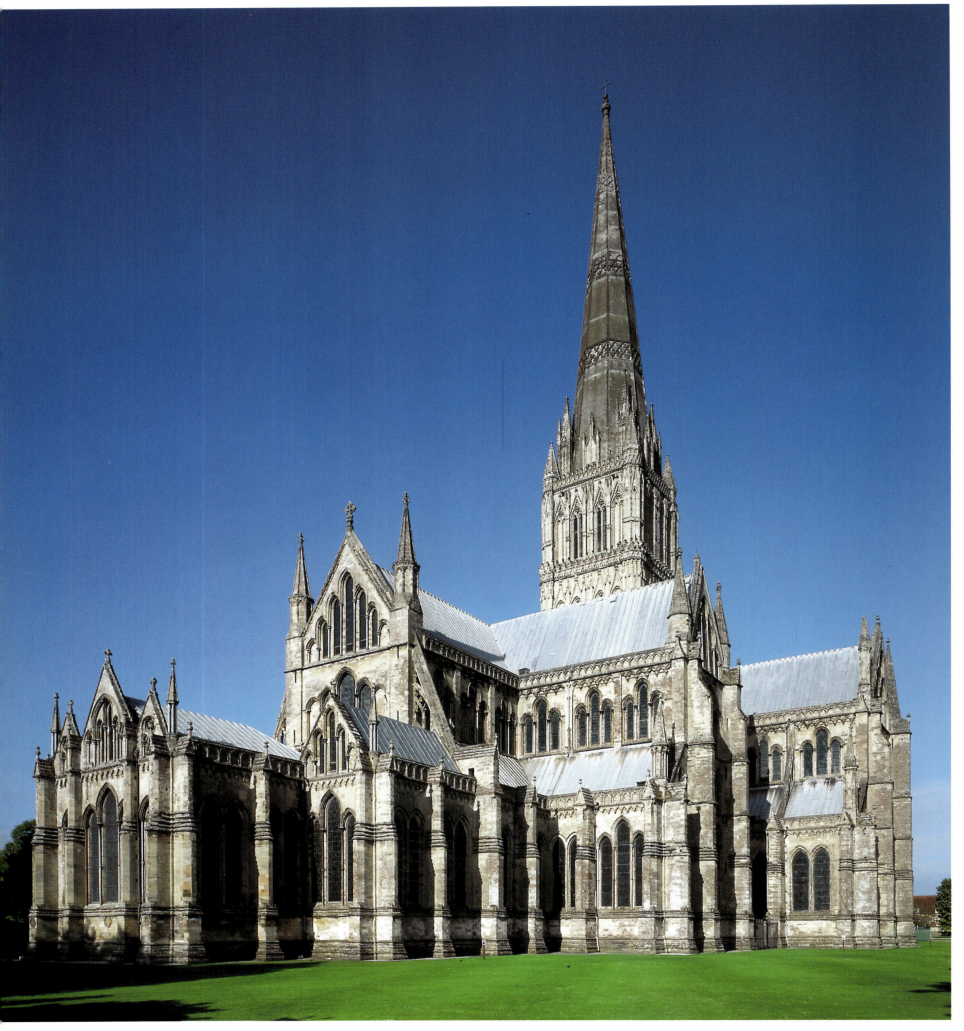

238   *England*

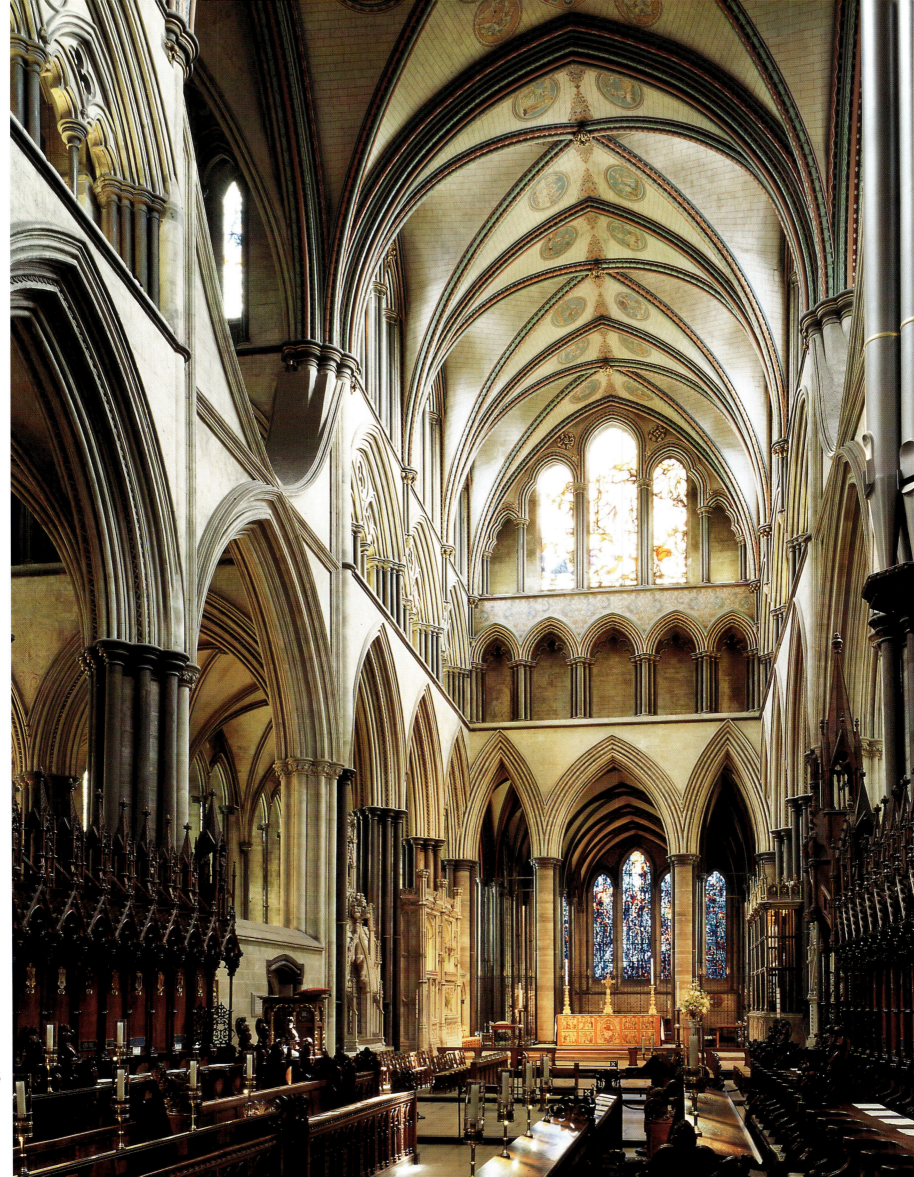

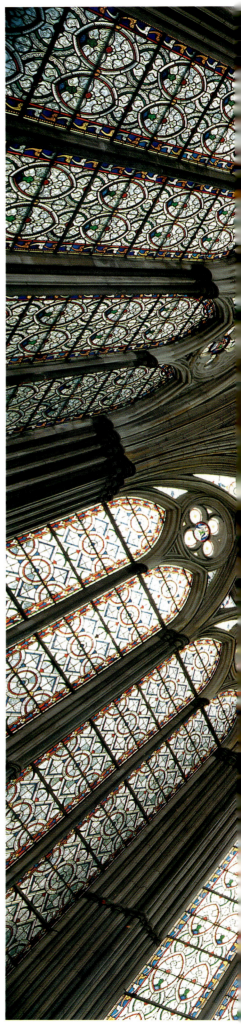

Wells

Wells, named for the springs that rise there, was only a mission at the time of its founding around 700. In 909, when the diocese of Sherborne was divided, Wells became the seat of a bishop. The first bishop of the Norman period, who came from Tours, moved his seat to Bath, but Wells remained the principal residence of the bishops, who to this day are the bishops of both Bath and Wells.

Construction of the present cathedral began at an unknown date under Bishop Reginald de Bohun, who was installed by Henry II in 1174. Building may have started shortly afterward, making it roughly contemporary with the Gothic choir of Canterbury. It was built from east to west. The main nave was consecrated in 1239, at which time the west facade was already being built. The architects during construction of the nave and facades were Adam Lock (d. 1229) and Thomas Norrey, who first completed the work on the facades. The upper parts of the towers were not built at that time: the south tower was raised in the 14th century and the north tower in the 15th century, but both remained incomplete.

The nave and three-aisled transept of the original structure have been preserved. The choir, however, which was an ambulatory choir with only three bays, was extended in the Decorated style to have six bays, and was given an extravagant new ambulatory. Later, the walls of the three original bays were altered to match the three new ones and unify the choir. Only the dividing arcades in the wall system of the first three choir bays have been preserved in their original form. They indicate that, for the most part, the choir had the same structure as the transept and nave. This means that the original structure was uniform from west to east.

The central nave has a notably severe style, with no trace of French Gothic or of Canterbury Cathedral. It is a typically English structure with three stories, all very distinct from one another. The architects preferred a blind triforium to the traditional gallery. It consists of arcaded walls with columns but no passage, and runs through from west to east like a continuous ribbon without even the smallest variation to the bays. The blind arcades, 33 of them on each side, travel through the nave like the flat wake of a ship; while other areas project upward, these arcades exert a strong horizontal emphasis. Nothing would have been more alien to the architect than to vary the columns he used. Rather than a rhythmic series, he preferred a regular beat, and the dividing arcades and vaulting provide it with metronomic precision. The vaults are transverse oblongs divided into four parts. This produces a rapidly repeating series of shapes,

entirely different from the sexpartite vaults of Canterbury Cathedral. The vaults arise almost from nothing, branching out from a cluster of three short, stubby engaged columns that begin on ornamental corbels set in the spandrels of the triforium. The clerestory, with its narrow lancet windows, retains the typically English passageway, although this has a sober meanness not usually associated with Norman architecture.

The dividing arcades are in complete contrast to this sobriety. The compound piers with an extremely fine profile are composed of numerous slender pillars that give an almost fluted appearance. The core of each pier is a simple cross shape. Their rich appearance comes from the triple clusters of columns attached to each of the four faces and angles. The clusters in the angles fill out the space to such an extent that the foremost projecting column, which is the only pointed one, actually delineates the edge of the pier. The undersides of the dividing arches are similarly multifaceted. The arches contain more than 25 profiles, and are by far the richest in European architecture. The profuse profiling of these arches remained a characteristic of English architecture from this time on; the trend was toward an overall profile, in which the individual shape was much less important than the total effect. The architects and stonemasons gave precedence to decoration, the richer the better, instead of the systematic approach favored in France. This was a legacy of Late Norman architecture.

The ambitious facade at Wells is also part of this trend. Its towers reach outward beyond the line of the side aisles, making the facade very wide, so wide in fact that it was scarcely possible to achieve a balance between width and height in the overall proportions. The main idea was to make the broad facade, with its stepped buttresses and tall lancet windows, the showplace for a collection of statues in niches. These are arranged one above the other over five stories, and crowned by a gabled centerpiece. The cycle of figures originally contained 176 statues, of which 127 have been preserved, and extends around the side and the rear of the towers. This parade of small niches with columns and gables was, and remains, unique. Only after the later addition of the towers, which because of the excessive width of the facade look stumpy, and in particular the crossing tower, did the exterior achieve the overall appearance typical of English cathedrals. The crossing tower was the first of the three towers to be built, between 1315 and 1322. Originally it had a tall spire made of wood sheathed in lead, which burned down in 1439.

As so often happened with English cathedrals, the weight of the crossing tower very soon led to damage to the load-bearing substructure. Only three decades after the tower was completed, the famous strainer arches were inserted with ingenious brutality between the columns of the crossing, each consisting of an inverted pointed arch sitting on a lower one to form an X-shape. The spandrels enclose open stone circles like large eyes. An additional point of interest derives from the fact that the curves of both pointed arches cross over, swinging from convex to concave curves. This was a shape known to everyone from everyday articles, like the bishop's folding chair or the pincers of the crane on a building site. Here the shape was produced in a gigantic format. The crossing is enclosed by these strainer arches on three sides, and separated by them from the adjacent spaces. They were omitted only on the east side, where their role was taken over by the rood screen. These strange and fascinating structures—in which imaginative observers can see a face with a gaping mouth—are the predominant focus in the nave and transept. When one looks up above them at the Late Perpendicular fan vaulting in the tower, the fascinating spectacle is complete. This part of the cathedral has a special quality that could hardly be more English.

The entire east end is also unusual, and at the same time typically English. It is a high point of the Decorated style, perhaps *the* high point. The Chapter House was built first, and was in use by 1319 at the latest. It is an octagon, and from its central column a fan vault with no fewer than 32 tightly packed ribs soars outward. The sheer radiancy of the vault could not be done better. The old theme of the octagonal English chapter house with a central column, fan vaulting, and surrounding band of windows here reaches the absolute height of richness.

The conversion and rebuilding of the choir came next. The retro-choir, which has rectangular chapels to the east as well as laterally to the north and south, is a two-aisled ambulatory, its special feature being the way the Lady Chapel (the eastern apsidal chapel) runs into it, like the Trinity Chapel in Salisbury. The Lady Chapel is, however, octagonal, and so the area where it runs into the ambulatory is not rectangular, as in Salisbury, but has triangular bays with correspondingly staggered columns. This space gives the impression of a forest of columns placed almost by chance where they stand. Each column also supports a fan of ribs, like those in the Chapter House, though these are not quite so profuse. The ribs reveal an endless, constantly changing series of patterns, as the trunks and branches of trees do when we walk through a forest. The visual charm of these patterns, which are widespread and much loved in England, is here taken to the ultimate degree, and visitors respond to the spectacle with visible delight.

The Lady Chapel is full of wonderful surprises. As we look into it through the ambulatory, we glimpse another world. It is higher than the ambulatory, with no central column, and has a wide-reaching fan vault consisting of several interlocking star shapes. In addition, the three eastern sides of the octagon are clearly longer than the other sides, and thus emphasized. Together with their tall windows they form a unique glasshouse, decorated with remarkable tracery employing the striking motif of trefoils deployed in four rows, one above the other. When viewed from the ambulatory, the effect is of looking into an apse.

The inner choir offers us yet another dimension. Its high wall has a triforium with a unique tracery grille that also provides a gallery of niches for statues. The clerestory windows are set back in a window niche with intrados deep enough to allow room for a passage. Both triforium and clerestory are enclosed within enormous arches, the triforium projecting forward like a shrine. Seen from directly in front, the slender columns between the niches prolong the uprights of the window tracery and run down to the spandrels of the dividing arcades. Because the eastern outer wall has the same shape, the choir area is completely unified. This effect is also furthered by the vaulting. Its basic shape, an east-west barrel with lierne vaulting, has its own unity, while the configuration of the ribs overides the transition through the transverse arches from one bay to the next. Here, octagons and squares alternate in a large web of ribs that has nothing in common with conventional rib vaulting. Rather like the superimposed trefoils in the window tracery of the Lady Chapel, the ribs are a simple surface ornament, as regularly and similarly shaped as the geometry of a honeycomb. It was an ideal way to unite the broad area of the ceiling.

If the east end at Wells was built by the same architect, then this man was the most versatile architect of the entire English Gothic period, and belongs on the Olympus of great inventors and creators.

Plates 129–137

129 Overall view from the northeast; in the foreground, the octagonal Chapter House
130, 131 West facade
132 Nave looking east
133 The crossing with the strainer arches
134 Central column and rib vaulting in the Chapter House
135 The choir looking through to the retro-choir and Lady Chapel
136 The forest of columns and fan vaulting in the retro-choir, looking through to the east apsidal chapel (Lady Chapel)
137 The octagonal Lady Chapel with fan vaulting

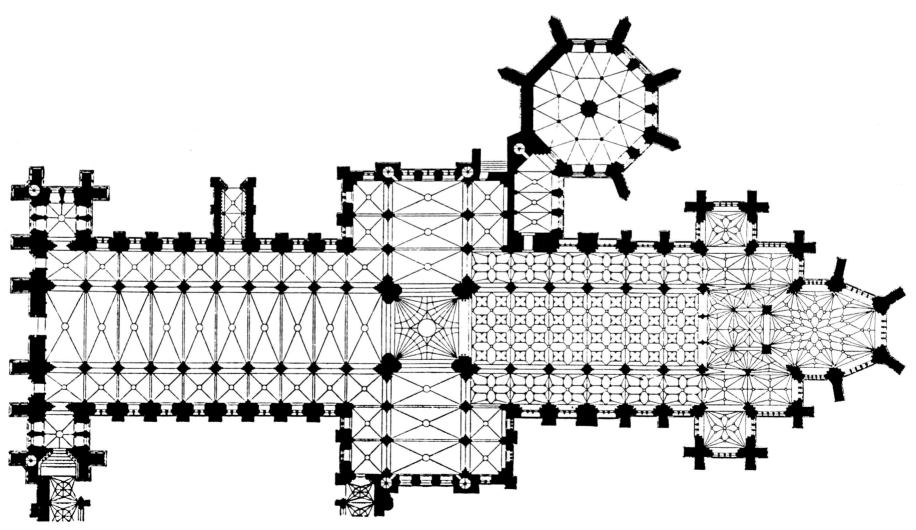

130, 131

Ely

Ely, near Cambridge, was once surrounded by impenetrable marshes. Only the middle of this area, the Isle of Ely, could be built on. Here, as early as the seventh century, a noble convent was built; its founder, Ethelreda, daughter of the Anglo-Saxon king, was canonized, and this soon made Ely a favorite place of pilgrimage. Following its destruction by Danish Vikings in the 10th century, the convent was converted into a monastery. After the Conquest, which Ely long resisted, a Norman abbot was installed. The second abbot, named Simeon, also a Norman by birth, had previously been a prior at Winchester. There, his brother, Bishop Walkelyn, had in 1079 begun the construction of a large, extremely elongated cathedral, which was consecrated as early as 1093. Simeon, who arrived in Ely in 1081, had been present when building began at Winchester. Gripped by building fever at the age of 90, he started building a similarly large church in Ely. As early as 1106, the sacred remains of Ethelreda were transferred to the new choir.

Shortly after, in 1109, Ely was raised to a bishopric, and separated from the diocese of Lincoln. This was not good for the new building, because the bishops secured the largest part of the monastic estates for themselves, while the financing of the church remained the concern of the priors and the monastery. Only later, in the Gothic period, would this change.

These events make the dimensions of around 426 ft. (130 m), the original overall length, all the more astonishing. In that sense, the monastery was certainly not poor. The nave has 13 bays, one more than Winchester, and seems to have been built over a roughly 20-year period, between 1110 and 1130. Toward the end of the 12th century, the extraordinarily lavish west part was added, with its abundance of towers. The nave and transept are almost in their original condition; the choir and the crossing, however, had to be rebuilt in the Gothic period.

The original choir, which was excavated in 1850, had an ambulatory but no radial chapels. The ambulatory was certainly intended for pilgrims, who could thus walk around the tomb of St. Ethelreda. The influence of Winchester can be seen in the transept, for it has the same number of bays, and also has three aisles. In the Norman architecture of England, Winchester and Ely are the only examples of a transept with three aisles.

The influence of Winchester, whose transept is the only original part of the building, can also be seen in the elevation. Here, as at Winchester, three-storied Norman arcading was used, with dividing arcades, paired gallery openings, and a clerestory with a passage and graduated triple arches.

The whole is held together by attached columns set between the bays to form vertical wall compartments. At Ely the elevation is significantly enriched by the variety of its structural elements. The stony severity of Winchester is softened by a certain restrained balance in the arcade walls, and by the harmony of the arches and columns. This represents a gain for refinement, but a loss in terms of power and originality.

At Ely the trend was toward not only a greater richness of forms, but also greater variety. The wall has two alternating forms of support, both in the dividing arcades and in the galleries: one is a compound pier, with no fewer than five circular projecting columns in the inner sides of the arches; the other is a solid circular column that is used only at ground level in the central nave and side aisles. The alternation of supports switches between the rich and the simple; it brings life and change to the seemingly endless arcade sequence, which is always slightly monotonous. At Ely, the Norman arcade wall reached its full beauty, achieving a balance between a crude display of strength and a cultivated distinction.

In contrast, the west front, built about half a century after the nave, has a very different character. It consists of a transverse block with an entrance hall in the middle, above which stands a mighty tower that was carried further upward in the Gothic period. Two additional towers were added to each of the fronts of the side arms. The northern arm, together with its towers, collapsed at the end of the 16th century, and was never rebuilt. Originally, therefore, the west front had five towers of which only three remain today. The side towers appear from a distance to be circular, but in fact are ten-sided, freestanding structures set at the corners of the side arm. The corners of the main tower are treated in a similar way, so that it seems to be enclosed within four satellite towers. Even in its present reduced form, the west front displays much of the powerful impact of earlier Norman architecture.

Equally noteworthy is the fact that the whole west front seems to be crammed with an enormous variety of multi-storied galleries. An ostentatious and apparently insatiable appetite for pomp is now mixed with the old display of strength. The motif of the arcade, in its infinite variety, here became a purely ornamental surface-covering pattern. No effort was spared to put on a show of might and tremendous opulence. Everything that a Norman architect had to say can be found here. But because the west front is so distinctive, this manifest opulence does not for a moment compromise the original Norman force of the central block and its towers. The intense richness of the decoration reflects a new kind of power with a quality of its own.

The Early English porch, added a little later, shows the same enthusiasm for arcaded galleries, and is so compatible with the transverse block that the differences are not immediately noticeable. The builders achieved their wish to create something spectacular, something sensationally inventive; today, the west front at Ely is justifiably numbered among the most famous works of world architecture. The fact that it made an impression even in its day is demonstrated by Kelso Abbey in Scotland; now in ruins, the five-towered west front was copied there in a simplified form.

By the 13th century the choir had become too small, so the bishop ordered the old choir and ambulatory to be demolished and extended the four-bay Norman choir with six more bays. This was done between 1234 and 1252, during the late phase of the Early English period. The new choir, which terminated in a flat windowed wall, vied visually with the imposing cathedral at Lincoln, not far away. However, the structural forms at Ely show a greater refinement than Lincoln, for example in the piers, where the eight projecting columns appear to encircle the core, and in the dividing arches, whose profiles descend in three distinct stages. Similarly, the gallery openings and the graduated triple arcades of the clerestory are truly magnificent examples of the exquisite artistry of the stonemasons.

The building of the Lady Chapel was begun in 1321; it is a spacious structure, 46 ft. (14 m) wide, which unusually stands adjacent to, rather than at the end of, the choir. It is a masterpiece of the mature Decorated style, with the now famous nodding ogee arches in the arcade running around it, and the unusual arches on the walls separating the windows. This chapel seems to have been created as a place for holding synods.

The Lady Chapel had hardly been started when the Norman crossing tower collapsed, shattering the piers and the adjacent bays of the choir. The architects who rebuilt these bays as far as the Early English choir, which had remained undamaged, gave free rein to a display of architectural magnificence. Here, the Curvilinear variant of the Decorated style reigns supreme, especially in the gallery, where the tracery abounds with extremely dense filigree designs, like nature in full profusion. Such a wonderful selection of finely worked pieces, such boundless virtuosity in the masonry cannot be found anywhere else, even in England. Here the Gothic almost takes on an Oriental, fairy-tale character reminiscent of the *Thousand and One Nights*. On the Continent, comparable work is not found until the Manueline Gothic of Portugal, that is, about 200 years later.

Detail of the wall of the facade between the west towers

The jewel in the crown of this restoration period is the world-famous and universally admired crossing. The old crossing was not simply rebuilt; rather the narrow, shaftlike space was replaced by a broad central area, an octagon in the middle of the cathedral's endless length. Where the aisles meet, the space suddenly broadens out into a massive central area like a piazza. The octagon is as wide as all three aisles together, and has a diameter of about 72 ft. (22 m). It has unequal sides, the diagonals being a good deal shorter than the other sides. The large windows in the diagonal sides make the octagon especially light. The pride of Ely soars above the octagon: the fantastic vault, like an enormous illuminated lantern, hovers weightlessly above the crossing; as wide as the central nave, it was intended to replace the old tower. The fascination of the lantern comes from the way it is supported: it stands at the center of an octagonal rib vault, which shoots upward in a series of fans, thereby developing a sprung tension, indeed whole fields of force, which raise the lantern up effortlessly to the light. The ribs are typical of English Gothic, but here they develop a dynamism like nowhere else. This creates a second, extremely eye-catching effect: the lantern octagon is turned by half a phase in relation to the lower octagon—the force fields appear to turn the lantern against the bays beneath. A pointed star vault shimmers in the ceiling of the lantern, bright like a real star above the shadowy lower vault. In this position, it is the star of all stars, the divine star of the firmament. Similarly, the circle at the apex contains the image of the Savior.

Technically, the octagon is made of wood, and as such is a masterpiece of the carpenter's craft. The load-bearing framework of the lantern, which projects freely into space, is made of oak beams in a triangular brace. In outward appearance, largely the result of restoration work in the 19th century, the octagon is broad and sturdy, and still gives the impression of a fortress installed on top of the cathedral. This, however, is no Norman stronghold, but rather a proud, heavenly citadel, crowned by a central crenellated tower.

It is one of Ely Cathedral's defining qualities that each phase of its building was handled with such marvelous skill, and this is why Ely is so beloved by friends of architecture.

Plates 138–144

138 Overall view from the northeast; in the foreground, the Lady Chapel
139 Nave, crossing tower, northern transept, and Lady Chapel from the northwest
140 West front
141 Nave looking east
142 View through the choir
143 The crossing (octagon) looking southeast to the choir and south transept
144 View upward into the crossing vault

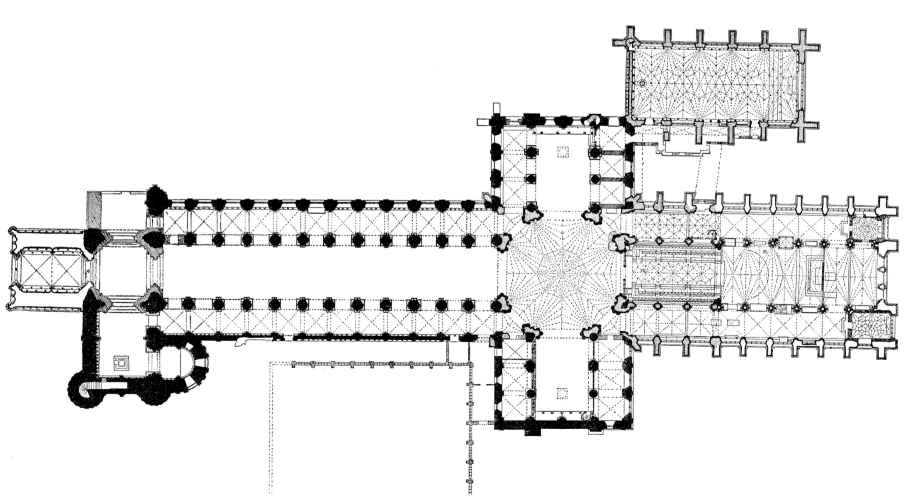

13

Peterborough

Below left:
Elevation of the nave wall

Below right:
North transept

Peterborough, with Ely and Norwich, is one of the large-scale Norman buildings of eastern England. Originally only an abbacy, in 1541 Peterborough was promoted to a bishopric, following the reorganization of the Church under Henry VIII. Here, too, Normans were installed as abbots after the Norman Conquest. The first Norman abbot started by building a fort against the rebellious monastery, but in 1116 it seems the second abbot set fire to it. The rebuilding of the church began two years later, and lasted for more than a hundred years until 1238, when, with the completion of the western part, the final consecration was celebrated. The financial position of the abbacy was weak; in 1177 the abbot gave valuable relics to Jews as collateral for large building loans. This was certainly the reason for his dismissal. Finally, however, the abbacy was in a position once again to extend the already elongated church by two more bays, and to erect a stately facade. With a total length just short of 459 ft. (140 m), the Norman structure was almost exactly the same size as Norwich Cathedral, and was slightly larger than the Norman Ely. On the east, the structure terminated quite prosaically with three apses. To provide the necessary altar positions, three eastern chapels were attached to both arms of the transept; they are open to one another, and structurally create a side aisle. Durham was the prototype for this arrangement; otherwise there is no trace of any influence from Durham. The decisive influences came from Norwich and Ely, with their three-storied arcade walls running evenly through the building, following the traditional practice of English Norman structures. Peterborough is a variant of Norwich and Ely, and as such is a direct expression of neighborly rivalry. Here, uniquely, even the original patterned wooden ceiling of the central nave has been preserved, admittedly in a very restored condition. The angled sections on either side give the ceiling a certain volume, which otherwise could be achieved only by a vault.

The builders of Peterborough valued uniformity: the design for the elevation was retained to the end, even though the nave was finished only four decades after the Gothic choir at Canterbury. The wall features the standard elements of the Norman period. The main story here is the gallery, with its strongly profiled paired openings. The clerestory, too, with its passage and graduated triple arcade, is typically Norman; this is a second version of the clerestory at Norwich. The three-storied nave offered more opportunity for variation, especially in the columns of the dividing arcades. The choir displays an alternation between two octagonal piers and one circular pier; the corners rather than the sides face into the choir, as the octagon had been turned half a phase. On the east side of the transept, the alternation of supports is reversed, giving two circular piers, then one octagonal pier. These variations were not taken up in the nave, which has many more sections. Here, circular piers with four engaged columns were used throughout. The differences in detail between the choir, transept, and nave do not disrupt the uniformity of the whole, but they do prevent an impression of complete monotony.

Like the east–west walls, the end walls of the choir and transept largely determine the shape of the building. They are three-storied window walls, rounded to an apse in the choir but flat in the transept. A special feature of the choir is that the choir wall, despite being rounded, does not have the usual cap vaulting but instead rises vertically to the ceiling. The effect is of a flat termination that curves outward, rather than of an apse with its half-dome omitted.

Although all the construction is of high quality, the first really creative achievement was to place a transverse block, rather like a transept, in front of the west end of the nave. This block was meant to have a tower above each of the end bays of the side aisles, that is, slightly indented, which would have resulted in a pair of towers rearing up behind the facade; but only the north tower was built. A wholly unusual screen front was placed in front of the block, consisting of three gigantic arches capped by gables with recessed side walls and flanked by two smaller towers, like outposts. The whole is a monumental version of a triple portal. Where the entrance doors are actually placed in relation to the arches seems to be quite immaterial. Part of the facade's special charm derives from the fact that the middle arch is narrower, and therefore less emphasized, than the lateral ones. This contradicts every visual convention, in which the emphasis increases from the sides to the center. The magnitude of the idea behind the arched portal, which has something immediately enthralling about it, conveys a sense of Norman power, even though

The choir from the southeast

the detailing, with its primarily decorative blind arcading, is pure Early English. There is a feeling that the abbacy wanted to produce a forceful and awe-inspiring status symbol that would match the mighty west front at Ely, which was a sensation in the region. In this the builders were totally successful.

The retro-choir of the New Building, a U-shaped ambulatory surrounding the high choir, looks rather boxy from the outside, making for an odd contrast with the powerful Norman architecture. The interior is a broad, light-filled space with a succession of six fan vaults on each side.

This vaulting, which is a masterpiece of the Late Perpendicular style, spans the room like light palm fronds, transporting the viewer into an enchanted palm grove that has been transformed into delicate filigree stonework. The New Building was completed in 1508. Its vaulting is so closely related to the rib vaults of King's College Chapel in Cambridge that one can assume it is by the same architect, James Wastell.

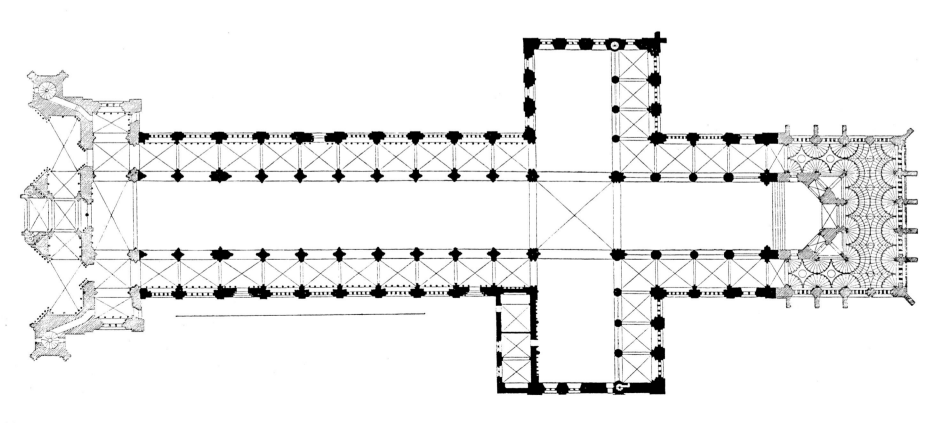

Lincoln

The first bishop of Lincoln was a Norman named Remigius. Earlier he had been the almoner of Fécamp Abbey in Normandy, and had financed a ship and soldiers for William the Conqueror for the forthcoming invasion of England; as a reward, William appointed him bishop of Dorchester-on-Thames. In 1072, the king transferred the bishop's seat to the hill of Lindum (Lincoln), which had been fortified since Roman times and was near a royal fortress. Here, Remigius immediately started to build a cathedral, which was consecrated in 1092, two days after the bishop's death. It was a three-aisled structure, about 328 ft. (100 m) long with a transept and two towers at the west end. Only the lower parts of the towers and, most importantly, the entrance facade have been preserved. The latter comprises a sequence of three gigantic arches, the tallest in the center, with a smaller arch on either side, suggesting that they are the "children" of the large one. The motif of a monumental entrance arch was not unusual on the Continent, following the erection of Charlemagne's palatine chapel in Aachen, but the idea of having three arched portals rather than one, and to extend this further with small lateral ones to make five in all, was unique. The facade thus became a powerful triumphal gateway, a cathedral's monument to supremacy.

The cathedral burned down in 1137 or 1139. Bishop Alexander, known as "the Magnificent," the third Norman bishop of Lincoln, authorized rebuilding, possibly with vaulting. The three portals on the west facade, with the frieze of statues above the central one, and the lower stories of the towers are from this period. The corners of the side towers were rounded off and strengthened with pierlike polygonal spiral staircases that project forward, while the walls were divided into tiers of delicate arcaded galleries. Here, the bishop really lived up to his nickname, "the Magnificent," for this work is in complete contrast to the simple, bare volume of the arches.

Around the middle of the 13th century, the facade was enlarged with a broad screen culminating in small octagonal towers. Its main motif is the blind arcading of the large upper gallery. It consists of narrow columned arcades with pointed lancets, which are as uniform as the strictly ordered phalanx of an army, and extend over the whole width of the facade. The wall of lancets is interrupted in the middle by the central arch, which was raised considerably in the same period and given a magnificent gable, which affirmed its status as the main motif in the screen front. The whole facade is uncompromisingly abrupt. In 1420, this effect was mitigated by raising the towers considerably and building up

the spiral staircases on the corners to such a height that the newels surround the body of the tower like upright lances. Contrasting with the width of the facade, the pair of soaring towers standing closely behind it display an almost arrogant pride, originally emphasized further by spires, which were removed in 1807. Seen from a distance, these are joined by the even taller and more massive crossing tower. From the west, the view offers a closed group of three towers above the main facade, one of the most imposing architectural landscapes that the Middle Ages produced.

The parts of the cathedral adjacent to the west facade were completely new Gothic additions, built in several phases. The first opportunity was provided by an earthquake in 1185, during which the Norman building was said to have burst apart, which indicates that it was vaulted. One year later, Hugh of Avalon, a Carthusian, was appointed bishop. He had been brought to England a decade earlier by the king from the Grande Chartreuse near Grenoble. In 1192, he commissioned the architect Geoffrey de Noiers to build a new choir; modeled on Canterbury, it had its own transept with two east chapels on each arm. It was completed by 1200, the year Hugh died. He was canonized in 1220.

The Hugh Choir is a more lavish version of the canons' choir in Canterbury Cathedral, which it surpassed by increasing the number of motifs employed. In every respect the architect showed himself to be unusually imaginative. The high point is provided by the vaulting in the high choir, the famous Crazy Vaults. Here the architect's passionate inventiveness veered toward the eccentric. According to the plan of the bays, the vaults should have been normal transverse ribbed vaults, but these were deliberately set at an oblique angle, the main cells offset at the apex, which is marked by a ridge rib. As a result, the diagonal ribs, instead of running all the way across, stop at the ridge. But there are two of these diagonal ribs rather than one, which gives the vault a rhomboidal shape that runs diagonally across its center. This shape is visually striking and, because it is not axially justified, it looks as if it is distorted. The Crazy Vaults, which are roughly contemporary with Chartres Cathedral, had no previous models and no successors.

An equally singular solution was the treatment of the end of the choir, which has not been preserved but has been excavated. As a result, we know it was polygonal, in the shape of half a hexagon, and surrounded by an ambulatory that at the apex of the choir opened onto a hexagonal chapel. Its size suggests that, like other chapter houses, it was vaulted from a central column. It is especially sad that this original structure was replaced later. The architect's talents are perhaps most clearly shown in the front walls of the choir transept, which combines pier buttresses, gables, and groups of lancet windows in the most harmonious way.

After the Hugh Choir, the main transept, with a series of eastern chapels, and the nave were built over a period of about 50 years, up to 1250. The works suffered a setback when, in 1239, the newly completed crossing tower collapsed. The Early English style was brought to an even greater level of opulence in the nave, especially in the gallery openings. Something new was also added to the central nave: a fine configuration of ribs. The customary ribbed vault was extended with additional ribs, on the one hand with a continuous ridge rib, as in the Hugh Choir, and on the other hand with tiercerons and clusters of triple ribs. No fewer than seven ribs fan out from every engaged column at the edges of the bays, including the transverse arch, which is matched in size and profile to the ribs and has completely lost its distinction as an arch separating the bays. This produced a series of vaults supported by a dense framework of ribs, with sharply pointed cells cutting in from the sides. All of this was done to make the vaulting as rich as the walls already were.

The glory of the cathedral's interior is first and foremost the present eastern part of the choir, the Angel Choir, so called after the angels in the spandrels of the triforium arcade. It was built between 1256 and about 1280 as a place to venerate St. Hugh, whose relics were moved there, and at the same time served as a retro-choir, ambulatory, and Lady Chapel. These functions were identified, not architecturally, but by the liturgical furniture installed there. The Angel Choir is without question the finest instance of the transition from the late Early English to the Decorated style.

The elevation of the east–west walls was essentially the same as in the nave, but its magnificent decoration was taken a step further toward perfection. The only new element was the tracery, which replaced the earlier lancets. This is especially clear on the straight east wall. In buildings in the Early English style, whole groups of lancet windows were installed on the east wall, which is the focus of the choir. These were arranged to produce fascinating effects in the front of the choir transept at Lincoln. Now, however, the east wall consisted of one gigantic window filled with tracery. Its component parts are the pointed arch, the circle, and the multifoil. The large format of the window is filled with two tracery windows, each with four lights, placed side by side and crowned by a large upper circle. The whole

Decorated Romanesque column shafts and Norman devil and chevron ornaments on the west portal

arrangement is clearly defined by a sober hierarchy of shapes using three different thicknesses of stone. This window, which sits within an elaborately profiled arch, is an ideal example of the Geometrical variant of the Decorated style.

Tracery also frames the openings in the triforium and the clerestory windows. The latter still have a double-arched outline in the old English tradition, and a passage. The tracery shapes are a purely French import, but blend effortlessly with the elevation, which follows the English tradition. It is surprising that tracery, which in France had reached its apogee, was so long absent from the lancet windows of England. But now the lancet window was constantly being used in various grouped or graduated combinations and in fact became the determining element of this form of architecture.

Lincoln is the best proof of this, most noticeably in the Chapter House, which was built around 1235. This 10-sided building has a central support surrounded by 10 extremely thin Purbeck shafts with double lancet windows in the enclosing walls. This building was the first masterpiece of its kind, and during the Decorated period would be followed by several others.

The cathedral had such an effect on its visitors that by the 13th century the unknown author of a *Life of St. Hugh*, published in 1220, broke into metaphorical raptures when describing the building. The Purbeck shafts, which were placed around the piers in the choir, reminded him of slender maidens dancing in a ring; the vaults reminded him of birds sitting on the columns and spreading their wings to fly high into the clouds. The descriptions of the two round windows in the transept, which the author called the Dean's Eye (the north one) and the Bishop's Eye (the south one) are still proverbial. The Dean's Eye has been preserved in its original form, but the Bishop's Eye was renovated in 1320 in the Curvilinear style, in which the tracery emulates the natural veins of leaves. This pattern is just as strange in the history of tracery as the Crazy Vaults are in the story of vaulting. The Early English style at Lincoln started with an eccentric design and the Decorated style ended with another. This idiosyncratic approach is found nowhere else.

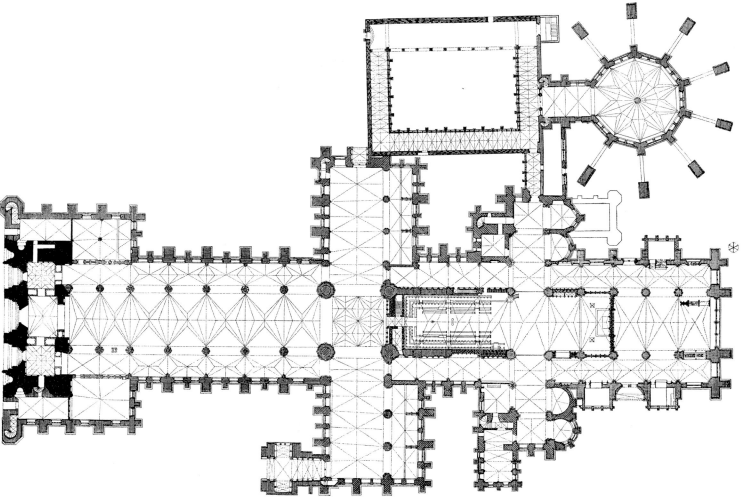

150

155

Durham

Durham was built thanks to St. Cuthbert, who was bishop of Lindisfarne on Holy Island off the northwest coast of England in the 7th century. Because of Viking raids toward the end of the 9th century, his holy remains were brought inland to the better-protected narrow ridge of Durham in the far north of England, which is enclosed on three sides by a river. The Normans gained a foothold here in 1071, when they built a border fortress against the Scots, which closed off access to the ridge. In the same year, William the Conqueror installed a bishop from France. When the bishop wanted to replace the monastery, with which he found himself in mounting conflict, he was killed by the monks.

From 1081 another bishop, also a Frenchman, took office and at the same time received from William the Conqueror the rights of a Count Palatine. With these privileges, he was able to enrich himself sufficiently to be able to vow to pay for the new cathedral building from his own pocket, while leaving the monks and prior responsible for the construction of the monastery buildings. The foundation stone was laid in 1093, but the bishop died only three years later. His successor, yet another Frenchman by birth, had been the king's tax collector, in which position he had acquired a good command of the art of intrigue. Nor was he a poor man. When the remains of St. Cuthbert were placed in his new burial site at the east end of the church in 1104, the choir may have been completed. Finally, after the second bishop to direct the building work died in 1128, the monks carried on building on their own during the subsequent five-year vacancy. They brought the construction to completion in 1133, although the west towers were not finished until 1220.

Shortly before this, a chapel with five aisles, the so-called Galilee Chapel, was built in front of the west facade and its three portals. Here, the mortal remains of the Venerable Bede were interred, which the sacristan of Durham had stolen in 1022 from the monastery at Jarrow, where the great historian had died in 735. As a space the Galilee Chapel is a remarkable invention; it consists of five parallel halls with longitudinal arcaded walls without any subdivision into bays. The motifs that determine the character of the chapel are typical Norman chevron arches, here as razor-sharp as shark's teeth and supported on quatrefoil columns. Because of the many columns and arches, people often are reminded of the forest of columns in a Moorish mosque, and in fact the chapel does have something unusually exotic about it, which makes it unique in England.

The Norman cathedral is for the most part well preserved.

Only the choir was substantially altered. From 1242, following the plans of the architect, Richard of Farnham, a transverse structure was added, a second transept from the same period as the retro-choir and ambulatory. This replaced the original termination of three graduated apses, because more altar sites were needed. To the east, facing the steep slope to the river below, the level, richly decorated facade, supported by buttresses, forms a frontage in which the brusque strength of the Norman legacy seems to live on. The transept is the Chapel of the Nine Altars, a building in the Early English style, in which each of the nine altars has its own lancet window. The direct prototype for this was the slightly earlier eastern part of the Cistercian church of Fountains Abbey. In conjunction with this addition, the stone vaults of the high choir, which had already shown the first signs of cracks and structural damage at the beginning of the 13th century—a hundred years after their creation—were replaced by the present rib vaults. Finally, from 1455, the present tower was erected in place of the Norman crossing tower, whose wooden spire had burned down after being struck by lightning in 1429. This powerful square structure, despite its late date, still has the same defiant force as earlier Norman architecture. The Norman influence appears to have remained quietly dominant long after the cathedral was founded.

Durham had an original overall length of 394 ft. (120 m), which puts it in the ranks of medium-sized Norman cathedrals. The steep slopes of the ridge to the east and west were a natural boundary, and from the outset prevented extension in depth, as usually happened elsewhere. The nave has only eight bays (as distinct from Winchester with 12, Ely with 13, and Norwich with 14). This makes Durham Cathedral much more compact and self-contained. It is indisputably the most powerful of the Norman cathedrals, not in size, but in the visual effect it has on the viewer.

The other Norman cathedrals, for example Ely, are characterized by their seemingly endless three-storied arcade walls and tightly packed piers running from east to west, sometimes with a variation in the types of pier used, and sometimes not. Their walls form sections, but not bays. It is different in Durham. The dividing arcades here, as tall as the gallery and clerestory put together, are powerfully emphasized. Moreover, their arches are broader, which is why the side aisles also make a spatial contribution. Above all, the variation in supports is given great emphasis. The main piers with their circular columns stand in the most severe contrast to the cylindrical circular piers. These veritable colossi are at their best when left freestanding, and clearly exhibit the massive weight of their stone cylinders. The Norman decorative elements—chevrons, flutes, and diaper patterns—densely enfold the faces of the cylinders like a tapestry. In this way the circular piers are treated as architectural sculptures. These piers, on which the structure is firmly and unshakably founded, are the unforgettable hallmark of Durham, a design well equipped to withstand the forces of nature.

Each main pier is faced with a cluster of triple engaged columns that continue up the wall. The alternation of piers thus involves the whole wall, as was done earlier at Jumièges in Normandy. They led the architect to make the crucial decision to connect the engaged columns straight across the nave with transverse arches that are strongly and richly molded. These transverse arches now subdivide the nave into double bays. The next decision was to vault the double bays. Because of the large intervals in the arcade, the double bays are not square, but have a longitudinal oblong plan that makes them visibly drawn out. Because of this, the architect did not vault the double bay with a single rib vault, but with two of them, which form transverse oblongs, as in the Late Gothic period. The vaults do not have a separating transverse arch in the middle of the bay; the transverse arches are confined to the edges of the bays. This form of vault could be termed a "double vault," corresponding to the "double bay."

The transverse arches are pointed, while the diagonal arches are rounded. This combined use of pointed and rounded arches was later used in French Gothic vaults, but these vaults are completely sensational, because they have cross ribs rather than the older groin vaults.

The rib vaults in the cathedral's nave were not created until after 1100. However, the choir, begun in 1093, already had vaults with cross ribs, which have been preserved in their original condition in the side aisles. In the vaulting of the choir, which in the 13th century replaced the old dilapidated vaults, the engaged columns suggest that the original shape of the vaults was retained apart from small differences of detail such as the newly added lateral arches. The choir vaults are, as in the nave, double vaults, but they have a separating transverse arch in the middle of the double bay.

In the choir, the vaults already had a system of engaged columns, which for their date is surprisingly early, and the original transverse arches and ribs of the choir side aisles are richly molded. The architect was far ahead of all his European colleagues; his work represents a solitary, pioneering achievement that is almost unprecedented. He success-

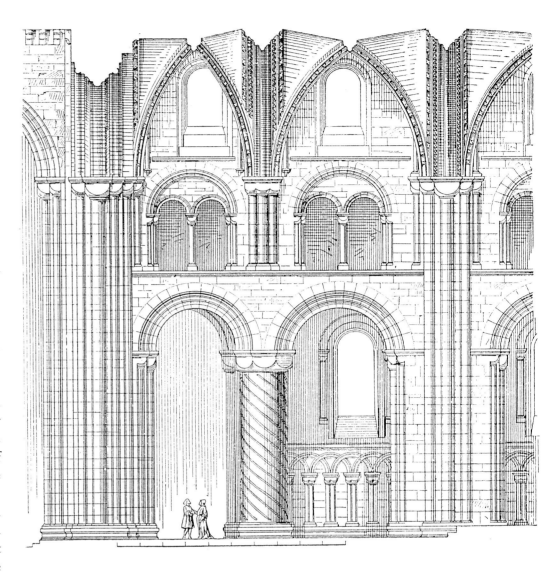

Choir elevation

fully built large-format rib vaults that are among the earliest in Europe, and may relate to Speyer Cathedral and perhaps constructions in northern Italy such as S. Abbondio in Como. In addition, he was the first to create a workable shaft-rib system; what is more, no sooner had he invented the ribs than he gave them sophisticated profiles. Finally, he used pointed transverse arches in conjunction with rounded diagonal ribs, thereby anticipating a crucial achievement of the Gothic style. All this had little to do with Norman architecture in England, and yet the architect maintained the closest ties with this tradition. Indeed, he added something further to the powerful effect of Norman buildings, so that Durham, although an exceptional case, has generally become the embodiment of the Norman style.

It is not certain whether the architect actually brought the building to completion. On the west wall of the transept and in the central nave, the vaulting plan seems to have been interrupted. There, on the upper wall, the engaged columns leading to the arches were omitted, although they had already been installed in the choir and east wall of the transept. In the end, however, vaults were also added in these locations, with corbels supporting the ribs. With these vaults, the full grandeur of the conception, as it had already been realized in the choir, was now achieved.

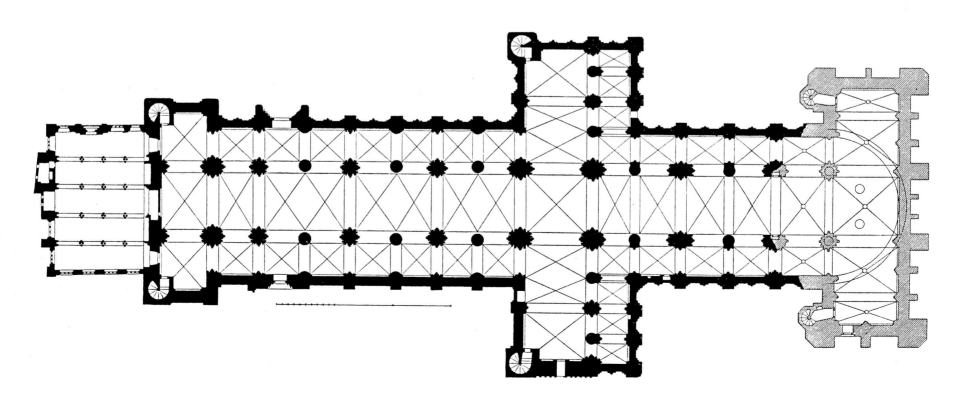

Italy

Architectural History

The medieval history of Italy begins with the Carolingian kings, Pépin and Charlemagne, who incorporated the northern Italian kingdom of Lombardy, with its capital at Pavia, into their own Frankish empire. After his decisive victory in 774, Charlemagne could then call himself *Rex Francorum et Langobardorum*. Pépin, who had been invited into the country by the pope to protect him against the Lombards, and had assumed patronage over the Roman church, founded the papal states in central Italy in 776 with the so-called Donation of Pépin. In southern Italy, meanwhile, the old Byzantine rule continued.

The subsequent history of Italy was somewhat chaotic. Split into numerous small states that vied constantly with each other, northern and southern Italy fell under foreign rule. From the time of Emperor Otto the Great (936–73), northern Italy was part of the Holy Roman Empire, though more and more of the cities, especially those in wealthy Lombardy, would fight for and gain their independence from the emperors, from the Salians to the Hohenstaufens.

The result of this turmoil was that the city-states, with their determined separatist movements, prevented any greater national unity, but produced a tremendous diversity of cultural and spiritual expressions. This was particularly true of Venice, whose fleet enabled it to become a world power; but it also applied to other coastal cities, like Genoa and Pisa, as well as powerful Milan in Lombardy, and Florence and Siena in Tuscany.

In southern Italy, Sicily was conquered by the Saracens in the ninth century, while Byzantium retained only Calabria and Puglia. The remaining principalities were spheres of influence of the Holy Roman Empire. From the beginning of the 11th century, the Normans poured into the country in large numbers and after countless battles conquered southern Italy and Sicily, legitimizing their rule as a papal fiefdom. With the coronation in Palermo of Roger II as king of Sicily, Calabria, and Puglia in 1130, the southern Italian Norman realm, the Monarchia Sicula, became a hereditary kingdom. In 1194, it fell to the Hohenstaufen emperor, Henry VI, who asserted the claims to inheritance of his wife, Constance, the daughter of Roger II. Henry's son, the Hohenstaufen heir to Sicily, and later Emperor Frederick II, made this southern empire a tightly organized and administered state.

After the fall of the Hohenstaufen emperors, Charles of Anjou, the son of Louis VIII of France, took possession of the southern Italian realm, and made Naples his capital. In 1282, Sicily fell to Peter of Aragon after the Sicilian Vespers rebellion. The mainland part of the kingdom remained with the House of Anjou until it passed to Naples in 1442 and finally to Aragon in 1504; from then on, until well into the 18th century, it was governed by Spanish viceroys.

The development of architecture in Italy is more coherent than the course of its history would lead one to expect. From the Late Classical period until into the 12th century, occasionally even into the Gothic period, the same building type appears again and again like a leitmotif throughout the architectural story: the three-aisled colonnaded basilica, with either open rafters or a flat ceiling. After the church of S. Giovanni in Laterano was established as the seat of the bishops of Rome in the fourth and fifth centuries, and both

Above:
Torcello Cathedral, interior looking east

Below:
Aquileia Cathedral, interior looking east

Opposite:
Lucca Cathedral, facade and campanile

Trani Cathedral

Above:
View from the southeast

Above right:
The nave looking east

the apostolic churches, St. Peter's and St. Paul's outside the Walls, had been built as enormous five-aisled colonnaded basilicas, the colonnaded basilica remained the favored type, although usually reduced to three aisles and on a considerably smaller scale. In Rome alone, more than 30 churches of this type were built before the end of the Romanesque period, including, from early Christian times, S. Maria Maggiore and S. Sabina. As early as Old St. Peter's, which Constantine the Great had been anxious to build, and particularly in the early Middle Ages, spoils from Classical times, which were abundantly available, especially in Rome, were used for the columns. In the rest of Italy, the cathedral in Grado, north of Venice, and four churches in Ravenna have retained features from the early Christian period, whereas Ravenna's five-aisled cathedral was replaced by a Baroque building.

Most colonnaded basilicas, for example, the cathedral of Torcello in the Venice lagoon (rebuilt 1008), have closely spaced arcades in the early Christian manner. Colonnades were installed in the earliest times, most importantly in Old St. Peter's, and these have a horizontal entablature instead of arches. When ancient entablature blocks were available, builders gladly incorporated them, which led to strangely patched-together colonnades, such as that of S. Prassede in Rome. The walls of the basilicas changed little in the course of the centuries, although the nave became steeper and narrower and the clerestory windows smaller in size. There were also arcades of columns with pointed arches, as in the cathedral at Aquileia.

The colonnaded basilicas were embellished both by galleries in the nave, which had small arcades opening onto the central nave, and by a transept with apses or with an attached quadrangular choir that terminated in an apse. Both galleries, which were frequently used in Byzantine architecture, and transepts were widely employed in the Romanesque church architecture of the Late Classical period. Typical examples are the galleries in S. Agnese and St. Lawrence outside the Walls and the transepts in the two large apostolic churches.

From the very beginning, the exteriors of these buildings had no towers; campaniles, or bell towers, were placed next to churches only from the beginning of the Middle Ages. These freestanding towers, sometimes of considerable height and structural complexity, have remained characteristic of Italian architecture. Several have achieved great fame, above all the Leaning Tower of Pisa, but also the campaniles of S. Marco in Venice and Florence Cathedral (see Plates 185, 164, 190, and ill. page 4).

The colonnaded basilica was certainly a time-honored institution sanctified by tradition, but as a building type it was very simple and offered only limited scope for architectural innovation. It was a relatively economical structure, especially when the shafts of the columns could be taken from older buildings. This might have been the decisive factor in the wide distribution and long life of this building type, not just for monastery churches but also for cathedrals. Italian bishoprics were considerably smaller than those in other European countries, and therefore had smaller incomes. This occasionally accounted for some colonnaded basilicas being very unassuming, even though they are cathedrals, as in Fiesole, Viterbo, and Tuscania. In others the arcades were at least given a variety of supports, for example in the cathedrals of Ferentino and Anagni. Many of these cathedrals were later converted or replaced by new buildings, probably because there was nothing remarkable anymore about the old colonnaded basilicas.

In southern Italy, the colonnaded basilica was equally widespread, and experienced a new flowering under Norman rule. Beginning with the Benedictine mother house at Monte Cassino, where from 1066 Abbot Desiderius built the abbey church as a colonnaded basilica with a nonprojecting three-apse transept, cathedrals with similar layouts were built in quick succession in Salerno, Amalfi, Capua, and Ravello, as well as in Taranto and Otranto. After construction had begun on a new basilica with a gallery in the harbor town of Bari in Puglia for the relics of St. Nicholas, brought there from Myra in 1087, the model was followed by the cathedrals of Bari, Trani, Bitonto, and Barletta. Gallery openings were installed above the column arcade with a symmetrical row of triple arches within an enclosing arch. A special feature of the Puglian buildings is the way that a distinctive arcade of columns, like an aqueduct, was added to the outer wall of the side aisles, topped by a dwarf gallery in the area usually occupied by the main gallery. The model for this was once again S. Nicola in Bari.

The earlier Byzantine building tradition of domed churches was taken up again in about 1080 in the Puglian cathedral at Canosa: a three-aisled columned church with a transept, its T-shaped layout is surmounted by domes. Three

sit over the transept and two over the nave. The three-aisled Molfetta Cathedral, begun after 1150, which has three broad bays with cruciform piers, each with a four-arched framework, is also vaulted with domes, some erected on squinches, and some on pendentives. The side aisles, on the

Above:
Bari, S. Nicola

Below:
Bitonto Cathedral

Palermo Cathedral, from the east (archive photograph)

The most important Norman buildings were Palermo Cathedral, which retains its orginal east side, with its powerful transept block flanked by turrets and the projecting apse, and the cathedrals at Monreale and Cefalù. The patron of Cefalù, begun in 1131, was Roger II, the first king of the Normans' southern empire, who wanted his tomb placed there. The east end has a three-part choir with graduated apses and a transept, and is partly rib-vaulted. Its width-to-height ratio of about 1:3 makes it seem extremely tall. The nave, in contrast, thanks to a change in plan, is a low-built colonnaded basilica with stilted pointed arches suggesting an Islamic influence.

The building of Monreale (see pages 394–405), begun in 1174, was initiated by King William II, the last legitimate Norman king before the rule of the Hohenstaufens. Here, the east end, as at Cefalù, has a graduated choir, but it forms a kind of cruciform central structure with the crossing and the transverse arms. The colonnaded hall of the nave is connected to it, and has a west facade with two towers. But what is most striking and precious about Monreale Cathedral is the ornamentation. On the inside everything is covered with a series of Byzantine-inspired mosaics; outside, the east end is decorated with intersecting pointed arches and ornamental bands and disks, forming a dense, tapestry-like pattern and conveying a fairy-tale impression of Oriental splendor.

Overall, the southern Italian and Sicilian Norman buildings have little in common with the Norman architecture of Normandy and England, apart from their general magnificence and the design of the arches in particular. Here in the south the Normans continued the indigenous tradition, but they were also open to both Byzantine and Islamic influences, readily adapting any foreign cultures to their own. Unlike other nations, the Normans remained undefeated by Mediterranean culture. In Normandy and England the Normans established their own distinct style, developing an architecture of power with a typical Norman character.

Under Hohenstaufen rule in the southern empire, which lasted just over half a century, the interests of the imperial house were directed not toward churches but toward castles and palaces, of which the most famous, Castel del Monte, became the "Crown of Puglia."

Pisa, which in politics always stood on the side of the emperor, arose almost overnight as a shining new center for architecture. After the Pisan fleet—at that time the strongest in the Tyrrhenian Sea—had annihilated the Saracen vessels off of Palermo in 1063, allowing the Pisans and Normans to

other hand, have barrel vaults with an internal buttressing system. The complicated vault shapes are all the more noticeable in Puglia, because large Norman buildings were not vaulted elsewhere. These dome structures, which show an unmistakable Islamic influence, are also found in Palermo. S. Giovanni degli Eremiti has five domes, each very distinct from the others, again arranged in a T-shaped configuration, while S. Cataldo, with its particularly Islamic appearance, has three domes, all using a squinch system to form the circular base.

jointly capture Palermo, building started on the cathedral in Pisa that same year (see pages 340–351). The Saracen loot provided unlimited materials, which can be seen in the building. The Byzantine emperor is said to have made the later highly praised architect, Buscheto, available to the people of Pisa, and this would explain why the cathedral resembles a Byzantine import, at least in its early stages and in the basic structural ideas. It was not completed until 1200. It is a five-aisled colonnaded basilica with a long, projecting three-aisled transept, and galleries on the north and south sides, which stand two aisles wide above the side aisles. It was the most extravagant medieval building in the whole of the country's architecture.

The building's love of splendor begins with the exterior, where it is expressed in tiers of blind arcading and ornamental pilasters, in colored bands, and in the squared-off profile—a Pisan hallmark. The cathedral's magnificent aspect is emphasized further on the facade and the main apse, where multistoried galleries of columned arcades are placed in front of passages. This style is completely dominant in the circular campanile, the Leaning Tower, where galleries cloak the cylindrical core above the pedestal in a continuous flow for an entire six stories. The cathedral, which was intended to be a proud symbol of victory, became a monument to extravagant wealth and luxurious excess, a showpiece of white and partially colored marble cladding designed to impress observers with its sumptuousness.

Cefalù Cathedral

Above left:
West facade

Above:
View from the northeast

Left:
View through the nave to the choir

Troia Cathedral, facade

The city of Florence was an aspiring competitor to Pisa; unlike Ghibelline Pisa, Florence was Guelph, opposing German imperial rule in Italy. Florence's stance soon showed itself in a different kind of architectural wealth: multicolored, ornamental paneled marble incrustations in combination with blind wall openings and arrangements of pilasters. It is so closely allied to the Classical period that this architecture is termed "Proto-Renaissance." It was in Florence that the "true" Renaissance of the 15th century got its start. The characteristic example is the principal state building, the Florentine baptistery, said soon after 1300 to be the old Roman Temple of Mars. Another example of rich cross-section facades is the colonnaded basilica of S. Miniato, while a third might have been the old cathedral of S. Reparata, which after only a little more than a century was replaced by the present, larger cathedral.

Almost at the same time as Pisa Cathedral, around 1063 or a little earlier, a second large, characteristically Byzantine structure was undertaken in Italy, although it was totally different. This was S. Marco in Venice, the private church of the Doges (see pages 310–321). S. Marco was not the seat of the patriarchs, and therefore was technically not a cathedral, but it could claim that status purely on the basis of its sumptuous, voluptuous appointments. Structurally, S. Marco is a duplicate of the Apostles church in Constantinople, the great building that was later destroyed by the Turks, and that after the Hagia Sophia was the second miraculous accomplishment of Justinian imperial architecture. The Apostles church lived on in S. Marco.

Both structures were Byzantine cruciform churches, that is, based on the plan of a Greek cross with five pendentive domes distributed above the cross. The west arm of the cross in S. Marco is additionally enclosed by a surrounding U-shaped narthex. In the Italian architecture of the 11th century S. Marco was a foreign body, yet the building found a successor to some extent in the "Santo" at Padua. This church of the Franciscan St. Antony was, and remains, one of the most popular places of pilgrimage. Less than a hundred years later, the design of S. Marco was repeated literally, using the cruciform design and even the same types of pier, in St. Front in Périgueux, one of the cruciform churches of Aquitaine, southern France. Here, the builders borrowed the pure architecture of S. Marco but omitted its mosaics and other ornamentation.

Ancona Cathedral on the Adriatic is also laid out as a Greek cross. Here, in the course of the 12th century, the older three-aisled colonnaded basilica was made into the transept of a new three-aisled colonnaded basilica. Both

This delight in ostentatious display was immediately taken up in a number of other cathedrals, from those in Lucca and Pistoia to Troia Cathedral in faraway Puglia. The outstanding features of the cathedral complex in Lucca are the mighty, richly constructed quadrangular campanile (unlike the circular Leaning Tower) and the facade (see ill. page 298). This cross-section facade, with its gable and sloping sides, mimics the cross-section of the basilica lying behind it, although it projects a little beyond it, like a screen. The facade is composed entirely of multistoried, superimposed arcaded galleries, some of which are blind, as in Pisa, but most of which open with a passage behind. The galleries, which have as many as five stories, form an arcaded curtain, an exuberantly triumphant variation on the arcade motif, which here covers every surface.

intersect at the center, and have a square crossing with a dome. The concept, which is reminiscent of Pisa Cathedral, may have been taken from Eastern cruciform churches—for example, those in Syria—which were laid out in a similar fashion. This is not surprising, given Ancona's coastal location.

The course of development in northern Italy, that is, in the regions that belonged to the Holy Roman Empire, and whose bishops not infrequently supported imperial politics, was entirely different from that in southern and central Italy. Here, around 1100, there was a changeover. New structures were no longer built as colonnaded basilicas; instead, vaulting was installed from the beginning. The vaulting generally followed the design invented a little earlier in the Salian emperor's cathedral in Speyer. This intersecting system comprised square double bays in the central nave, enclosed in the side aisles by two smaller square bays, a layout that made it necessary to alternate the supports, with massive main piers at the edges of the double bays and intermediate supports in between. The main piers had to support the engaged columns going up to the vault arches and connecting with the transverse and lateral arches, and, in the case of rib vaults, with the diagonal ribs as well. Over the crossing, or, in the absence of a transept, over the choir, many of these buildings have an octagonal dome with squinches, similar to the Rhenish imperial cathedrals.

Nave galleries were often employed in the wall structure, like those in southern Italian buildings. Their openings to the central nave have various forms: arcaded columns of four arches, as well as double and triple arcades, contained within a larger arch.

At the beginning of this developing trend, the very important monastic church of S. Abbondio in Como, probably begun about 1063, was laid out as a basilica with a flat ceiling in the nave and five graduated aisles. The usual columns in the central nave became tall circular piers. There was no transept; its place was taken by an apsidal choir, consisting of two square bays that form an unusually long east–west choir. Its importance in architectural history lies in its rib vaults, which, if not the earliest, are among the earliest large-scale rib vaults in Europe. The church of S. Abbondio had a great influence in northern Italy.

Some time after 1100, S. Lorenzo in Verona was built with a gallery and alternating supports in the nave with columns for the intermediate supports. The main supports had clustered piers with shafts running up the side of the central nave to the ceiling. Double bays were introduced because of the alternating supports and, in particular, because of the

Left:
Como, S. Abbondio, interior looking east

engaged columns employed. There was no vaulting, however, as was also the case at the earlier Abbey Church of Jumièges in Normandy. Soon afterward, around 1128, at S. Ambrogio in Milan, an unusually broad, low-built galleried church, the ceiling was vaulted using the new intersecting system with rib vaults. A similar method was employed at the Abbey Church of Rivolta d'Adda near Milan, which did not have a gallery, and at S. Michele in Pavia. With all these churches, the clerestory was either entirely absent or consisted of a small window in the lateral wall.

The intersecting system was used in a large format in the cathedrals of the aspiring cities of the Po River plain: Modena, Parma, Piacenza, and Cremona. These cities were economic and political rivals: in the battle between the papacy and the empire, Parma and Cremona stood on the side of the empire, while Piacenza was on the side of the pope. Modena was originally in the papal faction but eventually switched to that of the empire.

The cathedral of Modena (see pages 332–339) was begun in 1099 under the direction of the famous Lombard Lanfranc, who was, according to an inscription, *doctus et aptus*, that is, "learned and suitable." He built a basilica with a clerestory, which had paired gallery openings but no floors to the galleries, which were "false." Originally, the building had a flat ceiling, and every main pier on the edge of the double bays featured a massive pointed arch spanning the central nave. The central nave in this structure is strikingly reminiscent of that of the Abbey Church of Jumièges,

Parma Cathedral

Right:
Facade, campanile,
and baptistery

Below:
View through the nave

where the steep proportions seen in Modena have become lower and wider.

In Parma a cathedral was built beginning in about 1130, based on a square floor plan in the east end, with choir, crossing, and transept arms embellished with apses at the end of the choir, on the side walls, and on the east side of the transept arms. The square floor plan adopted in Parma was used far less in Italy than on the other side of the Alps. The cubic blocks of choir and transept, heightened by the octagonal crossing dome, produce a notably forceful, angular effect on the exterior. The central nave, on the evidence of the alternating supports and engaged columns, was originally intended to have sexpartite vaults, but quadripartite vaults were elected during the actual building process. These form oblong single bays within the double bays, conforming to the more modern bay system rather than to the older intersecting approach.

Fidenza Cathedral, previously Borgo S. Donnino, can be seen as a direct successor to Parma. It was built in 1180 with a similar side elevation, but here the sexpartite vaults originally planned at Parma above the double bays of the central nave have become quadripartite. The false galleries, on the other hand, repeat the model of Modena.

The cathedral at Piacenza, built over a period of more than 100 years, from 1122 to 1235, is marked by its massive circular piers, which in their stout, rollerlike weightiness relate to the colossal piers of Norman architecture in

England. Only the engaged columns alternate, not the piers themselves. They prepare the way for a sexpartite rib vault that is recognizably Gothic. The transept arms in Piacenza are remarkable: they each have three aisles of similar height and width, taller than the side aisles in the nave, but lower than the central nave. Each transept arm is a kind of hall church, with a tall triple arcade and bulky circular piers opening onto the central nave. The crossing, however, surmounted by an octagonal dome, includes only the two eastern arches of the triple arcade, rather than the whole of it. This pushes it eastward, relative to the centerline of the transept, an unusual solution with no obvious architectural reason behind it.

Finally, a cathedral was started in Cremona in 1107. Its internal structure relates equally to Parma and Piacenza: the cruciform main piers are like those at Parma, while the circular intermediate piers reflect Piacenza. The transept was added later, which is why the building, as originally conceived, had no crossing.

All these cathedrals in northern Italy are large brick structures, partially clad with freestone. An external hallmark of this group is the facade, which does not, as in Pisa, Lucca, or Florence, follow the outline of the nave but has its own shape with a large all-embracing gable. These are the so-called screen facades. A model was provided by S. Michele in Pavia. Only Modena conforms to the cross-section of the nave and side aisles (see Plate 178).

The exteriors are characterized by a structural richness typical of northern Italy generally and Lombardy in particular. This can be seen in the pilaster strips and circular engaged columns, the arch friezes and arcaded galleries, and the mostly two-storied porches in the form of a ciborium, or canopied row of columns. These structural forms had for a long time been a particular strength of stonemasons from the Alpine fringe, for example, the artisans from around Lake Como. As sought-after specialists, they were frequently called in to building projects on the other side of the Alps, such as the imperial cathedral in Speyer, where their main task was to create the freestone ornamentation.

The exterior of Ferrara Cathedral, begun around 1135, outshines all other northern Italian cathedrals. (Its interior was later totally changed.) Not just the facade, but the longitudinal elevations are completely covered with blind arcades and arcaded galleries. The concept of the facade is quite extraordinary: it employs recognizably Early Gothic shapes to form a triad of magnificent matching gables, a tripartite showpiece that gives architectural expression to the glory of the Trinity.

Piacenza Cathedral

Left:
West facade

Below left:
Central nave looking east

As in Germany, the Romanesque period in Italy lasted into the 13th century, and occasionally longer, for example at Trent, where the cathedral was not completed until the 14th century but still has an unquestionably Romanesque style. The bishopric of Trent, in fact, belonged to the Holy Roman Empire until 1803.

French-style Gothic was never really adopted in Italy, apart from the international Early Gothic of the Cistercians, for example in Fossanova, south of Rome, where the abbey church nave is almost identical to that of Pontigny in France and Ebrach in Germany. The mendicant Franciscans and Dominicans developed their own Italian Gothic style, building churches that were intended for large congregations; some of these structures are so austere that the expression "sermon barn" has been coined for them. Other churches of the mendicant orders, for example the Frari and Zanipolo (Ss. Giovanni e Paolo) in Venice, are more lavish, and reach dimensions that most Italian bishops and cathedral chapters could only dream of.

There is not one "French" instance among the Gothic cathedrals of Italy. All have strikingly individual characters, and therefore can hardly be compared even with one another. In Siena, the cathedral was begun in the 12th century to a Romanesque design, then raised and vaulted in the Gothic style; work on the east end continued until it was completed

in 1382 (see pages 370–383). Laid out with bays, the interior is characterized by broad, tall, round-arched arcades, the most conspicuous feature of which is the pattern of zebra stripes. In the middle of the cathedral, the arcades widen out from the nave at an angle with the sides, forming a hexagonal domed polygon (the former presbytery), the diameter of which is only a little smaller than the width of the three aisles together.

The cathedral's showpiece is the west facade, begun in 1284. This is rich beyond measure, with three large, round-arched portals crowned by Gothic gables, a central round window, and three pointed gables graduated to give the facade its striking tiered silhouette. Although the framing of the round window is extended sideways to make the window larger, the facade is a serene, complete masterpiece in both its forms and its proportions. Here, both the architecture and the sculpturally powerful reliefs are astonishingly diverse, a quality that is seldom found elsewhere. The facade at Siena is the Italian equivalent of the French type, with portals and a rose window. The design originated not from a professional architect but from a sculptor, Giovanni Pisano, at that time the best in Europe, who here showed himself to be one of the best architects, too.

A little later, in 1310, the facade of the cathedral at Orvieto, where the design was again created by a sculptor,

Lorenzo Maitani (see pages 384–393), emerged to rival the one in Siena. The result—which was believed to have immeasurably improved the prototype by introducing a more systematized structure—is a similar three-gabled frontage with three portals and a rose window. However, the front has become more faceted, and the diversity of relief has been exchanged for a tighter, more regular perpendicular framework. The winner in this competition, so typical of Italian art history, was indisputably Giovanni Pisano.

Orvieto Cathedral, a simple basilica with circular piers, rounded arches, and exposed rafters, is a surprising anachronism. It seems as though the architect was rejecting modern Gothic architecture and trying to revive the early Christian church.

Florence, too, came to rival Siena. Here, the Arte della Lana, the woodworkers' guild, financed the building (see pages 352–369), rather than the bishop and cathedral chapter. Building started in 1296, but the cathedral achieved its present size and shape only after 1357, when the master builder Francesco Talenti introduced a new design. In this cathedral everything is big and simple. The proportions, like the width and height of dividing arcades that reach up nearly to the springing line of the vaults, impart an astonishing hall-like spaciousness, which make the French cathedrals seem narrow and tightly proportioned.

The east end of Florence Cathedral was intended to be the masterpiece that demonstrated the genius of the city. It is a freestanding central structure, exceeding in size any previous ecclesiastical building. The core is an octagon with a diameter of 137.7 ft. (42 m), representing the width of all three aisles put together. Only the Roman Pantheon with its concrete dome has a greater diameter, surpassing Florence by 6.5 ft. (2 m). The octagon was extended by the addition of three polygonal apses, and finally heightened by the mighty dome, whose pointed outline was certainly in place by 1368. However, it was not until 1420, after 14 years of work, that one of the greatest engineering accomplishments of all time was successfully carried out under the direction of Filippo Brunelleschi. The dome above the four-part architectural mountain of a substructure, richly decorated with marble, made the Florentine cathedral one of the wonders of Europe, arousing constant admiration and astonishment (see ills. pages 4–5).

In 1390, even before the vaulting of the dome had begun in Florence, the citizens of neighboring Bologna entered the fray, with the parish church of S. Petronio. It was planned as a 597-ft. (182 m) -long, three-aisled basilica with a three-aisled transept that extends for 449 ft. (137 m). As in the east end at Florence, the crossing was supposed to become an octagon spanning the full width of the three aisles. If it had been completed, it would have been the largest church in the world. In the end, however, only the nave was completed, which is nevertheless very substantial, and in its location in the city S. Petronio looks like a cathedral.

The competition for the largest church had begun even earlier, in Milan under Duke Gian Galeazzo Visconti (see pages 322–331). Around 1386 the cathedral was undertaken to a French plan, although in fact the work looked less toward France than toward Cologne Cathedral, which ranked among the largest Gothic cathedrals ever, and now was clearly to be surpassed in Milan. The nave was laid out with five aisles and the transept with three. In the choir, however, the French cathedral model was reduced in size in favor of a simple 5/8 termination, and the chapels were omitted from the ambulatory. The five aisles were graduated in height, making it possible for the inner side aisles to have their own clerestory. However, the windows in the central nave and in the inner side aisles are too small for adequate illumination, which is why the interior is so dark that the vaults of the central nave are filled with shadows.

During the building works, renowned specialists were constantly brought to Milan from outside, including Frenchmen who are hardly known elsewhere, and, among those from Germany, some members of the Parler group, like Ulrich von Ensingen, the master builder of the titanic towers of Ulm and Strasbourg. But all these master builders left the masons' lodge under acrimonious circumstances, returning to their homelands after only a short period of activity. During construction of the dome above the crossing, Renaissance artists like Leonardo and Bramante were engaged. In 1572 the works were finished for the time being, but the exterior was not completed until the 19th century, which is why it exhibits more Gothic decorative work than any other building, to the point that it appears to be enclosed in a cocoon. This effect is, in part, the result of adding Neo-Gothic to the original Gothic.

Venice

Venice, located on islands in a lagoon, began as a refuge for inhabitants of the mainland during a period of mass migration. From about the year 1000 it grew in an unprecedented manner to become the most important maritime and trading power of the Mediterranean region. Nominally under the suzerainty of the Byzantine emperor, but in fact completely free, it was governed by a strict, self-regulating oligarchy under the leadership of its doges. Venice went on to enlarge its economic empire step by step, and founded numerous trading posts on the coasts of the eastern Mediterranean. In the 12th century, the city outstripped even the Byzantine empire. Finally, in 1204 the imperial capital of Constantinople was conquered by soldiers of the Fourth Crusade, who had been transported there on Venetian ships under the overall command of the venerable doge Enrico Dandolo. The newly installed Latin empire came under Venetian control. Although the empire lasted only until 1261, Venice, the *Serenissima*, had at last become a world power, a status it was to maintain for centuries. After the death of the duke of Milan, Gian Galeazzo Visconti, in 1402, left a power vacuum, Venice conquered northeastern Italy to the very gates of Milan, and a Venetian state was at last created with secure borders on the mainland.

There was a bishop's seat in Venice from the late eighth century, in the district of Olivolo-Castello on the edge of the city area; its cathedral church of S. Pietro in Castello probably dates from the ninth century. The bishops were subject to the Byzantine patriarchate of Grado, which had freed itself from the Lombard and later Frankish patriarchate of Aquileia. The patriarchs of Grado held sway only over maritime Venice, that is, over the coastal area of the lagoon, which was tiny in comparison to the ecclesiastical province of Aquileia. From 1156 the patriarchs of Grado lived on the Rialto in Venice. Pope Nicholas V did not react to this state of affairs until 1451, when he dissolved the old patriarchate of Grado and promoted the bishopric of Olivolo-Castello by transferring the title of Grado to the patriarchate of Venice with its seat at S. Pietro in Castello.

The bishops and patriarchs were of little importance politically in the republic of Venice. The ecclesiastical center was located not in S. Pietro in Castello, but in S. Marco, after a Venetian expedition in 828 had seized the relics of Mark the Evangelist in Alexandria, and brought them to Venice. The relics, among the most prized of all Christendom, did not come into the custody of the bishops or of the patriarchs, but instead, from the very beginning, were under the protection of the doges, at first kept in a chapel in the doges' palace. The doge, Agnello Partecipazio, commissioned a church to be built north of the palace in honor of St. Mark, whose mortal remains were ceremoniously laid to rest there in 836. St. Mark was the state's patron saint, protector, and guide. The deeds that Venice accomplished took place in his name, and were legitimized by him, including the city's unfettered economic imperialism and the wars it undertook to pursue its own interests. In the ecclesiastical hierarchy, S. Marco was subordinate to the bishops' cathedral of S. Pietro in Castello, but, as the state's holy shrine, it was without doubt the main church in the city. The precedence of S. Marco is clearly shown by the fact that after Napoleon brought about the end of the republic, the seat of the patriarchs was transferred in 1808 to S. Marco, which since then has been the cathedral church, rather than Pietro in Castello.

The original building of S. Marco was severely damaged in a citizens' revolt in 976, during which the doge lost his life. The worst thing about that event was that after the doge's death, no one knew where the relics of Mark were. Had they been burned? The next doge, Orseolo, ordered S. Marco to be rebuilt immediately. This second church, from the evidence of excavations, was built in the shape of a cross, and had a narthex, which for the most part corresponds to the present building. This was begun in 1063, in the same year as the cathedral in Pisa, on the initiative of the doge Domenico Contarini. Apparently, the Venetians of the day were given the choice between making war or building a church: they decided on the church. It was consecrated as early as 1071, the year in which Contarini died. But building was only completed in the year 1094, when the relics of St. Mark— which had been hidden in a pier—happily resurfaced. This miraculous event, the *apparitio*, is recorded on a mosaic in the interior of the church. In one source it is specifically noted that the new building was designed in a similar artistic style (*con simili constructione artificiosa*) as the Holy Apostles Church in Constantinople, that is, like the Emperor Justinian's large, Late Classical edifice, which was destroyed after the conquest of the city by the Turks in 1453, but until then had been as magnificent as Hagia Sophia. With the new building of S. Marco, Venice sought to equal the imperial city, even if their church did not match the size of Holy Apostles.

Contarini's church was built in brick, has been well preserved, and is clad with later, rich ornamentation both outside and inside. It is a Byzantine cruciform church with a dome, which is entirely consistent with the model of the Holy Apostles Church: a central body on the plan of a Greek cross with a pendentive dome above the crossing and a somewhat smaller dome of similar shape over each of the four arms of the cross. Barrel vaults were built between the domes, and the

Gentile Bellini's *Procession in St. Mark's Square* (from the series Legends of the Cross), 1496. (Galleria dell' Accademia, Venice)

load-bearing framework supporting the barrels is made from two-story piers of a complex shape, the so-called quadruple piers. They are not massive, but consist of four individual square piers connected by arches and enclosing a small space in the center. In the nave and in both transverse arms, the dome space is enclosed by barrel-vaulted side aisles connected to the central space by arcades running from pier to pier. Originally, galleries were added to the side aisles by means of intermediate ceilings that rested on the arcades, but the ceilings were later removed to give more light. Narrow passages, the so-called catwalks, are all that remain of the galleries.

In its original condition, the interior was plainer and lighter than today. In the 12th century a start was made on decorating the lower parts of the church with marble slabs and the upper areas with gold mosaics. The vault mosaics are particularly well lit. Light falls on them from the circle of windows at the base of the domes. It is this abundant, shimmering, all-enveloping gold that characterizes the interior, and makes it seem not quite of this world, with a ceremonial, sacred aura that has always been associated with the saints. The gold background, from which the individual depictions of figures and scenes somberly emerge, makes a decisive contribution to the building's atmosphere. The mosaic display was completed around 1300. Refurbishment was often necessary, but the use of paints and paintbrushes was prohibited under threat of punishment. The church's original condition was maintained until people became more concerned about the state of the western section in the 16th century, when mosaics designed by Titian, Tintoretto, Bassano, and others were added.

Although the external architecture of the Contarini building was made entirely of brick, from the very beginning, a narthex with large portals was placed in front of the west end, creating a frontage to St. Mark's Square. These recessed portals, actually a Classical motif, gave the facade an especially authoritative appearance. Typical Byzantine rounded gables one story higher echoed the arched portals, giving the building its unmistakable outline. The narthex, which in the interior is vaulted by a series of small cupolas, was wrapped in a U-shape around the north and south sides of the nave, although on the south it was soon altered again by the addition of a baptistery. All of these elements were decorated with mosaics, and the domes of the western narthex, depicting the Story of Creation, and the three cupolas of the north narthex, with the story of Joseph, are rated among the most outstanding works of mosaic art.

When the Byzantine empire was conquered in 1204, the Venetians brought whole ships' cargoes of booty back home, and decorated their state shrine with it. The exterior was embellished with marble cladding and countless splendid columns, those framing the portals being particularly outstanding in their dense profusion. The most important pieces of loot, however, were the four bronze horses from a Classical Roman quadriga (a two-wheeled chariot drawn by four horses abreast). The horses were set on columns over the central portal, in a position formerly occupied by the four Evangelists, like a sign of victory.

A further enhancement of the building's exterior involved the transformation of the cupolas. Because the five domes could hardly be seen from the outside, a wooden drum carrying a second cupola was placed on top of each of them. In this way, the whole dome area was substantially elevated. Now, for the first time, S. Marco could be seen in the general city skyline, even from a distance. Finally, around 1385, the semicircular gables of the Contarini building were enriched with towerlike niches containing statues and opulently adorned arched attachments. These gave the church a lively new outline and, at least in terms of height, an identifiably Gothic appearance. The result was to make the exterior, as seen from the square, look like a unique treasure house of pure Oriental legend. In his painting *The Procession in St. Mark's Square* (Galleria dell' Accademia, Venice), of 1496, Gentile Bellini captured every detail of the church exterior, down to the facade mosaics.

Finally, there is the isolated campanile on St. Mark's Square, which also belongs to St. Mark's Church. After it collapsed in 1902, an event that is recorded in a photograph, it was rebuilt as a replica. The original tower, with its vertical blind niches, was a 12th-century design, whose upper part was much changed and raised, attaining its final form in 1517. At a height of 312 ft. (95 m), the campanile is one of the tallest in Italy. With its cubic, angular strength, it forms a markedly Western contrast to the church's Byzantine domes and Oriental sumptuousness.

Plates 164–172

164 West facade and campanile from St. Mark's Square
165 The Classical bronze horses on the gallery above the main portal (now replaced by copies)
166 The main portal of the west facade (see Plate 164)
167 View though the western narthex; on the right is the entrance to the church; in the vaults are mosaic scenes of the episode of Noah
168 Small *Genesis* cupola in the western narthex, with a 13th-century mosaic
169 Top: The mortal remains of St. Mark are brought to the basilica in a procession, 13th-century mosaic from the northern portal of the west facade
Bottom: Prayer for the discovery of the relics of St. Mark, 13th-century mosaic in the west wall of the south transept
170 View through the church looking east
171 View from the crossing into the presbytery separated by an iconostasis
172 View upward to the vaulting and cupolas

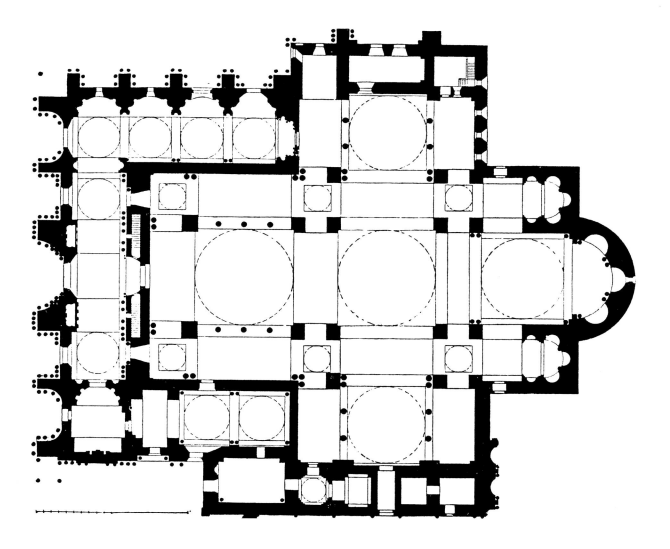

165

166

316 *Italy*

Milan

Milan, the Roman Mediolanum, enjoyed its first flowering in the fourth century, after Diocletian promoted General Maximian to co-emperor, and the city thus became an imperial residence. With the Edict of Milan in 313, Constantine the Great granted Christendom state recognition and freedom to practice its religion. From the fourth century, Milan, at that time a large city of about 130,000 inhabitants, had a special ecclesiastical position as the seat of a metropolitan, and one of the bishops of Milan, Ambrose, was one of the four Doctors of the Church. At the beginning of the period of mass migrations, the imperial residence was moved to Ravenna, which was better protected. The importance of Milan, which was destroyed by the Huns in 451, diminished even further when the later kings of Lombardy made Pavia their city of residence instead of Milan.

In the Middle Ages, Milan appointed itself the leader of the league of Lombard cities against the suzerainty of the Holy Roman Empire. As a result of this action, Emperor Frederick Barbarossa ordered the city to be razed to the ground in 1162, with the exception of the churches. Shortly thereafter, in 1176, Milan and the other cities of the League defeated Barbarossa decisively at Leganno. The number of inhabitants in Milan soon rose to about 60,000. Milan's position as the richest and greatest city in Lombardy has been unchallenged ever since. In the 14th century the city's rulers, the Visconti, became the most powerful dukes in northern Italy. Gian Galeazzo Visconti, who in 1397 was made the imperial representative for Italy by King Wenceslas, tried to establish a kingdom by conquering one northern Italian city-state after another. By the time of his death in 1402, he had half of Tuscany, including Pisa and Siena, in his grasp. The dream of a kingdom ruled from Milan ended at this point, and was not resurrected by the Sforza dukes, the successors of the Visconti.

During the rule of Gian Galeazzo Visconti, the present Milan Cathedral was begun with his strong support. The first cathedral was a columned basilica with five aisles and an eastern transept. Bishop Ambrose had this church built; it was only 223 ft. (68 m) long, which was very small for a cathedral of its time. It stood in the square to the west of the present cathedral facade. An octagonal baptistery located to the east also belonged to the original cathedral, again dating from the time of Ambrose; Ambrose baptized Augustine there in 387—a case of a later Doctor of the Church being baptized by an earlier one.

In the ninth century, a cathedral for winter services was built (consecrated in 836) where the present cathedral now stands and east of the first cathedral. In 1162, during the destruction of the city by Barbarossa, it was severely damaged, and after that repaired. The winter church received a new campanile in 1333, although just 20 years later this collapsed, destroying part of the nave. According to plans by the brothers Jacobello and Pier Paolo dalle Masegne, the facade appears to have been rebuilt in a style similar to that of the cathedral in Mantua.

Inscriptions mention the year 1386, the official date when building began in Milan. Other sources give different dates, indicating that the beginning of the works was somewhat chaotic. However, the story of the cathedral's construction and planning over the following years until the 15th century is extraordinarily well documented by detailed minutes of the meetings of the building commission. A gigantic building was planned from the outset, but the commission that elaborated the first plans lacked experience, which is why famous architects were repeatedly brought to Milan from Germany or France for advice. The discussions developed into an ongoing argument about good architecture and its principles, without reaching a consensus. In the end, the commission adopted practically none of the suggestions made by the foreigners.

After the building was begun, and its ground plan established, the Frenchman Nicolas de Bonaventure was brought to Milan in 1389. He appears to have conveyed his basic idea in a drawing by the architect Antonio di Vicenzo, the first Master of S. Petronio in Bologna. The drawing combines the ground plan and cross-section, and shows a five-aisled basilica with clustered piers of French inspiration, along with side aisles graduated in height from outside to inside. The height of the central nave equals the width of all five aisles together. The cross-section overall can be inscribed within a square. The dimensions and their relationships thus correspond to a very simple mathematical formula. This *ad quadratum* design scheme was commonly applied in northern Gothic buildings, such as the cathedral in Cologne, which also has five aisles.

After Nicolas de Bonaventure was dismissed, within a year, a German, Johann von Freiburg, came for a few months in 1391. He suggested the equally widespread *ad triangulum* scheme, as it had been applied in Strasbourg Cathedral, in place of the *ad quadratum* method. In the former, the height of the central nave is determined by an equilateral triangle raised from the full width of the aisles. With the *ad triangulum* scheme, the central nave is lower than it would be with the *ad quadratum* method. The proportional relationships are of a purely geometrical nature, which makes the mathematical calculations difficult. Shortly after Johann von Freiburg's brief "guest performance," the mathematician Stornalco from Piacenza calculated the measurements for the *ad triangulum* scheme in *braccia* (or "arms," the standard measurement). The results were accepted by the building commission.

At the end of 1391, after an envoy had been sent to Cologne to offer an appointment to a *maximus inzignerius*, Heinrich Parler from Gmünd arrived in Milan. At the time he was working on the minster choir at Ulm. Parler's suggestions were discussed in May 1392 by 14 specialists, including Parler himself, and, apart from Parler's vote, unanimously rejected. The master builder was sent home in disgrace. It appears that he had suggested a building like Cologne Cathedral, that is, with two side aisles of equal height and a triforium in the central nave. The commission stayed with the *ad triangulum* design, and fixed the graduated arrangement of the ceilings as well as the pier and vault heights in exact *braccia* measurements.

Now the height of the vaulting in the central nave related to the equilateral triangle in another way: formerly, the point of the triangle had marked the ridge of the vault, but now the whole of the vault was set so much deeper that the curves of the crowns of the vault were tangential to the sides of the triangle. This raised the point of the triangle some way above the top of the vaulting. This construction was published with a woodcut illustration by the Milan architect Cesare Cesariano in his commentary on Vitruvius (1521).

In 1394, Ulrich von Ensingen was called to Milan. He had been invited three years earlier, but at that time had preferred to take over the leadership of the masons' lodge at Ulm Cathedral. He enjoyed the highest reputation among German master builders. He not only began the mighty tower at Ulm Cathedral, but a little later, at the cathedral in Strasbourg, he built what became the tallest tower in the world, which was finally completed by his successor, Johann Hültz from Cologne. In comparison, the tasks that Ulrich von Ensingen took on in Milan were minor, restricted to the pier capitals and the apse windows. But the master builder achieved as little as his foreign predecessors, and returned to Germany six months later.

The disagreements came to a head in 1399 when three specialists were brought to Milan from Paris: Jacques Coene from the Netherlands (actually a famous master of illuminated manuscripts), Jean Campanosen, and his pupil Jean Mignot, who was the spokesman for the group. Mignot assured Gian Galeazzo that the structure would collapse if extensive safety measures were not implemented, for

example, strengthening the buttresses. The planned crossing tower, which was to be surrounded by four satellite towers (representing the throne of God surrounded by the thrones of the four Evangelists in the Apocalypse) was also said to be in great danger. Mignot warned that the satellite towers had no load-bearing subframe and that, in addition, the piers at the crossing were too weak. Mignot presented no fewer than 54 points of criticism so arrogantly that the local workforce deemed only 25 of them to be even worth answering. In all seriousness, they told Mignot that anything that was vertical could not fall; furthermore, Italian marble could bear twice the load of French stone, and, finally, a pointed arch exerted no lateral thrust. These observations indicate an astonishing ignorance, and yet the cathedral still stands today.

The main point of contention was fundamental. Mignot, insisting that architecture must follow geometric rules, formulated his now famous motto: *Ars sine scientia nihil est* (art without scientific knowledge is nothing). The Italians persevered with their position: *ars* was one thing, *scientia* another. In the end Mignot's fundamental statement was turned around to state the corollary: *scientia sine arte nihil est*. The French were more oriented toward theory and the Italians more toward experience. After Mignot's vehement demands that the building be reinforced and improved had been turned down, he was dismissed in 1401. The Milanese did agree with him on one point, however: the four towers around the crossing were removed even though construction on them had already begun.

Soon after the departure of the Frenchmen, the tracery was installed in the three gigantic windows of the choir ambulatory. The windows on the angled sides retained the design of Nicolas Bonaventure, but, in 1402, Filippino da Modena came up with a new proposal for the central window. In 1403, Antonio da Paderno finished the large windows in the transept facades. The eastern sections of the cathedral were well advanced, and the builders were now concerned with how to carry out the vaulting. In 1403, an attempt was made to secure the services of Wenceslas Parler, who was then employed at St. Stephen's Cathedral in Vienna, but he did not come.

The final vaulting of the choir was to have taken place in 1409, but Filippino da Modena, who in the meantime had been appointed site manager, had doubts about his own courage. The duke's ambassadors in Germany, France, and England looked for a first-class engineer, but failed to find one. Before tackling the vaulting, the builders applied a safety measure that many architects would have taken as a grievous slight. It was decided to bind the piers above the capitals, both

The facade of Milan Cathedral before its completion in the 19th century. 18th-century oil painting after an engraving by Marcantonio Dal Re, 1735 (Museo di Milano)

longitudinally and transversely, with iron ties that would be visible to all.

Meanwhile, around the middle of the 15th century, the Sforzas succeeded the Viscontis, and the east end of the cathedral, together with the three east bays of the nave, was completed. In 1452, the western sections of the previous church, including the facade, were pulled down so that the remaining bays of the new nave could be erected. At that time, the most difficult remaining section to build was the crossing tower, known as the *tiburio*. For this a German was summoned once again, although for this kind of engineering a master builder from Florence might have been the better choice as the cathedral dome in Florence, technically the greatest act of daring of the century, had been happily completed long before.

In Milan the choice fell on the chief foreman of the masons' lodge at Strasbourg Cathedral, Johannes Niesenberger, born in Graz, whose main task in Germany at that time was the vaulting of the minster choir in Freiburg. Niesenberger, who was paid a princely sum, arrived in 1483 with his own building crew of 15 workers and craftsmen. But, in 1486 he was accused of making structural errors, and, moreover, of having made similar errors in Freiburg. Niesenberger seems to have left Milan at that point. Only a year later, the Florentine architect Luca Fancelli, the builder of churches designed by Leon Battista Alberti in Mantua, reported that the original cupola should be demolished because it was threatening to cave in, and that a new one should be built.

Some of the greatest Renaissance artists—Francesco di Giorgio, Bramante, and Leonardo—were involved in the cathedral's planning. Francesco di Giorgio, Amadeo, and Dolcebuono, architects from northern Italy, were appointed in 1490 to realize the project. The tower was given an octagonal shape, surrounded on the diagonal sides by four satellite towers. The idea of the satellite towers, originally introduced during the early planning phases, was finally realized, after Mignot had given them up. How

Niesenberger's *tiburio* looked is not known. The *tiburio* of the Certosa di Pavia has similar satellites, although they are hemispherical. In Milan from that time onward, the rich Gothic ornamental style, as originally planned for the *tiburio* and reproduced in the woodcut in Cesariano's *Commentary*, was allied to the forms of the Lombard Renaissance, which also loved decorative effects, in a unique blended style. The octagonal vault above the crossing, illuminated by the windows in the lateral walls, nonetheless seems very Gothic because of its pointed arches.

For the time being, no more Gothic forms were used as the cathedral was completed. Outside, the facade, the flying buttresses, and large parts of the ornamentation were still unfinished. Unlike its appearance today, the outside looked rather bare until the 19th century. Political events also did little to encourage the continuation of construction. In 1499, the Duchy of Milan was occupied by troops of the French king; the occupation lasted (with interruptions) until 1525. After the duchy fell to the Spanish Habsburgs in 1535, the great archbishops and cardinals of the Counter-Reformation, Carlo and Federico Borromeo, led renewed efforts to complete the cathedral.

The main problem was the structure's facade, for which new designs were continually being developed, some of them with two massive towers, as had also been planned, briefly, for St. Peter's in Rome, even though there was hardly any tradition of west towers in Italy. The facade of Milan Cathedral had been a kind of playground for architectural fantasies for centuries. The main question was whether any new building should be in the Gothic or the Classical—that is, the Roman—style.

Under Carlo Borromeo it was decided in 1567 to adopt the design drawn up by the artist Pellegrino Pellegrini dei Tibaldi. In emulation of Michelangelo, Pellegrini was strongly influenced by Roman art, and in architecture he followed Vignola's strict Vitruvian adherence to rules. Pellegrini's project was related to Vignola's facade design for Il Gesù in Rome, which was built at nearly the same time. Unlike that design, this one featured pillars in front of the wall, providing both stories with an opulent, completely un-Roman display of columns. This project was reworked by Francesco Maria Ricchini, cathedral architect from 1631; an engraving of his work was published in 1635. However, only the rear wall of the porch was carried out with portals on the ground floor, and some of the windows in the upper story, but not the crucial aspect: the proposed "order" for the columns and entablature.

Milan's own traditional preference for the Gothic style

would prevail. Around 1650, the next master builder, Carlo Buzzi, delivered a new facade design with two towers, which employed Gothic forms covering not only the facade but also the *tiburio*. This design was accepted, and Buzzi gave the facade Gothic buttresses, even though it had already been started without them and was meant to be a model of Classical architecture. The buttresses were not completed, however, because building work was soon suspended. From then until the 18th century new "Baroque Gothic" designs were put forward, notably by Luigi Vanvitelli, the builder of the gigantic palace of Caserta in Naples, and the Piedmont architect Bernardo Vittone, who was the most important successor to Guarino Guarini in Turin.

The impetus for the completion of the exterior was provided by Napoleon, who entered Milan in triumph in 1796, ending Austrian rule. After his coronation in front of the cathedral with the iron crown of Lombardy in 1805, the final phase was begun under the direction of the architect Amati, who favored lavish Gothic ornamentation. His approach determined the exterior's final appearance, its graceful filigree stone architecture giving the cathedral a character that it had never had before. The facade was completed, too, although just a half a century later it no longer satisfied popular taste. As a result, an architectural competition for a more magnificent remake was held from 1883 to 1887. No fewer than 120 architects took part, including many from Germany and Austria. Nonetheless, neither this competition nor a later one in 1888 came to anything, so the facade was retained, as it had been finalized in the Napoleonic building campaign. It still stands today, after only slight changes in 1904.

The resplendent wealth of Gothic ornamentation, equaled by few other European cathedrals, among them Cologne, and the enormity of its dimensions make the cathedral impressively effective. With a total length of 515 ft. (157 m), about the same as Cologne Cathedral, a width of 216 ft. (66 m), a transept 288 ft. (88 m) long, and a total floor area of 125,942 sq ft. (11,700 sq m), Milan Cathedral is one of the largest in the world. Only the cathedral in Seville, which is generally considered to be the largest built in the Middle Ages, can match it, yet Milan may outstrip Seville in terms of its internal area. Its power is derived less from the exterior, enmeshed in detailed stone carvings, than from the central nave, which with a width just short of 62 ft. (19 m), is 157 ft. (48 m) high, the same height as the tallest French cathedral, Beauvais, in which the upper choir is clearly narrower. The central nave in Cologne Cathedral reaches 46 ft. (14 m) wide and 144 ft. (44 m) high. The difference in spatial effect is

much greater than the difference in measurements would suggest. In Milan, the space seems gigantic. Even just the east–west arcades, at more than 102 ft. (31 m), exceed all conventional dimensions. In comparison, the central nave at Notre-Dame in Paris is only about 3 ft. (1 m) higher, but in Lyon it is about 23 ft. (7 m) lower.

Its Gothic ornamentation makes Milan Cathedral a virtually unique achievement in Italian architecture, particularly because brick was customarily used for building in Lombardy, whereas marble was used for the cathedral. Nevertheless, as is already clear from the story of its genesis, the cathedral is much closer to local tradition than to the Gothic styles of France or Germany. The five-aisled ground plan with the three-aisled projecting transepts and an ambulatory still largely corresponds to a northern cathedral like Cologne or Beauvais. But, viewed against the background of northern and above all French cathedrals, the 5/8 termination of the choir is unusual, as is the lack of radiating chapels, which were obligatory in France. In Milan, the trapezoidal bays of the ambulatory, in comparison with the French 5/10 or 7/12 structures, are disproportionately large, yet the 5/8 termination allows the three projecting sides of the polygon to be so large that they each provide room for a gigantic window. They are the largest tracery windows in the world: each one is 39 ft. (12 m) wide, 92 ft. (28 m) high, divided into six double sections, and crowned by a large and very finely delineated rosette.

The cathedral's cross-section is most unusual for a north Alpine Gothic structure. Cathedrals with five graduated aisles are also found in France, for instance in Bourges, Beauvais, and Le Mans, but they are not as extreme as Milan, where there is so little room left for the clerestory and where the arcades extend upward to an extreme height. Despite the record height of the central nave—just short of 157 ft. (48 m)—it does not seem excessively high because its proportions are appropriate to its width. This preference for high side aisles and a low clerestory is typical of the indigenous architecture of Lombardy. The nearest comparable example is S. Maria del Carmine in Pavia, a Gothic three-aisled church from the period immediately before the start of building in Milan. There, rectangular chapels are attached to the side aisles, each with the same floor area as one bay in the side aisle. In Milan, too, although consideration was given to building such rows of chapels instead of the outer side aisles, especially since their dividing walls could have been used as internal buttresses, it was decided not to have dividing walls. Nevertheless, the bays of the outer side aisles continued to indicate chapels.

The typical Lombard division of the internal area meant that the windows in the central nave and the inner side aisles are very small; the aisles receive hardly any light from them, and therefore are permanently in a twilit obscurity. The gigantic windows of the ambulatory and the fronts of the transepts seem all the brighter in contrast. The latter were reduced in size in the 16th century when Gothic chapels were added instead of the transept portals, which seriously reduced the amount of light being admitted.

The defining characteristic of the cathedral's interior is provided by the piers. These are circular and clustered, with eight pointed engaged shafts. They are unusual in that, instead of capitals, they have completely original octagonal niches containing statues, an idea apparently introduced at the start of the original project. These architectural sculptures are distributed along the central nave in regular rows and give the piers an additional value. They provide space for 416 considerably larger-than-life-size statues. That, too, is a record. The cathedral that was supposed to outstrip all others has achieved that, but whether it does so in terms of architectural quality must be questioned.

Plates 173–177

173 View from the northwest
174 View into the north transept
175 View through the nave and crossing to the choir
176 Pinnacles in the roofscape
177 Crossing tower

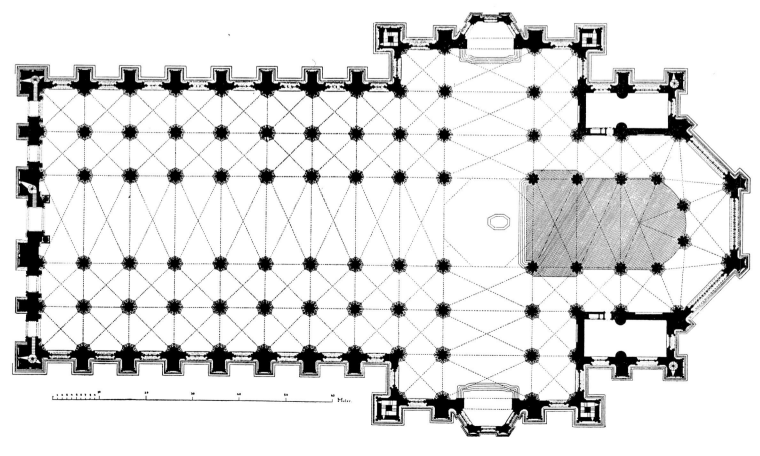

173

Modena

Modena, lying between Bologna and Parma in Emilia, was declared the Roman colony of Mutina in 183 B.C.E., and has been a bishop's see since the fourth century C.E. The first bishop, St. Geminianus (d. 397), was the patron saint of both the cathedral and the city. In the Late Classical period, the population deserted the settlement because of increased flooding and epidemics of fever. Only the center of worship remained standing. This was the burial church of St. Geminianus, which had been erected by his successor, Theodolus, near a necropolis, and lay outside the city on the Via Emilia. In Carolingian times it seems that the bishop's seat was transferred here from the deserted city. Gradually, a new settlement arose around it, eventually enclosed by walls in 891.

In the 11th and early 12th centuries, Modena's patron was the powerful margravine Matilda of Tuscany, who lived in the castle of Canossa. She not only held feudal powers of jurisdiction, but also supported building the new cathedral. The history of its construction is unusually well documented in several inscriptions and in a report on the building of the new church up to the year 1106; in that year, the mortal remains of St. Geminianus were transferred to the crypt of the new cathedral in the margravine's presence. The decision to build a new church was not taken by the bishop, because the seat was vacant at that time, but by the city's population and clergy. The reason for the new building was the dangerous structural deterioration of the earlier cathedral, which was described as old and ruinous. It was a five-aisled basilica with five apses, as evidenced by an excavation in 1913. The central aisle was 20 ft. (6 m) wide, the side aisles each 10 ft. (3 m) wide. The combined width of all five aisles was equivalent to the width of the present-day central nave of Milan Cathedral.

Two inscriptions report the start of building. One appears outside on the main apse, and proclaims that the cathedral was started in 1099, and that the master builder was called Lanfranc. He was *ingenio clarus* and *doctus et aptus*, in other words, famous for his abilities as well as learned and suitable. The inscription also tells us that the cathedral glowed with finely chiseled marble. According to the report, a master builder was initially sought out, then Lanfranc was found. Described as *designator* and *mirabilis artifex, mirificus edificator*, he was a wonderful artist; the design architect as well as master builder, he accomplished a real miracle.

The second inscription is on the cathedral's facade, where it is held by the figures of the prophets Henoch and Elias. The placing of the inscriptions at opposite ends of the cathedral, to east and west, was certainly intentional. The text of the second inscription is more modest. It names the year when construction began, and then, in a supplement—which the severely cramped lettering indicates was not initially planned—it names another artist, the sculptor Wiligelmus, rather than Lanfranc. The inscription was clearly intended to praise the sculptor's art, though the praise is left unstated. Once his works were completed, it was assumed that they would demonstrate his ranking among sculptors.

A third inscription, this one on the south side, reports the consecration of the cathedral in 1184 by Pope Lucius III. There is no mention here of the artists, although a later contract from 1244 states, among other things, that Maestri Campionesi worked on the cathedral for three generations, that is, master builders from Campione on Lake Lugano. The first generation probably arrived around 1170. Much of the rebuilding and many of the decorative works can be attributed to them: the rose window in the west facade, the addition of a transept, the building of a campanile and the rood screen, the so-called *pontile*, or "jetty."

When building began in 1099, there were problems obtaining materials, until excavation works stumbled upon a rich supply of stone from the ancient necropolis. This stone was raised mechanically, and worked into smoothly dressed blocks. At least 11 different types of stone can be identified. In some places, primarily in the upper parts of the exterior wall, ancient reliefs were lightly dressed and then inserted in the structure. Works began simultaneously at the east and west ends, and finally met on the south side at the second section of wall from the east, which is strangely abbreviated, because the measurements here did not work out exactly.

Lanfranc's cathedral is a three-aisled basilica, originally without a transept, with three parallel apses at the east end. The facade on the west does not, as so often in northern Italy, stand in front of the building like a screen but repeats the cross-section of the basilica. The presbytery, which originally had the same structure as the nave, occupies the east bay in front of the three apses. Its built-in crypt has nine aisles, presenting the spectacle of a dense forest of columns.

The exterior of the Lanfranc cathedral is a precisely calculated rectilinear design employing the same motif throughout: on the facade, along the north and south fronts, and on the three apses. Slim, columnlike shafts form arches that are backed by passages and enclosed by round arches forming a gallery of blind arcading that runs all the way around the cathedral. A special feature of these blind arcades is that they are echoed, section by section, by a dwarf gallery running above them in the form of a triple arcade, each section being crowned by a blind arch, and are supported

Genesis relief by Master Wiligelmus on the west facade: God the Father in the mandorla, the Creation of Adam, the Creation of Eve, and the Fall from Grace, 1099 to around 1110

below by a frieze of round arches. This motif uses the round arch, the principal Romanesque building form, to particularly good effect, showing its symmetrical beauty and variety through a constant repetition that makes the building completely harmonious. Only the portals, with their two-storied canopied porches, break the sequence of blind arches. The transepts, however, are out of keeping with the rest of the building. They were added later to the north and south sides of the presbytery of Lanfranc's building by the Maestri Campionesi. Because the walls of the side aisles of the Lanfranc building remain unchanged and run through to the apse, the arms of the transept become externally visible only in the area above the nave. Their side walls are lower than the clerestory onto which they abut, and their gable fronts rest on the walls of the side aisles with no vertical justification. This makes it clear that the transept arms are of a later date.

The dressed stones of the external walls are actually a cladding laid over brick walls, added to improve the cathedral's exterior. In contrast, all the interior walls, as well as the vaults, are unplastered exposed stonework, deep red in color. The interior is very dark because the windows are small, and it has been left largely in its original condition. Only the transept arms were added later, although they contribute little to the internal layout, and the rib vaults, which were added in the 15th century. Lanfranc's original church was not vaulted; it had either exposed roof timbers or a flat wooden ceiling.

The master builder Lanfranc planned the central nave with square double bays with alternating supports. The main piers at the edges of the bays have a cruciform core and four hemispherical engaged columns. The intermediate piers at the center of the bays, on the other hand, are monolithic marble columns. The hemispherical engaged columns facing the central aisle, each backed by a flat rectangular shaft, reach up the walls and divide the nave into bays. On the upper wall, they are joined to massive stepped arches that traverse the central nave from wall to wall. These arches are pointed and in modern terms would be called transverse arches, but because their cross-section is notably different from that of

the crowns of the vault, they must have been built before the vaulting. Originally, they would have served as supporting arches spanning the nave and bearing the thrust of the vertical walls in place of the crowns of the vault, a suspended wall providing a supporting base for the ceiling. The pointed style indicates that the arches had been introduced by the Maestri Campionesi, for Lanfranc would surely have made them with rounded arches. The idea behind them, however, was his.

The elevation of the nave walls is additionally embellished by two large blind round arches in the clerestory, which nowadays are partly overlapped by the vaulting and by gallery openings. These take the form of triple arcades within an enclosing arch, and are almost the same type as the galleries on the exterior. The galleries are clearly false, for there is no ceiling between the side aisles and the gallery area. Instead, massive arches span the aisle above the main piers. These arches correspond to the dividing arches, and carry a second arch at the level of the gallery openings, which incorporates a double arcade. The 15th-century rib vaulting rises above that. This two-storied arch construction, which effectively subdivides the side aisles into individual compartments, is the work of Lanfranc. The architect certainly favored galleries, which since time immemorial had been regarded as a sign of nobility, a status symbol, but he left out their floors because an upper gallery had no practical use. This led him to invest more in the side aisles—elsewhere little more than secondary corridors—and transform them into something special, a more sophisticated solution with greater visual variety.

Viewed overall, Lanfranc's cathedral is an important architectural creation of high quality. The sculptural work of Wiligelmus on the west facade is equally good. Here, the art of stone sculpture begins to regain the status that it had in ancient times. People in Modena were clearly aware that his work was a pioneering achievement: the inscription honors the sculptor alongside the architect. The main portal and the relief frieze on the facade are attributed to Wiligelmus. The portal, with its projecting, barrel-vaulted, columned canopy, or *protiro*, has ancient lions supporting its columns and is the earliest example of a type of portal that later became widespread, especially in Lombardy. Wiligelmus showed himself here to be a master not only of imaginative, amusing arabesques but also of mythical, burlesque, and stern figures in relief. Most famous of all is the large relief frieze depicting the story of the origin of humankind with concise brevity and directness. The Romanesque sculpture of northern Italy begins with these works.

The rood screen, or *pontile*, is another important northern Italian Romanesque work. It was built between 1170 and 1175, and renovated between 1916 and 1921; its projecting pulpit was added between 1208 and 1225. The balcony of the rood screen extends over the full width of the central nave, and is supported by columns that in turn stand on lions; it provides a unique site for reliefs of the Passion of Christ. In contrast with Wiligelmus's early Romanesque sculpture, however, these reliefs lack the freshness of a really schematic, tightly packed treatment, and represent a step backward into a coarse, at times distinctly raw primitivism.

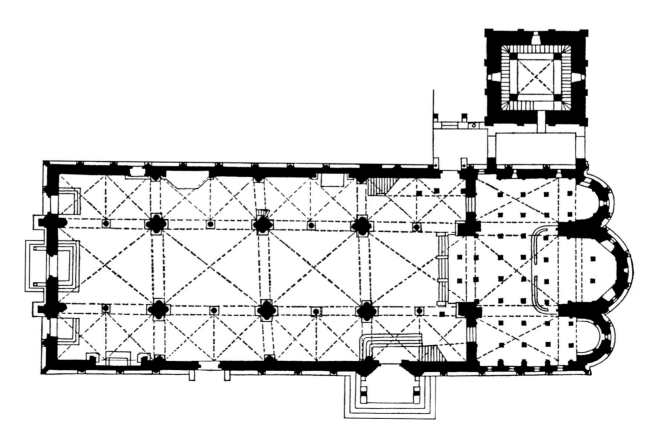

Pisa

Located on the Arno estuary, Pisa owes its historical importance to its port: even the Romans had a naval base there. The advance of Islam from North Africa into Europe caused the city to build its own fleet of warships, a fleet that continued to expand, thus facilitating Pisa's rise to the status of a world power. The city's period of greatness would be short, but all the more brilliant for that. As early as 828, the Pisans penetrated as far as Africa with fleets that at that time were still small. The year 1003 proved fateful: when the Saracens threatened Rome and Pope Silvester II, Pisa's ships came to the rescue, driving off the Saracens and taking Sardinia from them. When the Saracens unexpectedly forced their way into Pisa and razed the city to the ground, the Pisan fleet successfully counterattacked, drove off the Saracens, and gained undisputed mastery of the Tyrrhenian Sea. In the following decades, Pisa achieved one naval triumph after another: in 1051, the city conquered the Ligurian islands of Elba and Corsica. Pisa recorded its most triumphant victory in 1063, when after annihilating the Saracen fleet off Palermo, the Pisan troops, together with the Normans, conquered Palermo. That was the beginning of the end of Islamic rule in Sicily. Pisa occupied Sardinia two years later. In 1088, they conquered Tunis, and many Christian captives were freed. In 1099, Pisa made its fleet available for the First Crusade.

Economic expansion went hand in hand with military expansion, especially in the eastern Mediterranean, where Pisa, like Venice, maintained numerous trading posts. A binding trade and maritime law, enacted in 1075 for this commerce, was recognized not only by Pope Gregory VII but also in 1081 by Emperor Henry IV. A count (*conte*) stood at the head of the city government, but the feudal system was replaced by a municipal system in 1080, when the city, with support from the margravine Matilda of Tuscany introduced a consular government, which was ratified by the emperor in 1132.

Before the rise of Venice, Pisa was the most powerful city in the Mediterranean, a true world city, which, as a pious monk complained, teemed with heathens, from Turks, Africans, and Persians to Chaldeans. There were said to be 10,000 towers in the city, and even though these were required to be less than about 98 ft. (30 m) high, the cityscape must have made an overwhelming impression. In the 12th century, during the Hohenstaufen dynasty, Pisa was allied with the Ghibellines, and for that was granted an extended coastal area by Frederick Barbarossa in 1162. The area was secured with 554 castles and defensive towers. Pisa increasingly came into conflict with the neighboring Tuscan cities of Lucca and Florence and, above all, with the maritime power of Genoa. In 1284, Pisa's power came to an abrupt end. In the naval battle with Genoa off the island of Meloria, Pisa lost not just its entire fleet, but also the ships' crews. Without the protection of the fleet, the colonial empire collapsed quickly. In 1406, Pisa lost its freedom, too, when the city came under the rule of Florence.

Pisa was a bishopric from the fourth century. There are records of a cathedral in 748. In 1091, Pope Urban II, in gratitude for the liberation of Christians in Tunis in 1088, raised the bishopric to an archbishopric, and placed under it the bishoprics of Corsica, three of which had to be relinquished to Genoa in 1133. Politically, the bishops and archbishops of Pisa had very little importance.

The present cathedral is a monument to Pisa's shining past. An inscription on the facade relates that it was begun in 1063 after the naval battle off Palermo, and financed with the loot. In 1114, Pisa turned once again to the spoils of war to finance the cathedral after the city-state helped liberate the Balearic Islands from the Moors. The first consecration took place in 1118, although it seems that the cathedral was not completed until the second half of the 12th century.

Buscheto, the cathedral's architect, was reputedly lent to Pisa by the Byzantine emperor, and his work is highly praised in an epitaph on the facade. A second master builder, Rainaldus, is named in another inscription on the facade, for which, the text indicates, he was responsible.

The cathedral was erected in green fields on the periphery of the city, completely unrestricted by urban construction. The cathedral precinct also includes, to the east, the separate campanile famous worldwide as the Leaning Tower of Pisa; the walled cemetery, or Camposanto, on the north side; and the baptistery on the west. The cathedral precinct, a unique collection of magnificent buildings, is aptly named the Campo dei miracoli (the Court of Miracles).

An early baptistery was built on the north side. When building began on the present baptistery, the western site was chosen because of the way it aligned with the cathedral. It is reminiscent of the cathedral precinct in Florence, but also of the Temple Mount in Jerusalem, where the central structure of the Dome of the Rock, which the Crusaders called the Temple of the Lord, is in alignment with the multiaisled Al Aqsa mosque, formerly the Temple of Solomon. It is possible that when the new baptistery was built in Pisa, the planners took this precedent into account. In any case, the archbishop of Pisa in the early 12th century was simultaneously patriarch of the Kingdom of Jerusalem that had been founded after the First Crusade.

The cathedral at Pisa is one of the largest of its time, with a total length of 312 ft. (95 m) and a nave nearly 46 ft. (14 m) wide. In its magnificence, it is unique in the European Romanesque tradition. As a five-aisled columned basilica with tall, tightly spaced arcades in the central nave made of granite columns, it is related stylistically to the three large five-aisled columned basilicas in Rome: Old St. Peter's, St. John Lateran, and St. Paul outside the Walls. It is also related to the five-aisled Early Christian cathedral in Ravenna, which has since disappeared. However, Pisa is different from the Roman churches in that additional galleries, installed above side aisles, refer to the earlier Byzantine tradition. The galleries have two aisles that correspond to the side aisles below and open onto the central nave with a pair of openings for each bay in the nave and a central column between them. Originally, the aisles and galleries had flat ceilings; the side aisles were first vaulted after a fire in 1595.

Transverse arms with three aisles and galleries were added to the north and south of the east–west structure in a way unknown until then in Italian architecture. Earlier versions are found in the French pilgrim churches (for example, St. Rémi in Reims), but the closest parallels are in the Early Christian architecture of Syria and Asia Minor, such as, Qal'at Saman, or the Ecclesia Quadrifida in Shechem, which is known only from literary sources. In buildings of this type, four multiaisled basilica arms were arranged in a cruciform shape, giving a central space that was sometimes octagonal. Buscheto may well have been conversant with this Eastern tradition, because he came from Constantinople.

The central aisle of the tranverse arms, which terminate in an apse on the north and south faces, is 26 ft. (8 m) wide, clearly smaller and also lower than the nave and choir of the east–west nave. The crossing, therefore, does not have a square floor plan, but forms an elongated rectangle. Vaulted from the beginning, its elongated oval dome has a steep profile and was erected over squinches. There is nothing comparable to this cupola shape in the earlier European architecture.

The idea to partition off the transverse arms from the crossing is also highly original. Buscheto achieved this by allowing the inner side aisles and gallery to run through to the choir like a multistoried bridge. Thus, a rhythmical three-part arcaded wall rose over two stories facing the crossing, corresponding to the three aisles of the transverse arms. On the ground floor, it is a graduated triple arcade with four paired arches on the gallery level, each enclosed by a larger arch. Above the arcade wall, the clerestory also continues to the choir. Because they are partitioned off, the transverse

arms function almost like independent basilicas placed at right angles to the main body.

The appearance of the central nave is dominated by arcades of round arches, the east and west crossing arches being all the more conspicuous for being pointed, as are those of the columned arcades between the inner and outer side aisles. This has nothing to do with Gothic architecture, but rather shows the influence of Moorish forms. Buscheto also elaborated a very opulent style for the exterior. On the walls of the side aisles, he designed blind arcades with pilaster strips, and only pilaster strips at the gallery level, but spaced twice as close together. For the cathedral and the buildings that followed it he devised the decorative motif of a square standing on one corner, and this is repeated throughout the cathedral.

According to Buscheto's initial plan, the cathedral was actually supposed to have been shorter. Rainaldus gave the nave its final length by extending the aisles westward by three arcades, and outside—as can easily be seen from the pattern of the walls—by five units. Rainaldus's facade iterates the cross-section of the church. The seven-part blind arcading on the ground floor is aligned with the aisles lying behind it, the three central arcades corresponding to the central nave and the others to each of the side aisles. Rainaldus had a passion for multiple-columned arcades set closely together. Above the arcade is a single four-storied series of arcades, a trellis of small columns and arches that extends for a sequence of 19 arches, and then narrows so sharply with the pitch of the roof that at the top, beneath the gable of the central nave, only eight arches remain.

These repeating arcades are the pride of the building's exterior, significantly increasing the decorative magnificence of the cathedral and creating an impression of immeasurable wealth. The choir apse, too, acts as a counterpart to the facade as it closes the cathedral at the east end and takes up the motif of the arcaded gallery. The formal language employed appears to be so similar that it is justifiable to attribute the apse to Rainaldus, too. Perhaps, though, Buscheto left behind a plan for both parts of the building, which Rainaldus later adhered to.

The columned gallery was the key design feature of the campanile, a round tower with a cylindrical core surrounded by open galleries for six stories above the ground floor. As the art historian Vasari reported in the 16th century, the tower was started in 1173, apparently to plans by the sculptor and bronzesmith Bonanus (Bonanno Pisano), who would later be buried in the tower. The works had to be suspended as early as 1185, even before the third gallery was completed, because

Bronze door by Bonanus in the east portal of the south side aisle (*Porta S. Ranieri*) with reliefs representing scenes from the New Testament and Prophets, around 1180

the tower, which stands on soft alluvial soil, had already started to lean southward. Construction did not begin again until 1275 with Giovanni di Simone, who met his end in the naval battle off Meloria in 1284. He had tried to compensate for the existing inclination of the tower by placing the columns on the new stories vertically, and making those on the overhanging south side longer than those on the north side. This is why, when viewed from the east, the outline of the tower now describes a slight curve. The belfry, by Tommaso Pisano, the son of the sculptor, is much smaller in diameter and was added in 1350, only after the platform above the galleries had been brought back to the horizontal.

When completed, the tower, which is 184 ft. high (56 m), overhung by nearly 5 ft. (1.5 m); it stayed more or less as it was until the 19th century. Then, following earthworks undertaken in 1838, the groundwater table fell, and the tower began to tilt even more. In the 1930s, as the inclination increased to 16 ft. (5 m), it seemed only a matter of time before the tower fell. Instead, it was successfully underpinned

with concrete, with the result that the inclination increased by only 4/100 of an inch (1 mm) per year. The latest safety measures, completed in 2001, managed to reverse the inclination by about 1.3 ft. (40 cm). Since then the tower has once more been accessible to visitors.

Bonanus, the campanile's first architect, also created a bronze door for the cathedral's west portal. In the inscription on the portal, he proudly noted that because of his skill he had completed the door in a year—which was, apparently, record time. The door was ruined in 1595 in a fire at the cathedral, but a second door by Bonanus has been preserved. It stands in the east portal of the south transept, opposite the campanile in which he is buried. The double doors are made from individually cast relief panels with broad, flat frames mounted on a wooden backing. The panels depict scenes from the lives of the Virgin Mary and Christ in a terse, simple, but by no means primitive style of narration that reveals Byzantine influence, its design concentrating solely on the fundamentals. The figures stand out so strongly from the background that the themes are instantly recognizable, even without the aid of the explanatory inscriptions, which in their extreme clarity provide further evidence of Bonanus's skill at creating reliefs.

In 1153, two decades before building started on the campanile, and while the works on the west part of the cathedral were in full swing, the architect Diotisalvi, who had just erected the octagon of S. Sepolcro in Pisa, was commissioned to build a new baptistery to the west of the cathedral. He designed a circular structure, whose diameter, at 125 ft. (38 m), was slightly larger than the total width of the cathedral's nave. Evidently the round building was conceived, as were many other churches in this style, as a loose imitation of the Church of the Holy Sepulcher in Jerusalem. The interior with its ambulatory, gallery, and an unusual conical dome, which once opened to the sky by means of an oculus, like the Roman Pantheon, was simple, characterized architecturally by a double alternation of supports, with the piers and columns running in a sequence of a-b-b-a. Five of the columns were brought from Elba and Sardinia. The Norman kings of Sicily, Roger II and William I, gave financial support to the building.

The exterior of the baptistery has blind arcading on the ground floor, corresponding to that on the west facade of the cathedral. The columned gallery above it was probably built around 1265 by the sculptor Nicola Pisano, and crowned a little later by his son Giovanni with Gothic gables and pinnacles, and further embellished by a cycle of figures, statuettes, and busts in relief. The Gothic gables and

Representation of the Birth of Christ on the pulpit of the baptistery by Nicola Pisano (left) and on the pulpit of the cathedral by Giovanni Pisano (right)

pinnacles appear to be the earliest in Italy; they were a French import. The final story was added only after 1358, when an attempt was made to roof over the old dome, which rose like a cone with the top cut off. But the uppermost part of the old dome remained visible, and this now sits on the roof of the cupola like an ill-fitting cap. The open oculus was closed in 1394 with a flat vault. Only then was the baptistery completed. At 180 ft. (55 m), it is nearly as tall as the campanile.

The pièce de résistance of the baptistery is the pulpit, which according to an inscription was completed by Nicola Pisano in 1260. No longer rectangular, as had been customary until then, the body of the pulpit is a hexagon mounted on columns, with large marble reliefs on the balcony and more figures in the area of the arches. The reliefs were the basis of Nicola's claim to be not just the best but also the most revolutionary sculptor in Italy of his time. Referring clearly to ancient Roman sarcophagi, he created a sequence of reliefs in which the figures are packed tightly over the surface area but at the same time arranged behind one another and frequently overlapping. In this way, the scene is clarified spatially without depth of perspective. In his treatment of the human figure, Nicola sought to unify the Gothic style seamlessly with the ancient Roman tradition, and thereby create a new style, a renaissance of the Gothic. His enthusiasm for the Classical style is repeatedly expressed in the emotionless cool faces with their Junoesque harmony, and also in their athletic poses, which reflect a precise study of anatomy, drawn either from living models or antique sculpture.

The pulpit in the cathedral, created a generation later by Nicola's son Giovanni Pisano from 1302 to 1310–11, is even more extravagant than the baptistery pulpit. It replaced an older rectangular pulpit by Master Guilielmus dating from 1158–62, which was presented by the people of Pisa to Cagliari, and can be found there in the cathedral. Giovanni's pulpit was pulled down in 1599, and reassembled in 1926 from those parts of the original that had been preserved. Unlike the work of his father, Nicola, the scenes of Giovanni's late reliefs reflect human sensitivities and emotions, creating an impassioned excitement that imbues the entire panel with its unrestrained outbreaks of feeling. Giovanni's intense, barely controlled temperament made him a born dramatist, the opposite of Nicola, who was a quiet epic poet. With Giovanni, every scene is full of turbulent, emotionally charged activity. The basis for his art was his new, psychological way of looking at humankind. In this, Giovanni Pisano was the spiritual equal of his two great contemporaries, Dante and Giotto.

The Camposanto, or cemetery, was the fourth and last building in the Pisa cathedral precinct. To build it, 53 shiploads of earth were delivered from Golgotha in 1202. Giovanni di Simone, who was also occupied on the campanile, laid it out in 1278 in the form of a monumental cloister, which was structurally completed in 1350. An extensive series of wall frescoes (now removed to a museum), begun before the plague of 1348, includes the famous *Trionfo della Morte*, a vanitas that portrays the transitory nature of all earthly things. The fresco, by an unknown artist, was associated with

Francesco Traini, and also with Buonamico Buffalmacco. The latter was praised by Boccaccio as a particularly witty artist, who had long been believed to be a literary fiction because of his curious name, which in itself was held to be a joke (*buffa* means "funny"). The cycle of frescoes was finished in the 15th century by Benozzo Gozzoli from Florence. Out of gratitude, the city of Pisa granted him the right to be buried in the Camposanto. To lie there, within the Campo dei miracoli, was indeed a great honor.

Plates 183–189

183 Aerial view of the Campo dei miracoli with cathedral, campanile (Leaning Tower), baptistery, and Camposanto
184 View from the west of the facade, transept, and campanile
185 South transept and Leaning Tower
186 Nave and north transept from the south transept
187 View through the nave looking east
188 The pulpit in the baptistery by Nicola Pisano, completed in 1259–60
189 The cathedral pulpit by Giovanni Pisano, 1302–10/11 (see Plates 186, 187)

Plan of the cathedral. Above, gallery level; below, ground floor

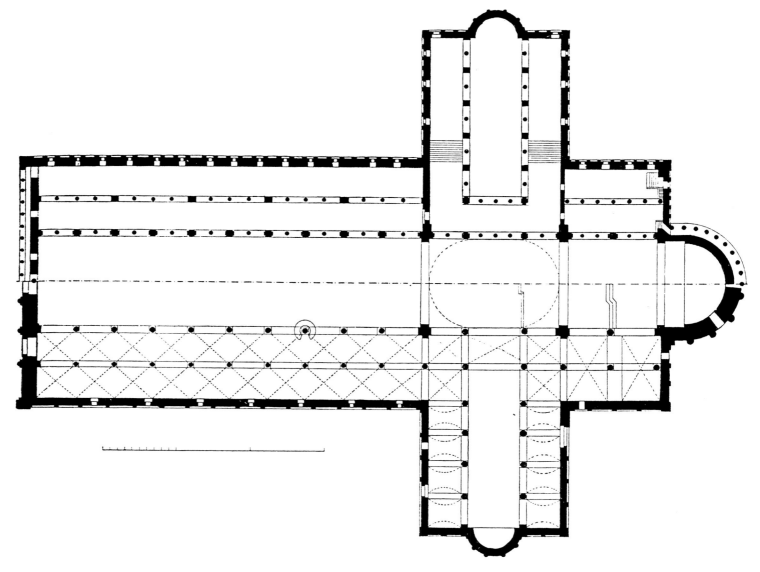

183

Florence

Florence, the largest city in Tuscany, lying on the River Arno, was the European capital of art and culture in the 15th century, when the reawakening of enthusiasm for antiquity was launching the new age that would come to be called the Renaissance. Florence had not been very important in ancient times. Caesar's veterans founded the colony of Florentia in 59 B.C.E. on the site of an Etruscan settlement; the basis for economic development was the extension of the Via Cassia through Etruria. The city's rise to become a center of trade and power began in the Middle Ages under the margraves of Tuscany—it was the Guelph margravine Matilda, who was strictly true to the pope, who made Florence a center of monastic ecclesiastical reform and anti-imperial politics. In the conflict between the Guelph and Ghibelline factions, which raged in nearly all Italian cities, the Guelphs finally prevailed in 1267, after the fall of the Hohenstaufen dynasty. The population organized into guilds, the leaders of which, from 1282, comprised the Signoria, that is, the chief administrative authority. This relatively democratic form of government was, however, severely restricted as early as 1293, when only the seven senior guilds (arti maggiori), to which merchants, bankers, and clothmakers belonged, were still entitled to govern, while the middle-ranking and junior guilds, including the artisan classes, were excluded. The population of Florence now grew rapidly to more than 100,000 inhabitants.

The Trecento (14th century) was dominated by continuous internal feuds not only between the parties, but also among the great families. However, in the Quattrocento (15th century) the Medici family assumed power, beginning with Cosimo, il Vecchio (the Elder), to whom government was transferred in 1434, and who cleverly preserved the old republic. The Medici, notably Lorenzo the Magnificent (il Magnifico), were able to maintain their ruling position, despite setbacks and even banishments. In 1530 they rose to be titular dukes of Florence, and in 1569 became grand dukes of Tuscany, after Florence became a territorial state following the incorporation of Siena in 1555. The Medici remained grand dukes until the dynasty died out two centuries later, in 1737.

Florence was a bishopric from the fourth century. The bishop's seat may have been located in the Church of S. Lorenzo that was consecrated by Ambrose, one of the bishops of Milan, in 393. Sometime between the ninth and the 11th centuries, the bishop's seat was transferred to the Church of S. Reparata, which until then had been merely a parish church. The bishopric of Florence was not raised to an archbishopric until 1419. At first, the baptistery, a truly magnificent structure that took almost a hundred years to build, beginning in about 1060, was far more important to the Florentine people than the cathedral.

The baptistery's present rectangular choir chapel dates from 1202, when it replaced an apse. As early as the 14th century, the Florentine historical author Giovanni Villani claimed that the baptistery was the ancient Roman Temple of Mars, built at the time of Augustus by workers sent to Florence by the Roman senate. The thesis of a Roman origin for the baptistery, which raised the status of Florence to that of Rome, was promoted and accepted as a state doctrine. Toward the end of the Trecento, it was used as grounds for the assertion that the Florentines were the true Romans of their age. In the 16th century the first grand duke, Cosimo de' Medici, commissioned a scientific study in an attempt to prove the Temple of Mars theory, but it was gradually recognized as being unsustainable and was finally discarded, even by Florentine patriots.

Even though the baptistery is not ancient, it is closer to antiquity than any other building of this period. In the 11th century nothing could compare with this monumental equal-sided octagon, with a diameter of 85 ft. (26 m). The structure of the internal walls is a two-story Classical Vitruvian "order," comprising pilasters, columns, and entablature. On the ground floor, each side of the octagon has a three-part colonnade with two salvaged Classical columns, with fluted pilaster piers on either side. These are placed in pairs at each corner of the room, leaving the corner itself free. The three-part Classical entablature (architrave, frieze, and cornice) runs around the room on both stories; it binds the octagon like a bracket. On the upper story, which is backed by a gallery, each side of the octagon consists of three pilaster bays, each of which has a pair of arches that make the story look like a gallery. The octagonal dome, made from eight individual hipped sections closed by a pointed arch, rises above the final cornice; this style is also called a "cloister vault" to differentiate it from a round dome.

The exterior is unified by a common motif: the irregular triple blind arcade of octagonal columns and round arches that distinguishes the upper story. The lower story is divided into bays by pilasters and an offset entablature; these are integrated with the blind arcades, creating great optical continuity. The large-scale design is enhanced by the small-scale decorative effect carried out within it. On the outer faces, smooth slabs of shining white Carrara marble and green serpentinite form an ornamental, strongly geometrical surface pattern of rectilinear panels that are punctuated by arcaded galleries.

The windows are set into this pattern like jewels. Some have rounded arches, and some are Classical edicola windows with flat triangular gables. In the early 13th century an attic story was added, consisting of pilaster bays and an entablature in which the architrave, in a non-Classical way, turns down vertically at the corners of the octagon, and so becomes a frame. This small detail has become famous: in the Renaissance, it was declared to be the only error made at the baptistery after the feature was copied at the foundling home in Florence, thereby repeating the "mistake." The attic story encases the dome vaulting of the interior, and supports a pyramidal pitched roof made of stone slabs. The internal construction between the dome and the pitched roof, on which the stone slabs rest, is not visible. The vaulting thus consists of two separate shells, the outer one acting as a kind of protective roof. Only in the uppermost zone do the two shells come together. The complete construction was reinforced in 1296, when Arnolfo di Cambio strengthened the eight corners of the octagon with projecting piers. These are especially conspicuous because of the alternation of light and dark stone layers, which changed the original appearance of the building to a considerable extent.

At the baptistery, the formal language employed both inside and outside, right down to details like the capitals, the fluting on the pilasters, and the triple division of the entablature, follows the Classical orders so closely that master builders at the beginning of the Renaissance, particularly Filippo Brunelleschi, were influenced much more by the baptistery than by ancient buildings. Perhaps it was they who invented the myth that the baptistery was the ancient Temple of Mars, and thus a first-class example of the building skills of the ancients, on a par with the Pantheon in Rome, with the additional advantage that it had been well preserved. The early Renaissance might in fact have been a rebirth, not of the Classical period but of medieval Florence. Scholars now use the term "Proto-Renaissance" to describe buildings of this era, like the baptistery, that are so close to the Classical period.

The importance of the baptistery to the Florentines is also demonstrated by the fact that, from the 1220s to around 1300, they gave the inner dome an expensive mosaic decoration, one of the most extensive after that of S. Marco in Venice. The city was not responsible for building and furnishing the baptistery—from the 12th century the rich guild of merchants and traders, the Arte di calimala o de mercanti, was responsible. The guild also provided another of the baptistery's claims to glory: its three bronze doors. The incentive for these, given the constant rivalry between cities,

The facade of Florence Cathedral before 1587, drawing by Bernardino Poccetti. (Museo dell'Opera di S. Maria del Fiore, Florence)

was the Bonanus doors at Pisa Cathedral. For the first door, the sculptor Andrea Pisano made the wax model, and casting specialists were brought in from Venice, since such skills were not available in Florence at that time. The models were finished in 1330, and both wings of the door on the east portal of the baptistery were ready to be hung in 1336. A competition for the second door between local and non-resident artists was announced in 1401. This first competition after the Classical, in which seven artists took part, was narrowly won by Lorenzo Ghiberti, who edged out the goldsmith Filippo Brunelleschi—a decision that would have great consequences, for Brunelleschi thereupon became the architect who not only vaulted the cathedral dome, but also founded Renaissance architecture.

Ghiberti produced the second baptistery door, which was formally based on the older door by Andrea Pisano, between 1403 and 1424. Soon afterward, he began work on the third door, which was completed in 1452. Michelangelo is alleged to have said that this door was worthy of decorating the gates of paradise, and ever since then it has been called the *Porta del paradiso*, the Paradise Door. The first program for the door

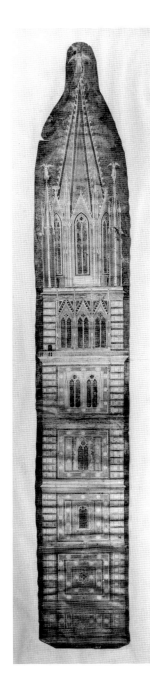

was elaborated by the humanist, and later state chancellor, Leonardo Bruni.

Ghiberti interpreted his scenes for the Paradise Door in a new way: they are almost paintings in bronze, rather than the reliefs of his first door, which reveal Gothic influences in their melody of gently curving lines. Among the scenes, in addition to distant landscapes, are architectural constructions that in their subject matter and in the arrangement of the perspective unmistakably indicate that they were not designed by Ghiberti, but by the theorist and later architect Leon Battista Alberti. The Paradise Door naturally received the place of honor on the east side, facing the cathedral's facade, while Ghiberti's other door was moved to the north side, and Pisano's was transferred to the south side.

Next to the magnificent baptistery, the old, modest-sized cathedral dedicated to S. Reparata must have looked like a stepchild. Its base level (as established in the excavations begun in 1965) lay about 10 ft. (2.9 m) deeper than at present, which indicates an early foundation. The church was a three-aisled Romanesque basilica, and extended farther westward than the present cathedral, but in the east only to the present third bay, that is, up to about the middle of the nave.

In 1296, the new cathedral was begun, on a much larger scale, and came under the patronage of S. Maria del Fiore. After a building period of 170 years, it was finally consecrated in 1467. In 1300, the sculptor Arnolfo di Cambio was nominated master builder. He may have worked out the first plan, which, contrary to earlier research findings, would have precluded a domed octagon at the east end. Instead, he intended a conventional choir with transept chapels, like that at S. Maria Novella. For the most part, the basic disposition of the west facade can be traced back to Arnolfo, as it is depicted in the drawing ascribed to Bernardino Poccetti, which originated before 1587. Arnolfo also began the sculptural decoration of the facade, some of which has been preserved.

In 1331, when the relics of the city's patron saint, St. Zenobius, were found beneath the crypt of S. Reparata, the Arte della Lana, the wool weavers' guild, took over the building. In 1334, the most famous artist of the time, the painter Giotto, was chosen as the architect of the cathedral and of the city defenses, and just three months later the foundation stone for the campanile was laid. Giotto's plan for the campanile is preserved in a sketch at the Cathedral Museum, Siena. The final tower conforms to this plan on the ground floor, but then deviates increasingly from it. For the top section, Giotto had envisaged a windowed octagon with gables, a steeple, and four large pinnacled towers, an idea that

demonstrates a remarkable relationship to the tower octagon of Freiburg Cathedral, and would have given Florence's cathedral overtones of northern Alpine Gothic. After Giotto's death in 1337, Andrea Pisano took over the building. He had certainly been active earlier on the reliefs of the base, and now took the construction of the tower up to the niche story. The four lower enclosed stories of the campanile were finished by the plague year of 1348. Francesco Talenti appeared as the new master builder in 1351. By 1359, he had built the three upper open stories of the campanile, and had raised it to a height of 279 ft. (85 m).

The final construction of the nave, begun long before, and for which the distribution of the piers had first been decided in 1357 and the number of bays in 1366, also happened in Francesco Talenti's time. The nave can, for the most part, be regarded as Talenti's creative accomplishment. We know that he designed the console passage in front of the clerestory and the piers, which effectively means the whole structural system. The dimensions of the nave, and even more the spatial relationships, are astonishing. Four square bays 66 ft. (20 m) wide and 131 ft. (40 m) high take up the whole of the central nave, which is 262 ft. (80 m) long. In comparison, Chartres has ten bays and the crossing within the same amount of space: 262 ft. (80 m). These numbers make it clear that the bays of Florence Cathedral are unusually massive, all the more so because the dividing arcades reach up very high, while the clerestory with its round windows is low. The longitudinal rectangular bays of the side aisles look like lateral extensions of the central nave rather than a sequence of bays in an east–west nave. The individual forms used in the structure are simple and large. Instead of being surrounded by clusters of Gothic shafts, the piers have pilasters on all four sides; only at the corners is there room for the shafts, from which the diagonal ribs spring. The transverse and lateral arches, on the other hand, are designed as flat strips, which are consistent with the pilasters.

While the interior is huge and bare, the exterior is covered with small, differently colored encrustations set in an endless series of rectangular ornamental enclosures, which are highly decorative but not systematically organized. On the outside of the cathedral, Florence demonstrates its wealth; on the inside, its stature. A sharper contrast between inside and outside is hardly imaginable.

In 1366, the planning of the cathedral reached its final phase: the choir. A year later—still with the support of the people—it was decided to accept the model prepared by a group of painters and sculptors, including Orcagna and Taddeo Gaddi. In 1368, all future site managers and

Representation of Florence Cathedral in the fresco by Andrea da Firenze in the Spanish chapel at the cloister in S. Maria Novella, Florence, around 1365–67

architects were required to swear to keep exactly to the model, a requirement that would have many consequences. This vow was faithfully kept until 1421, when Brunelleschi began the vaulting of the dome, and laid down the angles of elevation.

The design of the choir brought in a radical new idea: to add a massive central structure to the nave that combined two different types, the even-sided domed octagon and three apses. This addition increased the cathedral's overall length to 502 ft. (153 m) and its width to 295 ft. (90 m) in the eastern part. The diameter of the octagon was 137 ft. (42 m), equal to the total width of the three aisles, and only about 7 ft. (2 m) less than the largest dome in the world: that of the Roman Pantheon. However, while the Pantheon dome rests on a cylindrical wall, the much higher one in Florence had to rest on piers and arches. That meant it would be the greatest civil engineering risk in the history of European architecture. Even though the building was by now well advanced, no one knew how the vaulting problem would eventually be solved. Apparently, they trusted in the city's genius.

Three immense apses, the so-called tribunes, were added to the octagon at the intersection of the axes. Each has the ground plan of a 5/8 polygon and contains five square chapels set in a thick surrounding wall. On the outside, these also form a 5/8 polygon. Seen from the exterior, the apses appear to be surrounded by an ambulatory and are buttressed at the corners by upward slanting walls. Two sacristies are contained

between the apses, and these project outward on three sides of a 5/8 polygon. Overall, the east end looks from the outside like a veritable mountain, a pile of rounded and angular forms richly encrusted with ornamentation, and covered by domed tiled roofs above the apses.

The concept for the new choir was captured pictorially for the first time in the famous fresco by Andrea da Firenze in the Spanish Chapel in the cloister of S. Maria Novella. A church meeting is represented there, with Florence Cathedral in the background, as though it had already been completed. The fresco appears to have been painted before the final model of 1367, to which all building foremen were sworn, because it certainly shows the dome above the apses of the substructure, but not the drum that lifts the dome a good deal higher. The drum can be seen in a wooden model of the dome in the Florentine Museo dell'Opera di S. Maria del Fiore, and this may be a replica of the 1367 model.

The foundations of the choir were begun in 1379. After about thirty years, the octagon had progressed sufficiently so that in 1412–13 the drum—in reality, the windowed clerestory of the octagon—could be placed on it. Finally, the third apse, which had been held up, was added and completed in 1421.

At this point, faced with a giant hole up above the drum, the powers that be were in a quandary. The problem was that all previous experience of vaulting showed it was necessary to put in wooden scaffolding from which the eight parts of the dome could be constructed, but the builders feared that the scaffolding would not be able to support its own weight. Vasari reported two options that were considered: a provisional stone support column under the dome, and filling the entire octagon with earth. Finally, Brunelleschi suggested that the dome be vaulted with only a suspended scaffolding for the workers. This audacious proposal, which to many appeared to be madness, was accepted.

After three years of consultation over numerous submitted models, Brunelleschi and Ghiberti, rivals in the 1401 competition, jointly delivered a model, and in 1420 were nominated joint leaders with equal rights in the dome-building project. Ghiberti resigned this office in 1433. Despite their equal status, Brunelleschi has always been accepted as the master builder of the dome, largely because it was he who presented a written memorandum for the building, the so-called *Dispositivo*. Moreover, he invented the necessary machines, including a much admired windlass driven by oxen, with a cog drive that worked four different gears, including one in reverse.

The measurements and slope of the dome had been precisely stipulated in the resolution of 1367, and Brunelleschi kept to them. The height had been planned as 144 braccia, which is the holy number of the heavenly Jerusalem in the Apocalypse, and which also corresponded to the width of the substructure. The curvature of the dome at the corners was supposed to describe a pointed arch constructed according to the so-called *quinto acuto*, which meant that the radius of the arch should correspond to four-fifths of the diagonal of the octagon.

Brunelleschi's personal contribution to the dome lay not so much in determining its overall shape as in carrying out the construction. He did not place the vaulting as a single massive unit, as in the Pantheon, but subdivided it, following the model of the Florentine baptistery, into a strong inner shell and a thinner outer shell, which would act as a roof over the former. In fact, the outer shell is tiled, like a roof, which makes the dome look like the largest roof in the city. The shells were joined by ribs. On the outside they protrude at the eight corners and rise up in white marble, indicating the slope of the dome and at the same time framing the red-tiled roof panels. For each panel, two more ribs run between the shells,

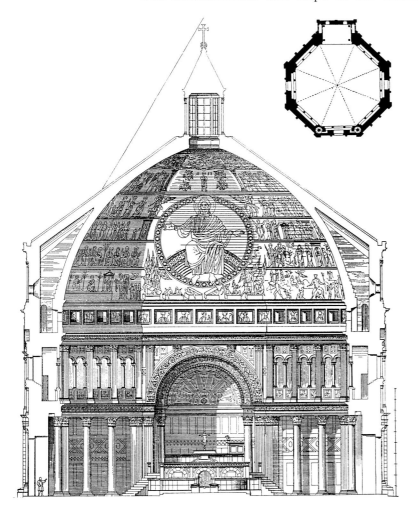

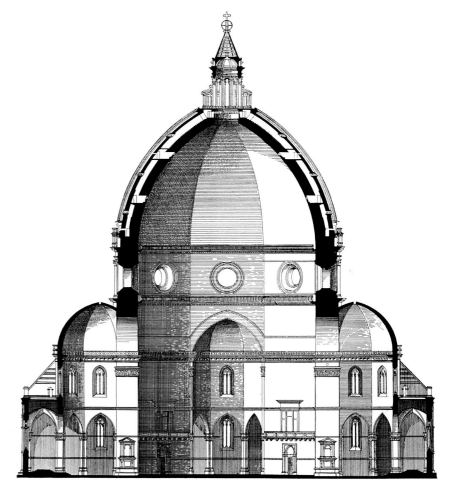

invisible from the outside. Numerous horizontal cross-ribs were added to these. The ribs build up a kind of grid that supports the thin outer shell, which could not bear such a load on its own. To increase stability further, and as far as possible to prevent cracks, Brunelleschi laid the brick courses in a herringbone pattern. In addition, the courses of bricks are not horizontal but curved, and rise from the middle of the roof panel to the corners, so that the latter are additionally supported by the strength of the brickwork. The slope of the dome was executed with the utmost precision. It was also possible to even out certain irregularities at the base, although the exact procedure remains unclear. Progress could have been assessed with a plumb line, course by course, or Brunelleschi, the inventor of scientific perspective, may have devised a system for taking visual bearings from below.

In 1436, at a height of 276 ft. (84 m), the final ring of the dome, on which the lantern would stand, was closed. A competition was staged for the lantern, which Brunelleschi's model won. However, the lantern was not begun until 1446 by Michelozzo and others, after Brunelleschi's death. When the dome was finished in 1467, it was 351 ft. (107 m) high. With its lateral buttresses and volutes, and its spire surrounded by rounded gables, it is a work that freely combines architecture and sculpture with creative imagination. But the dome is still not complete. On the sloping sides of the octagon, Brunelleschi designed semicircular exedras, or niches, as counterparts to the ceilings of the apses, but the uppermost part of the drum beneath the foot of the dome was left as unclad raw masonry. According to the *Dispositivo* of

1420, Brunelleschi had planned a two-storied gallery and a beautiful cornice. But when the drum was clad by Manetti in 1451–60, the difficult upper termination was left out. The present gallery, which was installed from 1508 on the southeast side to plans by Cronaca, Giuliano da Sangallo, and Baccio d'Agnolo, was not extended after Michelangelo— the absolute authority in such matters—had brusquely called it "a whimsical cage." An inexplicable puzzle is why the Florentines left this blemish on the dome of all places, itself a wonder of the world that, in Alberti's words, covers Tuscany with its shadow.

However, the facade also remained incomplete. In 1587, the torso, which had only reached half its planned height, was ripped off to create the foundation for a modern design. In the period following, several wooden models were created for the facade, for example, by Buontalenti, Giambologna, and Cigoli. They, however, limited themselves to proposing ephemeral showpieces and ceremonial decorative schemes for special occasions. The present facade was built from 1875 to 1887 to plans by Emilio de Fabris. No visitor pays any attention to it.

The fixtures of the cathedral are noticeably sparse. One reason for this was the wish of the state government to make the nave a hall of fame for Florence, and, indeed, four monuments were alloted to famous Florentines: Brunelleschi and Giotto, the Neoplatonist Marsilio Ficino, and the then very famous organist Squarcialupi. To these were added two painted equestrian statues of condottieri. In 1436, Uccello painted the Englishman John Hawkwood, known as

Reliefs from the campanile by Andrea Pisano, from 1334. From left: Noah, the inventor of winemaking; Tulbenkian, the first smith; Grammar

Giovanni Acuto in Florence, commander of the Florentine mercenaries toward the end of the 14th century. In 1456, Andrea del Castagno painted the memorial to Niccolò da Tolentino, commander of the Florentines in the Battle of San Romano.

From the liturgical fixtures the famous choir galleries of Donatello and Luca della Robbia went to the Museo dell'Opera di S. Maria del Fiore, as did the statues—the result of a competition—of the four seated Evangelists by Donatello, Nanni di Banco, and others, that were once erected on the west facade. The interior of the cathedral today conveys the impression that Florence, the capital of art, was opposed to having art in its cathedral.

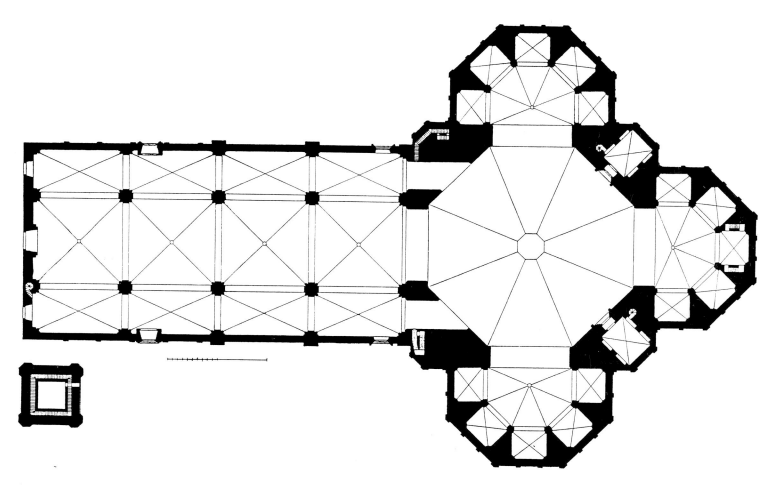

360 *Italy*

199

Siena

Siena, a hill town in the heart of Tuscany, was founded under Augustus as the Roman colony Saena Julia, and built on the site of an Etruscan settlement. However, the city claimed descent from Senus, the son of Remus, from whom the name Siena would be derived. Thus, Siena would rank directly after Rome. The city's insignia, the Capitoline she-wolf, which is seen here much more frequently than in Rome itself, is a reminder of this foundation myth.

In the Middle Ages, the city's banking houses were among the wealthiest in Europe. Politically on the side of the Ghibellines and loyal to the emperor, Siena came more and more into conflict with Florence. The Council of Nine, which governed the city from 1277 to 1355, concluded a peace treaty with Florence, and established the basis for further prosperity. Economically, this was Siena's most flourishing period. The decline began with the Black Death of 1348, which extensively depopulated the city. After eventful disputes between the common people and the nobility, Siena came under the rule of the Petrucci despots until in 1536 Charles V moved in and installed a governor, complete with Spanish garrison. The Spanish handed over Siena to Duke Cosimo I of Florence in 1555. With that, the city's freedom came to an end.

Siena Cathedral has been the seat of an archbishop since 1459. Its history, which is unclear on many points, is currently being extensively researched, and the results are not yet available. According to the very controversial present state of knowledge, a previous building was supposedly consecrated in 1178, but not completed until around 1215. The responsibility for building the cathedral passed from the bishop and cathedral chapter to the city around the end of the 12th century.

It is not known when the present cathedral was begun, but construction incurring considerable costs was in progress from 1226 to 1247. It is possible that at that time the old cathedral was just being extended. By 1258, in place of the city workers, Cistercian monks from the nearby monastery of S. Galgano were working at the cathedral, probably called in because they were experienced in the art of vaulting. By 1263 the dome was already sheathed in copper, and the east end was completed. Finally, the crypt under the choir was frescoed. According to an old, probably apocryphal belief held in Siena, the sculptor and architect Nicola Pisano was called in to build the choir, and later created the pulpit. The roofed-in campanile on the south side, dating from 1264, also belongs to this building phase; it is an unusual design, recessed into the side aisle, and thus appears to be still aligned to the outside of the earlier building.

The building of the nave followed, with bays larger than those of the choir, and the side aisles were extended. The west bay was begun first, in conjunction with the facade, which was ceremoniously started in 1284. The city exempted the architect and sculptor Giovanni Pisano, the son of Nicola, from all taxes and other such payments for life. To blend with the facade, the clerestory had to be heightened the length of the central nave. In 1290, Giovanni, the *caput magister*, was forgiven a fine he had been assessed for a misdemeanor, because it was deemed essential to retain him. However, in 1296–97, when only the lower story of the facade had been built, he went back to Pisa. It is not certain that the upper part of the facade can be attributed to Giovanni's design, but for artistic reasons it seems probable.

When the baptistery was begun in 1317 at the east end of the cathedral, the facade may have already been finished. The baptistery was not to be a detached structure; rather, the choir would be lengthened by two bays, and the baptistery placed beneath them. The sloping ground made extensive substructures necessary before it could be built; thus, it forms an underchurch in the eastern part of the choir, and so has three aisles and two bays. The east end was planned as a counterpart to the west facade. This was to be very much steeper, with three portals leading into the baptistery, and a magnificent Gothic rose window corresponding to the one in the west. A plan of the east facade, which remained incomplete at the top, is preserved in the Cathedral Museum at Siena.

In its original condition, before the eastward extension, the cathedral was a cruciform, three-aisled basilica with a flat east end with two bays and a projecting transept, which, unusually, was laid out with two aisles. The flat end to the choir could date back to the previous building, but may have originated with the Cistercians. The key idea, which makes the concept unique, was to have a hexagonal central structure instead of a conventional crossing. Two sides of its obtuse corners face each of the transverse arms, but it does not extend completely across the width of their three aisles. To carry it across to the transverse arms, triangular spandrels were added. Of the six pier arcades that connect the central structure to the adjoining areas, those on the east–west axis, which lead to the central nave and choir, are clearly higher and narrower than the others. Despite the hexagon, the emphasis of the longitudinal axis is preserved. The central structure is vaulted with an irregular 12-sided cupola, which uses squinches to adjust from the hexagon of the substructure to the cupola. The idea of installing a central structure in the basilica stemmed from the wish to create a sanctuary dedicated to Mary that would include not only the high altar—from 1311 Duccio's *Maestà*—but also the stalls of the canons' choir. Liturgically, the central structure served as the choir for divine office. Facing it, the nave and eastern part are simply designed with round-arched arcades of piers, which one could imagine being surmounted by a flat ceiling, as in Orvieto Cathedral. The most enduring spatial impression is of the repeated alternation between light and dark stone layers, which is quite penetrating, and reminds the modern observer of zebra stripes.

The cathedral is famous for its west facade, one of the great masterpieces of the art of proportion and balance. Here, Giovanni Pisano created a work that was not only intended to contain a series of sculptures by him, but also, in the strength and continuity of its organization, has its own sculptural character. The facade is perhaps the most striking example of sculptural architecture. It has three main motifs: on the ground floor a triple group of round-arched portals all the same size, and crowned with Gothic gables; above this a graduated group of three pointed gables; and, finally, the central motif of the large, rectangular frame containing the circular window in the center. The whole is enclosed on the sides by turrets, and in the center by tall pinnacles on a gigantic scale.

The width of the portals bears no relationship to the width of the aisles behind, just as in the upper story the frame does not stand vertically in line with the piers of the portals, but is pushed outward. This distribution is certainly not canonical; in fact, it goes against every visual principle. But it allows the portals the rhythm of being the same size, and in the upper story with the circular window creates a format that counterbalances the portals and gables. In the relation of the parts to one another, the facade achieves a pleasing and complete harmony. As the earliest Gothic church facade in Italy, it provides an answer to French cathedral facades with their figured portals and rose windows. Giovanni Pisano succeeded here with a work that is entirely independent, despite its French background.

For the facade, he created a sequence of larger-than-life statues of Old Testament patriarchs and prophets, ancient philosophers, and a sibyl (the original of which is in the Cathedral Museum). The cycle was conceived in a singular fashion for its time, not only because of its raised site, which allowed the figures to be viewed from a distance, but because of their interactions. The subject is not the individual prophets, but prophecy itself. All the figures are filled with an inner passionate excitement, which they express in the way their postures lean outward, in the movements of their turning and twisting bodies, in their looks and gestures, and in their emphatically open mouths. To a large extent, they are "talking" figures, demonstrating what it means to body and soul to be gripped by visionary prophecy.

In 1339, the council decided to build a new cathedral on the north side of the old cathedral and at right angles to it; the old cathedral was to serve as a transept. The proposed choir would have pointed north. Two plans for this project, probably by Lando di Pietro, are preserved in the Cathedral Museum, a richer version with a choir ambulatory and radiating chapels and a more modest version with a simple choir apse. The hexagonal central structure was to be retained. The nave of the new cathedral was started, but, because of the plague of 1348, work came to a standstill and was abandoned in 1355. The new cathedral remained no more than a torso, evidence of high-flying aspirations that Siena could no longer sustain.

Unlike the cathedral in Florence, the one in Siena is richly furnished throughout. The floor, made of priceless inlay work, on which more than 40 artists worked from 1369 until it was completed in 1562, embodies a sweeping pictorial world chronicle of heathen antiquity and the Old Testament. Vasari praised the work as the finest and greatest floor ever created.

The pulpit by Nicola Pisano is another masterpiece. He made the piece before 1268 with contributions from Arnolfo di Cambio, his son Giovanni Pisano, and others. Here, the magnificence of his pulpit in Pisa is raised to a still more opulent level. No longer as stylistically tied to the ancient reliefs, Nicola gives the scenes—each according to its subject—an animated new drama that supplants his earlier Classical coolness and indicates early signs of Giovanni's relief style.

The greatest sculptors conitnued to work on the cathedral's fixtures. Donatello, Ghiberti, and Jacopo della Quercia took part in designing the font in the baptistery (1414–34). With his *Salome* relief, Donatello achieved sensational success in the new perspective style as well as creating a thrilling drama. Ghiberti, in total contrast, portrayed the baptism of Christ so calmly and timelessly, and with such dignity, that the very act of baptism conveys a sacramental quality.

The Libreria Piccolomini has become the most popular of the pictorial fixtures on the cathedral's premises. The library was built in 1495 for the permanent collection of the humanist Enea Silvio Piccolomini, later Pope Pius II (1458–64); between 1502 and 1509, it was decorated with a series of frescoes comprising 10 pictures executed by the Umbrian painter Pinturicchio. They were commissioned by

Francesco Piccolomini, the nephew of Pius II, who became pope himself in 1503 (Pius III), but died just 10 days after his coronation. The theme of the series is the life of Enea Silvio Piccolomini, as diplomat, poet, humanist, and finally pope. Pinturicchio reveals himself here as a lovable, friendly narrator of expansive stories, rich in detail. Their peaceful demeanor suits Siena well, for the art of this city always tends to be in a similar vein.

1 Libreria Piccolomini
2 Duomo Nuovo

2OC

374 *Italy*

SOCRATES

HVC PROPERATE VIRI
SALEBROSVM SCANDITE
MONTEM
PVLCHRA LABORIS ERVNT
PREMIA PALMA QVIES

CRATES

382 *Italy*

Orvieto

The name of the city of Orvieto derives from *urbs vetus* (old city). The city is spread over a spectacular location on the plateau of a tuff cliff, which climbs to a height of 656 ft. (200 m) above the Paglia valley. The city, originally an Etruscan settlement, has been the seat of a bishop since 590, and in the 12th century became a community of free citizens. In the second half of the 13th century, from the time of Urban IV (1261–64), the popes and the Curia repeatedly stayed here; they resided in the southeast corner of the cathedral in a monumental two-winged palace, specifically built for this purpose. The papal sojourns ended abruptly with the fall of Boniface VIII in 1303.

Building started at the new cathedral in 1290, during Orvieto's papal period. The new building of the cathedral proceeded from the miracle of the mass at Bolsena, which is famous in part because of Raphael's representation of it in the Stanze (the suite of rooms decorated by Raphael in the Vatican). According to his depiction, a Bohemian priest who doubted the transubstantiation of host and wine into the body and blood of Christ experienced the consecrated host bleeding at a celebration of the mass in Bolsena. The altar cloth (*corporale*) marked by the blood, on which the chalice and paten stood, became a relic, evidence of the fact that Christ was actually present at the celebration of the Eucharist.

The Miracle of Bolsena and the *corporale* attained special importance and relevance in relation to the feast of Corpus Christi, when Pope Urban IV decreed a feast day on August 11, 1264, to commemorate the presence of Christ in the Eucharist. The pope commissioned the bishop to preserve the *corporale* in the cathedral at Orvieto, whereupon the influx of the pious increased so much that the old cathedral became too small. On October 15, 1290, Pope Nicholas IV laid the foundation stone of the new building. Construction was carried out first by the bishop, and then from 1296 by the newly installed guild government of seven consuls, which repeatedly supported the financing through the sale of papal indulgences. In 1338, Ugolino di Vieri, a goldsmith from Siena, delivered a magnificent enameled silver reliquary, which since then has contained the *corporale*, the cathedral's most important object of worship.

The new cathedral was to be worthy and splendid (*nobilis et sumptuosus*); this is mentioned several times in historical sources. The sculptor Ramo Paganelli from Siena, who had also worked beyond the Alps, was appointed for this purpose. In Siena he appears to have found a rival in Giovanni Pisano, and to have been driven from the building works by the latter. In 1293, Paganelli was named in Orvieto along with a large number of other master masons, including a Fleming, a Spaniard, a German, a Scot or Irishman, a Frenchman, six masons from Como, and a Roman: an international group of craftsmen. Because Paganelli was paid more than his colleagues, he may have been head of the masons' lodge. It is not clear whether the overall design of the cathedral was his.

Another artist, Lorenzo Maitani, who also hailed from Siena, was promoted to overseer (*caput magister universalis*) around 1300, and was finally contracted to Orvieto in 1310, when he was granted freedom from taxes and other such privileges. He died in 1330. The concept for the facade is generally attributed to Maitani, and the portals with their sculptural decoration were built under his leadership. Construction continued (with interruptions) until 1532, when the main gable, begun in 1513, was completed. The right corner tower was roofed over in 1590 and the left one in the 17th century. The most notable master builders after Maitani were Andrea Pisano (1347–48), Nino Pisano (1349), Orcagna (1359), and Antonio Federighi from Siena (1451–56).

Apart from the facade, the architecture of the cathedral is very simple both inside and out: a three-aisled basilica 292 ft. (89 m) in length with a transverse rectangular crossing, nonprojecting transept arms, and a rectangular (originally rounded) presbytery. Gothic rib vaults and the shafts supporting them are only in the eastern parts of the building. The nave, on the other hand, has a ceiling of exposed roof timbers, as Christian churches traditionally had from the time of Constantine the Great, some 1,000 years earlier. Given the European cathedrals that were being built at the time, the open roof timbers are an astonishing anachronism, especially in a cathedral that was supposed to be "worthy and splendid." It is possible that this original form of roofing was chosen in imitation of the papal basilicas in Rome, to emphasize the close connection of the pope to Orvieto. But perhaps the reason also lay in the bad experience suffered by the builders when they vaulted the east end: in both transverse arms, the walls bearing the vault were rapidly pushed so far outward that massive flying buttresses had to be added to shore up the north and south fronts of the transept. Later, chapels were built between the arches of the buttresses: the Cappella del corporale around 1350 on the north side and, from 1408, the Cappella nova in the south. The flying buttresses are clearly visible in the side walls of the chapels.

The nave and east end acquire their unmistakable identity, both inside and out, from the horizontal alternation of layers of pale and dark stone: layers of volcanic tuff and basalt (which were painted upon in the upper areas of the central nave). They form a uniformly regular pattern of zebra stripes that cover the cathedral, with the exception of the facade. In no other building is the zebra-stripe pattern, also much loved elsewhere, adhered to as rigidly and monotonously as it is here. The broad spans of the round-arched pier arcades in the nave are very simple and use large columns from older basilicas; these columns are circular except at the crossing, where they are octagonal. An additional characteristic feature of the nave was created by the five small apsidioles (apsidal chapels) on the outer side of the side aisles; these project outward and leave a space free for windows between them. This motif may have been copied, at the request of the pope, from the Laterano Palace in Rome, which originated in Carolingian times.

The desire for sumptuousness was realized only on the facade, which is one of the shining examples of Italian facade art, and has been praised as "daughter more of the heavens than of the earth." The impetus was to rival the cathedral facade in Siena, the masterpiece of Giovanni Pisano, which had been started a little earlier. The facade is, like the interior, very emphatically divided in three. At the bottom are three graduated portals, each of which has recessed side walls and archivolts, and uses small columns and circular lengths of stone to create a finely worked and magnificent assemblage. The central portal has a rounded arch, and the two side portals have pointed arches; all three are crowned by triangular gables. The upper part, which is sharply separated from the lower part by an arcaded gallery, has a large rectangular story in the center, a typical Italian *quadro*, crowned with a gable. Within it is a second *quadro*, which frames a tracery rose window.

The narrower side parts of the facade terminate in pointed gables that sit considerably lower than the central gable. The three gables give the facade a graduated, fanned-out silhouette, which is further emphasized by four tall supporting towers with pointed pinnacles. These supports, decorated with delicately carved shafts and slender columns, provide the vertical dividing elements in the overall pattern of the facade, and set out its division into three parts both clearly and precisely.

Two Gothic plan drawings proposed for the facade are preserved in the cathedral archives; the first shows only one gable, and the second, which is quite like the completed version, has three gables. Here the influence of French Flamboyant Gothic tracery is evident, somewhat on the lines of the transept at Notre-Dame in Paris, especially with the triangular gables, rose windows, and square gables. The designs can easily be attributed to two different master builders because of certain differences in the perspectival treatment. The three-gable design is by Lorenzo Maitani. The facade of the cathedral in Siena provided the starting point for the designs; it is different from Orvieto in that the story with the rose window is much wider than the middle portal beneath it. In Orvieto, the builders took care to keep all the elements exactly perpendicular to each other with clearly defined horizontals, which ultimately produced a geometrically defined grid that gives the facade an impression of precise order, but also of rigid severity. The grid, compared with Siena, was a correction. As a result, the facade has a greater clarity about it, which, however, came at the expense of variety and, particularly, visual excitement. Above all, the correction worked against the rose window which—even though its tracery, designed by Oragna, is very ornate—no longer has the centralizing power of the one in Siena because it is too small for the surrounding elements. Its effect is more that of an inlaid decorative piece.

The facade as a whole was improved when, in 1452, Antonio Federighi inserted a gallery of niches with statues—which was not anticipated in the earlier plan drawings—above the rose window, and so lifted the main gable higher. This gave the center of the facade a steeper and tighter verticality and enclosed the rose window more securely in the manner of a *quadro*. The interplay of architecture, sculpture, and, something rarely found, colored mosaics, which decorate the triangular gables, contributes to the effectiveness of the facade. The mosaics' bright colors increase the sense of sumptuousness.

The reliefs on the faces of the four piers on the ground floor are the most important sculptural decorations on the facade. These were made before 1330 by a group of sculptors led by Maitani. The central portal is flanked by piers depicting the Tree of Jesse and scenes from the Life of Christ. The left outer pillar has Genesis, and the right-hand one the Last Judgment, as its subect. The arrangement of the scenes between the tendrils of the Tree of Jesse is striking; there are parallels in Byzantine art. From a distance, the reliefs, a total of 162 marble panels, give the effect of a single large panel, artfully framed by the tendrils of the tree. Toward the top, the degree of completion diminishes: several clearly unfinished tablets are in place.

The cathedral fixtures include series of frescoes in the presbytery and in the Cappella del corporale, both by the minor 14th-century painter Ugolino di Prete Ilario. On the other hand, the frescoes in the Cappella nova are world-famous. They were started before 1450 by Fra Angelico in the vaults, but the works were soon suspended. In 1499, Luca

Signorelli took over, and he finished in 1503. The sequence is his masterpiece, as well as the most important Italian fresco painting from the period immediately preceding Michelangelo's ceiling in the Sistine Chapel. The theme, the Last Judgment, unfolds in individual scenes all around the upper wall. Most depict groups of athletic nudes in an unending variety of poses, which express the entire spectrum from dramatic despair to spiritual happiness. Interest is focused on the naked figures. The apocalyptic subjects, which include warnings about false prophets, create a many-layered scenario that lies somewhere between Dante's *Inferno* and Michelangelo's *Last Judgment*.

Dante himself and poets and philosophers from the Classical period are represented on the bottom part of the wall in the middle of panels in which the richly ornamented decoration simulates a leather wall covering. The thinkers are glimpsed at their work through the perspective provided by a window frame, as though through an oversized keyhole: Dante compares texts, Horace reflects, and Empedocles looks upward in surprise. These are perfectly controlled illusionistic paintings that, compared with the apocalyptic seriousness of the other frescoes, playfully present a series of joyful surprises.

Plates 211–217

211 General view across the city from the Torre del Moro
212 Facade relief by Lorenzo Maitani with scenes from Genesis, 1310–30 (see Plate 213)
213 West facade
214 Interior looking east
215 View from the right side aisle into the Cappella nova with the fresco cycle by Signorelli, 1499–1503
216 Relief from the Cappella nova with Dante and scenes from the *Divine Comedy* (see Plate 215)
217 *Hell*; scene from the fresco cycle by Signorelli in the Cappella nova (see Plate 215)

1 Cappella del corporale
2 Cappella nova

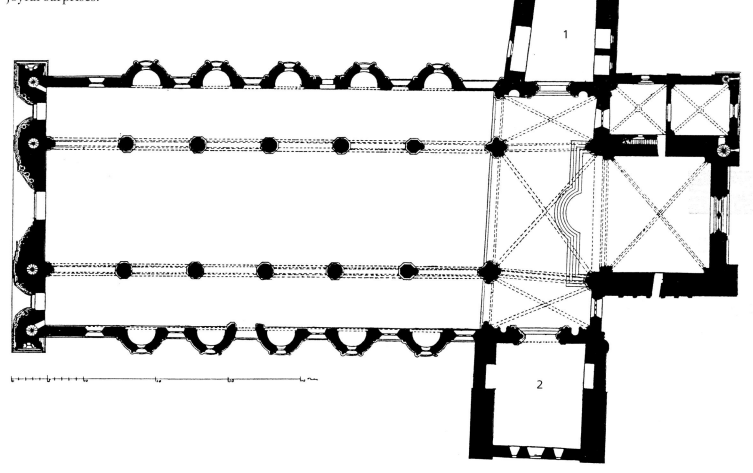

211

Monreale

Monreale is located on high ground, the *mons regalis*, or Royal Mountain, directly adjacent to Palermo, the capital of Sicily. Despite this proximity, there are archbishops' cathedrals in both places. The archbishopric of Palermo is the older of the two. It dates from the Late Classical period, and was subordinate to the patriarchs of Constantinople, and thus followed the Greek form of worship, not the Latin one. It continued under Saracen rule. The archbishops were still following the Greek form of worship when Palermo was conquered by the Normans in 1072, and became capital of the Monarchia Sicula under Roger II (1101–1154; king from 1130). Around 1170, Archbishop Gualtiero Offamilio (1169–90) started to build a new cathedral, a magnificent structure of substantial dimensions that was consecrated as early as 1185. This replaced an older basilica from the sixth century, which had been converted to a mosque by the Muslims, and later returned to Christian worship.

The cathedral of Monreale was built at the same time. In 1174, the young William II, the last of the Norman kings of southern Italy, founded a Benedictine abbey on this site. He granted it rich endowments and privileges, and declared it exempt from the rule of the archbishop of Palermo; instead, the abbacy was directly subordinate to the pope. Construction on the church, conceived as a burial place for the royal house, was started immediately, and completed in a suprisingly short time. As early as 1176, two years after the foundation of the abbacy, one hundred monks from the Cluniac cloister of La Cava near Salerno moved into the monastery. In 1183, at the king's request, Pope Lucius III raised Monreale to an archbishopric with the suffragan bishoprics of Catania and Syracuse. The monastery remained as it was, and the monks were not replaced by canons, which was unusual for Italy although it was customary in England. In the deed of elevation the pope praised King William, the new church, and the other buildings, and particularly emphasized that since the Classical period, no king had achieved a comparable work. In that same year, 1183, William's mother was interred in the church. It seems that the church, cloisters, and fixtures had been more or less completed by the time William died in 1189. The remains of the king, as well as those of his father, William I, were brought here. In the following period the church and cloisters remained virtually untouched. Not until the Renaissance was the whole complex enclosed by new buildings, including a royal palace. The church was almost certainly left unchanged because it was very famous; it was praised as unique, and sometimes even as the most magnificent undertaking in the world.

Structurally, the cathedral is composed of two conflicting parts: a cruciform eastern part and a three-aisled nave. The eastern part consists of a long, rectangular, very high crossing, the sanctuary, and two transverse arms that are wider than the sanctuary. All of these areas have wooden ceilings. The crossing even has a particularly pronounced wooden "stalactite" ceiling in the Islamic style. In contrast to the flat Romanesque ceilings, these rise up toward the center, like a low-pitched roof. The basic organization of the eastern part was developed from a Greek cross with what is ultimately a Byzantine central structure, to which another building type was added. The sanctuary is flanked by cross-vaulted ancillary choirs. The east terminations of these three rooms form a group of three graduated apses, with a short barrel-vaulted bay placed in front of the main apse. The subsidiary choirs and the three graduated apses conform much more to the tradition of Western Benedictine monastic churches than to the Byzantine type of central structure. Overall, Eastern and Western building styles were brought together here, and merge in a new, individual solution.

The formal language of the detail seems to be very plain, for all the walls have smooth surfaces, while the arcades, which have pointed arches, are simple incisions in the wall without moldings on the uprights. There are no subdivisions. The simplicity and flatness of the architectural surfaces show that from the outset the eastern part was meant to be covered with mosaics, which were indeed applied subsequently to the walls in all parts of the building.

As bare as the internal structures are in the east part, the outsides of the three apses are very richly decorated. Once, before the area around the cathedral was built up, these were visible from a distance, and in their raised position faced toward Palermo, which lies within sight on the plain on the edge of the Conca d'oro. Appreciating the church's exposed location, the king mounted a truly royal display of magnificence that has no equal anywhere. This takes the form of colored inlays, set in an ornamental pattern of bands and rosettes, and projecting blind arcades with small columns. The blind arcades are two-storied on the side apses and three-storied on the central apse. The unique overall appearance of the east section is achieved with a special kind of motif: the pointed blind arches intersect with each other and thus form more pointed arches, like steep lancet arches. The entire decoration is made up of these intersecting arches placed closely together. Together with the inlay work they make a magnificent spectacle of the east apses. Against the historical background of European Romanesque architecture, which is much more austere, they not only seem extremely rich but express something foreign—Islamic, in fact—as though the king had wanted to outperform the master builders and decorators of Islam, who were the greatest exponents of rich ornamentation. The old Saracen tradition of the country lived on, now allied to the Norman love of decoration to make something new and singular.

The nave is a three-aisled columned basilica, with a central nave three times as wide as each of the side aisles. This makes the central nave stand out as a broad, grand royal hall, enclosed on the sides by narrow corridors that lack the independence of real "aisles." The spatial relationships of the central nave recall early Christian basilicas. Prominent features are the open roof timbers, and the salvaged Classical columns. However, in their proportions the arcades seem entirely unclassical, because they reach up to more than half the height of the central nave—this height in relation to the clerestory is more of a medieval feature. Moreover, the arcade arches and the Western arch of the crossing are pointed, which is, again, not Classical but expresses once more the influence of Islamic architecture. Many styles come together in this nave.

On either side of the west facade are square towers in the shape of sturdy low blocks projecting out from the lines of the aisles, with a late Renaissance portico in between—a typical Norman structure, like that of Cefalù Cathedral east of Palermo (see ill. page 303). The porch, which replaces an older one, screens a main portal that is distinguished not just by a variety of graduated, voluptuously rich decorative borders, but also by a door with bronze reliefs. According to an inscription, this was made in 1185 by Bonanus of Pisa, the same Bonanus who a little earlier had also delivered a door, which has not been preserved, for the main portal of the cathedral in Pisa. Given his door at Monreale, the unsigned east door in Pisa (ill. page 342) can be ascribed to Bonanus.

The Monreale door is 11 ft. (3.4 m) wide and about 23 ft. (7 m) high, and is the largest medieval bronze door to have come down to us. It consists of a gridlike frame with 40 small reliefs with Old Testament and New Testament scenes and patriarchs and prophets. At the very top are two large panels with the enthroned Mary and Christ Pantocrator. These are the only panels to be cut into by the door arch; apparently the measurements that had been passed to Bonanus in Pisa were not exact. There is a second, clearly smaller bronze door in the portal of the north side aisle. This is from the same period, and is signed Barisanus of Trani, a bronze artist who also created doors for the cathedrals in Ravello and Trani.

However, it is above all the mosaics that really established

Double capital with dedication relief in the cloister

the worldwide fame of Monreale. They cover all the interior walls with a golden ground, occupying an area of about 38,751 sq. ft. (3,600 sq. m). The extensive cycles, with scenes from the Old Testament and the Life of Christ as well as the lives of Peter and Paul, further enriched by numerous figures of saints, are descended from the highly sophisticated Byzantine mosaic art; appropriately, the inscriptions are partly in Greek. Stylistically, the mosaics relate to contemporary Byzantine painting. The cycle culminates in the main apse with the oversized half-figure of Christ Pantocrator. His stern gaze, which misses nothing and from which no one can pull away, seems to fill the entire space of the church. This is one of the most forcible pictures of Christ's far-reaching power and omnipresence that has ever been created, comparable to the Christ Pantocrator in the main apse at Cefalù (see ill. page 303), but even more spellbinding.

King William had himself portrayed on the two east crossing piers in front of the main apse with Christ Pantocrator. On the north side of the sanctuary, above the royal lion throne that is a reference to the throne of Solomon, William is crowned by the enthroned Christ. Opposite, on the south side, above where the archbishop's throne formerly stood (it has not been preserved), William hands the finished church to the enthroned Mary. This dedication and the coronation are there to indicate that William's pious foundation is pleasing to God, and that his rule is God's wish. At the same time, they ensured his posthumous fame.

Finally, the famous cloister also demonstrated that no expense was too great for the king. With sides nearly 154 ft. long (47 m), and the almost endless sequences of 26 arches on each of the four sides, it is the largest cloister from medieval Italy. It is also one of the most magnificent, for the pointed arcades are decorated on the shafts of the double columns and on the stepped fronts of the arches with mosaic encrustations of tesserae made from lava and glass. The capitals, too, are decorated with extraordinary variety; figures include a relief representation of the dedication of the church to Mary by the king. It appears that five different studios worked on the capitals at the same time.

The grandest impression of the cloisters is provided by the south side, to which the rhythmic, evenly shaped, and continuous sequence of tall blind arcades on the ruins of the monastery dormitory make a monumental backdrop. The dormitory, with its severe monastic architecture, forms the greatest contrast imaginable to the splendor of the cloisters, especially to the fountain house in the southwest corner, which has its own tiny, intimate arcaded courtyard enclosed on all sides. One would prefer to imagine this fine jewel, filled with Eastern magic, in a royal Norman pleasure palace rather than in the cloisters of a Benedictine monastery—in Monreale, William was evidently more important than Benedict.

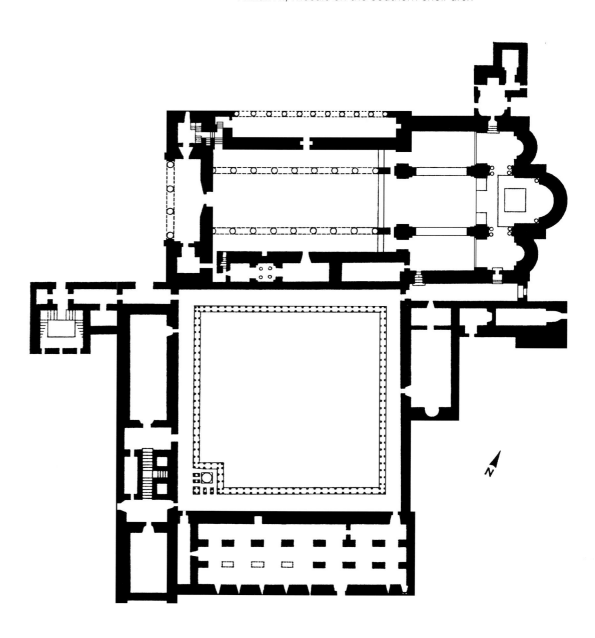

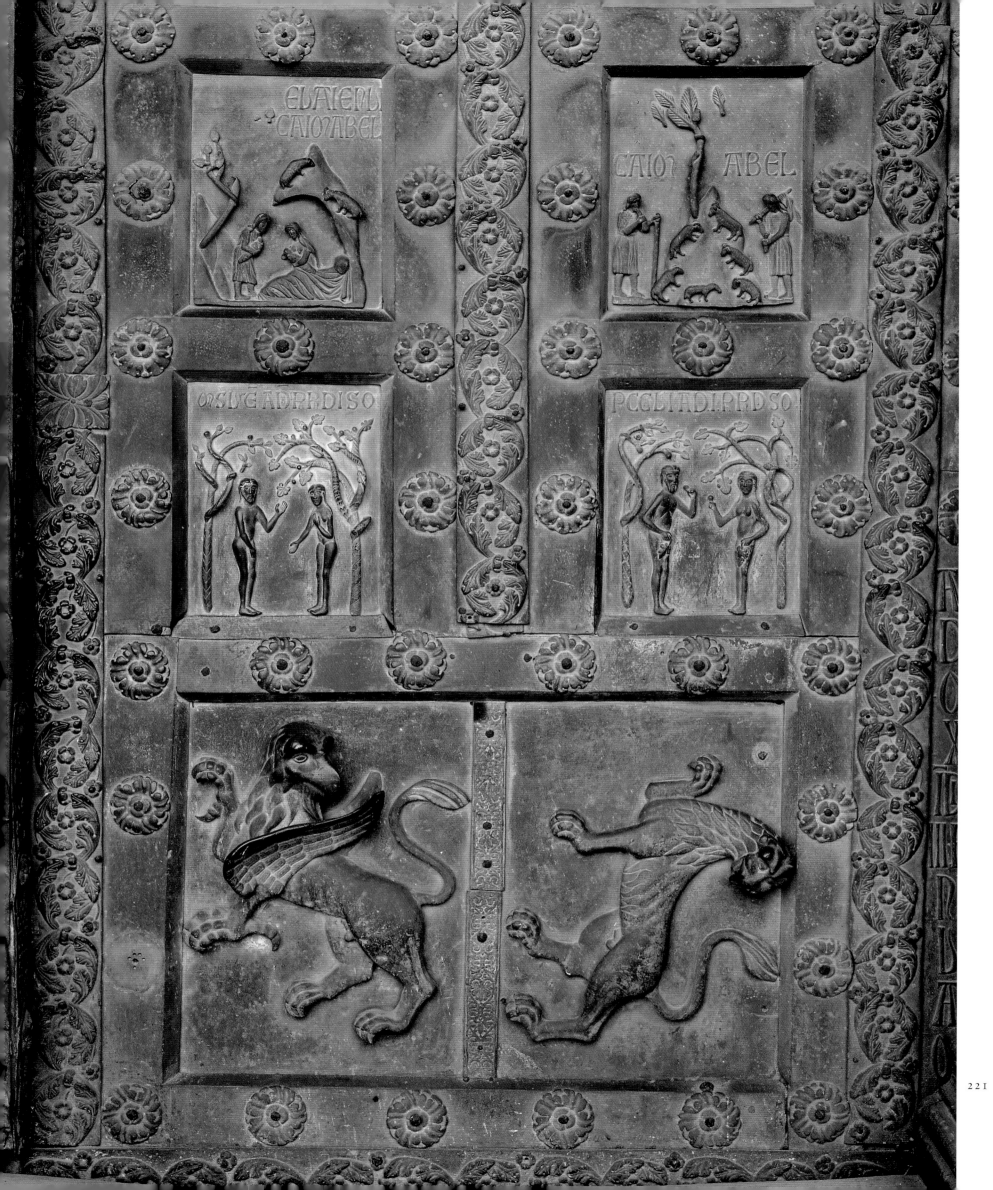

DUCAT AQ. REPTIL E AIE VIVETI IVOLA
E SUP TRA SUB FIRMAMTO CELI :

225

MP. ΘΥ.

REX
GVI
LIEL
MVS.
SCOS

226

FRANCE

Santiago de Compostela

Astorga

León

Burgos

Gerona

S P A I N

Lérida

Toro

Zaragoza

Zamora

Barcelona

Poblet

Salamanca

Segovia

Tarragona

Avila

PORTUGAL

Madrid

Coimbra

Palma de Mallorca

Plasencia

Toledo

Valencia

Lisbon

Granada

Seville

Málaga

N

100 km

ALGERIA

MOROCCO

Spain

Architectural History

For 600 years, the medieval history of Spain was defined by the Reconquista, the reconquest of the country by the Christians from the rule of the Muslim Moors. The Western Goths had made Roman Spain a kingdom of their own in the fifth century; in 711 the Arabs invaded, and very quickly conquered nearly the whole Iberian peninsula, which soon became a separate caliphate with its capital at Cordova. The Western Goths held out only in the mountainous northern regions of Asturias. In 778, in the northeast, Charlemagne conquered the area as far as the Ebro, the Spanish marches around Barcelona, which the Carolingians were able to retain despite a counterattack by the Moors.

Four empires gradually formed across northern Spain. In the northwest, there was the kingdom of Asturias, which several times broke down into the smaller states of Galicia, Asturias, and León. The capital was Oviedo, then, from 911, León. The territory of this empire reached as far as the Douro River. Castile, later to become so important, broke away from León and became a separate state in the 10th century. The second empire was the kingdom of Navarre in the Basque country, with its capital at Pamplona; the third was the state of Aragon, around the city of Jaca; and the fourth was the margravate of Barcelona, also known as Catalonia, which succeeded the former Carolingian Spanish marches.

By the 11th century, nearly the whole of Christian Spain, comprising Navarre, Castile, and Aragon, was temporarily united under one crown, and from these states two Spanish kingdoms took shape over time. These were Castile, finally united with León in 1230, and Aragon, which was joined through marriage with Catalonia as early as 1151. In the west of the Iberian peninsula, Portugal became an independent kingdom in 1129.

The Reconquista was facilitated by the fact that in 1031 the caliphate of Cordova was split into several smaller domains known as *taifas*: Seville, Toledo, Valencia, and Saragossa. The two Spanish kingdoms were now able to seize one city after another from the Moors. Castile conquered Toledo in 1085, which made the settlement of central Spain possible, then Cordova in 1236, Seville in 1248, and Cadiz in 1250. Aragon occupied Saragossa and the densely settled Ebro basin in 1118. After that, Aragon expanded seaward, and conquered the Balearic Islands from 1229 to 1233, then Valencia and Murcia on the coast; in 1282 they acquired Sicily, ruled until then by Anjou in France; Sardinia in 1326; and, finally, in 1443, the kingdom of Naples. After 1238, only the kingdom of Granada in the far south remained under Moorish rule, and that was a feudal vassal of Castile.

Spain first became a unified world power as a result of

Santiago de Compostela Cathedral, south transept

Opposite:
Zamora Cathedral, dome over the crossing from the northeast

the marriage of the heiress of Castile, Isabella, to Ferdinand of Aragon; the two kingdoms were joined in 1479. The Reconquista was finally concluded with the conquest of Granada. This happened in 1492, the same year in which America was discovered.

The cultural development, at least of northern Spain, owed much to a movement that embraced the whole of northern Europe: the pilgrimage to the tomb of the apostle James in Santiago de Compostela (*Santiago* means "St. James"), located near the west coast in Galicia. The route to it was difficult and dangerous in the ninth and tenth centuries. At that time, priests campaigned in their sermons for people to visit the apostle's grave, just as people would soon be summoned to join a crusade. From about the year 1000, a regulated pilgrims' organization developed and produced written pilgrims' guides to several routes through France, which then converged at Puente la Reina in Spain.

As a consequence, Spanish architecture in the north-western areas reveals close connections with France. The destination of the pilgrims, the cathedral of Santiago de Compostela (see pp. 418–27), begun in 1078, is architecturally

Salamanca, Old Cathedral

Right:
View from the north
transept into the crossing
dome

Far right:
Nave and south side
aisle looking east

almost a twin of St. Sernin in Toulouse: a cruciform structure with a choir ambulatory and radiating chapels, and a long, projecting transept with side aisles leading in a U-shape around the fronts of the transept. The chief characteristic is the galleries, which have paired openings onto the nave, and also run around the transept. Immediately above the galleries, the vaulting begins in the form of barrel vaults with transverse arches. There is no clerestory, so that the church is dimly lit. At the time, the galleries were perceived as making the two-storied walls rather grand, and one pilgrims' guide stated that the galleries were like something from a palace. As befits its cultic importance, Santiago is the largest Romanesque cathedral in Spain. Such was its status that the nave of the cathedral in Coimbra, the first capital city of Portugal, almost literally repeated the layout at Santiago with galleries and barrel vaults, although on a smaller scale; building at Coimbra dates from 1140, or earlier.

In the south of the kingdom, León quickly came to the fore as a result of its conquests, and was soon leading the way

with its Romanesque architecture, as though marking its acquisition of new territories by putting up large new buildings. The cathedrals of Zamora and Salamanca and the collegiate church of Toro were built around the middle of the 12th century. In these buildings, the architects abandoned the typical French-style choir with ambulatory, which Santiago still retains, in favor of a group of three graduated apses, attached directly to the transept. This layout had been common for some time farther north in the Pyrenean area. In the naves of these three buildings, the rectangular transverse bays were vaulted with either ribbed vaults or barrel vaults, and supported by a richer and stronger system of compound piers, a variant on the old cruciform pier.

The three buildings are famous for their round crossing towers, known as *cimborios*, which in the interior have a 16-part, umbrella-like ribbed dome mounted on a one- or two-storied drum. On the exterior they are surrounded on the diagonal sides by small round towers, like satellites. Both inside and outside, the atmosphere is one of seemingly unsurpassable splendor, a panoply of blind arcades, small columns, and friezes, as though the architects had sought to re-create the jewel-like luxury of a goldsmith's masterpiece. In their magnificence, the domes, sweeping upward into the heights, convey a vision of another world, perhaps the architects' idea of heaven.

Catalan architecture developed along similar lines. The cathedrals of Tarragona and Lerida, begun in the late 12th and early 13th centuries, are not very different from buildings like the cathedral in Salamanca in terms of the structure of the nave, with oblong transverse bays, ribbed vaults, and strong compound piers. The angular mass of the walls is typical of the Late Romanesque, and there are added Gothic elements such as the pointed arches.

Direct borrowings from French Gothic architecture are mainly found in those buildings that have a polygonal ambulatory and radiating chapels. The Cistercians pioneered this form of design. In the second half of the 12th century, in the monastic churches of Poblet (Catalonia) and Moreruela (Zamora province), they produced two closely related versions based on a clean-cut 5/10 polygon. The choir is

more extravagant in the monastic church at Alcobaça, in Portugal, begun after 1178 and with, surprisingly, a nave in the form of a hall church. When they built the choir, the Cistercians almost literally copied the choir and ambulatory of the Clairvaux monastery with its narrow 9/18 polygon, but widened the ambulatory to two aisles.

Avila in Castile, begun around 1170–80, is an earlier example of a cathedral with a choir and ambulatory with radiating chapels. This choir ambulatory also has two aisles. The columns of the ambulatory and the shallow convex shapes of the apses in the radiating chapels seem to derive from no less a source than St. Denis, the burial church of the French kings. The windows in the radiating chapels could not be repeated, however, because in Avila the whole choir forms a bastion of the city wall. The upper choir has a three-storied elevation, and the middle story has paired openings, the conventional style for galleries, although there is no gallery as such, the space being occupied by windows. The wall, with its sharply delineated graduated relief and small columns, is a fine example of the Late Romanesque flair for structural organization. On the other hand, the rib vaults are completely typical of early French Gothic.

Bourges, the outsider among the cathedrals of France, was used as the model for several buildings in Spain. One of these was the cathedral in Burgos, which was started in 1221; the ambulatory was already covered by 1230 (see pp. 436–45). Its bays originally had the same shape as those at Bourges—

Above:
Toro, Colegiata S. Maria la Mayor, view of the apses and crossing tower from the southeast

Left:
Salamanca, Old Cathedral, crossing tower from the east-southeast

Saragossa, La Seo
Cathedral, diagonal view

vaulted sections in the form of an inverted trapezium, facing small, narrow chapels. Much of the detailing at Bourges was also borrowed. For example, the circular piers are surrounded by slender shafts, one of which then continues up the wall as an engaged shaft and seems to divide the pier into two parts. Also, the multiarched compartments of the triforium are enclosed within larger arches, and there are small circular apertures at the foot of the vault crowns in the choir polygon. Clearly, the builders at Burgos were very familiar with the cathedral at Bourges. Burgos, however, has only three aisles, and so the extreme height of the piers and dividing arcades at Bourges, which has five graduated aisles, was not adopted. The wall elevation in the upper choir conforms more closely to that of classical French cathedrals such as Chartres.

The archbishop's cathedral in Toledo (see pp. 446–53), which dates from 1226, immediately following Burgos, kept even closer to the Bourges model. With five aisles and a three-aisled transept that derives from buildings such as Chartres, Toledo is the largest 13th-century cathedral in Spain. It has the same graduated form as Bourges, with narrower inner side aisles and wider outer ones. It also has similarly high dividing arcades and circular piers surrounded by shafts, as well as a separate triforium in the inner ambulatory with arches surmounted by an oculus.

A new treatment was adopted for the ground plan of the double ambulatory. In the inner ambulatory, there is an alternating sequence of rectangular bays with transverse ribs and triangular bays with three ribs. This alternation between rectangle and triangle, which ultimately derives from the ambulatory of Charlemagne's palatinate chapel in Aachen, means that the number of supports between the two ambulatories is doubled, unlike those in the inner polygon. In the outer ambulatory, rectangular bays alternate with, this time, very narrow triangular bays, similar to those of the cathedral in Le Mans. The radiating chapels are laid out in alternation to correspond with the structure of the bays. For each rectangular bay there is a larger chapel in the form of a polygonal apse. For every triangular span, there is a smaller rectangular chapel. As a result, two smaller chapels enclose a larger one, producing rhythmic groups of three facing each other. Originally, there were 15 chapels altogether, more than in any other cathedral ambulatory.

The architects at León were even more French than at Burgos and Toledo. The cathedral was begun in 1255 (see pp. 428–35), at a time when Gothic tracery in the Flamboyant style was favored in France, and León is a showpiece example of the manner. The ground plan for the east end of the High Gothic cathedral at Reims has a three-aisled transept, a short five-aisled choir, an ambulatory with radiating chapels, and a 5/10 polygon to terminate the choir. In León, the three-aisled nave is four bays shorter than in Reims, and the west towers are not integrated into the main body of the building, but stand next to it. Again, this is comparable to the transept towers at St. Denis, which were never finished. Also, the design of the west facade and the transept, with three large portals and a tracery rose window, is purely French. The three-storied wall elevation, with its pierced triforium and especially large tracery windows in the clerestory, reveals a clear relationship to the new building of St. Denis, begun in 1231, although the compound piers of Reims were preferred to the modern, tightly clustered piers of St. Denis. Nevertheless, the triple clusters of the main shafts in the nave continue down to the floor. In terms of architectural history, León is more French than Spanish, as French as the best buildings in France itself. This connects León to the nave in the cathedral at Strasbourg, at that time still German, and to Cologne Cathedral.

In Saragossa, the old capital of Aragon, the builders pursued another, highly unusual approach. Here, the cathedral of La Seo was built from 1300 as a three-aisled hall church with clustered piers, and extended to five aisles in the 15th century, which gives the interior a labyrinthine spaciousness.

After the first phase of Gothic cathedral architecture in Spain, which was influenced by France, a change began in Catalonia around 1300 that produced a completely new and individual Catalan architectural style. The only elements it shares with typically French cathedrals are the polygonal choir ambulatory and the radiating chapels. The structure is radically different, even anti-French.

The starting point was Barcelona, the new capital of the kingdom of Aragon. A new and highly inventive cathedral was begun here in 1298, which bravely attempted to unite two disparate types, the basilica and the hall church, the two most important and opposite building types of the Middle Ages. In the nave, the transverse rectangular bays are so close to square in shape that the piers of the dividing arcades, which are clustered piers surrounded by narrow shafts, are set far apart. The arcades themselves reach very high up. The imposts of the vaults in the side aisles and nave stand at the same height, as they do in hall churches. But, because the nave is twice as wide as each of the side aisles, the vaults in the nave reach up much higher than those in the side aisles, and higher than the dividing arcades. This is why a low wall runs between the dividing arcades and the crowns of the vaults in the nave. This is very high up, almost in the area of the vaults, but nonetheless—in the manner of basilicas—it has a triforium and a clerestory window in the form of an oculus. This solution gives the interior a hall-like breadth, quite unlike a basilica, but with lighting from on high, which is typically basilican.

On their outer side, the side aisles are enclosed by chapels and galleries set between the buttresses. The buttressing was thus brought inside, which is why the exterior looks so compact, like a fortress. This form of structure originated from a third and more rarely found building type: the single-aisled church with side chapels set between the piers of the buttresses and reaching up to the area of the vaults. The chief example of this is the cathedral at Albi in southern France, which was built from 1282. Taken as a whole, Barcelona Cathedral can be seen as a great synthesis combining the choir ambulatory with radiating chapels, the hall church, the basilica, and the lateral layout of single-aisle churches in a way that was new, and transcends every known category.

In Barcelona, the structural concept of the cathedral was again taken up in the parish church of Sta. Maria del Mar (1329–84), and brought to its final development. Here, the bays are even deeper than in the cathedral, the aisles even wider, the piers, now simple octagons without engaged shafts, even more slender, and the spatial relationships even more uniform. The apse, in the form of a polygon and with its tall, narrow, stilted arches, is completely different from the broad nave. The result is a spatial miracle, a place where visitors can breathe freely.

Left:
Barcelona Cathedral, view through the choir

Below left:
Barcelona, Sta. Maria del Mar, interior looking southeast

The cathedral in Palma de Mallorca is also a spatial miracle. From 1276 to 1349, Palma de Mallorca was the capital of the short-lived kingdom of Majorca, whose kings came from a branch of the House of Aragon; in addition to

Majorca, they also occupied Perpignan in the south of France. The cathedral was built on the site of the main mosque, which had been turned into a church for the bishop. A small Trinity chapel, the present east chapel, was added to the mosque in 1306 by King James II as a royal burial site. The much larger choir, now called the Capilla real, followed in 1314; the decision to replace the mosque with a new three-aisled nave was only made in 1386. (It was not consecrated until 1601, after building had been going on for more than 200 years.) The nave suddenly vastly increased the building's dimensions. The total length is 397 ft. (121 m); the width of the nave is around 59 ft. (18 m), its height about 138 ft. (42 m); the piers and side aisles are about 72 ft. (22 m) high. The dividing arcades are about 98 ft. (30 m) high, nearly as high as the nave of the cathedral in Soissons, and almost 23 ft. (7 m) higher than the nave in Noyon Cathedral.

The interior is dominated by the dividing arcades with their exceedingly slender octagonal piers that rise up sheer in a dizzying manner. Because of the arcades' great height, the side aisles are correspondingly high, like those of a hall church, and add to the building's air of spaciousness. Here, unlike Barcelona, the imposts in the nave are set farther up than in the side aisles, and there is also space for an unusual clerestory, which is large. The extreme contrasts of width and precipitousness are what make the interior so exhilarating. In addition to the piers, the gigantic, eye-catching rose window above the low choir arch provides a spatial motif of a different kind. Above the entrance, a second rose window acts as a pendant to the other; between them, they enclose the interior like polar opposites. The exterior, which formerly stood directly on the seashore, is very impressive: a mountain of soaring, tightly packed piers surround the base of the cathedral, as if protecting it like a phalanx. Their ordered regimentation seems to echo the structure of the old mosque.

The cathedral at Gerona, located close to Barcelona, is a unique piece of medieval architecture. Here, after 1312, the Romanesque nave was given a new polygonal choir with an illuminated ambulatory and a low series of radiating chapels. The choir is closely related to that of the cathedral in Barcelona, and has similar proportions, typical of Catalonia; the triforium and clerestory are pushed up high into the area of the vaulting, again because the dividing arcades are so high. In 1417, after several experts had been consulted about statics and aesthetic matters, the daring decision was made to build a single-aisled nave instead of a three-aisled one in the area between the side chapels, which were located between the buttresses. This would make the nave "more splendid and more striking," and would cause a greater sensation. Thus, a single-aisled nave was built, as had been done earlier in Albi, but this time with a width of about 76 ft. (23 m) and a height of about 112 ft. (34 m). These dimensions were risky, principally because the width of the vault bays defied every medieval standard, bringing them closer to the gigantic structures of the Late Classical period, such as Old St. Peter's in Rome, with a nave nearly 79 ft. (24 m) wide. The nave in Gerona is an immense open space, as big as three-aisled cathedrals plus chapels elsewhere. The choir, however, has all three aisles facing this enormous single nave, and is so overwhelmed by it that it seems to have been built for a much smaller race of people. As in the cathedral at Palma de Mallorca, a large round window, like a giant eye, is located above the choir arch. It seems, in fact, that Palma was the decisive influence in the nave's conception, for there, too, an enormous nave towers over a low choir. However, Gerona's choir is no small-scale single-aisled space, but a complete cathedral choir. This was what took its dimensions into a new and unknown world.

One hundred years later, the builders of Seville Cathedral in Andalusia (see pp. 454–63) were concerned with gigantic dimensions of a different kind. The cathedral was built on the site of a very famous 12th-century mosque that had been damaged by an earthquake; the mosque's minaret, a richly ornamented square tower, and the courtyard were retained. The new cathedral was designed to have no equal anywhere. Faced with this mania for gigantism, a member of the cathedral chapter voiced the fear that, on its completion, the builders would be thought mad.

The cathedral is rated the third largest historic cathedral in the world, after St. Peter's in Rome and St. Paul's in London. (If a different method of calculating size were followed, the third largest would be the cathedral in Milan.) The floor area occupies a rectangle almost 381 ft. (116 m) long and 249 ft. (76 m) wide. The rectangle recalls the ground plan of the old mosque on which it stands. The nave and choir have five aisles, and are enclosed on both sides by rectangular chapels; in contrast, the transept, which does not project beyond the chapels, has only a single aisle. The choir ambulatory with radiating chapels, long an obligatory feature of the larger Spanish cathedrals, is missing here. It was originally planned with two aisles, as in Toledo, but the plan was not carried out. If it had been, the floor area of the cathedral would have exceeded that of the cathedral in Milan, which although some 131 ft. (40 m) longer, is almost 33 ft. (10 m) narrower.

The dividing arcades, with their richly profiled compound

piers, reach up high in Seville, as they so often did in earlier Spanish cathedrals, which is why the clerestory is again very low. However, the side aisles are not graduated, as might be expected given the dimensions of the dividing arcades, and following the model of Toledo, but instead are the same height. At 118 ft. (36 m), they are nearly as high as the nave, each forming a majestic two-aisled hall with tightly spaced bays. Overall, the bays are aligned lengthwise, but this alignment lacks the strict differentiation found in other cathedrals. The interior loses its way a little, as though the old mosque were still there as a secret formative power, planted within the Gothic structure.

At the crossing, it is clear that something new was achieved in the design of the vaults, which are mostly simple ribbed vaults. Here, opulent star patterns of the Late Gothic period make their appearance, along with partially curved ribs. Cathedral Gothic has here developed into a style of decoration aimed at covering whole surfaces.

The art of decoration has a long tradition in Spain, going back to the Moors. Islamic ornamental forms, such as the horseshoe arch and the finely detailed multifoil, were combined with Christian forms as early as the Romanesque period and even more so in the Gothic. This led to the typically Spanish hybrid style known as "Mudejar," after the *mudéjares*, the Moors who stayed behind in Spain and became

Gerona Cathedral, view through the nave to the choir

Opposite:
Palma de Mallorca Cathedral

Top:
View from the south

Bottom:
View through the nave

Right:
Saragossa, La Seo
Cathedral, star vault in
the crossing dome

Far right:
Salamanca, New
Cathedral, view into
the crossing

Christians. This style, an art of finely detailed surface ornamentation, developed independently, parallel with the growth of cathedrals. In the Late Gothic period, it penetrated the world of cathedral architecture. In the 15th century, traditional Islamic elements were combined with the Flamboyant shapes of Late Gothic tracery from northern Europe, brought there by master builders and artisans who had come to Spain from Burgundy, Germany, and the Netherlands. The result was the so-called Hispano-Flemish style. This advanced quickly in the late 15th century under Queen Isabella of Castile to become the official state and court art, which is thus also known as the "Isabelline" style.

Burgos (see pp. 436–45) was one of the centers of the new trend toward ostentatious display. Around the middle of the 15th century, master builder Hans of Cologne was brought there; he worked on the pierced spire of the west tower, following the model of German spires such as those planned for Cologne Cathedral. In 1482, Simón de Colonia, the son of Hans of Cologne, built the incredibly rich octagonal Capilla del condestable, which, with its refined star vaulting, forms the choir termination at Burgos. The crowns of the vaulting reach up to the ridge, where a second star is formed. These vaults are made not of stone, but of glass, and are translucent. There are several more star vaults of this type in Burgos: they were a local specialty, as was the dome at the cathedral crossing. The dome vaulting originally designed by the same Simón collapsed in 1539, and was soon afterward

rebuilt in a similar form with glass crowns. At Seville Cathedral, the crossing tower that Simón built in 1506 collapsed just five years later. However, the magnificent star vault of the crossing in the cathedral of La Seo at Saragossa has been preserved.

Along with the development of architecture came an increasing refinement in stonemasonry, which finally reached a stage of unsurpassed finesse. It is reminiscent of delicate lacework or the filigree art of gold- and silversmiths. This latest Gothic phase was appropriately called the "Plateresque" style, derived from the word *platéro*, meaning "silversmith." The ornamentation, sometimes using a scale motif, now spread out prolifically to cover entire surfaces, even whole facades, independently of the building's design. In Portugal, where the Late Gothic style developed in its own individual way, this style was known as "Manueline," named for King Manuel I (1495–1521), under whom Portugal enjoyed its greatest period. The Plateresque style blossomed in the first half of the 16th century, at the same time as the High Renaissance in Italy.

During these late phases of the Gothic style, many Spanish cathedrals were given a cloister with opulent tracery, extravagant memorial chapels, and sometimes a high crossing tower, as for example at Valencia. In the interiors, there were large retable altars, in particular the highly artistic screens and railings that clutter up the space but are indispensable for the purposes of worship. Spanish cathedrals were like those in

England in this respect, whereas most such furnishings were later removed from French, German, and Italian cathedrals because they were felt to be obstructive.

In the late 15th and 16th centuries, as the Gothic period was drawing to a close in most other parts of Europe, it experienced a final heyday in Spain. A group of new cathedrals were built, all of them of considerable size and decorated with exquisite stonemasonry: first in Astorga, begun in 1477; then in Plasencia toward the end of the 15th century; then in Salamanca, where from 1513 a new and larger cathedral was built next to the old one; and finally in Segovia, begun in 1525, and Palencia, where the cathedral begun in 1321 was continued and completed in the early 16th century. These buildings, which in Segovia and Palencia still feature the traditional choir ambulatory with radiating chapels, are characterized by typically high dividing arcades with richly profiled compound piers, rich star and fan vaults, and most of all the strict tautness of the structure, which rhythmically encloses the interior. In this final Gothic period, the cathedrals still convey an astonishing vitality that maintains the high standards of quality of previous centuries.

At the same time, elsewhere, there was a transition toward building piers in which, in place of Gothic compound piers, the shafts were replaced by engaged columns in the shape of fluted Corinthian half-columns, which demonstrate an astonishingly exact knowledge of the Vitruvian rules for the Classical orders. The piers reached the necessary height by placing the columns on high Attic bases. The vaults, on the other hand, remained Late Gothic ribbed vaults. This happened in Granada and Málaga. Granada Cathedral, begun in 1523, is a five-aisled basilica in the older Gothic tradition, with a high rotunda for the choir instead of a polygon. In Málaga, the cathedral, begun in 1528, was built as a three-aisled hall church. Both buildings were started in the Gothic style by Enrique Egas, the master builder of the Late Gothic Capilla real in Granada, and then continued by Diego de Siloe in the "Roman" style. That was the beginning of the Renaissance in Spanish cathedral building, a period that began by grafting new facades based on Classical Roman types onto older Gothic cathedrals.

Above left:
Málaga Cathedral, choir

Above right:
Segovia Cathedral,
view of the choir

Santiago de Compostela

Above:
Portico de la gloria, trumeau in the middle of the portal, 1168–88

Opposite:
Puerta de las platerias, west recess on the left door: the Blessing of Christ; the Creation of Adam; King David, last decade of the 11th century

The bishopric of Santiago de Compostela (an archbishopric since 1124) has a special position among all the western bishoprics, because the bishop's seat was regarded as the burial place of the apostle James the Greater, which made it the destination of floods of pilgrims from all over Europe. According to legend, the apostle James the Greater, brother of John, did missionary work in Spain for seven years before he returned to the Holy Land, then ruled by the Jewish tetrarch Herod Agrippa; there he endured a martyr's death. James the Lesser took the mortal remains by ship to Spain. Miraculously, the wind drove the ship through the Straits of Gibraltar to the exact place where James had formerly preached, namely on the coast at Iria Flavia in Galicia in northwest Spain. Here, the mortal remains were buried. The gravesite was subsequently forgotten, until in the ninth century miraculous starlight from heaven appeared to a hermit in the countryside. Bishop Theodomiro of Iria was informed of this, and in 834 found the grave in an open field, and identified it as that of James.

The bishop and the Asturian ruler, Alfonso II "the Chaste," immediately arranged for a church to be built *supra corpus apostoli* (above the body of the apostle). As early as 862, the bishop of Iria had transferred his seat to the tomb of James, and in the same century the building of a new church was begun. It was commissioned by Alfonso III "the Great" (866–910), and by 899 the new cathedral was ready to be used for worship.

Since 1095, at the instigation of Pope Urban II, the burial site of St. James has been called Compostela, derived from *campus stellae*, the field of the star where the light miraculously appeared. From as early as the beginning of the 10th century, pilgrims streamed here in great numbers, even from the other side of the Pyrenees, and thus blessed the location with rapid growth. From 1072 there is evidence of pilgrim groups arriving not only from France, but also from Germany and Italy.

The church that was built toward the end of the ninth century, a basilica with a rectangular choir that enclosed the remains of a Roman tomb, appears to have been destroyed in 997 during the advance of the Moors against Galicia. After that, however, the influx of pilgrims continued to increase. It became essential to build a new church, one that was not only large enough but could also cope with the incoming and outgoing streams of people and indicate where they should go. Bishop Diego Peláez began construction in 1078, supported by Alfonso VI of Castille-León. The works were financed for the most part by pilgrims' donations. The pilgrims also lent a hand without payment by, for example,

laboring in the quarries. The master builder was the *mirabilis magister Bernardus*, assisted by a man named Robertus.

In 1088, ten years after the start of building, Bishop Peláez fell into disgrace with Alfonso VI, and was imprisoned. For the next 13 years the bishopric was vacant, and little work was done on the building. A new era began with Diego Gelmírez, a former administrator appointed bishop in 1101; under him Compostela was promoted to an archbishopric in 1124. The impressive bishop's palace is evidence of the power of this prince of the church in Galicia, whose rank was equal to that of a royal governor. Gelmírez energetically completed the church in 1128. The work was interrupted in 1117, when the population revolted against the bishop, and tried to burn him to death in the church. The side portal in front of the north transept, the Puerta de la azabacheria, was destroyed on this occasion. During the second building phase, Bernardo el Joven (Bernard the Younger), who is perhaps the same person as the treasurer Bernardo Gutierrez, worked in the masons' lodge. There are also mentions of a certain Esteban, an architect, who went to Pamplona in 1101 to design the cathedral there.

Santiago de Compostela was completed only after a third phase of building, when a porch with a gallery and an ornate three-part portal with statues, the Portico de la gloria, was built on the west facade between the towers. Ferdinand II of León commissioned the master mason Mateo for this purpose in 1168. Twenty years later, in 1188, according to the inscription, Mateo erected the door lintel of the middle portal beneath the tympanum. However, he was not able to complete the west facade until 1211, the same year as the final consecration of the church. The master mason was employed there for 43 years, and so must have been very young when he was appointed in 1168. The outer structure of the cathedral finally received its present, characteristically Baroque appearance after conversions and extensions in modern times, in particular the imposing west facade of 1738 with twin towers and the open double staircase in front of it that was already in place in 1606.

In the interior, the original Romanesque plan has been well preserved. With an overall length of 328 ft. (100 m), a transept extending over 230 ft. (70 m), and a nave height of almost 79 ft. (24 m), it is the largest Romanesque church in Spain. It is uniform in all its parts, and it is clear that, even after the interruption of the works in 1088, the builders kept to the original concept. The church has a three-aisled nave; an unusually long projecting transept, which also has three aisles with four chapels added to the east side; a short choir; and a choir ambulatory with five radiating chapels around the semicircular apse. Nave and transept, choir and ambulatory all have galleries, which above the ambulatory are lower and more like a triforium. A conspicuous feature of the layout is that the side aisles and galleries run in a U-shape around both arms of the transept. They and the choir ambulatory were arranged in this way to suit the requirements of a church much visited by pilgrims. The pilgrims were thus able to walk around the whole church, including past the burial place of St. James in the choir, as though they were in an all-enclosing ambulatory. The precise function of the galleries remains unclear. They could have been used in a great variety of ways, for example, as overnight accommodation for the pilgrims when the inns were full.

The elevation in the nave, transept, and choir is two-storied with, below, high dividing arcades with stilted, graduated round arches, and, above them, paired gallery openings forming a double arcade enclosed within a larger arch. This well-balanced, symmetrical motif gives the walls a particularly noble appearance, a feature that one medieval pilgrim praised and likened to the architecture of a palace, that is, fit for a lord. There is no clerestory; the vaults begin directly above the gallery. As a result, the main body of the church is only indirectly lit, and lies in a permanent sacred twilight. The vaults are half-barrels supported by box-shaped transverse arches. The side aisles, on the other hand, have cross vaults with transverse arches, while the galleries have half-barrel vaults running from outside to inside, thus forming a continuous brace against the lateral thrust of the main barrel vaults the length of the nave. The subdivisions of the structure are very simple. The slender piers have a square core, with a circular engaged column on all four sides connecting with the lateral and transverse arches; those facing the nave extend upward to the barrel vaults. The shape of the piers is varied: the corners of the square core are rounded off on every second pillar. This makes them look like compound piers made of eight sturdy round shafts. This variation means that although the supports alternate, the difference between them is not very noticeable.

Overall, the Romanesque cathedral looks like a French building on Spanish soil. An important predecessor was St. Etienne in Nevers, which was built a little earlier. In Santiago, the French building style reached a mature, classical form that was so satisfying that in the period immediately afterward it stimulated changes in style, definitely influencing several churches on the pilgrims' routes. Among these were Ste. Foy in Conques and, in particular, St. Sernin in Toulouse, a larger, five-aisled building that surpassed even the splendor of Santiago de Compostela.

Appropriately, in view of their great importance, the west facade and the facades of both transepts at Santiago were given extravagant portals decorated with sculptures. The south portal of the transept received the Puerta de las platerias. It was designed to fit in with the bays of the ambulatory inside the building, and is a double portal with ornamental columns and strongly molded archivolts enclosing a pair of tympanums decorated in relief. In the story above, both gallery windows are similarly surrounded by columns and archivolts, which were clearly added later and may originally have been intended for a portal. The design of the whole looks rather like a two-storied double portal. In the early 12th century there was hardly anything to compare with this in terms of magnificence. Some of the sculptures above the portal arches, and to the left of the portal, came from the north portals, and others from an earlier west portal that was later replaced by Master Mateo's present west portal. This is why the sculptural program of the Puerta de las platerias reveals such a variety of themes and artistic skill; it is almost a collection of heterogeneous elements.

The Portico de la gloria on the west side is much more uniform. It has three portals in the shelter of a porch, an original design unlike that of French portals of this or any preceding period. The upper parts of the recesses are filled with granite figures, which, as in France, stand forward of the columns and seem by their posture and movements to be ready to free themselves from them. They represent apostles and prophets, and stand above a substructure of short, sturdy columns. The tympanum in the middle portal, with the enthroned figure of Christ in Majesty, surrounded by the symbols of the four Evangelists and by angels carrying the instruments of the Passion, is enclosed by a semicircular arch of 24 enthroned elders. These figures are far more important than those in the recesses. The manifestation of Christ is the absolute ruling center, and is portrayed on a larger scale. Christ is shown here as the all-embracing Redeemer, Ruler of the Worlds, and Judge. The figure of St. James is placed on the trumeau, or central pier, directly below him, not standing, like other trumeau figures, but enthroned, like Christ. On his scroll is written *missit me dominus* (the Lord sent me), while his bearing and placement suggest that James is the instrument of Christ: a meaningful, immediately comprehensible idea.

The Portico de la gloria overall has a sculptural density and splendor that could hardly be improved on. Each individual figure in the recessess is also opulently, almost too richly portrayed. The coloring of the figures, which was revived in 1657, was meant to further emphasize their

animatedness. However, splendor is not the same thing as quality. In their formal language and spiritual expressiveness, these sculptures do not match the earlier marvelous achievements in France, as for example on the west portal in Chartres. Here, disciplined spiritual strength and ceremonious gravity have been replaced by a coarse realism, and by gestures that undermine the dignity of the figures.

Soon after the final consecration in 1211, the Romanesque cathedral, too, was found to be inadequate. In 1258, Archbishop Juan Arias, the chancellor of Alfonso X, began a French Gothic choir and ambulatory with 19 chapels. This was supposed to replace the Romanesque choir that in the meantime had become too small, and would have extended the church to a total length of some 427 ft. (130 m). The new choir would have been, like the one in the cathedral in León, a masterpiece of Flamboyant French Gothic tracery, but work on it ceased soon after the death of the archbishop in 1266.

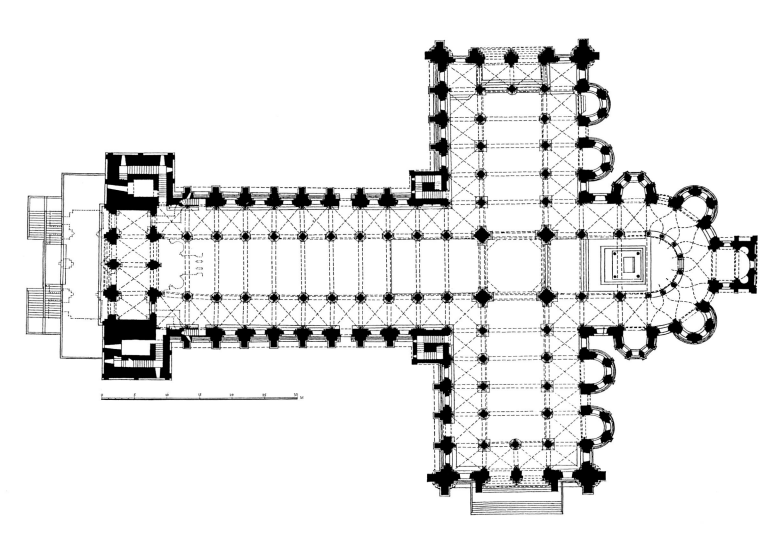

León

The site began as a Roman camp of the Seventh Legion. In the eighth century, León was conquered by the Moors, then won back again as early as the middle of the ninth century by the Asturian king Ordono. León has been the capital of Asturias since 911. The kings bore the title *imperator* to mark the precedence of Asturias over the other constituent kingdoms of Spain.

The kingdom of León emerged from the kingdom of Asturias. Galicia in northwest Spain belonged to it, as did Estramadura, which reached far to the south, and was retaken during the course of the Reconquista. León experienced its heyday under Ferdinand II (1157–88) and Alfonso IX (1188–1230), then united with the kingdom of Castile in 1230. There was already a bishopric in León in the Late Classical period, and again from 860. In 1105, the bishopric was freed from the church province of Toledo, and subordinated to the Holy See.

The construction of a new cathedral, called Pulchra Leonina, was conceived as early as 1205, but the present cathedral was not begun until around 1255 by Bishop Martin Fernandez, the chancellor and friend of Alfonso X "the Wise" of Castile (1252–84). The king supported the building with donations and privileges, as he did for the cathedral at Burgos and for the planned new cathedral choir at Santiago de Compostela. Under his government, these three buildings were directly influenced by the most modern

French architecture of the day, the tracery Gothic of the Flamboyant style. This was primarily found in churches with a close connection to the crown, for example St. Denis and Notre-Dame in Paris. It is possible that the king, by leaning toward the "royal" architecture of France, wanted to bestow some distinction on his own kingship, for there was no other political gain in it. Indeed, the politics of Alfonso X led to a protracted conflict with the nobility that plunged the country into economic crises and civil wars several times before the end of the 14th century. The building of León Cathedral was as far as the association with the French Flamboyant went; the style had no further influence on the development of Spanish architecture.

The cathedral was completed around 1300. It is the only example in Spain of a building constructed entirely in the Flamboyant style, and is indeed a purely French cathedral, particularly in the interior. León's purity of style was enhanced by a comprehensive restoration undertaken in the 19th century.

A certain Simón was named as the master builder in 1261, that is, shortly after construction began. It is not clear if he was French or Spanish by birth. A little later, Enricus, the same master builder identified at Burgos, was active in León. He died in 1277, and his name is entered in the register of deaths at both cathedrals. Perhaps Enricus was principally responsible for the portals with statues, which are for the most part closely related to those at Burgos. On the other hand, the cathedral at León shares hardly any structural features in common with Burgos, which was started much earlier; in Burgos the switch to tracery Gothic affected only the upper sections.

As a building type, León Cathedral is a three-aisled basilica with a double tower facade in the west; a three-aisled transept, which projects by only one bay on either side of the nave; and a short five-aisled choir with an ambulatory and radiating chapels. The choir terminates in a 5/10 polygon. Overall, the ground plan is most closely related to the cathedral in Reims, the coronation church of the French kings. The large rose windows on the west facade and south transept facade reveal French origins, as do the three portals with their abundant figures in the recesses, archivolts, and tympanums.

The placement of the towers in front of these French features is, however, unusual. The towers in France, regardless of whether they were on the west facade or on the fronts of the transepts, were mostly incorporated in the body of the building. But at León they are located outside the line of the side aisles, and separated from the gable front of the nave by

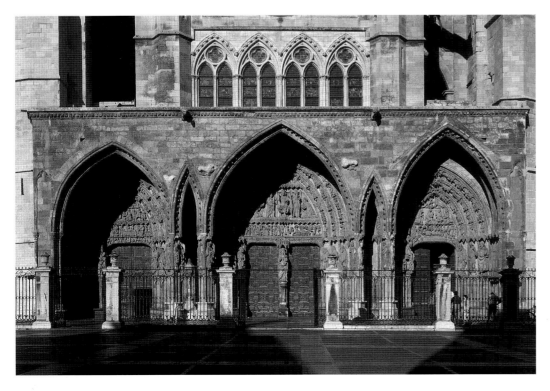

the width of the side aisles. The gable front thus becomes a facade on its own, isolated from the towers and rising up like a steep screen.

The blunt tower to the right of the south transept facade is similarly set to one side, standing above the bay of the outer side aisle in the choir. The tower is clearly incomplete, and does not reach above the eaves of the transept and high choir, like the transept towers of Chartres, Reims, and St. Denis or the choir towers of Chartres. Even if the lateral positioning of the tower does not feel French, there was at least one parallel shortly before, and a very prominent one: the Abbey Church of St. Denis, the royal burial site. This is one of the key buildings of the Flamboyant style, and there, in the course of additional building in the High Gothic style, towers were similarly sited beside the transept fronts, although they were left uncompleted.

The borrowings from France underline the main thrust of the cathedral's architecture. Because it was meant to be a royal cathedral, it specifically followed the lines of the two churches that were of greatest importance to French royalty: the coronation cathedral in Reims and the burial site of St. Denis. But because St. Denis was the more modern structure and had introduced more decisive innovations in its elevations than Reims, León really followed the former more than the latter.

The structure is uniform throughout the cathedral. It is three-storied with dividing arcades, a triforium about halfway up, and a clerestory. This three-story layout became the rule in France after Chartres Cathedral, and is also found in Reims and St. Denis. The most important innovations at St. Denis affected the triforium and the design of the piers. The triforium was illuminated by a glazed wall at the back, and in the front had a latticework of tracery windows. Stepped compound piers with multiple shafts were installed in the nave, instead of the conventional clustered piers typical of Classical cathedrals. The advantage of using these compound piers was that the shafts could run up from the floor level and connect with all of the arches and vault ribs that joined the pier from the central and side aisles. The nave vaulting was supported by a separate cluster of three continuous shafts.

In León, the idea of illuminating the triforium and covering the front of it with tracery was adopted because, technically, this approach was more suited to a country lower in rainfall than France. The lean-to roofs of the side aisles could be kept so flat that the outer walls of the triforium would stay free, and could therefore easily be pierced by windows. The compound piers at St. Denis were not adopted, however, although these were very modern. Instead, the architect at León fell back on clustered circular piers, which in the meantime had become dated, and built them in the style developed in Reims. On the side facing the nave, however, the piers were given the cluster of three continuous shafts from St. Denis, instead of just one engaged column, as would be normal for clustered piers. The resulting pier style is a synthesis that employs something of both royal buildings in France, and can be considered consistent with the intention to build a cathedral in León that was a monument to the monarchy.

The characteristic elements of the interior are provided by the shafts as they reach vigorously upward and the window tracery with stained glass, some of which is still original. The clerestory windows occupy the whole area of their wall, their glazed surfaces as large as was technically possible. This makes the upper part of the nave look like a glasshouse subdivided by the finest tracery. The triforium and clerestory window tracery consists of two double lights, each part surmounted by a multifoil circle. In the clerestory, double lights are crowned by a larger additional multifoil. Tracery like this, with double lights and several upper circles, was the standard pattern of French Flamboyant windows, and is especially striking in St. Denis and in the Sainte Chapelle in Paris, and also in the cathedrals of Troyes, Tours, and Châlons-sur-Marne. León, both in its design and the refinement of its execution, easily measures up to these French cathedrals.

In one respect the tracery at León is even more inventive than that of its French predecessors. In the clerestory, the tracery is enclosed by a narrow glazed light, which makes it possible for the tracery pattern to be narrower and steeper and to have an arch that is more pointed than the frame of the window opening in which it is located. The lateral lights are repeated in the triforium. The clerestory tracery appears to be a separate pattern, a window within a window, and this gives the clerestory an individual character, distinguishing it from other buildings of this type.

The portals and their range of statues also had to be of the highest quality if León was to be worthy of comparison with the French cathedrals. The portal statues, in addition to the statues of apostles and prophets in the recesses, traditionally included scenes from the Last Judgment and the Coronation of Mary. The relief in the tympanum of the Last Judgment, with its well-observed details from daily life, such as the organist and the bellows assistants before the gates of Paradise, is outstanding in the cycle. But overall, the sculpture fails to measure up to the highest French standards, as attained for example in Reims or the Sainte Chapelle in Paris. In its artistic quality, the sculpture at León clearly lags behind the architecture. In the end, it was not possible to transpose everything from France to live up to royal standards.

Plates 234–238

234 View of the cathedral from the southwest
235 Buttressing on the south side
236 South transept facade
237 View of the choir and north transept from the southwest
238 View from the nave into the choir

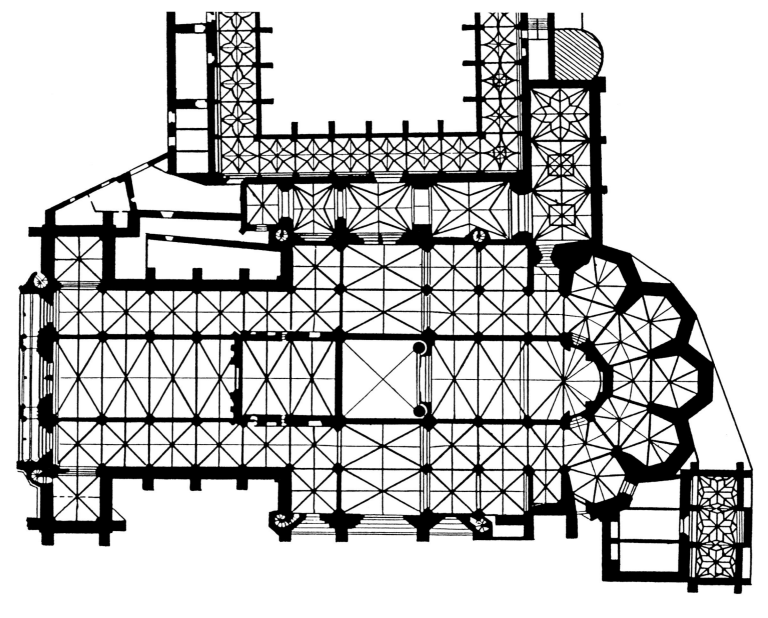

León 431

Burgos

Burgos was established as a bastion against the Moors in 884. From the middle of the 10th century, it was the capital city of Castile, and, after the latter was raised to a kingdom and united with León and Asturias under Ferdinand I (1035–65), it was an important center of Castilian royal rule, and of the Reconquista as it extended southward. A bishopric had been established at Oca in the fifth century; in 1075, Burgos became a bishopric in its own right, and was separated from Oca (Auca), which had been destroyed by the Moors. From 1086, the bishopric had the right of exemption, that is, it was not subordinate to any archbishop but was directly responsible only to the Holy See in Rome. In 1574, the bishopric was raised to an archbishopric. The kings of Castile had close ties with Burgos and so, in 1077, immediately after the relocation of the bishopric, Alfonso VI "the Valiant" set about building the first cathedral at his own expense. In 1178, Alfonso VIII founded the Cistercian memorial monastery of Las Huelgas outside the city gates as a royal burial site.

The present Gothic cathedral was begun in 1221 under Bishop Mauricio. Two years previously, Mauricio had traveled to Germany to conduct Beatrix of Hohenstaufen, the bride-to-be of his king, Ferdinand II, to Spain; the wedding took place in the old cathedral. The king supported the new building with endowments. As early as 1230, the cathedral chapter was able to move into the choir, and consecration followed in 1260, after a 39-year building period.

It is difficult to understand the true dimensions of the cathedral in its original state because of later alterations, extensions, and liturgical appointments, which obstruct the view. It is a three-aisled, twin-towered basilica with a single-aisled, long projecting transept, and a polygonal choir and ambulatory with a ring of radiating chapels. The choir termination and ambulatory form a slightly irregular polygon occupying five sides of a decagon. Originally, the radiating chapels were only small apsidioles and clearly narrower than the trapezoid bays of the ambulatory, to which they were attached. This plan came directly from that of Bourges Cathedral in France.

The wall of the choir, transept, and nave is three-storied, consisting of dividing arcades, triforium, and clerestory. The elevation is uniform throughout the church, and the piers are correspondingly uniform, with eight circular engaged columns surrounding a circular core. Part of the pier and three circular engaged columns continue upward to the base of the vaulting, where the shafts connect with the transverse arches and cross-ribs of the transverse quadripartite vaults. The lateral arches have their own shafts, which begin above the vault springers. The vaults also have a ridge rib, a motif

that was mainly used in England and is an unusual feature for a Spanish cathedral.

Characteristic of this cathedral's wall structure is the very high triforium with five, six, or eight smaller arches enclosed by a larger semicircular arch. Numerous rosettes with a trefoil or quatrefoil are cut into the upper part of the main arch. From a distance this format, with its circles, foils, and arcades, looks like purely surface decoration: and here, in fact, we can see the ornamental style of Islamic art working its way into a Gothic fabric, a trend typical of Spain.

Apart from this, the cathedral is entirely French in character. The model for the wall elevation, too, was the cathedral at Bourges, although the latter's five graduated aisles were here reduced to three. For the dividing arcades, this meant that the exaggerated height of the piers—a distinguishing feature of Bourges—could be avoided, and the piers brought back to a normal scale. Despite Burgos Cathedral's debt to Bourges, which is clear in the shape of the piers and the system of engaged columns, the architect here successfully gave the work an unmistakably individual character, which in its treatment of space is not at all reminiscent of Bourges.

Following the French model, around 1240 and thereafter the cathedral was given several portals, each with a program of figures. The three west portals were destroyed in the 18th century, although the south portal, with the pier statue of a bishop, and the north portal, with the Last Judgment in the tympanum and the apostles in the recesses, have been preserved. The iconographic model for the north portal was the Last Judgment portal at Chartres. A little later, the same master mason went to León, where he also worked on the portals.

One year after the consecration in 1260, a *magister operis* by the name of Enricus was mentioned as a citizen of Burgos, and he is also recorded as fulfilling a similar function at the cathedral in León. He died in 1277. Enricus was not the designing architect, in either Burgos or León. In Burgos, however, the extensions built between 1260 and about 1280 can be traced back to him: the third story of the west facade, the tracery gallery in the transept facade, the two-storied cloister, and a new, considerably enlarged ring of chapels surrounding the choir ambulatory. There, the small apsidioles were replaced by chapels, which occupy the full width of the bay between the buttresses, and protrude outside on three sides in an irregular polygon.

Around 1440, an energetic new building program was launched, mainly instigated by Bishop Alonso de Cartagena, a convert. The bishop, who had traveled to a church council in Basel in 1434, called the master builder Hans of Cologne to Burgos. Hans married a Spanish woman and became a citizen of Burgos. The Capilla de la visitación was the first building constructed under his leadership. In 1442, Hans of Cologne began the extension of the two west towers with their characteristic octagonal stone spires, which feature openwork tracery; here, the master builder kept to the Gothic of his native Germany. Following the gigantic project for the two-tower front of Cologne Cathedral, which came to an end before or around 1300, openwork stone spires had become fairly popular, for example, at Freiburg, Esslingen, and Rothenburg, as well as in the tower of St. Stephen's Cathedral in Vienna, and the designs for the cathedral tower in Ulm. Hans's main work in Burgos, however, was the octagonal crossing tower, crowned by eight pinnacles, built from about 1466, which evoked great admiration at the time. The last work by Hans of Cologne was the Capilla de la concepción, begun in 1457. When the master builder died in 1481, the chapel was unfinished; it would be completed by his son and successor, Simón, known as Simón de Colonia.

Simón's main work is the Capilla del condestable (1482–95), an octagon with a diameter of 49 ft. (15 m) that was built onto the choir ambulatory, slightly offset to the north from the apical chapel. The duchess Mencía de Mendoza endowed the priceless chapel as a burial place for her husband, Condestable Pedro Fernández de Velasco, the highest royal official in Castile. Outside, as inside, the chapel is a magnificent structure that frankly states how expensive it must have been to build. The exterior is closely related to the present crossing tower. In the interior, the blind arcades of the lower level, intended to display coats of arms, are decorated with the finest ornamentation, which is so delicate that it resembles embroidery in stone. The main attraction, and an unexpected surprise, is the eight-pointed-star vault, in the middle of which a small eight-pointed star is set, turned by half a phase in relation to the main star. Astonishingly, it is made not of stone, but of translucent glass with a perforated tracery pattern. In its radiance, this vault figure made of glass looks like a self-illuminating heavenly body. This was something that could have been done only in Spain, where it rains so little.

The use of glass in vaulting would became a specialty of the masons' lodge in Burgos. The Capilla de la presentación, erected in 1519 for the canon and protonotary Gonzalo de Lerma, is also vaulted with an eight-pointed star, and has a perforated glazed ornamental figure at the top. It is quite likely that Hans of Cologne's crossing tower, much admired by his contemporaries, had featured such a star shape, but this

tower collapsed in 1539. The load-bearing crossing piers, erected in the first building phase, had never been intended for such a tower; they were too weak, and so gave way. The adjoining vaults in the choir, transept, and nave were also destroyed in the collapse.

Soon afterward, from 1544 to 1568, after the crossing piers had been strengthened, Juan de Vallejo built the present crossing tower, clearly influenced by the structural designs of his predecessor. The damaged adjacent vaults were redesigned with ribs that were now curved. Outside, the tower was decorated with pointed Plateresque ornamentation that more closely resembles the art of a confectioner than that of a stonemason. The observer wonders with amazement whether such an opulent display could ever be surpassed. Faced with an exterior like this, it is hardly believable that Michelangelo's drum in the dome of St. Peter's in Rome was built at the same time.

The interior of the crossing tower is no less extraordinarily lavish. The vaulting also features an eight-pointed star, but this one is perforated with an ornamental pattern and glazed throughout, not just in the upper part. The whole vault is now illuminated, going beyond what was achieved in the Capilla del condestable and indeed the limits of what was then possible. This crown in the cathedral's star vault amounts to a unique, completely innovative technical miracle that delights the eye with a scarcely believable spectacle. In the 1990s, the translucency of the vault was restored when a protective glass roof was placed over it.

The crossing tower is a stylistic anachronism, no doubt because of its predecessor's influence and that of the Gothic tradition of the stonemasons. However, before the tower was built, a pioneering work in the new architectural style had been created in the cathedral: the Escalera dorada, the golden staircase of Diego Siloe in the northern transept, which dates from 1519. The staircase leads from the interior of the transept to the coronation portal, located in the north front wall of the transept. In an unusual arrangement, the portal is not at ground level but is located a good deal higher up, because the ground outside the cathedral on the north side is higher than the floor of the church. The function of the steps was to create a dignified way for the king to process between the portal and the church. The architect achieved this in a masterly manner. The staircase as a whole is laid out with the symmetry of a mirror image. The ascent begins in the middle with a single flight, and at the first landing divides into two flights at right angles to the first, and then, after a second landing, each flight switches back to come together at the final landing in front of the portal. The prototype for this dividing double staircase was Bramante's drawing for the staircase in the Cortile del belvedere in the Vatican from just 10 years earlier. That was an outside staircase, however; in Burgos it was brought inside. Later stairways of the Baroque period also followed this model. The most important of these was the famous, but no longer surviving Ambassador's Stairs in Versailles, which became the paragon for stately staircases throughout Europe. The basic concept of the staircase in Burgos stands up well relative to the demands of the Baroque style. Its simplicity, combined with the perfection of the idea, had something timeless about it. It was a concept that would be extended and embellished, but never bettered. That is the essence of a great design.

1 Capilla de la concepción
2 Escalera dorada
3 Capilla del condestable
4 Capilla de la visitación

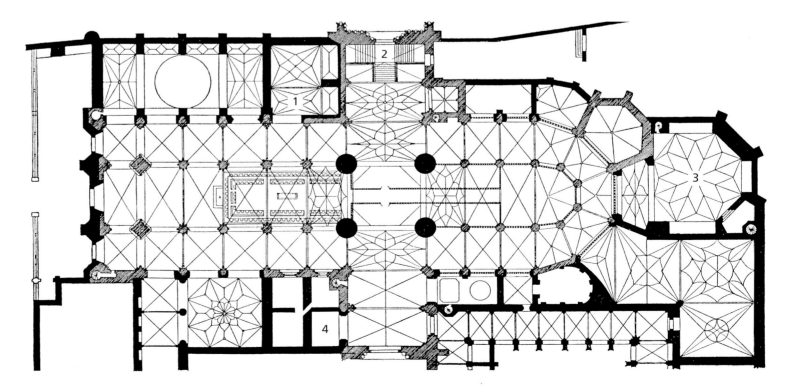

242

Toledo

Toledo, the former Roman Toletum, was the religious center of the Iberian peninsula beginning in the Late Classical period. It became a bishopric around 300, although at that time it still belonged to the North African ecclesiastical province of Carthage. In the early sixth century, the bishop of Toledo became a metropolitan, that is, he attained the rank of an archbishop. As the capital city of the kingdom of the Western Goths, who after the defeat of their Toulousan empire in southern France at the Battle of Vouillée (507) drove across the Pyrenees into the Iberian peninsula, Toledo also assumed a leading political and cultural role until 712. In 589, with the renunciation of Arianism by the Western Goths at the Third Council of Toledo, a single uniform Catholic faith extended throughout Spain. The councils, which had been held in Toledo since 400, were also imperial conventions, and even the king had to adhere to their decisions. In 681, as bishop of the court, the archbishop was designated primate of the Church of the Western Goths, but never officially adopted this title. He had the right not only to consecrate the king and all Spanish bishops, but, together with the king, to appoint bishops. This right of appointment gave the primate the decisive position of power within the Church in the Iberian peninsula.

The Moors conquered Toledo in 712. However, unlike the Western Goths, the caliphs made Cordova, not Toledo, the capital of the new Moorish empire. Only in 1035 did Toledo at least become the capital of a *taif*, that is, an imperial province. The Reconquista strove mightily to win back Toledo because it was the old Christian center of Spain, and Alfonso VI "the Valiant" succeeded in the same century, in 1085. Muslims, Jews, and Mozarabs (Moorish Christians) were allowed to remain and to practice their religions until 400 years later, when the Inquisition ordered the forcible conversion, first, of the Jews in 1492, and then of the Muslims in 1502.

Shortly after its recapture by Alfonso, Toledo was finally confirmed as an archbishopric in 1088. Even earlier, in 1085, Pope Urban II had awarded the bishop of Toledo the primacy over the Spanish church, which for a short time had been claimed by Santiago de Compostela, yet without all the old rights that had existed before the Moorish conquest. The bishops of Castile, with the single exception of the bishop of Burgos, were subordinated to the archbishop.

The main mosque, after its consecration to Mary, initially served as a cathedral for the archbishop and the cathedral chapter, whose membership in the 12th century grew from 30 to 90. A new building was begun in the 13th century, at the same time as Burgos. Its initiator was Archbishop Rodrigo Ximénez de Rada, who had been in office since 1209. He had studied in Paris, and so may have had personal knowledge of several French Gothic constructions, including the building sites of some cathedrals that were not yet completed. The archbishop was a confidant of Ferdinand III "the Saintly" of Castile, and also of Bishop Mauricio of Burgos, who at around the same time began the cathedral there, and who had earlier been an archdeacon in Toledo. It is an indication of the consolidation of royal power that expensive new cathedrals could be built simultaneously in both seats of the royal court, Toledo and Burgos.

The king and archbishop together laid the foundation stone in Toledo in 1226, although the building had already been started in 1222/23, that is, immediately after the foundation stone of Burgos had been laid in 1221. The cathedral in Toledo was erected on the site of the old mosque, and its ground plan largely follows the foundations of the mosque. The first master builder, named Martin, was probably not Spanish by birth, but more likely French. Another master builder, identified by his epitaph, was Pedro Perez, evidently a Spaniard.

The choir of the cathedral was completed around the middle of the 13th century. Work on the nave continued into the 14th century, and the vaults in the eastern parts of the nave were built as late as 1493. At that time, the upper choir was also fitted out with splendid side screens, a massive retable high altar that practically fills the apse, and star-shaped vaulting. As so often in Spain, the interior has been substantially affected by new additions, changes, and rebuilding, as happened with the choir chapels, which explains why the spatial concept of the original plan is not immediately recognizable.

Even if Toledo Cathedral is closely associated with the one in Burgos, the higher quality of Toledo can be seen even in the ground plan: not only does the cathedral have five aisles, it also has a three-aisled transept, although it does not project. The choir, which is unusually short, consists of a single transverse rectangular bay and an apse in the form of a 5/10 polygon. The two aisles of the choir ambulatory surround the apse, and the inner ambulatory continues into the eastern side aisle of the transept. The architect devised a plan for the bays in the ambulatory that elegantly solves the main problem of a double ambulatory, namely, the continuous increase in size of the trapezoid bays from inside to outside. The problem first arises in the outer ambulatory: if the number of bays there were to be the same as the number of sides in the apse polygon, then the plan of each

span would be a gigantic trapezoid that could hardly be vaulted. The architect circumvented this problem by dividing the bays of both aisles of the ambulatory into smaller individual bays with different configurations. He doubled the number of piers separating the bays in the inner ambulatory, in opposition to the piers in the apse polygon, from four to eight. It was then possible to arrange alternating rectangular bays with diagonal ribs and triangular vaults with three radiating ribs in place of the trapezoid bays that were the rule in choir ambulatories in French Gothic buildings. In the outer ambulatory, the number of supporting shafts on the wall was increased from eight to 16 in opposition to the piers between the two aisles. There, too, triangular and rectangular vaults were alternated, but in the reverse order of that in the inner aisle.

The outer triangular bays are narrow and wedge-shaped. This is strikingly analogous to the outer ambulatory in Le Mans Cathedral, and the likelihood that the architect of Toledo knew Le Mans is confirmed by the external buttressing: the way in which the flying buttresses in Le Mans are divided in two to match the triangular bays is repeated exactly in Toledo. Each one of the bays of the outer ambulatory has a radiating chapel attached to it: the rectangular bays have a chapel in the form of a semicircular apse and the triangular bays have a smaller rectangular chapel. The result is a ring of 15 chapels that alternate in shape and size and, without exception, are very small; the rectangular chapels are in fact tiny. Looking out from the inner ambulatory, a viewer sees two rectangular chapels attached to one semicircular chapel to create a rhythmic group of three. The ring of chapels has been only partly preserved; its sequence was considerably disturbed by two larger chapels that were attached later.

The overall arrangement of the choir ambulatory, with the continuous increase in bays from inside to outside, is as unique in European architecture as the form of the radiating chapels. The architect used French models to develop a completely independent new concept. In the elevation, however—as can be seen in the choir and its ambulatory—he was clearly influenced by Bourges Cathedral, which also has five aisles. From the latter, he adopted the height differential between the outer and the inner ambulatory, and also the idea of giving the inner ambulatory its own clerestory and triforium, because it is higher than the outer ambulatory. The arcading of the triforium, which here is illuminated, and the rosette-shaped clerestory windows form a window group in the same area of wall. The influence of Islamic art is noticeable in details like the multifoil arches of the triforium

and the overlapping arches every second rosette. This influence is even clearer on the triforium of the upper choir, where pierced, multifoil arches were used. This triforium, unlike that in the ambulatory, is not illuminated.

The style of the piers and the system of engaged columns around them are also derived from Bourges. Eight circular columns surround a circular core, and a part of the circular core and three of the columns climb the inner choir up to the vault springers. This is consistent with the system in both Bourges and Burgos. However, the column system in Toledo and Burgos is different from that in Bourges. It is no longer designed for the sexpartite choir and nave vaulting that was customary in the Early Gothic period, but for the modern quadripartite vaulting that had become the norm after Chartres and the other Classical cathedrals in France.

The adoption of the graduated aisle heights of Bourges meant that the dividing arcades are very high, but not as extreme as they are in the French cathedral. In Toledo the structural system that was an experiment in the choir was retained for the whole cathedral. Only the window shapes were changed. In the inner side aisle, nave, and transept, the clerestory windows merged with the triforium and were made into a single opening. Despite these changes, the overall concept remained uniform.

The proportions of the aisles and arcades in Toledo had a considerable influence on subsequent Spanish cathedral architecture. Even if the buildings had only three aisles and could have been lower, the great height of Toledo was retained, and indeed even increased, particularly in Catalan Gothic buildings.

Of the later conversions and alterations at Toledo Cathedral, Narciso Tomé's famous *Transparente*, completed in 1732, was a stroke of genius. Because the inner sanctum of the Late Gothic altar could not be seen from beyond the choir ambulatory, an opening was made in the altar and the inner sanctum placed within a glazed shrine so that it was visible from both sides, hence its name, *El Transparente*. On the side facing the choir ambulatory, the opening was given a highly expressive collection of columns, entablatures, and countless figures, with the outward-curving entablatures resembling deep niches. To bring his "production" to work, the architect created a new overhead light source, a skylight that effectively illuminated the *Transparente* like a spotlight. In the inner ambulatory, the crown was taken out of half a Gothic vault, and above it a shaft was built with a large window to the outside, through which not only light but also the whole heavenly angelic host streamed in. This stage management of the light brought the *Transparente* to perfection: the spectacle of an ardent *theatrum sacrum*. The precedents for such effects had been created in the Roman Baroque style by the theatrical Gianlorenzo Bernini, but Narciso Tome's architectural drama put to shame anything that had gone before. Tome was fortunate that the Gothic construction of the ambulatory was solid enough to support the skylight housing newly placed in it.

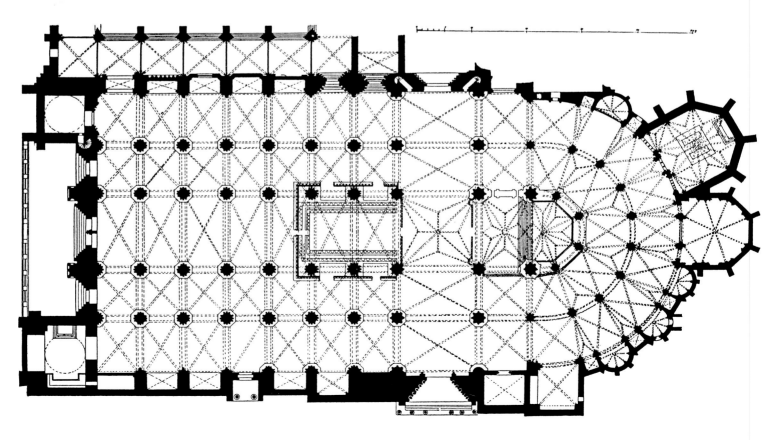

Toledo   449

Seville

Seville began as a Phoenician harbor city on the lower reaches of the Guadalquivir in southern Spain, and became Roman territory in 206 B.C.E. The city has been the seat of an archbishop since the end of the fourth century. At the time of the Western Goths' empire in Spain (507–711), the authority of the Church was decisively stamped on the state, mainly by Archbishop Isidore of Seville (594–636). Although in 712 Seville was conquered by the Moors, the archbishops were permitted to exercise their office for 400 years, until Seville became an independent realm after the fall of the caliphate of Cordova, and then in 1146 came under the rule of the Almohades. The new rulers immediately dissolved the archbishopric and, in 1193, when they made Seville the capital of al-Andalus, drove out all the Christians and Jews.

During the Reconquista, Seville remained one of the most important Moorish bulwarks against the Christians, but Ferdinand III "the Saintly" of Castile succeeded in conquering the city in 1248 and, because of its importance, made it his residence. His son and successor, Alfonso X "the Wise," who during the interregnum was nominally also king of the Holy Roman Empire, without ever having set foot in the empire, drove the rebellious population out of Seville and its surrounding countryside, and replaced them with Castilians. Both kings designated Seville as their burial place. In the subsequent period the city rose to be one of the richest ports in the world: the discovery of America by Christopher Columbus, who is buried in Seville Cathedral, helped the city's growth in an unforeseen manner. The cathedral chapter, which was made up of more than 80 members, also received a large income. Only in Toledo were the membership and income higher, but Seville ran a very close second.

The grand mosque, erected under the direction of the architect Ahmed ben Basso between 1172 and 1198 as a prestige building for the Almohades, was the precursor to the present cathedral. In style it corresponded to the slightly older Kutubiya mosque in Marrakesh in what is present-day Morocco: a large walled rectangle with a courtyard on the north side for ritual washing and a prayer room attached to the south side. A few small remnants of the doors in the surrounding wall, which led into the courtyard and the prayer hall, have been preserved. The prayer hall itself had 17 aisles aligned north–south; the middle one was wider and higher than the others. The aisles were separated by arcades of columns and horseshoe arches.

In 1184, it was decided to build a minaret at the northeast corner of the prayer hall. When the cathedral was built, the minaret was retained but made into a bell tower. The present-day multistory extension was added, in rich Renaissance style, in the 16th century, including the now famous crowning metal weather vane, a figure representing Faith that has given the tower the name La Giralda (from *girar*, "to turn"). The total height of the tower is now 305 ft. (93 m). The original minaret reached a height of some 230 ft. (70 m).

Differing from the minarets in the eastern part of the Islamic world, where they are circular and extremely narrow and rise up like pointed needles, La Giralda conforms to the massive square building tradition of the western Islamic regions like Morocco and Algeria. The minarets in Marrakesh and Rabat in Morocco are similar, as is the imposing Mansuriah in Tlemcen in Algeria. Originally, the top platform of La Giralda carried another, smaller turret with four gilded spheres at the top that gleamed from a long way off. The square tower is made of brickwork, with all four sides characterized by surface ornamentation, forming closely woven lozenge shapes. A vertical run is left in the middle of each side for columned arcades with multifoil arches. In the way the angular solidity of the building fabric blends with the refined surface pattern, and in the harmony between the square tower and the upper extension, La Giralda is without question one of the most impressive towers in world architecture.

After the conquest of Seville by Ferdinand III, 11 of the 15 mosques in the city were given to the Christians and three to the Jews; only one remained Muslim. The main mosque served as the cathedral for 150 years. Only when it was damaged by an earthquake in 1401 did the cathedral chapter decide to build a new, much larger cathedral in its place. Its massive size was intended to express the great importance of both city and bishopric, and would be unmatched anywhere. In response to the megalomania apparent from the very beginning, a member of the cathedral chapter expressed his fear that the builders would be declared mad after the cathedral had been built.

Until the consecration in 1519, many master builders, most of them foreign, oversaw the works: 1421–34, Pedro García; 1435, the Fleming Ysambert; 1439–49, the Frenchman Carlin; 1454–72, the Frenchman Juan Norman, and after him, Juan de Hoces; in 1496 Master "Ximon," that is, Simón de Colonia from Burgos, who apparently built the crossing tower, which was completed in 1506 but collapsed as early as 1511. From 1515, the works were directed by Juan Gil de Hontañón, who previously had worked in Salamanca, and later would go to Segovia. Foreign artists from Germany and Flanders created the stained-glass windows in the first half of the 16th century. In the course of the 16th and 17th centuries, numerous fixtures were added and conversions effected, which enrich the interior but make it impossible to obtain an overall view. In 1888 the crossing vaults collapsed for a second time, and were rebuilt.

In addition to La Giralda, the large courtyard was also retained from the old mosque, with its crenellated surrounding wall and gallery, although both were later modernized. The courtyard, known today as the Patio de los naranjos (Courtyard of the Orange Trees), was originally the entrance court, and now embraces the north side of the cathedral. As in Toledo, Seville Cathedral's dimensions were determined by the foundations of the mosque. The cathedral itself stands on the area of the north–south–oriented prayer hall, but was turned through 90° to have an east–west alignment. It takes the form of a five-aisled basilica with a single-aisled, nonprojecting transept and a row of rectangular chapels on both the long sides. Originally, a two-aisled choir with ambulatory and radiating chapels was planned, as in Toledo, but the entire east end remained unbuilt after Henry III (1390–1406) gave up the idea of installing the royal burial chamber there. Thus, the cathedral overall has a rectangular ground plan, similar to the former prayer hall of the mosque.

A choir ambulatory and radial chapels would have made the building considerably larger, clearly larger than any other church in the world, which was certainly the intention of those building it. Now two cathedrals, Milan and Seville, can dispute the title of being the largest medieval church, depending on whether the calculation is based on the surface area or the space enclosed. Such calculations have never been precisely carried out. Generally, Seville is considered to be larger, and the measurements are very impressive: total length 384 ft. (117 m)—with choir ambulatory and radial chapels it would have been about 509 ft. (155 m)—total width about 249 ft. (76 m); width of nave 53 ft. (16 m); height of nave 118 ft. (36 m); width of individual side aisles 36 ft. (11 m); and height of side aisles 85 ft. (26 m).

The internal space has an amazing feeling of enormous width. The width is almost more impressive than the length because the nave and upper choir, cluttered with obstructive additions, cannot be fully viewed. All four side aisles are of the same height, but tower so far above the chapels that there is room above them for windows. The nave, on the other hand, is only slightly higher than the side aisles. The dividing arcades reach up so high that the clerestory in the lateral wall is located in the area of vaulting, and therefore

View through the Patio de los naranjos to the north transept facade

makes little impact. Unusually high, richly molded compound piers make a strong spatial impact, giving the twin-aisled halls of the side aisles a taut upright profile. Because the nave is only very slightly higher, all five aisle together form something like an extemely wide hall church, despite the basilica-like cross-section. At Seville it seems as though the basilica and the hall, the two most important basic types of medieval east–west structures, have been synthesized into one.

Within this vast space, which threatens to lose its cohesiveness because of the extreme width, an element of centering is provided by the transept, which intersects the multiple sequence of bays and creates a crossing. This does not lie in the geometric center of the building, but provides the interior with a balance that holds the spatial continuity together. This center is further enhanced by the vaults all around the crossing, and in the crossing itself after 1511, when the tower collapsed. At that time the vaults were renewed by fan vaults, which are extremely richly decorated with the finest tracery, and display an opulence that is not found in the architecture of the other parts of the cathedral. The splendid vaults are in fact a treasure raised on high that emphasizes the crossing even more.

On the outside of the building, apart from La Giralda, another magnificent feature is the luxuriant ornamentation that completely covers the transept facade facing the courtyard. The rest of the exterior is plainer. The gigantic cube of the cathedral is flanked by numerous flying buttresses, which rise up at an unusually acute angle, so that they appear almost horizontal. Together with the piers and pinnacles, they divide up the blocklike outlines of the building. Viewed from La Giralda, the buttressing is especially impressive. From the tower, a viewer can also see that the cathedral has no roofs above the vaulting; this is unimaginable in any northern European city, but typical for Seville, which lies much closer to North Africa—and thus Islam—than to central Europe. The powerful influence of Islam in Seville is still evident in the cathedral, despite all its Gothic features.

Plates 251–257

251 View of the cathedral from the south
252, 253 La Giralda
254 View from the north transept into the nave
    with the canons' choir
255 Nave looking northeast
256 View through the crossing into the south transept
257 View into the crossing vaults

1 La Giralda

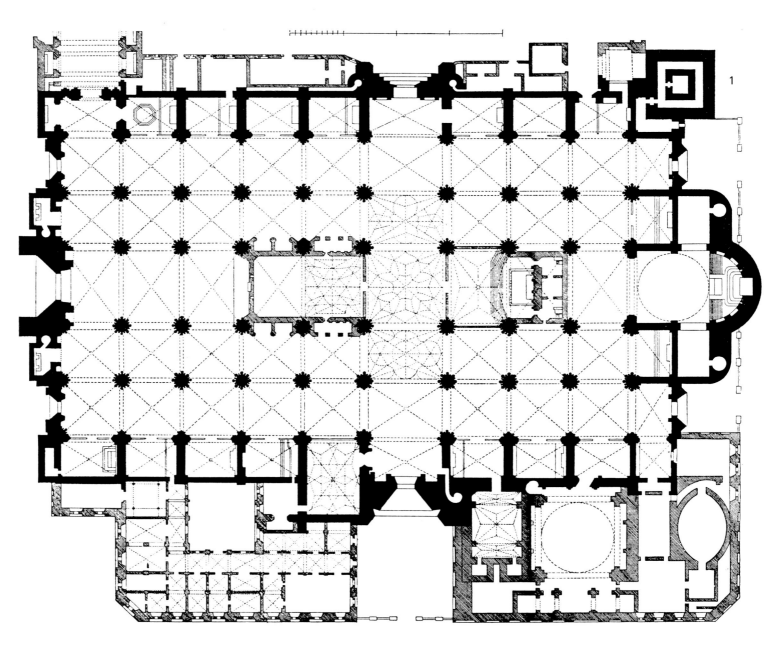

1

254

Appendix

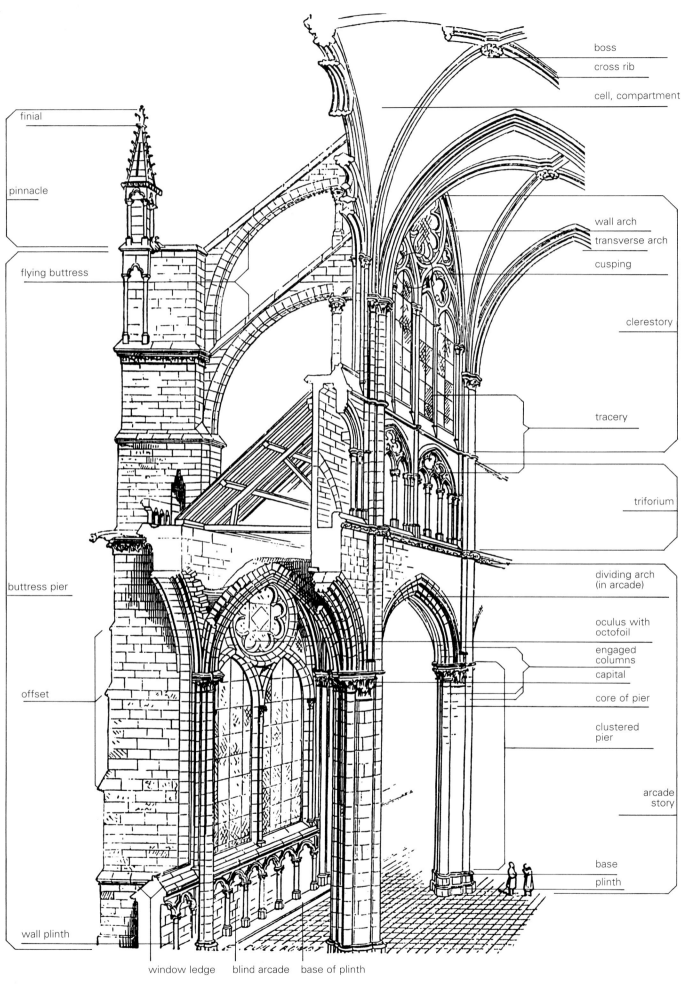

boss

cross rib

cell, compartment

finial

pinnacle

wall arch

transverse arch

cusping

flying buttress

clerestory

tracery

triforium

buttress pier

dividing arch
(in arcade)

oculus with
octofoil

engaged
columns

capital

core of pier

offset

clustered
pier

arcade
story

base

plinth

wall plinth

window ledge   blind arcade   base of plinth

Explanation of terms using the example of a bay in the nave of Amiens Cathedral, with a reconstruction of the original side wall (isometric drawing after Viollet-le-Duc)

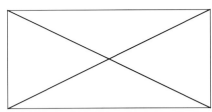

Quadripartite vault with transverse arch and cross ribs

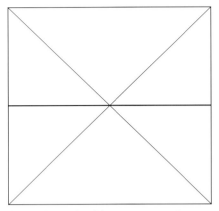

Sexpartite vault with transverse arch, cross ribs, and transverse rib

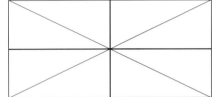

Vault with transverse arch, cross ribs, and ridge ribs going lengthwise and across

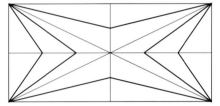

Vault with transverse arch, cross ribs, ridge ribs, and tiercerons

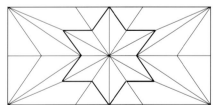

Vault with transverse arch, cross ribs, tiercerons, and liernes

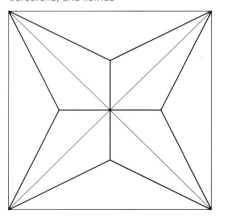

Four-pointed star with cross ribs and gable ribs

Select Bibliography

General

Acland, James H., *Medieval Structure: The Gothic Vault*, Toronto 1972

Barral i Altet, Xavier, et al., *Romanische Kunst*, Vol. 1: *Mittel- und Südeuropa*; Vol. 2: *Nord- und Westeuropa* (Universum der Kunst), Munich 1983 and 1984

Binding, Günther, *Masswerk*, Darmstadt 1989

——, *Hochgotik: Die Zeit der grossen Kathedralen*, Cologne 1999

Cali, François, *L'ordre ogival: Essai sur l'architecture gothique*, Paris 1963

Castelfranchi Vegas, Liana (ed.), *Cantieri Medievali*, Milan 1995

Châtelet, Albert, and Roland Recht, *Ausklang des Mittelalters* (Universum der Kunst), Munich 1989

Dehio, Georg, and Gustav von Bezold, *Die kirchliche Baukunst des Abendlandes, historisch und systematisch dargestellt*, 2 text vols. and 5 of plates, Stuttgart 1884–1901; rep. Hildesheim 1969

Duby, Georges, *Die Zeit der Kathedralen: Kunst und Gesellschaft 980–1420*, Frankfurt am Main 1992

Erlande-Brandenburg, Alain, *Triumph der Gotik 1260–1380* (Universum der Kunst), Munich 1988

Fitchen, John, *The Construction of Gothic Cathedrals: A Study of Medieval Vault Erection*, Chicago/London 1961

Frankl, Paul, *Gothic Architecture* (The Pelican History of Art), Harmondsworth 1962

Franz, Heinrich Gerhard, *Spätromanik und Frühgotik* (Kunst der Welt), Baden-Baden 1969

Gall, Ernst, *Die gotische Baukunst in Frankreich und Deutschland*, Part 1: *Die Vorstufen in Nordfrankreich von der Mitte des 11. bis gegen Ende des 12. Jahrhunderts*, Leipzig 1925

Grodecki, Louis, Anne Prache, and Roland Recht, *Gothic Architecture*, London 1986

Jantzen, Hans, *Die Gotik des Abendlandes: Idee und Wandel*, Cologne 1962; new ed. Cologne 1997

Kubach, Hans Erich, and Peter Bloch, *Früh- und Hochromanik* (Kunst der Welt), Baden-Baden 1964

Nussbaum, Norbert, and Sabine Lepsky, *Das gotische Gewölbe: Eine Geschichte seiner Form und Konstruktion*, Munich/Berlin 1999

Prache, Anne, *Cathédrales d'Europe*, Paris 1999

Recht, Roland (ed.), *Les Bâtisseurs des cathédrales gothiques* (exh. cat.), Strasbourg 1989

Rüdiger, Wilhelm, *Die gotische Kathedrale: Architektur und Bedeutung*, Cologne 1979

Sauerländer, Willibald, *Das Jahrhundert der grossen Kathedralen, 1140–1260* (Universum der Kunst), Munich 1990

Segger, Jürgen, *Zur Statik gotischer Kathedralen: Dargestellt am Kölner Dom und an statisch verwandten Kathedralen* (dissertation), Aachen 1969

Swaan, Wim, *Die grossen Kathedralen*, Cologne 1969

Toman, Rolf (ed.), *Die Kunst der Romanik: Architektur, Skulptur, Malerei*, Cologne 1996

—— (ed.), *Die Kunst der Gotik. Architektur, Skulptur, Malerei*, Cologne 1998

Wilson, Christopher, *The Gothic Cathedral: The Architecture of the Great Church 1130–1330*, London 1990

England

Böker, Hans Josef, *Englische Sakralarchitektur des Mittelalters*, Darmstadt 1984

Bony, Jean, *The English Decorated Style: Gothic Architecture Transformed 1250–1350*, Ithaca, N.Y. 1979

Clifton-Taylor, Alec, *The Cathedrals of England*, London 1967; 2nd ed. 1986

Escher, Konrad, *Englische Kathedralen*, Munich/Berlin 1929

Harvey, John, *English Medieval Architects: A Biographcal Dictionary down to 1550*, London 1954

——, *The Perpendicular Style 1330–1485*, London 1978

Hürlimann, Martin, *Englische Kathedralen*, Zurich 1948

Kowa, Günter, *Architektur der englischen Gotik*, Cologne 1990

Pevsner, Nikolaus, and Priscilla Metcalf, *The Cathedrals of England*, 2 vols., New York/Harmondsworth 1985

Rickman, Thomas, *An Attempt to Discriminate the Styles of English Architecture from the Conquest to the Reformation*, London 1817; 7th ed. 1881

Schäfke, Werner, *Englische Kathedralen: Eine Reise zu den Höhepunkten englischer Architektur von 1066 bis heute*, Cologne 1983

France

Aubert, Marcel, *Gotische Kathedralen und Kunstschätze in Frankreich*, Wiesbaden [n.d.]

Bony, Jean, *French Gothic Architecture of the 12th and 13th Centuries*, Berkeley/London 1983

Büchsel, Martin, *Die Geburt der Gotik: Abt Sugers Konzept für die Abteikirche Saint-Denis*, Freiburg im Breisgau 1997

Combier, Pierre du, *Les chantiers des cathédrales*, Paris 1953

Freigang, Christian, *Imitare ecclesias nobiles: Die Kathedralen von Narbonne, Toulouse und Rodez und die nordfranzösische Rayonnantgotik im Languedoc*, Worms 1992

Jantzen, Hans, *Kunst der Gotik: Klassische Kathedralen Frankreichs: Chartres, Reims, Amiens*, Hamburg 1957; rep. Berlin 1987

Kimpel Dieter, and Robert Suckale, *Die gotische Architektur in Frankreich 1130–1270*, Munich 1985; rev. college ed. Munich 1995

Male, Emile, *Die Gotik. Die französische Kathedrale als Gesamtkunstwerk*, Stuttgart/Zurich 1994

Schäfke, Werner, *Frankreichs gotische Kathedralen: Eine Reise zu den Höhepunkten mittelalterlicher Architektur in Frankreich*, Cologne 1979

Schlink, Wilhelm, *Die Kathedralen Frankreichs*, Munich 1978

Sedlmayr, Hans, *Die Entstehung der Kathedrale*, Zurich 1950; new ed. Freiburg im Breisgau 1993

Simson, Otto von, *Die gotische Kathedrale*, Darmstadt 1968; 2nd ed. Darmstadt 1972

Germany

Böker, Hans Josef, *Die mittelalterliche Backsteinarchitektur Norddeutschlands*, Darmstadt 1988

Busch, Harald, *Deutsche Gotik*, Vienna/Munich 1969

Klotz, Heinrich, *Geschichte der deutschen Kunst*, Vol. 1: *Mittelalter 600–1400*, Munich 1998

Kubach, Hans Erich, and Albert Verbeek, *Romanische Baukunst an Rhein und Maas*, 4 vols., Berlin 1976 and 1989

Legner, Anton, *Deutsche Kunst der Romanik*, Munich 1982

Möbius, Friedrich, and Helga Scurie (eds.), *Geschichte der deutschen Kunst 1200–1350*, Leipzig 1989

Mrusek, Hans-Joachim, *Drei sächsische Kathedralen: Merseburg, Naumburg, Meissen*, Dresden 1976

Nussbaum, Norbert, *Deutsche Kirchenbaukunst der Gotik*, Darmstadt 1994

Schütz, Bernhard, *Deutsche Romanik: Die Kirchenbauten der Kaiser, Bischöfe und Klöster*, Freiburg im Breisgau 1989

Ullmann, Ernst, *Gotik: Deutsche Baukunst 1200–1550*, Leipzig 1994

Winterfeld, Dethard von, *Die Kaiserdome Speyer, Mainz, Worms und ihr romanisches Umland*, Wurzburg 1992.

——, *Romanik am Rhein*, Stuttgart 2001

Italy

Brucher, Günter, *Die sakrale Baukunst Italiens im 11. und 12. Jahrhundert*, Cologne 1987

Decker, Heinrich, *Gotik in Italien*, Vienna 1964

Kubach, Hans Erich, *Architektur der Romanik* (Weltgeschichte der Architektur), Stuttgart 1974

Pace, Valentino, and M. Bagnoli (ed.), *Il gotico europeo in Italia*, Naples 1994

Wagner-Rieger, Renate, *Die italienische Baukunst zu Beginn der Gotik*, Part 1: *Oberitalien*; Part 2: *Süd- und Mittelitalien*, Graz/Cologne 1956 and 1957

Willemsen, Carl A., *Apulien: Kathedralen und Kastelle. Ein Kunstführer durch das normannisch-staufische Apulien*, Cologne 1971

Spain

Durliat, Marcel, *Romanisches Spanien*, Würzburg 1995

Hänsel, Sylvaine, and Henrik Karge (eds.), *Spanische Kunstgeschichte*, Vol. 1: *Von der Spätantike bis zur frühen Neuzeit*, Berlin 1992

Harvey, John, *The Cathedrals of Spain*, London 1957

Karge, Henrik, *Die Kathedrale von Burgos und die spanischer Architektur des 13. Jahrhunderts: Französische Hochgotik in Kastilien und Leon*, Berlin 1989

Lambert, Elie, *L'art gothique en Espagne: Aux XIIe et XIIIe siècles*, Paris 1931

Palol, Pedro de, *Spanien: Kunst des frühen Mittelalters vom Westgotenreich bis zum Ende der Romanik*, Munich 1965; Munich 1991

Index

Places, Names, *Terms*

Photograph Credits

Plates

Airdiasol Rothan, Strasbourg plate 49
Atélier Paul, Prague plates 104, 105, 109, 110
Bamberg, Diözesanmuseum page 11; plates 86 (photograph: Gaasch), 90 (photograph: Ingeborg Limmer)
Achim Bednorz, Cologne plates 11, 12, 18, 20, 24, 34, 58
Constantin Beyer, Weimar plates 95–103
Caisse Nationale des Monuments Nationaux, Paris (photograph: François Lauginie) plates 38, 39; (photograph: Patrick Müller) plates 1, 26, 56
Camerafoto, Venice plates 170–72
Citadelles & Mazenod, Paris (photograph: Jean Mazenod) pages 2, 10; plates 9, 19, 33
Fridmar Damm, Cologne plate 76
Uwe Dettmar, Frankfurt/M plates 8, 13, 25, 47
Deutsches Archäologisches Institut, Madrid (photograph: Jens-Peter Wisshak) plate 252
Editions Valoire plate 40
Joachim Feist, Pliezhausen plates 65, 66, 69
Rainer Gaertner, Wiehl plates 63, 64, 67, 68, 75, 78, 80, 82
Gallimard Photothèque, Paris plate 54
Kurt Gramer, Bietigheim plate 73
Jochen Helle (Bildarchiv Monheim) plates 2, 3, 6, 7, 14, 15, 16, 17
Markus Hilbich, Berlin plate 106
Albert Hirmer (Hirmer Fotoarchiv, Munich) pages 1, 8, 9; plates 4, 5, 10, 21, 22, 23, 27, 30, 31, 32, 35, 36, 37, 41, 42, 44, 45, 46, 53, 55, 70, 84, 85, 87, 91, 92, 181, 188, 189, 193, 195, 196, 201 (2), 202, 205, 209, 210, 212, 213, 220–22
Michael Jeiter, Morschenich plate 50
Kraichgau Verlag, Ubstadt-Weiher plate 59
Fabio Lensini, Siena plates 200, 206–08
Ingeborg Limmer plates 88, 93, 94
Mainz, Bischöfliches Diözesanmuseum (photograph: M. Hankel-Studio, Bodenheim) plates 72, 74
Joseph Martin, Madrid page 6; plates 228–51, 253–57
Paolo Marton, Treviso plate 190
Ministero per i beni culturali ed ambientali dell'Umbria, Perugia plates 215–17
Florian Monheim, Meerbusch page 12, front jacket; plates 79, 83, 89, 112–19, 121–28, 130–37, 139–63
Werner Neumeister, Munich plates 107, 108
Panini Editore, Modena plates 184–87, 197, 199
Pubbliaerfoto, Varese plates 43, 183
Antonio Quattrone, Florence plates 191, 192, 194, 211
Ghigo Roli, Modena plates 173–80, 182

Caroline Rose, Paris back jacket; plates 28, 29
Scala Istituto Fotografico, Florence /Antella pages 4–5; plates 164–69, 198, 203, 204, 214, 218, 219, 223, 224
Eugen Uwe Schmitz, Hamm plates 51, 52, 57, 61, 62, 71, 77, 81
Marco Schneiders, Lindau plates 48, 60
Toni Schneiders, Lindau plate 227
Simmons Aerofilms, Borehamwood plates 111, 120, 129, 138

Text illustrations

Achim Bednorz (Bildarchiv Monheim) pages 413 (2), 414 (2), 415, 416 right, 220 bottom
Louis Berenger, Aspet/Pujos page 22 bottom
Constantin Beyer, Weimar pages 122, 128 bottom (2), 189 (2)
Bildarchiv Foto Marburg pages 35 left, 45, 107, 128 top, 132 bottom
Bildarchiv Monheim pages 30 (2) (photograph: Achim Bednorz); 218 (2), 221 top (photograph: Roman von Goetz)
Jutta Brüdern, Brunswick pages 125, 126 top, 127 top, bottom right, 130 top, 131
Caisse Nationale des Monuments Historiques, Paris page 61
Camerafoto, Venice pages 299 (2), 311
Foto Saporetti, Milan page 324
Fratelli Alinari, Florence pages 298, 303 (3), 304, 307 (2), 308
Frick Collection, New York page 235
Kurt Gramer, Bietigheim page 130 bottom
Graphische Sammlung Albertina, Vienna page 140
W. Hege, Gelsenkirchen pages 177 right, 188
Konrad Helbig page 302
Markus Hilbich, Berlin page 200
Albert Hirmer (Hirmer Fotoarchiv Munich) pages 20, 22 top, 24 (2), 26 (2), 27 (3), 28, 29 (2), 31 (2), 33 right, 35 right, 51, 71, 83, 126 bottom, 141 top, 151 top, 156, 177 left, 333, 343 (2), 357 (3), 395, 408, 409, 410 (2), 411 (2), 418, 419
Martin Hürlimann pages 214 left, 215, 219 (2), 247, 259, 269, 277
Michael Jeiter, Morschenich pages 33 left, 131 bottom (2)
Fabio Lensini, Siena page 354
Joseph Martin, Madrid pages 428, 455
Mainz, Bischöfliches Diözesanmuseum page 157 top
Florian Monheim, Meerbusch pages 32 (2), 133 (2), 212, 214 right, 216, 217, 220 top, bottom, 221 bottom, 268
Erich Müller, Kassel page 127 bottom left
Oronoz, Archivo Fotográfico, Madrid pages 412, 416 left, 417 (2)

Panini Editoriale, Modena page 342
Paris, Bibliothèque Nationale page 16
U. Pfistermeister, Nuremberg page 132 top
Publisher's archive page 353
Antonio Quattrone, Florence page 355
Eugen Uwe Schmitz, Hamm pages 135 (2), 157 bottom
Wilkin Spitta, Loham/Mariaposching page 129 (2)
Werner Stuhler, Hergensweiler b. Lindau page 301 (2)
Trompette (from Sauerländer, *Gotische Skulptur in Frankreich*) page 15
Hans Weber, Lenzburg page 300 (2)
Zodiaque Fotothèque, St. Léger-Vauban pages 305, 306 (2)

Cartography: Computerkarthographie Carrle, Munich
The plans and sections were taken from relevant specialist literature.